Saint Peter's University Library
Withdrawn

D1219141

THE LOEB CLASSICAL LIBRARY

FOUNDED BY JAMES LOEB 1911

EDITED BY
JEFFREY HENDERSON

EDITOR EMERITUS
G. P. GOOLD

CICERO

XXV

LCL 205

CICERO

LETTERS TO FRIENDS

VOLUME I

EDITED AND TRANSLATED BY

D. R. SHACKLETON BAILEY

HARVARD UNIVERSITY PRESS
CAMBRIDGE, MASSACHUSETTS
LONDON, ENGLAND
2001

Copyright © 2001 by the President and Fellows
of Harvard College
All rights reserved

LOEB CLASSICAL LIBRARY® is a registered trademark
of the President and Fellows of Harvard College

Library of Congress catalog card number 00-047259
CIP data available from the Library of Congress

ISBN 0-674-99588-0 (volume I)
ISBN 0-674-99589-9 (volume II)
ISBN 0-674-99590-2 (volume III)

CONTENTS

CICERO'S
LETTERS TO FRIENDS

INTRODUCTION

The Roman, at any rate the upper-class Roman, was a letter writer. In ancient Greece a man's circle was apt to be mainly confined to a single small town and the countryside adjoining. But the well-to-do Roman might well have connections up and down Italy as well as in the provinces. He himself spent much time in his country houses (villas). Business, public or private, might take him abroad for long periods. Although there was no postal system, bearers could usually be found: his own slaves, his friends' slaves, casual travellers, or the couriers of business companies.

Hardly any specimens of this activity survive except for Cicero's correspondence, consisting almost entirely of private letters written without any idea of future publication and published, as it seems, almost exactly as they stood. (The omission in one letter to Atticus of a scandalous story about Cicero's nephew may have been deliberate, but it is hard to find any other evidence of expurgation, let alone falsification.) As such they are uniquely interesting, even apart from their value as a source of historical and other kinds of information.

What remains of Cicero's correspondence has come down in two large collections, the Letters to Atticus and the so-called Letters to Friends, and two much smaller

ones, to his brother Quintus and to M. Brutus. Many more were extant in antiquity of which only stray fragments now survive. Except for a few of the earliest letters to Atticus they were all written in the last twenty years of Cicero's life. We know from Cornelius Nepos that Atticus preserved Cicero's letters dating from his consulship in 63 in eleven papyrus rolls and that friends were allowed to read them. What happened after his death is unknown, but they were probably not published until the middle of the first century A.D., though the rest of the correspondence seems to have come out much earlier.

The collection of Letters to Friends *(Epistulae ad Familiares)* did not originally appear as such. Our MSS have it in sixteen "Books." Some of these consist entirely or mainly of letters to or from a single correspondent: Lentulus Spinther in Book I, Appius Claudius in Book III, Caelius in Book VIII, Terentia or Terentia and children in Book XIV, Tiro in Book XVI. Book XIII consists of letters of recommendation, Books X–XII of correspondence relating to the struggle with Antony in 44–43. The rest show more or less internal cohesion. Evidence suggests that they were arranged and published separately or in groups during the Augustan period by a single editor, who was in all probability Cicero's faithful secretary, Tiro; he is also likely to have produced the now lost collections of letters to individual correspondents other than Atticus known to have existed in antiquity: Caesar, Pompey, Octavian, and others, as well as those surviving to Quintus Cicero and Marcus Brutus. At what time the collection of sixteen books came into being is unknown. The title "Letters to Friends" seems to be no older than the Renaissance.

The "friends" are a motley group. Some of them, like

Trebatius Testa, Caelius, and Papirius Paetus, really were familiars, to whom Cicero could write as informally, though not as intimately, as to Atticus or to his brother. With powerful aristocrats like Cato, Lentulus Spinther, and Appius Claudius he was on no such easy footing, so that his letters to them are in as elaborate a style as his published works. The high sentiments, stately flatteries, and courteously veiled rebukes might have transposed naturally into eighteenth-century English, but put a modern translator at a disadvantage. Other letters fall somewhere in between these two types, including two dispatches from Cilicia, both models of elegant, straightforward language. Cicero's correspondents are briefly described in the register of The Friends that follows.

Cicero's letters only come fully to life against a historical and biographical background, though a bare outline is all that can be offered here.[1]

Historical Background

Marcus Tullius Cicero was born on 3 January 106 B.C. at his family home near the hill town of Arpinum (still Arpino) about seventy miles to the east of Rome. For nearly a century the Arpinates had been citizens of Rome, a status attained by most of Italy south of the Po only after the bloody 'Social War' of 90–88. The family was old and well-to-do, and like many locally prominent Italian families, had good Roman connections; but from the standpoint of a Roman aristocrat Cicero was a nobody, a 'new

---

[1] The Historical Background that follows is reproduced from my Loeb Classical Library edition of the Letters to Atticus.

man,' a fact of lasting practical and psychological importance.

About ten years after Cicero's birth his father took up
residence in a fashionable part of Rome. Cicero and his
younger brother received the best education money could
buy, and he is said to have easily outshone his socially
superior classmates. On coming of age at sixteen or seven-
teen he served for a short time in the Roman army against
the insurgent Italian allies. He lived in stormy times. Roman political institutions were turning out to be inadequate for the government of an already large empire. The
authority of the Senate, the only permanent governing
body, had been seriously shaken in the last three decades
of the second century. The career of the great general
Marius, also a native of Arpinum and a family connection
of the Ciceros, had pointed the way to future army commanders who were to build positions of personal power on
the loyalty of their troops.

The Social War was followed by the terrible internal
struggles of the eighties. In 88 the Consul Sulla, a brilliant
general from an impoverished noble family who combined
conservative sympathies with a contempt for constitutional
forms, set a fateful precedent by marching his army on the
capital in rebuttal of a personal injustice. His chief opponents were killed or, like Marius, escaped into exile. But
Sulla had business elsewhere. Later in the year he left for
the East to deal with a foreign enemy, the redoubtable
Mithridates of Pontus. Turmoil ensued. Rome stood a
siege before being captured again by the forces of the
anti-Sullan Consul Cinna and old Marius, emerging from
banishment like an avenging ghost. The resulting massacre

was the bloodiest of its kind so far known in Roman history. Marius died a few months later, but Rome and Italy remained under the control of Cinna and his associates for the next four years.

In 83 Sulla brought his victorious legions home. Fighting followed up and down the peninsula, and Rome had another Marian bloodbath before Sulla came out master of the situation. His ruthless reprisals left a grim memory, but to people of traditional outlook he was the restorer of the Republic. As Dictator he produced a new constitution guaranteeing control of affairs to an enlarged Senate, and, this task completed, he retired voluntarily into private life (79). His work was not wholly undone for thirty years.

Despite close Marian connections Cicero seems to have disliked and despised Cinna's regime and only began his public career, as an advocate, after Sulla's victory. He scored a sensational triumph with his defence of a certain Roscius, the victim of persecution by an influential freedman of Sulla's, and his services in court became much in demand. But in 79 his voice was suffering from overstrain and for this and perhaps other reasons he left Rome for three years of travel in Greece and Asia Minor. After a fresh start in 76 his star rose rapidly and steadily. The next thirteen years brought him the two great objects of his ambition, primacy at the Roman bar and a political career culminating in the Consulship. Without one setback he climbed the official ladder, elected Quaestor, Plebeian Aedile, and Praetor by handsome majorities and at the earliest age allowed by law. The Consulship at this period was almost a preserve of the nobility, consisting of descendants of Consuls, though now and again a man of praeto-

rian family was let in. For more than a generation before Cicero's candidature in 64 new men had been excluded. Nevertheless he easily topped the poll.

His year of office would not have been particularly memorable but for a timely attempt at a coup d'état by his unsuccessful fellow candidate Catiline, a patrician champion of the bankrupt and disinherited. The plot was discovered and suppressed by Cicero. Catiline had left Rome to join his armed followers, and had to be defeated and killed next year, but five of his chief associates were arrested and brought before the Senate. After a memorable debate they were executed under Cicero's supervision. In and out of the Senate he was hailed as the saviour of Rome, but the legality of the action was disputed, and it brought him into lasting unpopularity with the have-nots.

Cicero's prestige had reached a peak (from which it gradually declined), but the principal figure of the Roman world was not in Rome. Gnaeus Pompeius Magnus (Pompey the Great) rose early to fame by his brilliant military exploits against the adversaries of Sulla. His reputation was consolidated by years of finally successful warfare against the Marian leader Sertorius in Spain and the suppression of Spartacus' slave revolt in Italy. In 70 he became Consul in defiance of legal qualifications as to age and previous offices. Three years later, against the opposition of the senatorial leaders, he received an extraordinary commission to clear the Mediterranean of piracy. Prompt and complete success was followed by something even bigger — an overall command in the East where Mithridates and his ally the King of Armenia were still defying the empire. Pompey's campaigns established Roman control over a vast area of western Asia, which he reorganized as he saw fit.

In 62 he returned to Italy and, to the relief of the home authorities, at once disbanded his army.

Pompey had two demands, both reasonable: ratification of his arrangements in the East and land for his veteran soldiers. But the senatorial conservatives, now tending to centre around a strong-minded young nobleman called M. Porcius Cato, distrusted his intentions and resented a career so conspicuously out of conformity with oligarchical norms. Several, in particular his predecessor in the eastern command, L. Lucullus, and a Metellus (Creticus) who had fallen foul of him in Crete, nursed bitter personal grudges. Their unwisely stubborn obstructiveness resulted in a coalition between Pompey and two prominent politicians, both out of sympathy with the post-Sullan establishment: C. Julius Caesar and M. Licinius Crassus. The former, son of a Marian Praetor and former son-in-law of Cinna, was a favourite with the city populace, none the less so because he came from one of Rome's most ancient families; the latter, also a nobleman and Pompey's colleague in 70, was, next to Pompey himself, the richest man in Rome. This alliance, often called the First Triumvirate though it had no official status, dominated the scene for years to come. Cicero could have made a fourth, but although much dissatisfied with the 'optimates,' who were apt to remember his origins rather than the public services of which he so often reminded them, his principles would not let him take part in a conspiracy against the constitution.

In 59 Caesar became Consul. Almost literally over the dead body of his optimate colleague Bibulus, in defiance of senatorial opposition and constitutional procedures, he pushed through a legislative program which satisfied his two associates and gave himself a five-year command in

northern Italy and Gaul. In the event it lasted until 49 and enabled him to annex modern France (apart from the old Roman province in the south) and Belgium to the Roman empire. There were even expeditions across the Rhine and the English Channel. Before leaving Rome he had arranged for the elimination of Cicero, who had rejected several tempting overtures. Early in 58 the patrician demagogue and Tribune P. Clodius Pulcher, following a personal vendetta, was allowed to drive him into exile with the passive connivance of Pompey, despite earlier professions of friendship and support. Distraught and desperate, Cicero fled to Greece. Eighteen months later the tide had turned. Clodius had fallen out with Pompey, who, with Caesar's rather reluctant consent, arranged for a triumphal restoration. For a while thereafter Cicero tried to play an independent political hand, taking advantage of rifts in the triumviral solidarity. But these were patched up at the Conference of Luca (Lucca) in 56, and Cicero received a sharp warning from Pompey, which took prompt effect. A eulogy of Caesar's victories in the Senate, described by himself as a palinode, was his last important political gesture for several years. He continued active forensically, but his choice of clients now had to include creatures of the dynasts, some of them enemies of his own. Meanwhile his personal relations with Caesar developed a new cordiality, and in 54 his brother Quintus went to Gaul to make a military reputation and, as he hoped, his fortune as one of Caesar's lieutenant generals.

The year 55 saw Pompey and Crassus together again in the Consulship. Caesar's tenure in Gaul was extended for another quinquennium, and the Consuls were appointed to commands in Spain and Syria for a like period (Pompey

remained in Italy, governing Spain through deputies). But the later fifties produced a realignment. Pompey was the devoted husband of Caesar's daughter Julia; she died in 54 and in the following year Crassus was defeated and killed by the Parthians. Caesar and Pompey were left in what began to look like confrontation. After the conquest of Gaul Pompey could no longer feel secure in his position of senior while at the same time Cato and his friends were losing their hostility to Pompey in face of the threat from Caesar. The rapprochement between Pompey and Senate, which Cicero had once unsuccessfully tried to promote, came about under the pressure of events. In 52, at the behest of the Catonians, Pompey took power as sole Consul (the term Dictator was avoided) to restore law and order, which had broken down in a welter of street warfare and electoral corruption. This accomplished with no less efficiency than the clearance of the seas in 67, the question of Caesar's future came uppermost. After protracted maneuvring the upshot was another civil war, which broke out at the beginning of 49, when Caesar led his troops across the river Rubicon into the homeland. Hardly more than two months later, after Caesar had encircled and captured a large republican army at Corfinium, Pompey, the Consuls, and a large part of the Senate crossed the Adriatic with their remaining troops, leaving Caesar in undisputed control of Italy and Rome.

Cicero had missed the political preliminaries. In 51 he found himself unexpectedly saddled with the government of a province (a thing he had twice avoided in the past), namely Cilicia, comprising almost all the southern seaboard of Asia Minor and a large part of the interior, together with the island of Cyprus. He entered it at the end

of July for his year's tenure. He proved an excellent, if reluctant, governor and with the assistance of his brother and other experienced military men on his staff he even campaigned against the untamed people of the mountains with enough success to win the title of Imperator from his troops and a Supplication (Thanksgiving) from the Senate — the usual preliminaries to a Triumph. Arriving in Italy during the final stage of the crisis he pleaded for peace in public and in private. When that failed, after many waverings recorded in almost daily letters to Atticus, he sailed from Italy in June and is next heard of early the following year in Pompey's camp near Dyrrachium (Durazzo).

Caesar's victory at Pharsalia[2] in August 48 was virtually the end of Pompey, who was killed shortly afterwards in Egypt, but it was not the end of the Civil War. Thinking it was, Cicero accepted Caesar's invitation (conveyed through his own son-in-law Dolabella) to return to Italy and spent an unhappy year in Brundisium (Brindisi) pending decisions on his future, while Caesar was involved in Egypt and Asia. On Caesar's return in September 47 his anxieties were relieved in a gracious interview and he was able to take up life again in Rome.

It was almost entirely a private life. Caesar showed him much kindness and he was on outwardly friendly social terms with most of Caesar's principal followers, but his advice was not required and he rarely appeared in the Forum or the Senate House. Paradoxically he now had most

---

[2] 'Pharsalus, the modern title of the battlefield, is not merely in itself an error both gross and gratuitous; it is implicated with another that is more serious still': J. P. Postgate; see his discussion in *Lucan, De Bello Civili VIII* (Cambridge 1917), Excursus C.

to fear from a republican victory. For Cato and others had established a new position of strength in Africa, where Caesar's lieutenant Curio had lost his life and army early in the war; and after that was destroyed by another Caesarian victory at Thapsus in April 46, Pompey's sons were able to fight another day in Spain. Even their defeat in the hard-fought battle of Munda (March 45) was not the end.

Meanwhile, especially after his daughter's death in February 45, Cicero took refuge in literary work. In his young days he had published verse, with temporary acclaim, and many carefully edited speeches. The works *On the Orator* and *On the Republic* appeared in the fifties. In 46–44 he turned to philosophy. Without any pretensions to original thought, he put the ideas he found in his Greek sources into elegant Latin in a rapid succession of treatises which made a greater impact on the minds of men to come than perhaps any other secular writings of antiquity.

Cicero had no prior knowledge of the conspiracy against Caesar's life in 44, though its leader M. Brutus was his intimate friend. But when Caesar fell in the Senate House on the Ides of March, Brutus waved his blood-stained dagger and shouted Cicero's name. Certainly the act had Cicero's wholehearted approval. But a little while later he ruefully recognized that though the king was dead the monarchy survived. The conspirators, an assortment of republican loyalists and disgruntled place-seekers, had not planned ahead, and the Consul Mark Antony, who in Cicero's opinion ought to have been eliminated along with his colleague Caesar, soon made it evident that he intended to take Caesar's place. The 'liberators' were driven out of Rome by mob violence.

Disgusted at the scene, Cicero set out in July for

Greece, where his son was a student in Athens, but reports from Rome made him turn back. On 2 September he delivered in the Senate the first of a series of attacks on Antony which he jestingly called Philippics, after Demosthenes' speeches against Philip of Macedon. There were no immediate consequences and for some time Cicero again lay low. But by the end of the year the situation had been transformed. Antony was at Mutina (Modena) besieging the legal governor of Cisalpine Gaul, Decimus Brutus, who was one of Caesar's assassins. Soon he found himself opposed by three republican armies. Their commanders were the two Consuls of 43, Hirtius and Pansa, both Caesarians but hostile to Antony's ambitions, and Caesar's youthful grandnephew and adopted son, Caesar Octavianus, who had returned to Italy the previous April and emerged as Antony's rival for the loyalty of Caesar's veterans. At this time Cicero professed complete confidence in Octavian's loyalty to the Republic. Meanwhile, he himself had taken the lead in Rome as the acknowledged embodiment of the Senate and People's will to resist the new despotism. M. Brutus and his brother-in-law and co-conspirator Cassius had left for the East, where they succeeded in taking over the entire Roman empire east of the Adriatic in the republican interest. The West, however, was in the hands of four Caesarian governors, none of whom, except perhaps Cornificius in Africa, was wholly reliable from Cicero's standpoint. It was his business to make the Senate a focus for their loyalties and to maintain a stream of hortatory correspondence.

In April the situation at Mutina was resolved. Antony suffered two heavy defeats and was forced to raise the siege

and escape westwards. But both Consuls lost their lives in the fighting. The game in Italy now lay in Octavian's hands, but Antony was not finished. Joined by a large contingent under his lieutenant Ventidius he crossed the Alps into southern Gaul, now governed by Caesar's former Master of the Horse, M. Lepidus. The news that they had joined forces caused consternation in Rome, where the war had seemed as good as won. In northern Gaul Cicero's family friend L. Plancus professed loyalty and was joined by Decimus Brutus. But the armies remained inactive until August or September, when Plancus, along with Pollio, the governor of Further Spain, joined the opposition. Decimus' men deserted and he was killed in flight.

In Italy Octavian had begun to assert himself, demanding the vacant Consulship—at nineteen years old! When the Senate refused, he marched his army on Rome and occupied the city without bloodshed. His election followed on 19 August. Then came a meeting with Antony and Lepidus in October at which a common front was established. The three dynasts became 'Triumvirs for the Constitution of the Republic' and parcelled out the western part of the empire between them. Funds were raised and vengeance satisfied by a revival of Sulla's Proscriptions. The victims were numerous, many of them eminent, and Cicero was naturally among the first. After an abortive attempt to escape by sea he was hunted down and killed at his villa near Formiae on 7 December 43. His brother and nephew met a similar fate.

In 42 the republican cause finally went down to defeat at Philippi, where Brutus and Cassius perished. Eleven

years later monarchy was established by Octavian's victory over Antony at Actium.

The complexities of Cicero's career and personality hardly appear in a mere summary of events. In his various phases he became what circumstances made him, sometimes paltry, sometimes almost heroic. His ambition was rooted in insufficiency. Carrying all his life a set of traditional ideas which he never consciously questioned, he seldom ignored his code, but was easily swayed and perplexed by side issues and more or less unacknowledged personal inducements. His agile mind moved on the surface of things, victim of their complexity. Always the advocate, he saw from ever-shifting angles, and what he saw he rarely analysed.

Often confused himself, he perplexes us. He failed to realise that self-praise can defeat its end. Alongside the image of the wise and dauntless patriot which he tried to project into posterity has arisen the counterimage of a windbag, a spiteful, vainglorious egotist. And that is not because, as some of his admirers have urged, the survival of his private correspondence has placed him at a disadvantage. His published speeches reveal him to a generation intolerant of his kind of cliché. The flabbiness, pomposity, and essential fatuity of Ciceronian rhetoric at its too frequent worst does him more damage than any epistolary 'secrets.' No other antique personality has inspired such venomous dislike. In antiquity Asinius Pollio's son wrote a book comparing Cicero with his own father to the disadvantage of the former. This may have criticized him mainly as an orator and stylist, like another production entitled 'Cicero whipped.' His modern enemies hate and

despise him as a man—from titanic Mommsen, obsessed by scorn of political inadequacy, romantic worshipper of 'complete and perfect' Caesar, to Kingsley Amis' young schoolmaster who had the bad luck to be reading the Second Philippic in class.[3] The living Cicero was hated by some, but not despised. His gifts, matching the times, were too conspicuous. And many opponents were disarmed; Mommsen himself might have capitulated to a dinner party at Tusculum.

Cicero's Family

In later life, after the death of his parents and a cousin, Lucius Cicero, to whom he was much attached, Cicero's family circle at one time or other included the following.

1. His wife Terentia. She was rich and well connected, possibly even of noble family; we hear only of a half-sister, a Vestal Virgin who probably belonged to the patrician Fabii. The marriage apparently worked well for many years, but after Cicero's return from exile there are signs of strain. The differences seem to have mainly had to do with money. In 46 they ended in divorce. Terentia is alleged to have lived to 103 and twice remarried.

2. His daughter Tullia. Probably born in 76 or 75 rather than 79 or 78, as usually supposed. Cicero was devoted to her and distraught with grief at her death in February 45. On her marriages see items 7–9.

3. His son Marcus, born in 65. He turned out a disap-

---

[3] 'For a man so long and thoroughly dead it was remarkable how much boredom, and also how precise an image of nasty silliness, Cicero could generate.' (*Take a Girl Like You,* Chapter V.)

pointment to his father, an unremarkable young man who was happier commanding a troop of cavalry than studying philosophy. He escaped the Proscriptions, being in Greece at the time, and served in Brutus' army. Later Octavian made him Augur, Consul in 30, and governor of Asia. He also gained a reputation as the hardest drinker in Rome.

4. A brother Quintus, about two years his junior. Following in Cicero's wake he held the usual offices up to Praetor and was Proconsul in Asia from 61 to 59. In 54 he took service under Caesar in Gaul, but like his brother followed Pompey in the Civil War. Pardoned by Caesar after Pharsalia, he perished in the Proscriptions of 43. His relations with his brother were close and generally affectionate until 48. The story of their quarrel and superficial reconciliation can be found in Chapter 19 of my biography. A number of Cicero's letters to him written between 59 and 54 survive.

5. Quintus' wife Pomponia, sister of Atticus. The marriage took place in 70 or thereabouts and ended with divorce in 45. It was never a success. Pomponia was several years older than her husband and apparently of a shrewish disposition. Cicero's letters contain many references to their domestic difficulties.

6. Their son, the younger Q. Cicero, born about the end of 67. Much more gifted intellectually than his cousin, he grew up to be a thorn in his elders' flesh. Like his father and uncle he perished in the Proscriptions.

7. Tullia had three husbands, all young men of noble family. She was betrothed to the first, C. Calpurnius Piso Frugi, in 67 and married in 62. He was Quaestor in 58, but died the following year before Cicero's return. He seems

to have been a model son-in-law, and Cicero writes warmly of his loyalty in the bad times.

8. Tullia married Furius Crassipes in 55. They were divorced within a few years, but nothing is known of the circumstances.

9. Tullia married P. Cornelius Dolabella in 50, a rake and a Caesarian. Divorce followed in 46, but Cicero remained on good terms with him until he allied himself with Antony, having succeeded Caesar as Consul in 44. He committed suicide in the East in 42 to avoid capture by Cassius.

10. In January 45 Tullia bore a son, who lived only a few months. He was called Lentulus after Dolabella's adoptive name.

11. Not long after divorcing Terentia Cicero married his young and wealthy ward, Publilia. Another divorce followed after a few months. She had a brother(?), Publilius, and a mother living.

12. Pomponia's brother, T. Pomponius Atticus. He married Pilia in 56; her brother, Pilius Celer, was a noted speaker and a Caesarian. Their daughter, Caecilia Attica, was probably born in 51.

Manuscripts, Text, and Translation

The text of Books I–VIII (in the traditional arrangement) depends almost entirely on the ninth or tenth century Mediceus 48.7, which arrived in Florence in 1392 and remains there in the Laurentian Library. Two others, G and R, both of the twelfth century, correct many of its errors and introduce many of their own, but their contributions almost without exception appear to be medieval

conjecture. They are, or should be, quoted in critical editions as the earliest known sources for readings, not as having independent authority.

In the last eight Books, however, the situation is different. Three other MSS, H of the eleventh century and DV of the fifteenth, together represent an independent tradition (χ) of value almost equal to M. For a full account, see the introduction to my Cambridge edition (1977).

The text of this edition is almost the same as my Teubner text (1988), differences being indicated by asterisks in the critical notes. In these I have not particularized the manuscript sources, but rather aimed to give warning where the reading in the text has little or no manuscript support (excluding some too obvious or generally accepted to need mention). The notes in such cases give the transmitted reading followed in parenthesis by the name of the corrector; if that does not follow, ς is to be assumed, the comprehensive siglum for inferior MS(S) or early editions(s).

The fullest apparatus criticus is in L. Mendelssohn's edition of 1893, covering MGRDH and certain fragments, but for most purposes those of W. S. Watt (Oxford Text), myself, or J. Beaujeu (where available) will serve. The last named completed the Budé edition of the correspondence in vols. VI–XI, covering letters dated to 25 March 49 and after. These volumes are valuable not only for their admirable introductions and notes but also for a text which, if containing little in the way of convincing novelties, deserves praise for thorough scholarship and independent, open-minded judgment. I have reviewed the work volume by volume in *Gnomon*.

The only modern commentary on the entire correspon-

dence before my Cambridge edition, that of Tyrrell and Purser (1904–33), though highly readable, has not unfairly been described as a mine of honest misinformation.

It has, of course, been impossible here to argue controversial readings and interpretations, or the many difficult problems of dating. The arrangement and numbering of the letters is as in my Cambridge edition: partly chronological, partly by grouping according to correspondent or genre.

The translation that follows has been revised from my translation published as number 1 in the Classical Resources series of the American Philological Association (1988), a takeover from the two-volume edition that appeared in the Penguin Classics series (1978).

Throughout, all dates are B.C. unless otherwise specified.

Abbreviations in Critical Notes

Corr. = *Corradus.*
Crat. = *Cratander.*
Ern. = *Ernesti.*
Gron. = *Gronovius.*
Gul. = *Gulielmius.*
Lamb. = *Lambinus.*
Man. = *Manutius.*
Mart. = *Martyni-Laguna.*
Mend. = *Mendelssohn.*
Or. = *Orelli.*
SB = *Shackleton Bailey.*
T.–P. = *Tyrrell–Purser.*
Vict. = *Victorius.*
Wes. = *Wesenberg.*

BIBLIOGRAPHICAL NOTE

Editions

Jean Beaujeu, *Cicéron: Correspondance* (Paris: Budé), vols. VI–XI, 1980–1996.

D. R. Shackleton Bailey, *Cicero: Epistulae ad Familiares* (Cambridge Texts and Commentaries), 1977.

W. S. Watt, *Cicero: Ad Familiares* (Oxford Classical Texts), 1988.

Biographies

M. Gelzer, *Cicero: ein biographischer Versuch*, Wiesbaden, 1969.

Elizabeth Rawson, *Cicero*, London, 1975.

D. R. Shackleton Bailey, *Cicero*, London, 1975.

D. Stockton, *Cicero: A Political Biography*, Oxford 1971.

Study

G. O. Hutchinson, *Cicero's Correspondence: A Literary Study*, Oxford University Press, 1998. Contains an extensive bibliography.

THE FRIENDS

Acilius Caninus, M. Caesarian officer, Proconsul in Sicily 46–45.

Aemilius Lepidus, M. Consul in 46 and one of Caesar's leading followers. Succeeded him as Chief Pontiff and became governor of Narbonese Gaul and Hither Spain. In 43 joined Antony and became Triumvir; Consul again in 42; governor of Africa 40–36. Forced by Octavian to retire from public life.

Aemilius Paullus, L. Elder brother of the above and Consul in 50. Allegedly bought by Caesar. Probably neutral in the Civil War, he was proscribed by the Triumvirs but escaped to end his days in Miletus. On the problem of his name see my *Onomasticon to Cicero's Speeches* (1992).

Allienus, A. Friend of the Ciceros and one of Quintus' legates in 59. Praetor in 49, he supported Caesar. Proconsul in Sicily 48–46; Legate of Trebonius, then Dolabella 44–43; last heard of handing over his army to Cassius.

Ampius Balbus, T. Praetor in 59; apparently governor of Asia the following year as successor to Q. Cicero; later transferred to Cilicia. Adherent of Pompey and friend of Cicero, who probably obtained permission for him to return to Italy in 46. Called 'the trumpet of the Civil War'

21

SAINT PETER'S COLLEGE LIBRARY
JERSEY CITY, NEW JERSEY 07306

by Caesarians for reasons unknown, he wrote 'on the deeds of brave men.'

Ancharius, Q. As Tribune in 59 he opposed Caesar. Praetor in 56; succeeded L. Piso as governor of Macedonia in the following year.

Antonius, C. Cicero's colleague in the Consulship of 63, suspected of Catilinarian leanings; he had previously been expelled from the Senate for rapacity and insolvency. Governor of Macedonia 62–60. Condemned after his return to Rome, he went into exile but lived to become Censor (!) in 42. Mark Antony was his nephew.

Antonius, M. Caesar's Quaestor in 52 and one of his principal lieutenants in the Civil War. Tribune in 49. Consul with Caesar in 44 and would-be successor to his power, he eventually formed the Triumvirate of 43 along with Octavian and Lepidus. As ruler of the eastern half of the empire he quarrelled with Octavian and committed suicide after defeat at Actium in 31.

Appuleius. Proquaestor in Asia in 46. He may have been Sex. Appuleius, Consul in 29, or P. Appuleius, Tribune in 43.

Asinius Pollio, C. Born about 76, Praetor in 45, Consul in 40. Soldier, orator, author of tragedies and historian. Governor of Further Spain at the time of Caesar's death, he joined Antony in 43 and remained his supporter, but lived on under Augustus until 5 A.D.

Caecilius Metellus Celer, Q. As Praetor in 63 cooperated with Cicero against Catiline. Governor of Cisalpine Gaul in 62, Consul in 60. Died in 59. His wife was the notorious Clodia, who was half-sister to his half-brother P. Clodius.

Caecilius Metellus Nepos, Q. Younger brother to the fore-

SAINT PETER'S COLLEGE LIBRARY
JERSEY CITY, NEW JERSEY 07306

going. As Tribune in 62 agitated against Cicero and was suspended from office. Consul in 57, then governor of Hither Spain.

Caecina, A. Friend of Cicero, who defended his father in an extant speech; of noble Etruscan family. Noted orator and author among other things of a treatise on divination by lightning.

Caelius Rufus, M. Born about 88. Placed by his father under Cicero's patronage and successfully defended by him on a criminal charge in 56 (subject of the speech *Pro Caelio*). One of the leading orators of the period. Tribune in 52, Curule Aedile in 50. Previously an opponent of Caesar, he changed sides just before the outbreak of the Civil War and was made Praetor in 48. As such he started an agitation in favour of debtors; this ended in an attempted rising against Caesar in which he and his associate Milo lost their lives.

Caesius, P. Nothing is known about him but the Caesii were prominent in Arpinum.

Cassius Longinus, C. As Proquaestor took charge of Syria after Crassus' death at Carrhae in 53. Gained a success against invading Parthians in 51. As Tribune in 49 joined Pompey. Pardoned and favoured by Caesar, he became Praetor in 44 and one of the leading conspirators against Caesar's life. Subsequently organized forces against the Triumvirs in the East and perished with Brutus at Philippi in 42. Married to Brutus' half-sister, Junia Tertia (Tertulla).

Cassius Parmensis, C. ('Of Parma'; such descriptives were sometimes treated as *cognomina*). Quaestor in 43. According to Velleius (who may, however, have confused him with someone else), he was one of Caesar's assas-

sins and the last of them to die (killed at Athens after Actium). Author of elegies (Horace *Epistles* 1.4.3) and other poetry.

Claudius Marcellus, C. Praetor in 80 and governor of Sicily. An Augur, he wrote a book on the subject.

Claudius Marcellus, C. Son of the foregoing. As Consul in 50 in opposition to Caesar, but neutral in the Civil War. Married Caesar's great-niece Octavia.

Claudius Marcellus, C. Consul in 49, cousin of the foregoing. Naval commander under Pompey in 48, he seems to have died before Pharsalia.

Claudius Marcellus, M. Elder brother of the foregoing and Consul in 51. A steady opponent of Caesar, he joined Pompey in the war but retired to Mytilene after Pharsalia. Publicly pardoned by Caesar in 46 (hence Cicero's extant speech of gratitude), he was murdered by a friend on his way home. Distinguished orator.

Claudius Pulcher, Ap. Brother of P. Clodius and hence inimical to Cicero in 57 but later reconciled. Consul in 54; Cicero's predecessor in Cilicia; Censor in 50. Supported Pompey in the Civil War, but died before Pharsalia. One of his daughters married Pompey's elder son, another married M. Brutus. Cicero's letters build up the picture of an arrogant, corrupt, and unscrupulous magnate. Author of a treatise on Augury, his interests allegedly extended to less respectable forms of divination as well as agriculture.

Claudius Pulcher (maior), Ap. Nephew of the foregoing. Probably served under Caesar in Gaul, after whose death he joined Antony, but temporarily regretted it. Later a triumviral partisan and Consul in 38.

Cluvius (or Clovius? See my Commentary, vol. II, p. 460). Apparently in charge of land assignments in Cisalpine Gaul in 46 or 45.

Coelius Caldus, C. Quaestor to Cicero in 50 and left by him in charge of Cilicia.

Cornelius Dolabella, P. (after adoption Cn.? Cornelius Lentulus Dolabella?). Defended by Cicero on two capital charges, he became his son-in-law in 50 but was divorced in 46. A favoured follower of Caesar (despite demagogic activities as Tribune in 47), whom he succeeded as Consul in 44. After some wavering joined Antony and left for his province of Syria late in the year, killing C. Trebonius, governor of Asia, on his way. Soon afterwards committed suicide to avoid capture by Cassius.

Cornelius Lentulus Spinther, P. As Consul in 57 took a leading part in Cicero's restoration. Governor of Cilicia 56–54. A steady supporter of Pompey before and in the Civil War, he was killed in Africa in 46, perhaps by Caesar's orders. The name Spinther, derived from an actor who resembled him, is used by Cicero only for his son.

Cornelius Lentulus Spinther, P. Son of the foregoing. Falsely claimed to have taken part in Caesar's murder. Went to Asia in 43 as Trebonius' Quaestor, after whose death he was an active supporter of Brutus and Cassius. Probably put to death after Philippi.

Cornificius, Q. Quaestor in 48; served Caesar in and after the Civil War. Governor of Africa 44–42, until defeated and killed by the neighbouring governor T. Sextius. A notable orator and poet.

THE FRIENDS

Culleolus. Proconsul in Illyricum, probably in 61 or 60. Perhaps the Culleolus mentioned slightingly in *Letters to Atticus* 117(VI.3).6.

Curius. Proconsul, when or where is unknown.

Curius, M'. Man of business resident in Patrae, a close friend of Atticus, later also of Cicero.

Domitius Ahenobarbus, Cn. Son of the Consul of 54. With Pompey in the Civil War. Returned to Italy after Pharsalia. Later a partisan of Antony (becoming Consul in 32), whom he finally deserted. Shakespeare's Enobarbus.

Fabius Gallus, M. Formerly miscalled Fadius. Author, Epicurean, connoisseur of art.

Fadius, T. Found guilty on a bribery charge, probably in connection with his election to the Praetorship in 58. He had been Cicero's Quaestor in 63 and as Tribune was active for his recall.

Furfanus Postumus, T. Proconsul in Sicily in 46.

Furius Crassipes. Patrician. Married Cicero's daughter Tullia in 56 or 55, but divorced before 51. May have been Quaestor in Bithynia in 54.

Furnius, C. Friend of Cicero, Tribune in 50. A Caesarian, he was Munatius Plancus' Legate in 43 and later supported Mark Antony and his brother Lucius. Pardoned and dignified by Octavian, he lived to see his son Consul in 17.

Gallius, Q. As Praetor in 43 deposed by Octavian. On the addressee of Cicero's Letters 268 and 270 see note to the former.

Julius Caesar, C. The Dictator.

Junius Brutus, M. After adoption by his uncle Q. Servilius Caepio sometimes called (Q. Servilius) Caepio

(Brutus). A leader in the conspiracy that led to Caesar's assassination. The collection of his correspondence with Cicero in 43 appears in a separate volume.

Junius Brutus Albinus, D. Not closely related to the foregoing. Served under Caesar in Gaul and the Civil War; governor of Transalpine Gaul 48–46. Regarded with special favour by Caesar, who named him Consul for 42 along with L. Plancus; nevertheless took a leading part in the conspiracy against Caesar's life. Later besieged by Antony in Mutina in his province of Cisalpine Gaul; after Antony's defeat and escape followed him across the Alps to join Plancus with his army. When the latter went over to Antony and Lepidus he fled, but was tracked down and killed on Antony's orders.

Licinius Crassus, M. Fought for Sulla against the Marians; later Consul in 70 and 55. In 60 he joined Pompey and Caesar to form the so-called First Triumvirate. Left for Syria in 55. Defeated and killed at Carrhae in 53 leading an invasion of Parthia. Next to Pompey the richest man in Rome. Despite some surface cordiality, Cicero disliked and disapproved of him.

Ligarius, Q. Pompeian, whose conduct in the Civil War was defended by Cicero before Caesar in an extant speech. Allowed to return to Rome, he joined the conspiracy in 44.

Lucceius, L. (son of Quintus). Praetor in 67 and unsuccessful candidate for the Consulship in 60. On amicable terms with Cicero and one of Pompey's closest friends and advisers until Pharsalia, he was pardoned by Caesar but may have perished in the proscriptions of 43. His history of the Social and Civil Wars of the eighties, perhaps in Greek, may have been published in part only

or not at all. His promise to write about Cicero is not known to have been kept.

Manlius Torquatus, A. Praetor perhaps in 70 and a long-standing friend of Atticus, also of Cicero, who tried through Dolabella to get Caesar's permission for him, as an ex-Pompeian living in Athens, to return to Italy, whether successfully or not is uncertain; but according to Cornelius Nepos (*Atticus* 11.2) in 42 he was with the republicans in Greece and survived their defeat at Philippi.

Marcius Philippus, Q. Probably a son or nephew of L. Philippus. Consul in 56; in charge of Cilicia probably as Quaestor pro consule 47–46.

Marius, M. Probably one of the Marii of Arpinum with a family link to Cicero, certainly an old friend. What is known of him suggests a cultured valetudinarian, living at his ease in his villa on the Bay of Naples.

Matius C. Old friend of Cicero and closely attached to Caesar, whom he accompanied in Gaul without official rank. Cicero calls him by nickname referring to his baldness, not a token of regard.

Memmius, C. (son of Lucius). First husband of Sulla's daughter Fausta, who was a ward of L. Lucullus, hence perhaps an enemy of the two Luculli. An erratic political career ended in exile after conviction for bribery in 52. Noted orator and poet, generally assumed to be the friend to whom Lucretius dedicated his poem on the doctrines of Epicurus, with which this Memmius seems to have had little sympathy to judge by Cicero's letter.

Memmius, C. Perhaps son of the foregoing, Consul in 34.

Mescinius Rufus, L. Cicero's Quaestor in Cilicia. Seems to have joined Pompey in the Civil War but was allowed to

return to Italy in 46. The highly unflattering reference in *Letters to Atticus* 117(VI.3).1 puts the amicability of the letters in perspective.

Minucius Basilus, L. Legate of Caesar in Gaul and the Civil War and Praetor in 45; joined the conspiracy against him. Murdered by his slaves the following year. A friend of Cicero and firmly to be dissociated from a namesake who followed Antony in 44.

Minucius Thermus, Q. Governor of Asia 51–50. A Pompeian in the Civil War and proscribed in 43, he escaped to join Sex. Pompeius and then Antony.

Munatius, T. Apparently held office in a province some time after 57.

Munatius Plancus, C. *see* Plautius Plancus.

Munatius Plancus, L. Family friend of Cicero. Served under Caesar in Gaul and the Civil War. City Prefect during Caesar's absence 46–45. As governor of Transalpine Gaul (except the Narbonensis), he finally joined Antony in 43. Consul in 42. Changed sides again before Actium and became Censor in 22. Founder of Lyons.

Nigidius Figulus, P. As a senator assisted Cicero in 63. Praetor in 58. Joined Pompey in the Civil War and died in 45. A prolific writer on various branches of learning, he was chiefly remembered as an astrologer and magician.

Oppius, C. Roman Knight, friend and agent of Caesar, often mentioned in conjunction with Cornelius Balbus and like him a friend of Atticus and Cicero.

Paconius Lepta, Q. Cicero's Prefect of Engineers in Cilicia.

Papirius Paetus, L. Wealthy resident of Naples and an old friend of Cicero.

Plancius, Cn. Befriended Cicero when Quaestor in Macedonia in 58. Curule Aedile in 55 or 54, defended by Cicero on a bribery charge in an extant speech. Last heard of in 45 as a Pompeian awaiting pardon in Corcyra.

Plautius (or Plotius) Plancus, L. Originally C. Munatius Plancus, brother of Cicero's correspondent. He appears in July 44 as in charge of assignment of land to Caesar's veterans. Praetor in 43 and intermediary between his brother in Gaul and the senate, he somehow ended up on the triumviral Proscription list and perished, as described by Valerius Maximus (6.8.5).

Pompeius Bithynicus. Friend of Cicero, Propraetor in Sicily 44–43. After some resistance he accepted Sex. Pompeius Magnus as co-governor, who later had him executed.

Pompeius Magnus, Cn. Pompey the Great.

Porcius Cato, M. 'Of Utica.' Leader of conservative opposition to the 'First Triumvirate.' Later made common cause with Pompey against Caesar, and after Pompey's death became the life and soul of die-hard resistance. Committed suicide at Utica after the republican defeat in 46.

Rex. Perhaps son of Q. Marcius Rex, Consul in 68 or perhaps a Rupilius Rex (see my Commentary, vol. I, p. 479). He seems to be a pardoned Pompeian holding a position of authority (Quaestor?) in Sicily.

Rutilius, M. (or Sempronius Rutilius, M.?). Very likely we should read RUTILUS, i.e. Caesar's former Legate M. Sempronius Rutilus (*Gallic War* 7.90.4), as suggested by Syme.

Sallustius, Cn. Proquaestor in Syria in 50; but the name is doubtful.

Scribonius Curio, C. Cicero's relations with him went back a long way, but the tone of the letters makes it obvious that Cicero stood on a much less intimate footing with this young nobleman than with Trebatius or Caelius Rufus, men of his own social type. In politics Curio played unpredictable, appearing as Tribune in 50 in the role of fervent optimate but suddenly going over to Caesar allegedly for a vast bribe. Defeated and killed in 49 leading an expedition to Africa.

Servilius Isauricus, P. Earlier aligned with Cato and married to his niece, he joined Caesar in the Civil War and was his colleague as Consul in 48. Governor of Asia in 46–44. Moderate opponent of Antony after Caesar's death, but later reconciled, becoming Consul again in 41.

Sestius, P. Quaestor in Macedonia in 62. As Tribune in 57 took a leading part in promoting Cicero's recall and was defended on charges in this connection by Cicero in 56 (speech extant). Later Praetor and Cicero's successor as governor of Cilicia in 49. Went over to Caesar after Pharsalia. Supported Cicero in 43 but kept life and status in the thirties. A notoriously wearisome speaker and writer.

Sextilius Rufus, C. Quaestor (?) in Cyprus in 49; perhaps the Sextilius Rufus who commanded Cassius' fleet in 43.

Silius, P. Governor of Bithynia 51–50; owner of a suburban property which Cicero wished to buy in 45.

Sittius, P. Roman Knight, who left Italy for Further Spain and then Mauretania in 64, where, according to our

sources, he became a military adventurer. In 57 condemned in absence on an unknown charge. Brought a force to join Caesar in 46 and received a principality in reward. Murdered in 44, not to Cicero's distress (*Letters to Atticus* 394(XV.17).1).

Sulpicius Galba, Ser. Legate to C. Pomptinus, then to Caesar in Gaul and Praetor in 54. Supported Caesar in the Civil War and joined the conspiracy against him in 44. Fought against Antony in the battle of Forum Gallorum. Probably perished in the Proscriptions.

Sulpicius Rufus, Ser. Friend and contemporary of Cicero's and one of the most famous of Roman jurists. Consul in 51, he strove to avert the coming conflict with Caesar, but in 49 after initial wavering joined Pompey (the common view that he stayed neutral is mistaken). After Pharsalia retired to Samos, but was appointed governor of Achaea by Caesar in 46. Died in 43 on a mission from the senate to Antony.

Terentia. Cicero's wife from about 80 to 46.

Terentius Varro, M. Of Reate, the most learned and prolific author of his time. Born in 116. Had a distinguished military and political career under Pompey's aegis; gave up the republican cause after Pharsalia and became head of Caesar's new library. Narrowly escaping proscription in 43 he lived on until 27 in tireless literary activity. Of his vast and various output only a small part, and that perhaps the least interesting (treatises on agriculture and the Latin language), survives, numerous fragments apart. Fragments of his *Menippean Satires* suggest that this was a real loss to Latin literature.

Trebatius Testa, C. Of Velia, an eminent jurist and a friend

of Cicero, about twenty years his junior. Recommended by him to Caesar in 54. Supported Caesar in the Civil War, remaining however on excellent terms with Cicero, who dedicated to him his *Topica,* a work full of illustrations taken from Roman law. He lived to a ripe old age and figures in the first Satire of Horace's second book.

Titius. Not identified.

Titius, T. Legate in a grain-exporting province (Sicily?). Perhaps one with the foregoing.

Titius Rufus, C. City Praetor in 50.

Toranius, C. Cicero writes to him as a Pompeian exile in 45. As Curule Aedile in 64 (?) he had C. Octavius as colleague, who left him guardian to his son, the future Augustus. That did not save him from proscription in 43, though he may have survived.

Trebianus. Another Pompeian exile.

Trebonius, C. Tribune in 55, put through a law extending Caesar's command. Legate to Caesar in Gallic and Civil Wars and Praetor in 48. Governor of Further Spain 47–46 and Suffect Consul in 45. Joined the conspiracy against Caesar in 44. Brutally murdered by Dolabella soon after arrival in Asia as governor.

Tullius Cicero, M. Cicero's son. He survived the troubles to be favoured by Octavian with a Consulship in 30 and Proconsulate in Asia, also earning a reputation as the hardest drinker in Rome.

Tullius Cicero, Q. Cicero's younger brother.

Tullius Tiro, M. Slave, later freedman, and confidential secretary and literary assistant to Cicero, after whose death his long life was largely devoted to fostering Cicero's memory and works.

Valerius, L. A jurist, later recommended to Ap. Claudius (Letter 64). Not certainly the mimographer of Letter 34 (see note to letter).

Valerius Orca, Q. Praetor in 57, thereafter governor of Africa. A Caesarian in the Civil War, he remained on good terms with Cicero.

Vatinius, P. Tribune in 59, carried through legislation on behalf of Caesar, to whom he later owed an Augurate and the Consulship in 47. Cicero attacked him in an extant speech, but in 54 became reconciled under pressure and defended him in court. From then on they were on friendly terms.

Volumnius Eutrapelus, P. Roman Knight and celebrated wit. After Caesar's death an adherent of Antony.

CICERO'S
LETTERS TO FRIENDS

1 (V.1)

Scr. in Gallia Cisalpina c. prid. Id. Ian. an. 62

Q. METELLUS Q. F. CELER PRO COS. S. D. M. TULLIO CICERONI

1   Si vales, bene est.[1]

Existimaram pro mutuo inter nos animo et pro reconciliata gratia nec absente‹m umquam me abs te›[2] ludibrio laesum iri nec Metellum fratrem ob dictum capite ac fortunis per te oppugnatum iri. quem si parum pudor ipsius defendebat, debebat vel familiae nostrae dignitas vel meum studium erga vos remque publicam satis sublevare. nunc video illum circumventum, me desertum a quibus minime conveniebat.

2   Itaque in luctu et squalore sum, qui provinciae, qui exercitui praesum, qui bellum gero. quae quoniam nec ratione nec maiorum nostrum clementia administrastis, non erit mirandum si vos paenitebit. te tam mobili in me

---

[1] benest *(recte, sed vide comm.; item in ep. sequenti*
[2] *(SB)*

---

[1] Q. Caecilius Metellus Nepos. Since entering office as Tribune on 10 December 63 he had demonstrated hostility to Cicero and his handling of the Catilinarian crisis. See next letter.

[2] Probably the one reported in para. 8 of Cicero's reply ('that one who had punished others' etc.).   [3] Customary when, for

1 (V.1)
METELLUS CELER TO CICERO

Cisalpine Gaul, ca. 12 January 62

Q. Metellus Celer, son of Quintus, Proconsul, to M. Tullius Cicero greetings.

I hope you are well!

In view of our reciprocal sentiments and the restoration of our friendly relations I had not expected that I should ever be held up by you to offensive ridicule in my absence, or that my brother Metellus[1] would be attacked at your instance in person or estate because of a phrase.[2] If his own honourable character did not suffice for his protection, the dignity of our family and my zeal on behalf of you and your friends and the commonwealth should have been support enough. Now it seems that he has been beset, and I deserted, by those whom it least behoved.

So I wear the black of mourning[3]—I, in command of a province and an army conducting a war![4] Well, you and your friends have managed it so, without reason or forbearance. It was not like this in our forbears' time, and it will not be surprising if you all come to be sorry.[5] I did not

example, a close relative faced prosecution on a capital charge. Many Romans put on mourning for Cicero when threatened by Clodius in 58. Metellus Nepos had been suspended from office by the Senate.   [4] Against Catiline.   [5] Perhaps a hint of what might happen when Pompey returned from the East.

meosque esse animo non sperabam. me interea nec
domesticus dolor nec cuiusquam iniuria ab re publica
abducet.

2 (V.2)

Scr. Romae med. m. Ian. an. 62

M. TULLIUS M. F. CICERO Q. METELLO Q. F. CELERI
PRO COS. S. D.

1 Si tu exercitusque valetis, bene est.

Scribis ad me te existimasse pro mutuo inter nos animo
et pro reconciliata gratia numquam te a me ludibrio laesum iri. quod cuius modi sit satis intellegere non possum;
sed tamen suspicor ad te esse adlatum me in senatu, cum
disputarem permultos esse qui rem publicam a me conservatam dolerent, dixisse a te propinquos tuos, quibus ne-
gare non potuisses, impetrasse ut ea quae statuisses tibi in
senatu de mea laude esse dicenda reticeres. quod cum dicerem, illud adiunxi, mihi tecum ita dispertitum officium
fuisse in rei publicae salute retinenda ut ego urbem a domesticis insidiis et ab intestino scelere, tu Italiam et ab
armatis hostibus et ab occulta coniuratione defenderes,
atque hanc nostram tanti et tam praeclari muneris societatem a tuis propinquis labefactatam, qui, cum tu a me rebus
amplissimis atque honorificentissimis ornatus esses, ti-

---

[1] It was usual to include the army in this formula when writing
to a commanding general.   [2] As Praetor in 63 Celer had
raised troops in northern Italy and cut off Catiline's retreat to
Gaul.

think to find your own disposition so changeable towards me and mine. In the meantime neither domestic unhappiness nor any man's ill usage shall turn me away from the commonwealth.

2 (V.2)
CICERO TO METELLUS CELER

Rome, mid January 62

From M. Tullius Cicero, son of Marcus, to Q. Metellus Celer, son of Quintus, Proconsul, greetings.

I hope all is well with you and the army.[1]

You write that you had not expected ever to be held up to offensive ridicule by me, in view of our reciprocal sentiments and the restoration of friendly relations. What that means, I cannot precisely tell. But I suspect you have heard a report to the effect that, while arguing in the Senate that there were very many who regretted my saving of the commonwealth, I remarked that relatives of yours, to whom you could not say no, had prevailed upon you to suppress what you had decided you ought to say in the Senate in commendation of myself. In making this observation, I added that you and I had made a division of duty in the preservation of the commonwealth: my part was to guard Rome from domestic plots and the enemy within the gates, yours to protect Italy from armed force and underground conspiracy.[2] This partnership of ours in so vital and splendid a task had been impaired by relatives of yours, who feared you might make me some gesture of mutual good

muissent ne quae mihi pars abs te voluntatis mutuae tribueretur.

2 Hoc in sermone cum a me exponeretur quae mea exspectatio fuisset orationis tuae quantoque in errore versatus essem, visa est oratio non iniucunda, et mediocris quidam est risus consecutus, non in te sed magis in errorem meum et quod me abs te cupisse laudari aperte atque ingenue confitebar. iam hoc non potest in te non honorifice esse dictum, me in clarissimis meis atque amplissimis rebus tamen aliquod testimonium tuae vocis habere voluisse.

3 Quod autem ita scribis, 'pro mutuo inter nos animo,' quid tu existimes esse in amicitia mutuum, nescio; equidem hoc arbitror, cum par voluntas accipitur et redditur. ego si hoc dicam, me tua causa praetermisisse provinciam, tibi ipse levior videar esse; meae enim rationes ita tulerunt, atque eius mei consili maiorem in dies singulos fructum voluptatemque capio. illud dico, me, ut primum in contione provinciam deposuerim, statim quem ad modum eam tibi traderem cogitare coepisse. nihil dico de sortione vestra; tantum te suspicari volo, nihil in ea re per collegam meum me insciente esse factum. recordare cetera, quam cito senatum illo die facta sortitione coegerim, quam multa de te verba fecerim, cum tu ipse mihi dixisti orationem meam non solum in te honorificam sed etiam in colle-

---

3 Macedonia and Cisalpine Gaul had been assigned by the Senate as consular provinces for 62. Cicero enlisted support against Catiline from his unreliable colleague C. Antonius by letting him have Macedonia instead of drawing lots. Later he an-

will in response to the ungrudging warmth of my tributes to yourself.

When in the course of my remarks I explained how eagerly I had been looking forward to your speech and how egregiously I had been astray, my speech caused some amusement and a moderate amount of laughter ensued—not directed at you, but rather at my mistake, and at the artless candour with which I admitted my desire to be praised by you. Really there could be nothing but compliment to you in my saying that at the very height of my glory I still hankered for some testimonial from *your* lips.

As for your reference to 'our reciprocal sentiments,' I do not know how you define reciprocity in friendship. I conceive it to lie in good will equally received and returned. If I were to say that I forwent a province[3] for your sake, you would think me less than sincere. It suited my purpose to do so, and I draw more pleasure and profit every day from my decision. What I do say is, that having announced the relinquishment of my province at a public meeting, I lost no time in planning how to transfer it to you. Of the lottery among the board of Praetors I say nothing. I only invite you to surmise that I was privy to all my colleague's actions in the matter. Be pleased to recall what followed, how promptly I called the Senate together on the day the lottery had taken place, and at what length I spoke about you. You said to me yourself that my speech was flattering to you to the point of being less than complimen-

nounced that he would not take a province at all, leaving Cisalpine Gaul to be allotted to one of the eight Praetors. He goes on to imply that Antonius, instigated by himself, had manipulated the lottery in Celer's favour.

41

4 gas tuos contumeliosam fuisse. iam illud senatus consultum quod eo die factum est ea praescriptione est ut, dum id exstabit, officium meum in te obscurum esse non possit. postea vero quam profectus es, velim recordere quae ego de te in senatu egerim, quae in contionibus dixerim, quas ad te litteras miserim. quae cum omnia collegeris, tu ipse velim iudices satisne videatur his omnibus rebus tuus adventus, cum proxime Romam venisti, mutue respondisse.

5 Quod scribis de reconciliata gratia, non intellego cur reconciliatam esse dicas quae numquam imminuta est.

6 Quod scribis non oportuisse Metellum, fratrem tuum, ob dictum a me oppugnari, primum hoc velim existimes, animum mihi istum tuum vehementer probari et fraternam plenam humanitatis ac pietatis voluntatem; deinde, si qua ego in re fratri tuo rei publicae causa restiterim, ut mihi ignoscas (tam enim sum amicus rei publicae quam qui maxime); si vero meam salutem contra illius impetum in me crudelissimum defenderim, satis habeas nihil me etiam tecum de tui fratris iniuria conqueri. quem ego cum comperissem omnem sui tribunatus conatum in meam perniciem parare atque meditari, egi cum Claudia, uxore tua, et cum vestra sorore Mucia, cuius erga me studium pro Cn. Pompei necessitudine multis in rebus perspexe-
7 ram, ut eum ab illa iniuria deterrerent. atqui ille, quod te

---

4 The decree (ca. October 63) will have appointed Celer to a command in north Italy prior to his taking over the governorship of his province. Cicero's name would appear in the preamble with a complimentary reference to Celer's services as Praetor.

5 This visit must have taken place at the end of 63 while Celer was still Praetor.

tary to your colleagues. Moreover, the senatorial decree[4] passed that day contained a preamble which, as long as the document survives, will plainly testify to the friendly office I did you. Then, after you left Rome, I would ask you to recollect my speeches in the Senate with reference to yourself, my deliverances at public meetings, and the letters I sent you. When you have put all this together, I leave to your own judgement whether your conduct on the occasion of your recent visit[5] to Rome adequately reciprocated mine at all these points.

You refer to 'the restoration of friendly relations.' I fail to understand why you should speak of a restoration of relations which have never been impaired.

You write that your brother Metellus should not have been attacked by me because of a phrase. Now in the first place I would ask you to believe that your sentiment here, your fraternal spirit redolent of good feeling and natural affection, has my warm approval. Secondly, if in any matter I have opposed your brother on public grounds, I ask you to forgive me—in public spirit I call no man my superior. But if I have defended my existence as a citizen in face of a savage onslaught on his part, you should be content that *I* do not protest to *you* about your brother's ill usage. When I learned that he was planning and preparing his entire program as Tribune with a view to my destruction, I addressed myself to your lady wife Claudia[6] and your sister Mucia[7] (her friendly disposition towards me as a friend of Cn. Pompeius had been plain to me in many connections) and asked them to persuade him to give up his injurious design.

[6] See Index under Clodia.
[7] Actually half-sister, married to Pompey.

audisse certo scio, prid. Kal. Ian., qua iniuria nemo umquam in ullo[1] magistratu improbissimus civis adfectus est
ea me consulem adfecit, cum rem publicam conservassem,
atque abeuntem magistratu contionis habendae potestate
privavit. cuius iniuria mihi tamen honori summo fuit; nam
cum ille mihi nihil nisi ut iurarem permitteret, magna voce
iuravi verissimum pulcherrimumque ius iurandum, quod
populus idem magna voce me vere iurasse iuravit.

8   Hac accepta tam insigni iniuria tamen illo ipso die misi
ad Metellum communis amicos qui agerent cum eo ut de
illa mente desisteret. quibus ille respondit sibi non esse
integrum; etenim paulo ante in contione dixerat ei qui in
alios animum advertisset indicta causa dicendi ipsi potestatem fieri non oportere. hominem gravem et civem egregium, qui, qua poena senatus consensu bonorum omnium
eos adfecerat qui urbem incendere et magistratus ac senatum trucidare, bellum maximum conflare voluissent,
eadem dignum iudicaret eum qui curiam caede, urbem
incendiis, Italiam bello liberasset! itaque ego Metello, fratri tuo, praesenti restiti. nam in senatu Kal. Ian. sic cum eo
de re publica disputavi ut sentiret sibi cum viro forti et
constanti esse pugnandum. a.d. III Non. Ian. cum agere
coepisset, tertio quoque verbo orationis suae me appella-
bat, mihi minabatur, neque illi quicquam deliberatius fuit
quam me, quacumque ratione posset, non iudicio neque

---

[1] animo *(SB (noluit Or.))*

---

8 The usual oath taken by a retiring magistrate, that he had observed the laws during his term of office. Cicero neatly adapted it
to the occasion by swearing that he alone had saved Rome and the
Republic.

And yet, on the last day of the year, as I am sure you have heard, he put upon me, Consul and saviour of the commonwealth, an insult which has never been put upon any holder of any magistracy, no matter how disloyal: he deprived me of the power to address an assembly before retiring from office. This affront, however, redounded greatly to my honour. In face of his refusal to let me do more than take the oath,[8] I swore in loud tones the truest and finest oath that ever was, and the people likewise in loud tones swore that I had sworn the truth.

Even after receiving so signal an insult I sent common friends to Metellus that very same day to urge him to change his attitude. He replied that his hands were no longer free; and in fact he had declared at a public meeting a little while previously that one who had punished others without a hearing ought not to be given the right to speak himself. What sense of responsibility, what civic virtue! To judge the preserver of the Senate from massacre, of Rome from arson, of Italy from war, worthy of the same penalty as was inflicted by the Senate with the approbation of all honest men upon those who had designed to set fire to Rome, slaughter magistrates and Senate, and kindle a terrible conflict![9] Accordingly, I stood up to your brother Metellus face to face. On the Kalends of January we had a political disputation in the Senate which let him feel that he had to deal with a man of courage and resolution. In a speech on 3 January he named me in every sentence with threats; he had thoroughly made up his mind to bring me down by hook or by crook—not through due process of

---

[9] The Senate had decreed a public Thanksgiving in honour of Cicero's services almost in these terms.

disceptatione sed vi atque impressione evertere. huius ego temeritati si virtute atque animo non restitissem, quis esset qui me in consulatu non casu potius existimaret quam consilio fortem fuisse?

9 Haec si tu Metellum cogitare de me nescisti, debes existimare te maximis de rebus a fratre esse celatum; sin autem aliquid impertivit tibi sui consili, lenis a te et facilis existimari debeo qui nihil tecum de his ipsis rebus expostulem. et si intellegis non me dicto Metelli, ut scribis, sed consilio eius animoque in me inimicissimo esse commotum, cognosce nunc humanitatem meam, si humanitas appellanda est in acerbissima iniuria remissio animi ac dissolutio. nulla est a me umquam sententia dicta in fratrem tuum; quotienscumque aliquid est actum, sedens iis adsensi qui mihi lenissime sentire visi sunt. addam illud etiam, quod iam ego curare non debui sed tamen fieri non moleste tuli atque etiam ut ita fieret pro mea parte adiuvi, ut senati consulto meus inimicus, quia tuus frater erat, sublevaretur.

10 Qua re non ego oppugnavi fratrem tuum, sed fratri tuo repugnavi; nec in te, ut scribis, animo fui mobili, sed ita stabili ut in mea erga te voluntate etiam desertus ab officiis tuis permanerem. atque hoc ipso tempore tibi paene minitanti nobis per litteras hoc rescribo atque respondeo: ego dolori tuo non solum ignosco sed summam etiam laudem tribuo (meus enim me sensus quanta vis fraterni sit amoris

---

10 Perhaps the decree allowed Nepos to leave Italy, as in fact he did.

law, but by aggressive violence. If I had not offered a spirited and manly resistance to his indiscretions, nobody could have believed that my record as a courageous Consul was aught but a freak of chance.

If you were unaware of Metellus' intentions towards me, you must recognize that your brother has kept you in the dark about matters of the highest consequence. On the other hand, if he told you something of his plans, you ought to appreciate how mild and easygoing I show myself in not expostulating with you on this very subject. And if you recognize that I was not upset by a phrase of Metellus but by the bitter hostility of his purpose and attitude towards me, I must ask you now to note my forbearance—if that is the right word for laxity and weakness in the face of the most severe provocation. I have never once spoken in the Senate for a motion against your brother; on all such occasions I have kept my seat and supported those who appeared to me to make the most lenient proposal. I will add something else: although I could not be expected, after what had passed, to be active in the matter, I was not sorry to see my enemy relieved[10] (because he was your brother) by a senatorial decree, and I even assisted, so far as in me lay, to bring this about.

Thus I made no attack upon your brother, but repelled his attack on me; and my disposition towards you, so far from being changeable, has been eminently stable, so much so that my feelings remained the same even when friendly actions on your part were no longer forthcoming. Even now, though you have written to me in almost menacing terms, this is the answer I have to make: I not only pardon your irritation, I highly commend it—my own experience of the power of a brother's affection is my

admonet); a te peto ut tu quoque aequum te iudicem dolori meo praebeas; si acerbe, si crudeliter, si sine causa sum a
tuis oppugnatus, ut statuas mihi non modo non cedendum
sed etiam tuo atque exercitus tui auxilio in eius modi causa
utendum fuisse.

Ego te mihi semper amicum esse volui, me ut tibi amicissimum esse intellegeres laboravi. maneo in voluntate et,
quoad voles tu, permanebo, citiusque amore tui fratrem
tuum odisse desinam quam illius odio quicquam de nostra
benevolentia detraham.

3 (V.7)

Scr. Romae m. Apr. an. 62

M. TULLIUS M. F. CICERO S. D. CN. POMPEIO CN.F.
MAGNO IMPERATORI

1   S. t. e. q. v. b.; e. ⟨v.⟩[1]

Ex litteris tuis quas publice misisti cepi una cum
omnibus incredibilem voluptatem; tantam enim spem oti
ostendisti qua⟨nta⟩m ego semper omnibus te uno fretus
pollicebar. sed hoc scito, tuos veteres hostis, novos amicos,

---

[1] *(Lamb).*

---

[1] Pompey's cognomen Magnus (the Great), conferred by his
victorious troops in 81 and confirmed by Sulla, was used officially,
and in a formal address like this it would have been discourteous
to omit it. Otherwise Cicero does not normally use it simply as a
name, without further implications.

monitor. In return, I ask you to be fair in your judgement of a similar feeling on my part, and to take the view that, if I have been the victim of a bitter, savage, and unprovoked attack by a member of your family, it was not incumbent on me to give way—that, on the contrary, I was entitled in such a situation to your support and that of the army you command.

I have ever wanted you to be my friend, and have tried to let you see that I am a very good friend of yours. My sentiments remain the same, and shall, as long as you so desire. I shall sooner give up my resentment against your brother out of affection for you than abate a jot of the good will between us out of animosity towards him.

3 (V.7)
CICERO TO POMPEY

Rome, April 62

From M. Tullius Cicero, son of Marcus, to Cn. Pompeius Magnus,[1] son of Gnaeus, Imperator, greetings.

I hope all is well with you and the army, as it is with me.

Like the rest of us I was immeasurably delighted with your dispatch,[2] in which you have held out the bright prospect of a peaceful future; such a prospect as I have ever been promising to all and sundry in reliance on your single self. I must tell you, however, that it came as a severe blow

---

[2] To the magistrates and Senate, no doubt announcing the writer's return to Italy in the near future. He actually arrived at the end of the year.

vehementer litteris perculsos atque ex magna spe deturbatos iacere.

2   Ad me autem litteras quas misisti, quamquam exiguam significationem tuae erga me voluntatis habebant, tamen mihi scito iucundas fuisse. nulla enim re tam laetari soleo quam meorum officiorum conscientia; quibus si quando non mutue respondetur, apud me plus offici residere facillime patior. illud non dubito, quin, si te mea summa erga te studia parum mihi adiunxerint, res publica nos inter nos conciliatura coniuncturaque sit.

3   Ac ne ignores quid ego in tuis litteris desiderarim, scribam aperte, sicut et mea natura et nostra amicitia postulat. res eas gessi quarum aliquam in tuis litteris et nostrae necessitudinis et rei publicae causa gratulationem exspectavi; quam ego abs te praetermissam esse arbitror quod verere‹re›[2] ne cuius animum offenderes. sed scito ea quae nos pro salute patriae gessimus orbis terrae iudicio ac testimonio comprobari; quae, cum veneris, tanto consilio tantaque animi magnitudine a me gesta esse cognosces ut tibi multo maiori quam Africanus fuit [a] me non multo minore‹m› quam Laelium facile et in re publica et in amicitia adiunctum esse patiare.

[2] *(Vict.)*

---

[3] Who these were is disputed. Probably Caesar and perhaps Crassus were in mind, also subversives generally who hoped to see Pompey take their part against the senatorial establishment.

[4] These had been described in a lengthy letter sent to Pompey the previous December.

to your old enemies, nowadays your friends;[3] their high hopes dashed, they despond.

Your personal letter to me evinces but little of your friendly sentiments towards me, but you may be sure that it gave me pleasure all the same. My chief joy is apt to lie in the consciousness of my services to others. If these fail of a like response, I am perfectly content that the balance of good offices should rest on my side. I have no doubt that if my own hearty good will towards you does not suffice to win your attachment, the public interest will join us in confederacy.

Not to leave you in ignorance of the particular in which your letter has disappointed me, let me speak plainly, as becomes my character and our friendly relations. My achievements[4] have been such that I expected to find a word of congratulation upon them in your letter, both for friendship's sake and that of the commonwealth. I imagine you omitted anything of the sort for fear of giving offence in any quarter.[5] But I must tell you that what I have done for the safety of the country stands approved in the judgement and testimony of the whole world. When you return, you will find that I have acted with a measure of policy and a lack of self-regard which will make you well content to have me as your political ally and private friend—a not much lesser Laelius to a far greater Africanus.[6]

[5] I.e. to people like Caesar who condemned the execution of the Catilinarian conspirators.

[6] Scipio Africanus the Younger, destroyer of Carthage in 146. His lifelong friend was C. Laelius, called Sapiens (the Wise). Both figure in Cicero's Dialogues.

4 (V.6)

Scr. Romae med. vel ex. m. Dec. an. 62

M. CICERO S. D. P. SESTIO L. F. PRO Q.

1 Cum ad me Decius librarius venisset egissetque mecum ut operam darem ne tibi hoc tempore succederetur,
quamquam illum hominem frugi et tibi amicum existimabam, tamen, quod memoria tenebam cuius modi ad me
litteras antea misisses, non satis credidi homini prudenti
tam valde esse mutatam voluntatem tuam. sed postea
quam et Cornelia tua Terentiam convenit et ego cum Q.
Cornelio locutus sum, adhibui diligentiam, quotienscumque senatus fuit, ut adessem, plurimumque in eo negoti
habui ut Q. Fufium tribunum pl. et ceteros ad quos tu
scripseras cogerem mihi potius credere quam tuis litteris.
omnino res tota in mensem Ianuarium reiecta erat, sed
facile obtinebatur.

2 Ego tua gratulatione commotus, quod ad me pridem
scripseras velle te bene ⟨e⟩venire quod de Crasso domum emissem, emi eam ipsam domum ⌐xxxv⌐ aliquanto
post tuam gratulationem. itaque nunc me scito tantum habere aeris alieni ut cupiam coniurare, si quisquam recipiat.
sed partim odio inducti me excludunt et aperte vindicem
coniurationis oderunt, partim non credunt et a me insidias

---

[1] Assumed throughout as provenance, not only where evidence so points but in the absence of evidence to the contrary.

[2] Cornelia, daughter of L. Scipio Asiaticus, Consul in 83, was
Sestius' wife. Q. Cornelius may have been a client of her family.

[3] A very large sum, though there is evidence that much larger

LETTER 4 (V.6)

4 (V.6)
CICERO TO P. SESTIUS

Rome,[1] *mid or late December 62*

From M. Cicero to P. Sestius, son of Lucius, Proquaestor, greetings.

When your secretary Decius called on me and asked me to do my best to ensure that no successor to you is appointed for the present, despite my estimation of his honesty and loyalty to yourself, I hardly believed him. I remembered how you had written to me earlier on, and here was this sensible fellow telling me that you had completely changed your mind! But after your Cornelia met Terentia and I had a word with Q. Cornelius,[2] I took care to attend whenever there was a meeting of the Senate; and I had a deal of trouble to make Tribune Q. Fufius and the others to whom you had written believe me rather than your letters. The whole question has been deferred till January, but we are carrying our point without difficulty.

You wrote to me some time ago about Crassus' house, wishing me luck in my bargain. Stimulated by your felicitations I actually bought the house some time after I received them, for HS3,500,000.[3] So take notice that I am now so deeply in debt that I should be glad to join a plot, if anyone would have me. But some of them bar me out of prejudice—they hate me as a plot-breaker and make no bones about it. Others do not trust me. They fear a trap,

amounts were sometimes paid for houses in Rome. Cicero's purchase, situated on the Palatine above the Forum, was considered ostentatious (cf. *Letters to Atticus* 16 (I.16).10). It had belonged to Crassus' father.

metuunt nec putant ei nummos deesse posse qui ex obsi-
dione feneratores exemerit. omni<no> semissibus magna
copia est; ego autem meis rebus gestis hoc sum adsecutus
ut bonum nomen existimer.

3   Domum tuam atque aedificationem omnem perspexi
et vehementer probavi.

Antonium, etsi eius in me officia omnes desiderant,
tamen in senatu gravissime ac diligentissime defendi sena-
tumque vehementer oratione mea atque auctoritate com-
movi.

Tu ad me velim litteras crebrius mittas.

5 (V.5)

Scr. Romae c. VIII *Kal. Ian. an. 62*

M. CICERO S. D. C. ANTONIO M. F. IMP.

1   Etsi statueram nullas ad te litteras mittere nisi com-
mendaticias (non quo eas intellegerem satis apud te valere
sed ne iis qui me rogarent aliquid de nostra coniunctione
imminutum esse ostenderem), tamen, cum T. Pomponius,
homo omnium meorum in te studiorum et officiorum
maxime conscius, tui cupidus, nostri amantissimus, ad te
proficisceretur, aliquid mihi scribendum putavi, praesertim cum aliter ipsi Pomponio satis facere non possem.

2   Ego si abs te summa officia desiderem, mirum nemini
videri debeat. omnia enim a me in te profecta sunt quae ad

---

4 Monthly.

1 Cf. *Letters to Atticus* 12 (I.12) and 13 (I.13).1. Atticus no
doubt took the letter with him to Greece.

and won't believe that the man who got the capitalists out of a tight corner can be short of cash! To be sure there's plenty of money to be had at ½%;[4] and my exploits have at least got me the reputation of being a good risk.

I have inspected your house and all the new building, and heartily approve.

The lack of friendship towards me on Antonius' part is universally remarked; notwithstanding which, I have defended him in the Senate in the most weighty and conscientious style. The House was strongly impressed by what I said and the fact that I said it.

Please write to me more often.

5 (V.5)
CICERO TO C. ANTONIUS

Rome, ca. 23 December 62

From M. Cicero to C. Antonius, son of Marcus, Imperator, greetings.

I had not intended to write you any letters except of recommendation—not that I had any reason to suppose they carry any particular weight with you, but because I did not wish to show the persons who asked for them that our connection was less close than formerly. However, T. Pomponius[1] knows my zeal and friendly offices on your behalf better than any man; he is a well-wisher of yours and a very devoted friend of mine. Since he is setting out to join you, I think I ought to write a few lines, especially as Pomponius himself would be disappointed if I did not.

Nobody could fairly wonder if I were to expect great favours from you, for everything has been forthcoming on

tuum commodum, quae ad honorem, quae ad dignitatem pertinerent. pro his rebus nullam mihi abs te relatam esse gratiam tu es optimus testis, contra etiam esse aliquid abs te profectum ex multis audivi; nam comperisse me non audeo dicere, ne forte id ipsum verbum ponam quod abs te aiunt falso in me solere conferri. sed ea quae ad me delata sunt malo te ex Pomponio, cui non minus molesta fuerunt, quam ex meis litteris cognoscere. meus in te animus quam singulari officio fuerit, et senatus et populus Romanus testis est; tu quam gratus erga me fueris ipse existimare potes, quantum mihi debeas ceteri existiment.[1]

3 Ego quae tua causa antea feci, voluntate sum adductus posteaque constantia; sed reliqua, mihi crede, multo maius meum studium maioremque gravitatem et laborem desiderant. quae ego si non profundere ac perdere videbor, omnibus meis viribus sustinebo; sin autem ingrata esse sentiam, non committam ut tibi ipsi insanire videar. ea quae sint et cuius modi poteris ex Pomponio cognoscere. atque ipsum tibi Pomponium ita commendo ut, quamquam ipsius causa confido te facturum esse omnia, tamen abs te hoc petam ut, si quid in te residet amoris erga me, id omne in Pomponi negotio ostendas. hoc mihi nihil gratius facere potes.

[1] existimant

---

[2] 'Learned' (*comperisse*) was the word used by Cicero when reporting to the Senate what he had discovered about Catiline's plot. His enemies took it up against him, no doubt with the implication that the intelligence had been manufactured or doctored by Cicero himself. The word 'untruly' (*falso*) seems to be in denial of such an implication.

my side which might conduce to your interest, honour, and prestige. To the fact that I have received nothing from you in return you are the best witness; that in some measure you have even shown a disposition to the contrary I have heard from many sources—I dare not say 'learned'[2] in case I might be using the very word which they tell me you often bring up against me (untruly). But I had rather you heard of the stories which have reached me from Pomponius (he has been no less vexed by them than I) than from a letter of mine. The Senate and People of Rome stand witness to my conspicuously friendly disposition towards you. Of your gratitude yourself can judge, of your debt to me let the world judge.

What I have already done for you was done at first out of good will and later for consistency's sake. But I assure you that the future will make far larger demands on my zeal, loyalty, and energy. I shall persevere with all my might, provided I do not seem to be throwing my trouble away. But if I find that it gets me no thanks, I shall not let myself be taken for an idiot—even by you. Pomponius will inform you of what I mean and explain its nature.[3] As for Pomponius himself, I recommend him to you, though I am confident that you will do all you can for his own sake. Still, I will ask you to show any regard for me that you may retain in Pomponius' affair.[4] You can do nothing that will oblige me more.

---

[3] Antonius might, and in the event did, have to face charges when he returned to Rome, and Pompey was rumoured to intend getting him recalled.

[4] The money owed to Atticus by the town of Sicyon (cf. *Letters to Atticus* 13 (I.13).1).

6 (XIV.4)

Scr. Brundisii prid. Kal. Mai. an. 58

TULLIUS S. D. TERENTIAE ET TULLIAE ET CICERONI SUIS

1 Ego minus saepe do ad vos litteras quam possum propterea quod cum omnia mihi tempora sunt misera, tum vero, cum aut scribo ad vos aut vestras lego, conficior lacrimis sic ut ferre non possim. quod utinam minus vitae cupidi fuissemus! certe nihil aut non multum in vita mali vidissemus. quod si nos ad aliquam alicuius commodi aliquando reciperandi spem Fortuna reservavit, minus est erratum a nobis; si<n>[1] haec mala fixa sunt, ego vero te quam primum, mea vita, cupio videre et in tuo complexu emori, quoniam neque di, quos tu castissime coluisti, neque homines, quibus ego semper servivi, nobis gratiam rettulerunt.

2 Nos Brundisi apud M. Laenium Flaccum dies XIII fuimus, virum optimum, qui periculum fortunarum et capitis sui prae mea salute neglexit neque legis improbissimae poena deductus est quo minus hospiti et amicitiae ius officiumque praestaret. huic utinam aliquando gratiam
3 referre possimus! habebimus quidem semper. Brundisio profecti sumus a. d. II[2] Kal. Mai. per Macedoniam Cyzicum petebamus.

O me perditum, o me adflictum! quid nunc? rogem te ut venias, mulierem aegram, et corpore et animo confec-

----

[1] *(Rut.)*   [2] v *(Corr.)*

----

[1] See *Letters to Atticus* 49 (III.4).

6 (XIV.4)
CICERO TO HIS FAMILY

Brundisium, 29 April 58

From Tullius to his dear Terentia and Tullia and Marcus greetings.

I send you letters less often than I have opportunity, because, wretched as every hour is for me, when I write to you at home or read your letters I am so overcome with tears that I cannot bear it. If only I had been less anxious to save my life! Assuredly I should have seen no sorrow in my days, or not much. If Fortune has spared me for some hope of one day recovering some measure of well-being, my error has not been so total. But if these present evils are to stay, then, yes, I want to see you, dear heart, as soon as I can, and to die in your arms, since neither the Gods whom you have worshipped so piously nor the men to whose service I have always devoted myself have made us any recompense.

I have stayed in Brundisium for thirteen days with M. Laenius Flaccus, a very worthy gentleman. He has disregarded the danger to his own property and status in his concern for my safety, and refused to be deterred by the penalties of a wicked law[1] from carrying out the established duties of hospitality and friendship. I pray that one day I may be able to show him my gratitude. Grateful I shall always be. I am leaving Brundisium on 29 April and making for Cyzicus by way of Macedonia.

Ah, what a desperate, pitiful case is mine! What now? Shall I ask you to come—a sick woman, physically and spir-

tam? non rogem? sine te igitur sim? opinor, sic agam: si est spes nostri reditus, eam confirmes et rem adiuves; sin, ut ego metuo, transactum est, quoquo modo potes, ad me fac venias. unum hoc scito: si te habebo, non mihi videbor plane perisse. sed quid Tulliola mea fiet? iam id vos videte; mihi deest consilium. sed certe, quoquo modo se res habebit, illius misellae et matrimonio et famae serviendum est. quid? Cicero meus quid aget? iste vero sit in sinu semper et complexu tuo.[3] non queo plura iam scribere; impedit maeror.

4   Tu quid egeris nescio, utrum aliquid teneas an, quod metuo, plane sis spoliata. Pisonem, ut scribis, spero fore semper nostrum. de familia liberata, nihil est quod te moveat. primum tuis ita promissum est, te facturam esse ut quisque esset meritus; est autem in officio adhuc Orpheus, praeterea magno opere nemo. ceterorum servorum ea causa est ut, si res a nobis abisset,[4] liberti nostri essent, si obtinere potuissent; sin ad nos pertinerent, servirent, praeterquam oppido pauci. sed haec minora sunt.

5   Tu quod me hortaris ut animo sim magno et spem habeam reciperandae salutis, id velim sit eius modi ut recte sperare possimus. nunc miser quando tuas iam litteras accipiam? quis ad me perferet? quas ego exspectassem Brundisi si esset licitum per nautas, qui tempestatem praetermittere noluerunt.

6   Quod reliquum est, sustenta te, mea Terentia, ut potes honestissime. viximus, floruimus; non vitium nostrum sed

---

[3] meo *(Tyrrell)** [4] abesset *(Lambini amicus)*

---

[2] Tullia's husband, C. Calpurnius Piso Frugi.

itually exhausted? Shall I *not* ask then? Am I to live without
you? Perhaps I should put it like this: if there is any hope of
my return, you must build it up, and help in the campaign.
On the other hand if all is over, as I fear, then come to me
any way you can. Be sure of one thing: if I have you, I shall
not feel that I am utterly lost. But what is to become of my
Tulliola? You at home must take care of that—I have nothing to suggest. But assuredly, however matters turn out,
the poor little girl's marriage and good name must be a pri-
mary consideration. Then there is my son. What will he
do? I hope that he will always be clasped to your bosom. I
cannot write any more now. Grief clogs my pen.

How you have fared I do not know—whether you still
have something left, or, as I fear, have been stripped of all.
Yes, I trust that Piso[2] will always be faithful. You need not
worry about the freeing of the household. In the first place,
the promise made to your people was that you would treat
each case on its merits (Orpheus, in fact, is loyal so far,
none of the others very noticeably so). The position of the
other slaves is that if it turned out that my property was no
longer mine, they would be my freedmen, provided they
could make good their claim to the status; whereas, if I still
had a hold on them, they would remain my slaves except
for just a few. But these are minor matters.

You urge me to hold my head high and hope for restoration. I wish the facts may give ground for reasonable hope.
Meanwhile, as matters wretchedly stand, when am I going
to get your next letter? Who will bring it to me? I should
have waited for it at Brundisium if the sailors had let me,
but they did not want to lose the fair weather.

For the rest, dearest Terentia, bear up with all the dignity you can muster. It has been a good life, a great career.

virtus nostra nos adflixit. peccatum est nullum, nisi quod non una animam cum ornamentis amisimus. sed si hoc fuit liberis nostris gratius, nos vivere, cetera, quamquam ferenda non sunt, feramus. atqui[5] ego, qui te confirmo, ipse me non possum.

Clodium Philhetaerum, quod valetudine oculorum impediebatur, hominem fidelem, remisi. Sal<l>ustius officio vincit omnis. Pescennius est perbenevolus nobis; quem semper spero tui fore observantem. Sicca dixerat se mecum fore, sed Brundisio discessit.

Cura, quod potes, ut valeas et sic existimes, me vehementius tua miseria quam mea commoveri. mea Terentia, fidissima atque optima uxor, et mea carissima filiola et spes reliqua nostra, Cicero, valete.

Prid. Kal. Mai. Brundisio.

7 (XIV.2)

Scr. Thessalonicae III Non. Oct. an. 58

TULLIUS S. D. TERENTIAE SUAE ET TULLIOLAE ET CICERONI SUIS

1   Noli putare me ad quemquam longiores epistulas scribere, nisi si quis ad me plura scripsit, cui puto rescribi oportere. nec enim habeo quid scribam nec hoc tempore quicquam difficilius facio. ad te vero et ad nostram Tulliolam non queo sine plurimis lacrimis scribere. vos enim video esse miserrimas, quas ego beatissimas semper esse

---

[5] atque *(Wes.)**

The good in me, nothing bad, has brought me down. I have
done nothing wrong, except that when I lost the good
things of life I did not lose life itself. But if it was more for
our children's happiness that I should live, let us bear what
remains, intolerable though it be. And yet, while I tell you
to be strong, I cannot tell myself.

I am sending Clodius Philhetaerus back, because he is
hampered by eye trouble. He is a faithful fellow. Sallustius
is the most forward of all. Pescennius is full of kindly feeling towards me; I think he will always be attentive to you.
Sicca had told me that he would stay with me, but has left
Brundisium.

Take care of your health as best you can, and believe
that your unhappiness grieves me more than my own. My
dear Terentia, loyalest and best of wives, my darling little
daughter, and Marcus, our one remaining hope, good-bye.

29 April, from Brundisium.

7 (XIV.2)
CICERO TO HIS FAMILY

Thessalonica, 5 October 58

From Tullius to his dear Terentia and his dear Tulliola and
Marcus greetings.

You are not to suppose that I write letters of any length
to anyone, unless somebody has written a lot to me and I
feel I ought to reply. In fact I have nothing to write about,
and at the present time I find it the most intractable of
tasks. To you and our Tulliola I cannot write without many
tears, for I see that you are very unhappy—you, for whom I
wished all the happiness in the world. I ought to have given

volui idque praestare debui, et, nisi tam timidi fuissemus, praestitissem.

2   Pisonem nostrum merito eius amo plurimum. eum, ut potui, per litteras cohortatus sum gratiasque egi, ut debui. in novis tribunis pl. intellego spem te habere. id erit firmum, si Pompei voluntas erit; sed Crassum tamen metuo.

A te quidem omnia fieri fortissime et amantissime video, nec miror, sed maereo casum eius modi ut tantis tuis miseriis meae miseriae subleventur. nam ad me P. Valerius, homo officiosus, scripsit, id quod ego maximo cum fletu legi, quem ad modum a Vestae ad Tabulam Valeriam ducta esses. hem, mea lux, meum desiderium, unde omnes opem petere solebant, te nunc, mea Terentia, sic vexari, sic iacere in lacrimis et sordibus, idque fieri mea culpa, qui ceteros servavi ut nos periremus!

3   Quod de domo scribis, hoc est de area, ego vero tum denique mihi videbor restitutus si illa nobis erit restituta. verum haec non sunt in nostra manu; illud doleo, quae impensa facienda est, in eius partem te miseram et despoliatam venire. quod si conficitur negotium, omnia consequemur; sin eadem nos fortuna premet, etiamne reliquias tuas miseras[1] proicies? obsecro te, mea vita, quod ad sumptum attinet, sine alios, qui possunt si modo volunt, sustinere; et valetudinem istam infirmam, si me amas, noli vexare. nam mihi ante oculos dies noctesque versaris.

---

[1] misera ⌐, *vulg. olim*

---

[1] In the Comitium, called after a painting set up by M. Valerius Messalla (nothing to do with P. Valerius) to commemorate a victory in the first Punic War. The Tribunes met there officially and it seems that Terentia had been summoned before them in

it to you, and should have done so if I had not been such a coward.

I have a great affection for Piso, as he deserves. I have written encouraging him as best I could and thanking him as was proper. I gather that you pin hopes on the new Tribunes. That will hold good, if Pompey is friendly; but I am still afraid of Crassus.

I see that courage and love shines in all you do, nor does that surprise me. But it is a heartbreaking situation when my distresses are relieved at the cost of so much distress to you. P. Valerius (he tries to help) has written to me an account, which I wept bitterly to read, of how you were taken from the Temple of Vesta to the Tabula Valeria.[1] Ah, my beloved, my heart's longing! To think that you, dearest Terentia, once everybody's refuge in trouble, should now be so tormented! There you are, plunged in tears and mourning, and it is my fault! In saving others, I ruined you and me.

As for what you say about the house, or rather the site on which it stood, indeed I shall not feel myself truly restored until that is restored to me. But these things are not in our hands. What grieves me is that in your unhappy and impoverished state you should be contributing to any necessary outlay. If the thing goes through, we shall win all. But if Fortune stays my enemy, are you going to throw away what poor little you have left? My darling, I beg you, where expense is concerned, let others bear it who can, if only they will; and do not overstrain that frail health of yours, if you love me. For you are before my eyes night and

connection with a financial matter. Her half-sister Fabia was a Vestal Virgin.

omnis labores te excipere video; timeo ut sustineas, sed
video in te esse omnia. quare, ut id quod speras et quod
agis consequamur, servi valetudini.

4   Ego ad quos scribam nescio, nisi ad eos qui ad me
scribunt aut ad eos de quibus ad me vos aliquid scribitis.
longius, quoniam ita vobis placet, non discedam; sed velim
quam saepissime litteras mittatis, praesertim si quid est
firmius quod speremus.

Valete, mea desideria, valete.

D. a. d. III Non. Oct. Thessalonica.

8 (XIV.1)

Scr. partim Thessalonicae med. m. Nov. partim Dyrrachii VI
Kal. Dec. an. 58

TULLIUS TERENTIAE SUAE TULLIOLAE SUAE CICE-
RONI SUO S. D.

1   Et litteris multorum et sermone omnium perfertur ad
me incredibilem tuam virtutem et fortitudinem esse teque
nec animi neque corporis laboribus defatigari. me miserum! te ista virtute, fide, probitate, humanitate in tantas
aerumnas propter me incidisse, Tulliolamque nostram, ex
quo patre tantas voluptates capiebat, ex eo tantos perci-
pere luctus! nam quid ego de Cicerone dicam? qui cum
primum sapere coepit, acerbissimos dolores miseriasque
percepit. quae si, tu ut scribis, fato facta putarem, ferrem
paulo facilius; sed omnia sunt mea culpa commissa, qui ab
iis me amari putabam qui invidebant, eos non sequebar

day. I see you are shouldering every burden. I fear you may not have the strength. Yet clearly everything depends on you. So in order that we may win the prize of your hopes and efforts, take good care of your health.

I do not know whom I should write to, except those who write to me or who are mentioned in letters from home. Since it is your joint wish, I shall not go further away. But I hope you will send me letters as often as possible, especially if we have grounds for reasonable hope.

Good-bye, my absent loves, good-bye.

Dispatched 5 October, from Thessalonica.

8 (XIV.1)

CICERO TO TERENTIA

Thessalonica, mid November 58, and Dyrrachium, 25 November

From Tullius to his dear Terentia and to dear Tulliola and to dear Marcus greetings.

Many folk write to me and everybody talks to me about you, what amazing courage and fortitude you show, how no trials of body or spirit wear you out. Ah me, to think that my brave, loyal, true, gentle wife should have come by such misery because of me! And to think that our Tulliola should be suffering so much grief on account of her papa, who used to give her so much pleasure! As for Marcus, what can I say? Bitter sorrow and suffering has been his portion since the earliest dawn of intelligence. If I thought all this was the work of fate, as you say, I should find it a little easier to bear. But I am to blame for everything. I thought I was loved by people who were only jealous of my

2   qui petebant. quod si nostris consiliis usi essemus neque apud nos tantum valuisset sermo aut stultorum amicorum aut improborum, beatissimi viveremus. nunc, quoniam sperare nos amici iubent, dabo operam ne mea valetudo tuo labori desit. res quanta sit intellego quantoque fuerit facilius manere domi quam redire. sed tamen, si omnis tribunos pl. habemus, si Lentulum tam studiosum quam videtur, si vero etiam Pompeium et Caesarem, non est desperandum.

3   De familia, quo modo placuisse scribis amicis faciemus. de loco, nunc quidem iam abiit pestilentia, sed quam diu fuit me non attigit. Plancius, homo officiosissimus, me cupit esse secum et adhuc retinet. ego volebam loco magis deserto esse in Epiro, quo neque Piso veniret nec milites, sed adhuc Plancius me retinet; sperat posse fieri ut mecum in Italiam decedat. quem ego diem si videro et si in vestrum complexum venero ac si et vos et me ipsum reciperaro, satis magnum mihi fructum videbor percepisse et vestrae pietatis et meae.

4   Pisonis humanitas, virtus, amor in omnis nos tantus est ut nihil supra possit. utinam ea res ei voluptati sit! gloriae quidem video fore. de Quinto fratre, nihil ego te accusavi, sed vos, cum praesertim tam pauci sitis, volui esse quam

5   coniunctissimos. quibus me voluisti agere gratias egi et me a te certiorem factum esse scripsi.

      Quod ad me, mea Terentia, scribis te vicum vendituram, quid, obsecro te (me miserum!), quid futurum est? et

---

[1] P. Cornelius Lentulus Spinther.   [2] L. Calpurnius Piso Caesoninus, Consul in 58 and incoming governor of Macedonia. Distinguish from Cicero's son-in-law in the next paragraph.

success, while I refused to follow those who sought my friendship. If only I had relied upon my own judgement instead of paying so much attention to the talk of friends, whether fools or knaves, how happy I might have been! As things are, since our friends tell us to hope, I shall take care not to let my health let your efforts down. I well understand the magnitude of the task, and how much easier it would have been to stay at home than it is to return. However, if we have all the Tribunes on our side, if Lentulus[1] is as zealous as he seems, and if we also have Pompey's and Caesar's good will, we ought not to despair.

As to my household, I shall do as you tell me our friends think best. As to my place of residence, the epidemic has now disappeared, but while it lasted it did not touch me. Plancius, who is untiring in his good offices, is anxious to have me with him, and keeps me here. I wanted to stay in some less frequented place in Epirus out of the way of Piso[2] and his soldiers, but Plancius still keeps me here. He hopes it may turn out that he leaves for Italy in my company. If I live to see that day, and return to my family's embraces, and get all of you and my own self back again, I shall feel that your devotion to me and mine to you have been sufficiently rewarded.

Piso's kindness, manliness, and affection for us all is quite superlative. I pray it may bring him happiness; certainly it will bring him honour. As regards my brother Quintus, I meant no criticism of yourself; but I wanted you all to be as close to one another as possible, especially as you are so few. I have thanked the persons you wished me to thank, and written that my information came from you.

Dearest, you tell me that you are going to sell a row of houses. This is dreadful. What in the name of heaven, *what*

si nos premet eadem fortuna, quid puero misero fiet? non queo reliqua scribere, tanta vis lacrimarum est; neque te in eundem fletum adducam. tantum scribo: si erunt in officio amici, pecunia non deerit; si non erunt, tu efficere tua pecunia non poteris. per fortunas miseras nostras, vide ne puerum perditum perdamus. cui si aliquid erit ne egeat, mediocri virtute opus est et mediocri fortuna ut cetera consequatur.

6   Fac valeas et ad me tabellarios mittas ut sciam quid agatur et vos quid agatis. mihi omnino iam brevis exspectatio est. Tulliolae et Ciceroni salutem dic. valete.

7   Dyrrachium veni, quod et libera civitas est et in me officiosa et proxima Italiae. sed si offendet me loci celebritas, alio me conferam, ad te scribam.

D. a. d. vi Kal. Dec. Dyrrachi.

9 (XIV.3)

Scr. Dyrrachii prid. Kal. Dec. an. 58

TULLIUS S. D. TERENTIAE SUAE ET TULLIAE ET CICERONI

1   Accepi ab Aristocrito tris epistulas, quas ego lacrimis prope delevi. conficior enim maerore, mea Terentia, nec meae me miseriae magis excruciant quam tuae vestrae-

---

3 Para. 7 is a postscript added at Dyrrachium. The letter proper was written before Cicero left Thessalonica in mid November (cf. *Letters to Atticus* 67 (III.22).4).

is to happen? And if no change of fortune comes to my relief, what is to become of our poor boy? I cannot go on, the tears overcome me, and I would not wish to draw yours. Just this I will say: if my friends are loyal, money will not be lacking; if not, you cannot achieve results with *your* money. For pity's sake, pitiable that we are, don't let our unfortunate boy be utterly ruined! If he has something to keep him above penury, he only needs a modicum of ability and a modicum of luck to gain the rest.

Take care of yourself and send me couriers, so that I know what is doing and what you and the children are doing. To be sure, I have not long to wait now. Give my love to Tulliola and Marcus. Good-bye to you all.

I have come to Dyrrachium[3] because it is a Free City, and anxious to serve me, and the nearest point to Italy. But if I find there are too many people about for my liking, I shall go somewhere else and send you word.

Dispatched 25 November, Dyrrachium.

9 (XIV.3)
CICERO TO HIS FAMILY

Dyrrachium, 29 November 58

From Tullius to his dear Terentia and Tullia and Marcus greetings.

I have received three letters from Aristocritus, and almost blotted them out in tears. I am overwhelmed with grief, dearest Terentia; and my own distresses do not tor-

que. ego autem hoc miserior sum quam tu, quae es miserrima, quod ipsa calamitas communis est utriusque nostrum, sed culpa mea propria est. meum fuit officium vel legatione vitare periculum vel diligentia et copiis re-

2 sistere vel cadere fortiter. hoc miserius, turpius, indignius nobis nihil fuit. qua re cum dolore conficiar, tum etiam pudore. pudet enim me uxori [mae]¹ optimae, suavissimis liberis virtutem et diligentiam non praestitisse. nam mi ante oculos dies noctesque versatur squalor vester et mae-ror et infirmitas valetudinis tuae. spes autem salutis perte-nuis ostenditur. inimici sunt multi, invidi paene omnes. eicere nos magnum fuit, excludere facile est. sed tamen, quam diu vos eritis in spe, non deficiam, ne omnia mea culpa cecidisse videantur.

3 Ut tuto sim quod laboras, id mihi nunc facillimum est, quem etiam inimici volunt vivere in tantis miseriis. ego tamen faciam quae praecipis. amicis quibus voluisti egi gratias et eas litteras Dexippo dedi meque de eorum officio scripsi a te certiorem esse factum. Pisonem nostrum miri-fico esse studio in nos et officio et ego perspicio et omnes praedicant. di faxint ut tali genero mihi praesenti tecum simul et cum liberis nostris frui liceat! nunc spes reliqua est in novis tribunis pl. et in primis quidem diebus. nam si

4 inveterarit, actum est. ea re ad te statim Aristocritum misi ut ad me continuo initia rerum et rationem totius negoti

---

¹ *(Ern.)*

---

¹ See Glossary under Legate.

ture me more than yours and my family's. But my wretchedness is greater than yours (and yours is bitter enough)
because, while we both share the disaster, the blame for it
is mine and mine only. It was my duty either to avoid the
impending danger by taking a Commissionership[1] or to
oppose it by careful provision or to fall bravely. Nothing
could have been more miserable, dishonourable, and unworthy of me than *this*. So I am overwhelmed by shame as
well as grief. Yes, I am ashamed to have been found wanting in the courage and carefulness that the best of wives
and most enchanting of children had the right to expect of
me. Night and day I have before my eyes the sorry spectacle of my family in grief and mourning and the frailty of
your health. The hope of restoration held out to me is very
slender. Many are hostile, almost all are jealous. To drive
me out was a feat, but to keep me out is easy. However, as
long as my family continues to hope, I shall do my part, for
I would not wish to seem responsible for *every* fiasco.

You need not be concerned for my safety. That is no
problem now, for even my enemies want me to stay alive in
my present wretchedness. However, I shall do as you advise. I have thanked the friends you named and given the
letters to Dexippus, and I have written that my information about their good offices came from you. Our dear
Piso's extraordinary devotion and activity on my behalf is
evident to me and everyone talks of it. The Gods grant that
I may enjoy the blessing of such a son-in-law in person with
you and our children! Our last hope now lies in the new
Tribunes—and in the first few days; for if novelty is lost, we
are finished. I am therefore sending Aristocritus to you
straight away, so that you can write me an immediate account of the initial stage and a conspectus of the whole

posses scribere; etsi Dexippo quoque ita imperavi statim ut recurreret, et ad fratrem misi ut crebro tabellarios mitteret. nam ego eo nomine sum Dyrrachi hoc tempore ut quam celerrime quid agatur audiam, et sum tuto; civitas enim haec semper a me defensa est. cum inimici nostri venire dicentur, tum in Epirum ibo.

5   Quod scribis te, si velim, ad me venturam, ego vero, cum sciam magnam partem istius oneris abs te sustineri, te istic esse volo. si perficitis quod agitis, me ad vos venire oportet; sin autem—sed nihil opus est reliqua scribere. ex primis aut summum secundis litteris tuis constituere poterimus quid nobis faciendum sit. tu modo ad me velim omnia diligentissime perscribas; etsi magis iam rem quam litteras debeo ‹ex›spectare.

Cura ut valeas et ita tibi persuadeas, mihi te carius nihil esse nec umquam fuisse.

Vale, mea Terentia; quam ego videre videor itaque debilitor lacrimis. vale.

Prid. Kal. Dec.

10 (V.4)

Scr. Dyrrachii c. med. m. Ian. an. 57

M. CICERO S. D. Q. METELLO COS.

1   Litterae Quinti fratris et T. Pomponi, necessari mei, tantum spei dederant ut in te non minus auxili quam in tuo

business. To be sure, Dexippus also has my orders to hurry back straight away, and I have written to my brother asking him to send couriers at short intervals. I am staying in Dyrrachium at the present time expressly so that I get the quickest possible news of what goes on. Also I am quite safe, having always been a patron of this town. When my enemies are reported to be on their way, it will be time to go to Epirus.

As regards your offer to join me if I wish, well, I know that a large share of this burden rests upon your shoulders, and so I want you to stay in Rome. If you and the others succeed in your efforts, it is for me to join you. If not—but there is no need to go on. I shall be able to decide what to do from your first letter, or at latest from your second. All I ask is that you write me the most comprehensive and detailed accounts—though it is results rather than letters I should be expecting now.

Take care of your health, and rest assured that nothing in the world is more precious to me than you, or ever has been.

Good-bye, dearest Terentia. I seem to see you, and my weeping exhausts me. Good-bye.

29 November.

10 (V.4)
CICERO TO METELLUS NEPOS

Dyrrachium, mid January 57

From M. Cicero to Q. Metellus, Consul, greetings.

Letters from my brother Quintus and my friend and connection T. Pomponius had so raised my hopes that I

75

collega mihi constitutum fuerit. itaque ad te litteras statim misi, per quas, ut fortuna postulabat, et gratias tibi egi et de reliquo tempore auxilium petii. postea mihi non tam meorum litterae quam sermones eorum qui hac iter facie-bant animum tuum immutatum significabant; quae res fecit ut tibi litteris obstrepere non auderem.

2   Nunc mihi Quintus frater meus mitissimam tuam orationem, quam in senatu habuisses, perscripsit; qua inductus ad te scribere sum conatus et abs te, quantum tua fert voluntas, peto quaesoque ut tuos mecum serves potius quam propter adrogantem crudelitatem tuorum me op-pugnes. tu, tuas inimicitias ut rei publicae donares, te vicis-ti; alienas ut contra rem publicam confirmes adduceris? quod si mihi tua clementia opem tuleris, omnibus in rebus me fore in tua potestate tibi confirmo. si mihi neque magis-tratus neque senatum neque populum auxiliari propter eam vim quae me cum re publica vicit licuerit, vide ne, cum velis revocare tempus omnium [re]servandorum,[1] cum qui servetur non erit, non possis.

[1] *(Man.)*

---

[1] Lentulus Spinther.

[2] On 1 January 57. In his defence of Sestius (para. 72) in 56 Cicero says that Metellus declared himself ready to give up his personal enmity (dating from 63–62) in deference to the Senate and in the public interest.

[3] I.e. P. Clodius. It has been ascertained that he was half-brother to the Metelli, not cousin, as once supposed.

counted on your assistance no less than on your colleague's.[1] Accordingly, I wrote to you at once in terms
proper to my present position, both expressing my gratitude and soliciting your assistance in the future. Later it
was conveyed to me, not so much by letters from home as
by the talk of travellers passing this way, that your attitude
had changed. That is why I did not venture to importune
you with letters.

Now my brother Quintus has sent me the text of your
speech in the Senate[2] in which you express yourself in the
gentlest terms. It has emboldened me to write to you and
to beg you, with whatever urgency your own sentiments
make acceptable, to preserve those near to you[3] along with
myself rather than attack me on account of *their* high-
handed cruelty. In giving up a grudge of your own for the
sake of the public interest you have won a victory over
yourself. Are you prevailed upon to support the grudges of
others against that interest? If you will find it in your heart
to help me, I give you my word that I shall be at your disposition in all things. If the violence which has overcome me
and the commonwealth together shall prevent magistrates
and Senate and People from assisting me, may I say a word
of warning? When you would fain call back the time for
saving all, you may call in vain, because there will be none
to save.[4]

---

[4] Cicero evidently did not care to put his meaning directly, but
Metellus was to understand that (a) he, Cicero, could be saved
without ruining Clodius, and (b) if rescue did not come soon it
would be too late. The final words, though general in form, point
to Cicero himself (not Clodius). His letters from exile hint more
than once at suicide if hopes of return did not materialize.

11 (V.3)

Scr. in Hispania Citeriore parte post. an. 56

Q. METELLUS NEPOS S. D. M. CICERONI

1 Hominis importunissimi contumeliae, quibus crebris contionibus me onerat, tuis erga me officiis leniuntur et, ut sunt leves ab eius modi homine, a me despiciuntur, libenterque commutata persona te mihi fratris loco esse duco.

2 de illo ne meminisse quidem volo, tametsi bis eum invitum[1] servavi.

De meis rebus, ne vobis multitudine litterarum molestior essem, ad Lollium perscripsi de rationibus provinciae quid vellem fieri, ut is vos doceret et commonefaceret.

Si poteris, velim pristinam tuam erga me voluntatem conserves.

12 (I.1)

Scr. Romae Id. Ian. an. 56

M. CICERO S. D. P. LENTULO PRO COS.

1 Ego omni officio ac potius pietate erga te ceteris satis facio omnibus, mihi ipse numquam satis facio. tanta enim

---

[1] invitus *coni. SB*

---

[1] Clodius.

[2] During his Consulship the previous year, when he thwarted Milo's attempts to bring Clodius to trial.

11 (V.3)
METELLUS NEPOS TO CICERO

Hither Spain, latter half of 56

From Q. Metellus Nepos to M. Cicero, greetings.

The insults heaped upon my head by an unmannerly individual[1] in speech after speech are softened by your acts of friendship. From such a person they are of small account, and I despise them accordingly; and, welcoming the change of roles, I take *you* for my brother. Of him I do not even want to think, though I saved him twice over in spite of himself.[2]

As for my concerns, not wanting to trouble you and my other friends with a spate of letters, I have written in detail to Lollius,[3] telling him my wishes with regard to the administration of my province and asking him to inform and remind you all accordingly.

If you can, I hope you will keep your friendly sentiments towards me as in the past.

12 (I.1)
CICERO TO LENTULUS SPINTHER

Rome, 13 January 56

From M. Cicero to P. Lentulus, Proconsul, greetings.

In all that is due to a friend, or rather a benefactor, my efforts on your behalf seem adequate to everyone except myself; for me they are never enough. Your services to me

---

[3] Probably L. Lollius, formerly fellow Legate of Nepos under Pompey. They captured Damascus together in 65 or 64.

magnitudo est tuorum erga me meritorum ut, quoniam tu
nisi perfecta re de me non conquiesti, ego quia non idem in
tua causa efficio vitam mihi esse acerbam putem. in causa
haec sunt: Hammonius, regis legatus, aperte pecunia nos
oppugnat. res agitur per eosdem creditores per quos, cum
tu aderas, agebatur. regis causa si qui sunt qui velint, qui
pauci sunt, omnes rem ad Pompeium deferri volunt. senatus religionis calumniam non religione sed malevolentia et
2   illius regiae largitionis invidia comprobat. Pompeium et
hortari et orare et iam liberius accusare et monere ut
magnam infamiam fugiat non desistimus. sed plane nec
precibus nostris nec admonitionibus relinquit locum. nam
cum in sermone cottidiano tum in senatu palam sic egit
causam tuam ut neque eloquentia maiore quisquam nec
gravitate nec studio nec contentione agere potuerit, cum
summa testificatione tuorum in se officiorum et amoris
erga te sui. Marcellinum tibi esse iratum sc<rib>is;[1] is hac
regia causa excepta ceteris in rebus se acerrimum tui de-
fensorem fore ostendit. quod dat, accipimus; quod instituit
referre de religione et saepe iam rettulit, ab eo deduci non
potest.
3   Res ante Idus acta sic est (nam haec Idibus mane scrip-

---

1 scis (*de* M *vide comm.*) (*Hartman*)

---

1 This refers to the affair of the exiled King of Egypt, Ptolemy
XII, nicknamed the Piper, father of the famous Cleopatra. In September 57 the Senate had commissioned Lentulus, as proximate
governor of Cilicia, to restore him to his throne. But in January the
custodians of the Sibylline prophecies produced an oracle forbid-
ding the employment of a host. This was no doubt also a move
against Pompey, who came more and more to be suspected of

have been so great that my life turns sour when I think that I am failing to achieve in your case[1] what you achieved in mine, never relaxing short of complete success. The relevant facts are as follows: The king's representative, Hammonius, is openly working against us with money. His intermediaries are the creditors who played the same role when you were in Rome. The king's well-wishers (there are not many of them) all want to see the business handed over to Pompey, whereas the Senate is approving the religious subterfuge;[2] not for religion's sake, but out of ill will and the odium aroused by the royal largesse. I never stop urging and begging Pompey, even going so far as to take him pretty frankly to task and warning him to steer clear of a major scandal. But truth to tell, he leaves no opening for appeals or warnings on my part, since both in day-to-day conversation and publicly in the Senate he has pleaded your cause as eloquently, impressively, zealously, and vigorously as anybody could possibly have done, with the fullest acknowledgement of your services to himself and his affection for you. You write that Marcellinus is annoyed with you. He promises that he will be your most ardent champion in all respects, except this affair of the king. We take what he offers, but there is no diverting him from his determination to refer the religious point to the Senate, as he has already done on a number of occasions.

Up to the Ides this is the record (I am writing on

wanting to handle the restoration himself. The business dragged on for a while, but in the end Lentulus did nothing, and Ptolemy was reinstated by the enterprising governor of Syria, A. Gabinius, in 55.

[2] The aforesaid Sibylline oracle.

si): Hortensi et mea et Luculli sententia cedit religioni de exercitu; teneri enim res aliter non potest. sed ex illo senatus consulto quod te referente factum est tibi decernit ut regem reducas, quod commodo rei ⟨publicae⟩[2] facere possis, ut exercitum religio tollat, te auctorem senatus retineat. Crassus tris legatos decernit nec excludit Pompeium; censet enim etiam ex iis qui cum imperio sint. Bibulus tris legatos ex iis qui privati sint. huic adsentiuntur reliqui consulares praeter Servilium, qui omnino reduci negat oportere, et Volcacium, qui Lupo referente Pompeio decernit, et Afranium, qui adsentitur Volcacio. quae res auget suspicionem Pompei voluntatis; nam ⟨anim⟩advertebatur[3] Pompei familiaris adsentiri Volcacio. laboratur vehementer; inclinata res est. Libonis et Hypsaei non obscura concursatio et contentio omniumque Pompei familiarum studium in eam opinionem rem adduxerunt ut Pompeius cupere videatur; cui qui nolunt, idem tibi, quod eum ornasti, non sunt amici.

4   Nos in causa auctoritatem eo minorem habemus quod tibi debemus, gratiam autem nostram exstinguit hominum suspicio, quod Pompeio se gratificari putant. ut in rebus

[2] rem (*Crat.* (rei p.))
[3] (*Lamb.*)

---

[3] M. Terentius Varro Lucullus. His brother Lucius had died earlier in the year. He and the orator Hortensius, both senior Consulars, were Spinther's principal backers in the Senate along with Cicero.

[4] Pompey at this time held proconsular *imperium* in virtue of his extraordinary office as controller of grain supplies.

[5] Bitterly hostile to Pompey at this period.

the morning of the Ides): The resolution put forward by Hortensius, myself, and Lucullus[3] gives way to the religious objection as regards an army; we cannot gain our point in any other way. But in accordance with the decree which was passed on your own motion it gives you authority to restore the king, if you can do so without prejudice to the public interest. While an army is precluded by the religious obstacle, the Senate would thus retain you as the person responsible. Crassus proposes a Commission of Three, from which he does not exclude Pompey, since he provides that persons holding military command[4] shall be eligible. Bibulus[5] proposes a Commission of Three to be selected from those *not* holding command. He is supported by the other Consulars excepting Servilius,[6] who is against *any* restoration, Volcacius,[7] who is for authorizing Pompey on Lupus'[8] motion, and Afranius, who supports Volcacius. The last circumstance intensifies suspicion as to Pompey's wishes—support for Volcacius by Pompey's intimates did not go unmarked. It is a hard struggle, and things are going against us. Energetic lobbying by Libo and Hypsaeus, which is no secret, and the interest shown by all Pompey's friends have led to the opinion that Pompey is anxious for the assignment. Those who are against him are no friends to you either, because of what you have done for him.

I carry less weight in the matter because of my obligations to you, and my private influence is nullified by the prevailing suspicion—they think they are obliging Pompey. We are dealing with a business that was inflamed in se-

[6] P. Servilius Vatia Isauricus, Consul in 79.

[7] Consul in 66.

[8] P. Rutilius Lupus, Tribune. On his motion see the next letter.

multo ante quam profectus es ab ipso rege et ab intimis ac
domesticis Pompei clam exulceratis, deinde palam a consularibus exagitatis et in summam invidiam adductis, ita
versamur. nostram fidem omnes, amorem tu[4] absens, praesentes tui cognoscent. si esset in iis fides in quibus summa
esse debebat, non laboraremus.

13 (I.2)

Scr. Romae XVI *Kal. Febr. an. 56*

⟨M. CICERO S. D. P. LENTULO PRO COS.⟩

1 Id. Ian. in senatu nihil est confectum propterea quod
dies magna ex parte consumptus est altercatione Lentuli
consulis et Canini tribuni pl. eo die nos quoque multa verba fecimus maximeque visi sumus senatum commemo-
ratione tuae voluntatis erga illum ordinem permovere.[1]
itaque postridie placuit ut breviter sententias diceremus.
videbatur enim reconciliata nobis voluntas esse senatus,
quod cum dicendo tum singulis appellandis rogandisque
perspexeram. itaque cum sententia prima Bibuli pronuntiata esset, ut tres legati regem reducerent, secunda
Hortensi, ut tu sine exercitu reduceres, tertia Volcaci, ut
Pompeius reduceret, postulatum est ut Bibuli sententia
divideretur. quatenus de religione dicebat, cui quidem[2] rei
iam obsisti non poterat, Bibulo adsensum est; de tribus

[4] tui *(SB)*
[1] removere *(Lamb.)*   [2] cuique *(Lamb.)*

---

[1] Marcellinus.   [2] L. Caninius Gallus, Tribune.

cret long before you left Rome by the king himself and by Pompey's close friends and familiars, and has subsequently been stirred up in public by the Consulars. It has now gained a highly invidious notoriety. My loyalty will be recognized by all, and my affection for you by your absent self and present friends. If others whose loyalty should have been beyond reproach were not falling short, we would not be in such difficulties.

13 (I.2)
CICERO TO LENTULUS SPINTHER

Rome, 15 January 56

From M. Cicero to P. Lentulus, Proconsul, greetings.

Nothing was settled in the Senate on the Ides of January because a large part of the day was taken up by an altercation between Consul Lentulus[1] and Tribune Caninius.[2] I spoke at length that day myself, and I think I made a very considerable impression on the Senate when I dwelt on your attachment to that Order. We therefore thought best to make only short speeches on the day following, feeling that we had regained the House's good will—I had clear evidence of that both during my address and in approaches and appeals to individuals. Accordingly three proposals were put forward: first Bibulus', that the king be restored by a Commission of Three, second Hortensius', that he be restored by you without an army, and third Volcacius', that he be restored by Pompey. There was a demand that Bibulus' motion should be split. So far as it concerned the religious issue it was agreed, opposition on this point being now out of the question, but on the Commission of Three it

2 legatis frequentes ierunt in alia omnia. proxima erat
Hortensi sententia, cum Lupus tribunus pl., quod ipse de
Pompeio rettulisset, intendere coepit ante se oportere dis-
cessionem facere quam consules. eius orationi vehementer ab omnibus reclamatum est; erat enim et iniqua et
nova. consules neque concedebant neque valde repugna-
bant; diem consumi volebant, id quod est factum. perspi-
ciebant enim in Hortensi sententiam multis partibus pluris
ituros, quamquam aperte ut Volcacio adsentirentur multi
rogabantur, atque id ipsum consulibus invitis; nam ii Bibuli
3 sententiam valere cupierant.[3] hac controversia usque ad
noctem ducta senatus dimissus est.[4]

Ego eo die casu apud Pompeium cenavi nactusque
tempus hoc magis idoneum quam umquam antea, quod
post tuum discessum is dies honestissimus nobis fuerat in
senatu, ita sum cum illo locutus ut mihi viderer animum
hominis ab omni alia cogitatione ad tuam dignitatem tuen-
dam traducere. quem ego ipsum cum audio, prorsus eum
libero omni suspicione cupiditatis; cum autem eius familiaris omnium ordinum video, perspicio, id quod iam
omnibus est apertum, totam rem istam iam pridem a certis
hominibus non invito rege ipso consiliariisque eius esse
corruptam.

4 Haec scripsi a. d. XVI Kal. Febr. ante lucem. eo die
senatus erat futurus. nos in senatu, quem ad modum spero,
dignitatem nostram, ut potest in tanta hominum perfidia et
iniquitate, retinebimus. quod ad popularem rationem attinet, hoc videmur esse consecuti, ut ne quid agi cum popu-

3 cupierunt *(Wes.)*
4 et *(Wes.)*

was heavily defeated. Hortensius' motion stood next, when Tribune Lupus began to insist that, having himself consulted the House earlier concerning Pompey, he had the right to take a vote before the Consuls. His speech was received with loud protests from all sides—it was unfair and without precedent. The Consuls did not give way, but neither did they put up much of a fight. They wanted the sitting talked out, which is what happened, because it was plain to them that Hortensius' motion would get a thumping majority despite much open canvassing in support of Volcacius—which again was not to the liking of the Consuls, who had wished Bibulus' motion to win the day. The argument was prolonged till nightfall, and the House rose.

I happened to be dining with Pompey that evening. It was a better moment than had ever come my way before, because we had just had our most successful day in the Senate since your departure. So I talked to him, and I could flatter myself that I led his mind away from all other notions and focused it upon upholding your position. When I listen to him talking, I quite acquit him of all suspicion of selfish aims. But when I look at his friends of all classes, I see what is now plain to everyone, that this whole business has for a long while past been bedevilled by certain individuals, not without the connivance of the king himself and his advisers.

I am writing this on 15 January before daybreak. The Senate is to meet today. At the meeting, as I hope, we shall maintain our position, so far as practicable in the general ambience of treachery and unfair play. As for the role of the People,[3] I think we have so managed that no proceed-

[3] I.e. the popular legislative assembly.

lo aut salvis auspiciis aut salvis legibus aut denique sine vi posset. de his rebus pridie quam haec scripsi senatus auctoritas gravissima intercessit; cui cum Cato et Caninius intercessissent, tamen est perscripta. eam ad te missam esse arbitror. de ceteris rebus quicquid erit actum scribam ad te et ut quam rectissime agatur omni mea cura, opera, diligentia, gratia providebo.

14 (I.4)

Scr. Romae XIV *Kal. Febr., ut vid., an. 56*

‹M. CICERO S. D. P. LENTULO PRO COS.›

1   A. d. XVI Kal. Febr. cum in senatu pulcherrime staremus, quod iam illam sententiam Bibuli de tribus legatis pridie eius diei fregeramus, unumque certamen esset relictum sententia Volcaci, res ab adversariis nostris extracta est variis calumniis. causam enim frequenti senatu non magna varietate magnaque invidia eorum qui a te causam regiam alio traferebant obtinebamus. eo die acerbum habuimus Curionem, Bibulum multo iustiorem, paene etiam amicum. Caninius et Cato negarunt se legem ullam ante comitia esse laturos. senatus haberi ante Kal. Febr. per legem Pupiam, id quod scis, non potest, neque mense
2   Februario toto nisi perfectis aut reiectis legationibus. haec

---

4 See Glossary.
5 C. Porcius Cato, Tribune.
1 The elder, Consul in 76.

ings in that quarter are possible without violation of the auspices and the laws, in fact without violence. Yesterday a senatorial resolution[4] in very impressive terms went through on these matters, and although Cato[5] and Caninius cast vetoes, it was placed on record. I think you have been sent a copy. On other matters I shall write to tell you whatever takes place, and shall use all my care, pains, diligence, and influence to ensure that things go as much as possible on the right lines.

14 (I.4)
CICERO TO LENTULUS SPINTHER

Rome, 17 (?) January 56

From M. Cicero to P. Lentulus, Proconsul, greetings.

We were holding up magnificently in the Senate on 15 January. Already on the previous day we had smashed that motion of Bibulus on the Commission of Three, and the only battle left to fight was Volcacius' motion. However, our opponents dragged the proceedings out on various pretexts, because we were carrying our point in a full House, which showed little difference of opinion and no little irritation against those who were trying to put the king's affair out of your hands and into someone else's. We found Curio[1] bitterly hostile to us that day, Bibulus much fairer, almost friendly even. Caninius and Cato undertook not to bring forward any legislation before the elections. As you know, the Senate is debarred by the lex Pupia from meeting before the Kalends of February, and throughout February there can be no sitting until embassy

tamen opinio est populi Romani, a tuis invidis atque
obtrectatoribus nomen inductum fictae religionis ‹idque
susceptum ab aliis›[1] non tam ut te impediret quam ut ne
quis propter exercitus cupiditatem Alexandream vellet ire.
dignitatis autem tuae nemo est qui‹n› existimet habitam
esse rationem ab senatu. nemo est enim quin sciat, quo
minus discessio fieret, per adversarios tuos esse factum;
qui nunc populi nomine, re autem vera sceleratissimo
tribunorum[2] ‹pl.›[3] latrocinio si quae conabuntur agere,
satis i‹a›m provisum est ut ne quid salvis auspiciis aut legibus aut etiam sine vi agere possent.

3   Ego neque de meo studio neque de non nullorum iniuria scribendum mihi esse arbitror. quid enim aut me osten-
tem, qui, si vitam pro tua dignitate profundam, nullam
partem videar meritorum tuorum adsecutus, aut de aliorum iniuriis querar, quod sine summo dolore facere non
possum? ego tibi a vi, hac praesertim imbecillitate ma-
gistratuum, praestare nihil possum; vi excepta, possum
confirmare te et senatus et populi Romani summo studio
amplitudinem tuam retenturum.

[1] *(SB)*
[2] tiranno G *(sed del.)*: *om.* MR *(Purser)*
[3] *(SB)*

business has been completed or deferred.[2] However, the belief of the Roman People is that the religious pretext was trumped up by your ill-wishers and detractors, and then adopted by others not so much to stand in *your* way as to stop anyone from wanting to go to Alexandria for the sake of a military command. Everyone judges that the Senate has taken proper account of your honour, since everybody knows that your opponents prevented a decision. If they now make any move, nominally through the People but in reality by a criminal act of tribunician freebooting, sufficient means have now been taken to ensure that they can do nothing without violating the auspices and the laws, or indeed without the use of force.

I do not think it would be appropriate for me to describe my own zeal or the ill usage of certain persons. There is no occasion for me to parade myself, for if I were to sacrifice my life in defence of your honour, I should not appear to have balanced a fraction of what I owe you; nor yet to complain of the wrongs done you by others, which I cannot do without heartfelt distress. I can offer you no guarantee against violence, especially in the present weakness of our magistrates, but, violence apart, I can say with confidence that you will maintain your high standing through the zealous good will of the Senate and People of Rome.

[2] All days in January after the 15th were comitial days, on which it was illegal for the Senate to meet except by special dispensation. Another law (lex Gabinia) provided that during February the hearing of deputations from abroad should take precedence over other business.

15 (I.5a)

Scr. Romae c. Non. Febr. an. 56

< M. CICERO S. D. P. LENTULO PRO COS. >

1   Tametsi mihi nihil fuit optatius quam ut primum abs te ipso, deinde a ceteris omnibus quam gratissimus erga te esse cognoscerer, tamen adficior summo dolore eius modi tempora post tuam profectionem consecuta esse ut et meam et ceterorum erga te fidem et benevolentiam absens experirere. te videre et sentire eandem fidem esse hominum in tua dignitate quam ego in mea salute sum expertus ex tuis litteris intellexi.

2 nos cum maxime consilio, studio, labore, gratia de causa regia niteremur, subito exorta est nefaria Catonis promulgatio quae nostra studia impediret et animos a minore cura ad summum timorem traduceret. sed tamen, in eius <modi> perturbatione rerum quamquam omnia sunt metuenda, nihil magis quam perfidiam timemus; et Catoni quidem, quoquo modo se res habet, profecto resistemus.[1]

3   De Alexandrina re causaque regia tantum habeo polliceri, me tibi absenti tuisque praesentibus cumulate satis facturum. sed vereor ne aut eripiatur causa regia nobis aut deseratur; quorum utrum minus velim, non facile possum existimare. sed, si res coget, est quiddam tertium, quod neque Selicio nec mihi displicebat, ut neque iacere re[ge]m pateremur nec nobis repugnantibus ad eum deferri ad quem prope iam delata existimatur. a nobis agen-

---

[1] resistimus

---

[1] To deprive Lentulus of his province. It had been promulgated by C. Cato as Tribune.

15 (I.5a)
CICERO TO LENTULUS SPINTHER

Rome, ca. 5 February 36

From M. Cicero to P. Lentulus, Proconsul, greetings.

It was my dearest wish that my gratitude to you should be abundantly demonstrated, first to yourself, and then to the world. But I am deeply sorry that conditions since your departure have been such as to give you in your absence a trial both of my loyalty and good will towards you and of other people's. I see from your letter how keenly you are aware that the same brand of loyalty has been forthcoming on behalf of your honour as I experienced when my existence as a citizen was at stake. While I was striving my utmost in the king's matter, by dint of thought, zeal, hard work, and personal influence, Cato's abominable bill[1] suddenly made its appearance to hamper our efforts and divert our attention from the lesser concern to a grave alarm. However, although no unwelcome possibility can be ruled out in such an imbroglio as this, my main fear is treachery; as for Cato, we shall of course oppose him in any circumstances.

With regard to Alexandria and the king's business, I can promise you this much, that your absent self and your friends here present will be more than satisfied with my conduct. But I am afraid that the king's business will either be snatched out of our hands or let drop, and I find it hard to judge which of the two I like less. But if the worst comes to the worst, there is a third possibility, which neither Selicius nor I find inadmissible—namely not to let the matter go by the board, and at the same time not to let it be assigned *in the teeth of opposition from our side* to the

tur omnia diligenter ut neque, si quid obtineri poterit, non
contendamus nec, si quid non obtinuerimus, repulsi esse
videamur.

4   Tuae sapientiae magnitudinisque animi est omnem amplitudinem et dignitatem tuam in virtute atque in rebus
gestis tuis atque in tua gravitate positam existimare; si quid
ex iis rebus quas tibi Fortuna largita est non nullorum hominum perfidia detraxerit, id maiori illis fraudi quam tibi
futurum. a me nullum tempus praetermittitur de tuis rebus et agendi et cogitandi. utor ad omnia Q. Selicio; neque
enim prudentiorem quemquam ex tuis neque fide maiore
esse iudico neque amantiorem tui.

16 (I.5b)

Scr. Romae paulo post v *Id. Febr. an. 56*
‹M. CICERO S. D. P. LENTULO PRO COS.›

1   Hic quae agantur quaeque acta sint [ea][1] te et litteris
multorum et nuntiis cognosse arbitror; quae autem posita
sunt in coniectura quaeque videntur fore, ea puto tibi a me
scribi oportere.

    Postea quam Pompeius et apud populum a. d. vii[2] Id.
Febr., cum pro Milone diceret, clamore convicioque
iact‹at›us est in senatuque a Catone aspere et acerbe

[1] *(Wes.)*
[2] at octavo *(Sjögren)*

---

[2] Pompey.

person[2] to whom it has almost been assigned (so people think) already; throughout taking care on the one hand not to lose any possible success by default, and on the other to avoid the appearance of a rebuff in any failure.

As a wise and high-minded man, you must regard your status and honour as depending entirely upon your own qualities and achievements and your moral dignity. If any of the gifts which Fortune has showered upon you is abstracted by the treachery of certain persons, you will judge that they more than yourself will be the sufferers. I am losing no opportunity of acting and planning in your interests. In all matters I am availing myself of Q. Selicius' services. None of your friends in my judgement surpasses him in shrewdness or loyalty or affection for you.

16 (I.5b)
CICERO TO LENTULUS SPINTHER

Rome, shortly after 9 February 56

From M. Cicero to P. Lentulus, Proconsul, greetings.

I expect you have heard what is happening and has happened here from plenty of informants, both by letter and word of mouth. It is my business, I think, to write to you about matters of surmise and forecast.

Pompey appeared to me much shaken after his rough reception—noise and abuse—when he spoke for Milo[1] at the public meeting on 7 February, and Cato's bitter and vehement attack in the Senate, which was received in por-

---

[1] Arraigned by Clodius before a popular assembly. Letter 7 (II.3). 2 of the letters to Quintus gives a full account.

nimium[3] magno silentio est accusatus, visus est mihi vehementer esse perturbatus. itaque Alexandrina causa, quae
nobis adhuc integra est (nihil enim tibi detraxit senatus nisi
id quod per eandem religionem dari alteri non potest),
videtur ab illo plane esse deposita.

2   Nunc id speramus idque molimur ut rex, cum intellegat
sese quod cogitabat, ut a Pompeio reducatur, adsequi non
posse et, nisi per te sit restitutus, desertum se atque abiec-
tum fore, proficiscatur ad te; quod sine ulla dubitatione, si
Pompeius paulum modo ostenderit sibi placere, faciet. sed
nosti hominis tarditatem et taciturnitatem. nos tamen nihil
quod ad eam rem pertineat praetermittimus. ceteris iniuriis quae propositae sunt a Catone facile, ut spero, resistemus. amicum ex consularibus neminem tibi esse video
praeter Hortensium et Lucullum; ceteri sunt partim ob-
scurius iniqui, partim non dissimulanter irati. tu fac animo
forti magnoque sis speresque fore ut fracto impetu levissimi hominis tuam pristinam dignitatem et gloriam consequare.

17 (I.6)

Scr. Romae fort. m. Mart. an. 56

‹ M. CICERO S. D. P. LENTULO PRO COS. ›

1   Quae gerantur accipies ex Pollione, qui omnibus negotiis non interfuit solum sed praefuit.

---

3 inimicorum *Weinhold (cf. Leg. 1.27 nimis arguti)**

---

1 Probably C. Asinius Pollio, though then only about 21.

tentous silence. He seems to me to have quite given up the Alexandrian business. Our position is intact, because the Senate has taken nothing from you except what cannot, on account of the same religious scruple, be given to anybody else.

What we are now hoping and working for is that when the king realizes that his plan of a restoration by Pompey is impracticable and that unless he is brought home by you he will be left totally in the lurch, he will go to you. Without the smallest doubt he *will* do this, if Pompey makes a sign, however slight, to show his approval. But you know how slow and uncommunicative Pompey is. However, I am letting nothing slip which might have a bearing on this question. As for the other outrages threatened in Cato's proposal, I hope we shall have no difficulty in resisting them. I do not find any of the Consulars to be your friend except Hortensius and Lucullus. The rest are either more or less overtly ill-disposed or undisguisedly in dudgeon. You must keep your courage and spirit high and be of good hope that, when we have crushed this irresponsible fellow's attack, you will flourish in your old dignity and repute.

17 (I.6)
CICERO TO LENTULUS SPINTHER

Rome, March (?) 56

From M. Cicero to P. Lentulus, Proconsul, greetings.

You will learn what is toward from Pollio,[1] who has taken not only part but the leading part in every transaction.

Me in summo dolore quem in tuis rebus capio maxime scilicet consolatur spes, quod valde suspicor fore ut infringatur hominum improbitas et consiliis tuorum amicorum et ipsa die, quae debilitat cogitationes et inimicorum et proditorum tuorum.

2 Facile secundo loco me consolatur recordatio meorum temporum, quorum imaginem video in rebus tuis; nam etsi minore in re violatur tua dignitas quam mea adflicta est, tamen est tanta similitudo ut sperem te mihi ignoscere si ea non timuerim quae ne tu quidem umquam timenda duxisti. sed praesta te eum qui mihi a teneris, ut Graeci dicunt, unguiculis es cognitus. illustrabit, mihi crede, tuam amplitudinem hominum iniuria. a me omnia summa in te studia officiaque exspecta. non fallam opinionem tuam.

18 (I.7)

Scr. Romae ex. m. Iun. vel m. Quint. an. 56

< M. CICERO S. D. P. LENTULO PRO COS. >

1 Legi tuas litteras, quibus ad me scribis gratum tibi esse quod crebro certior per me fias de omnibus rebus et meam erga te benevolentiam facile perspicias; quorum alterum mihi, ut te plurimum diligam, facere necesse est, si volo is

In the keen distress which I feel in your affairs hope is naturally my greatest comforter, since I have a strong inkling that the evil disposition now current will be worn down by the countermeasures of your friends and by mere lapse of time, which is weakening the devices of your enemies and betrayers.

I have a second comforter ready to hand in the recollection of my own experience, which I see mirrored in yours. True, your standing is injured in a smaller concern than that which brought mine so low. None the less, the similarity is so close that I hope you forgive me if I decline to fear contingencies which you never thought formidable. Only show yourself the man I have known you since your nails were tender,[2] as the Greeks say. Trust me, the wrong men do you will add lustre to your greatness. Expect from me at every turn the uttermost in zealous service; I shall not disappoint your good opinion.

18 (I.7)
CICERO TO LENTULUS SPINTHER

Rome, late June or July 56

From M. Cicero to P. Lentulus, Proconsul, greetings.

I have read your letter, in which you say you are glad to be kept informed through me on all points at such frequent intervals and to see such plain evidence of my good will towards you. As for the latter, I must needs hold you in the highest regard, if I want to be such as you have wanted

[2] I.e. from childhood. In Greek the expression can also mean 'from the fingertips inward,' i.e. all through.

esse quem tu me esse voluisti; alterum facio libenter, ut, quoniam intervallo locorum et temporum diiuncti sumus, per litteras tecum quam saepissime colloquar. quod si rarius fiet quam tu exspectabis, id erit causae quod non eius generis meae litterae sunt ut eas audeam temere committere. quotiens mihi certorum hominum potestas erit quibus recte dem, non praetermittam.

2   Quod scire vis qua quisque in te fide sit et voluntate, difficile dictu est de singulis. unum illud audeo, quod antea tibi saepe significavi, nunc quoque re perspecta et cognita scribere, vehementer quosdam homines, et eos maxime qui te et maxime debuerunt et plurimum iuvare potuerunt, invidisse dignitati tuae, simillimamque in re dissimili tui temporis nunc et nostri quondam fuisse rationem, ut quos tu rei publicae causa laeseras palam te oppugnarent, quorum auctoritatem, dignitatem voluntatemque defenderas non tam memores essent virtutis tuae quam laudis inimici. quo quidem tempore, ut perscripsi ad te antea, cognovi Hortensium percupidum tui, studiosum Lucullum, ex magistratibus autem L. Racilium et fide et animo singulari. nam nostra propugnatio ac defensio dignitatis tuae propter magnitudinem benefici tui fortasse plerisque offici maiorem auctoritatem habere videatur quam sen-

3 tentiae. praeterea quidem de consularibus nemini possum aut studi erga te aut offici aut amici animi esse testis. etenim Pompeium, qui mecum saepissime non solum ⟨a⟩

to think me. As for the former, it is a pleasure to talk to you by letter as often as possible, separated as we are by distance of place and time. If I do so more rarely than you expect, the reason will be that my letters are such as I should not dare to hand to the first comer. Whenever I find reliable persons, to whom I can safely entrust them, I shall not let the opportunity slip.

You wish to know how this person and that has behaved and felt towards you. It is difficult to speak of individuals. I only venture now to report in the light of ascertained fact what I have often intimated to you in the past, that certain persons, particularly those most bound in duty to help you and best able to do so, have been jealous of your standing, and that despite differences of circumstance there has been a remarkably close parallel between your present experience and mine in days gone by. Those whom you offended in the public interest have been your open adversaries, whereas those whose prestige, position, and purposes you supported have shown themselves less mindful of your manly conduct than hostile to your credit. In this crisis, as I have already informed you in detail, I have found Hortensius most anxious to serve you. Lucullus has shown good will, and among those in office L. Racilius' loyalty and courage have been outstanding. My own role as champion and defender of your honour may perhaps with most minds count rather as a fulfilment of obligation than as an expression of opinion in view of the magnitude of your services to me. Aside from those mentioned, I cannot testify to any good will or service or friendly disposition on the part of any of the Consulars. You know, of course, that Pompey was not much in the Senate during the period in question. He talks to me about you very frequently, not

me provocatus sed etiam sua sponte de te communicare solet, scis temporibus illis non saepe in senatu fuisse; cui quidem litterae tuae quas proxime miseras, quod facile intellexerim, periucundae fuerunt. mihi quidem humanitas tua, vel summa potius sapientia, non iucunda solum sed etiam admirabilis visa est. virum enim excellentem et tibi tua praestanti in eum liberalitate devinctum non nihil suspicantem propter aliquorum opinionem suae cupiditatis te ab se abalienatum illa epistula retinuisti. qui mihi cum semper tuae laudi favere visus est, etiam ipso suspiciosissimo tempore Caniniano, tum vero lectis tuis litteris perspectus est a me toto animo de te ac de tuis ornamentis et commodis cogitare.

4   Qua re ea quae scribam sic habeto, me cum illo re saepe communicata de illius ad te sententia atque auctoritate scribere: quoniam senatus consultum nullum exstat quo reductio regis Alexandrini tibi adempta sit eaque quae de ea <re per>scripta est[1] auctoritas, cui scis intercessum esse, ut ne quis omnino regem reduceret, tantam vim habet ut magis iratorum hominum studium quam constantis senatus consilium esse videatur, te perspicere posse, qui Ciliciam Cyprumque teneas, quid efficere et quid consequi possis, et, si res facultatem habitura videatur ut Alexandream atque Aegyptum tenere possis, esse et tuae et nostri imperi dignitatis, Ptolomaide aut aliquo propinquo loco

1 (ς *et Lamb.*)

---

1 He had promulgated in December a bill authorizing Ptolemy's restoration by Pompey with two lictors.

2 Literally 'the Alexandrian king,' Cicero's usual way of referring to Ptolemy. So too Caelius at the end of Letter 81.

only when I prompt him but of his own accord. I could easily see how much your latest letter pleased him. For my part, I was not only pleased but struck with admiration at your forbearance, or rather your excellent good sense. Bound to you as he was for your signally handsome behaviour to himself, he was inclined to suspect an estrangement on your side due to the notion some people entertained about his own aspirations. Now by that letter you have kept this eminent man's friendship. I always thought he wished you to emerge with credit, even during that highly suspicious episode of Caninius;[1] and now that he has read your letter, I am clear that his one thought is for you and the honours and advantages to come to you.

So please regard what I am about to write as written with his approval and authority after frequent consultation between us. No decree of the Senate exists under which the restoration of the king of Egypt[2] is taken out of your hands. The recorded resolution, which as you know was vetoed, against the king's restoration by any person whomsoever, should be regarded as an ebullition of bias and spite rather than as the firm policy of the Senate, and its authority is to be measured accordingly. I therefore say that *you,* as governor of Cilicia and Cyprus, are in a position to judge what you can do and achieve. Should circumstances appear to furnish a fair prospect of your controlling Alexandria and Egypt, your honour and the Empire's will be well served if you proceed to Alexandria with a naval and military force, after first settling the king at Ptolemais[3] or some

---

[3] Cicero will have meant Ptolemais Hormos, an important Nile port at the southern entrance of the Fayum (not Ptolemais in Cyrenaica or Ptolemais in Phoenicia (Acre)).

rege collocato, te cum classe atque exercitu proficisci
Alexandream ut, eam cum pace praesidiisque firmaris,
Ptolomaeus redeat in regnum; ita fore ut et per te restitua-
tur, quem ad modum senatus initio censuit, et sine multi-
tudine reducatur, quem ad modum homines religiosi
Sibyllae placere dixerunt.

5   Sed haec sententia sic et illi et nobis probabatur ut ex
eventu homines de tuo consilio existimaturos videremus; si
cecidisset ut volumus et optamus, omnis te et sapienter et
fortiter, si aliquid esset offensum, eosdem illos et cupide et
temere fecisse dicturos. qua re quid adsequi possis non
tam facile est nobis quam tibi, cuius prope in conspectu
Aegyptus est, iudicare. nos quidem hoc sentimus, si ex-
ploratum tibi sit posse te illius regni potiri, non esse cunc-
tandum; si dubium sit, non esse conandum. illud tibi
adfirmo, si rem istam ex sententia gesseris, fore ut absens a
multis, cum redieris ab omnibus collaudere; offensionem
esse periculosam propter interpositam auctoritatem reli-
gionemque video. sed ego te ut ad certam laudem adhor-
tor sic a dimicatione deterreo redeoque ad illud quod
initio scripsi, totius facti tui iudicium non tam ex consilio
tuo quam ex eventu homines esse facturos.

6   Quod si haec ratio rei gerendae periculosa tibi esse
videbitur, placebat illud, ut, si rex amicis tuis, qui per provinciam atque imperium tuum[2] pecunias ei credidissent,
fidem suam praestitisset, et auxiliis eum tuis et copiis adiu-
vares; eam esse naturam et regionem provinciae tuae ut
illius reditum vel adiuvando confirmares vel neglegendo

[2] imperi tui (*R. Stephanus*)

other place in the vicinity; then, when you have established order in the city and stationed troops to secure it, let Ptolemy come back to his throne. In this way he will be restored by you, as the Senate originally resolved he should be, and he will be restored without a 'host,' which according to our pious politicians is how the Sibyl wants it done.

But both Pompey and I approve this view with the qualification that we realize your policy will be judged by results. If all turns out as we wish and pray, there will be universal praise for your good judgement and courage. If anything goes wrong, those same voices will say you acted ambitiously and rashly. That being so, it is not as easy for us as for you, almost within sight of Egypt as you are, to judge what you can accomplish. Our feeling is that if you are certain you can take over the kingdom, you should lose no time; but if this is doubtful, you ought not to make the attempt. I do guarantee that if you bring it off satisfactorily, many will applaud you in your absence, and everyone when you return. But I recognize that a setback would be dangerous because of the Senate's contrary resolution and the religious aspect. Well then, I am urging you forward to a certain success and at the same time I am warning you back from a doubtful conflict; and I return to my starting point: your entire action will be judged by results, rather than by your own policy.

If the above way of proceeding seems to you too risky, we suggest the following: provided the king fulfils his engagements to your friends who have lent him money in your province and sphere of command, you should help him with auxiliary troops and supplies. The nature and situation of your province enable you either to support his restoration by lending him assistance or to hinder it by

impedires. in hac ratione quid res, quid causa, quid tempus ferat, tu facillime optimeque perspicies. quid nobis placuisset ex me potissimum putavi te scire oportere.

7   Quod mihi de nostro statu, de Milonis familiaritate, de levitate et imbecillitate Clodi gratularis, minime miramur te tuis, ut egregium artificem, praeclaris operibus laetari. quamquam est incredibilis hominum perversitas (graviore enim verbo uti non libet), qui nos, quos favendo in communi causa retinere potuerunt, invidendo abalienarunt; quorum malevolentissimis obtrectationibus nos scito de vetere illa nostra diuturnaque sententia prope iam esse depulsos, non nos quidem ut nostrae dignitatis simus obliti sed ut habeamus rationem aliquando etiam salutis. poterat utrumque praeclare, si esset fides, si gravitas in hominibus consularibus; sed tanta est in plerisque levitas ut eos non tam constantia in re publica nostra delectet quam splendor

8   offendat. quod eo liberius ad te scribo quia non solum temporibus his, quae per te sum adeptus, sed iam olim nascenti prope nostrae laudi dignitatique favisti, simulque quod video non, ut antehac putabam, novitati esse invisum meae; in te enim, homine omnium nobilissimo, similia invidorum vitia perspexi, quem tamen illi esse in principibus facile sunt passi, evolare altius certe noluerunt. gaudeo tuam dissimilem fuisse fortunam; multum enim interest utrum laus imminuatur an salus deseratur. me meae tamen

withholding the same. In this context nobody will perceive so readily and accurately as yourself just what is best in the particular circumstances of the case and time. I thought you ought to know *our* views from me rather than another.

You felicitate me on the state of my affairs, on Milo's friendship and Clodius' irresponsibility and impotence. Well, it does not at all surprise me to see a fine artist delighting in his own masterpieces. And yet the perverseness (I prefer not to use a stronger word) of folk is beyond belief. With good will they could have kept me in the common cause; instead, their jealousy has estranged me. For I must tell you that their venomous backbiting has pretty well succeeded in turning me away from my old, long established principles and brought me to the point, not indeed of forgetting my honour, but of paying some belated attention to my vital interest. The two could have run perfectly well in harness, if our Consulars had known the meaning of good faith and responsibility. But the majority are such fribbles that they are less pleased by my steadfastness in public affairs than irritated by my distinction. I write this to you the more frankly because you supported my public credit and standing almost from their earliest beginnings long ago as you do today—and that there *is* a today I owe to you. I can also write so because I find that it is not my birth, as I always used to think, that has aroused ill will. For the evils of envy have been similarly manifest in your case, *crème de la crème* as you are. In your case, however, they were willing enough to see you figure among the leaders of the community, but as for any higher flight—no, no! I am glad that your lot has been different from mine; for it is one thing to lose some prestige and quite another to be left alone when one's existence is at stake. However,

ne nimis paeniteret tua virtute perfectum est. curasti enim ut plus additum ad memoriam nominis nostri quam demptum de fortuna videretur.

9   Te vero [e]moneo cum beneficiis tuis tum amore incitatus meo ut omnem gloriam, ad quam a pueritia inflammatus fuisti, omni cura atque industria consequare magnitudinemque animi tui, quam ego semper sum admiratus semperque amavi, ne umquam inflectas cuiusquam iniuria. magna est hominum opinio de te, magna commendatio liberalitatis, magna memoria consulatus tui. haec profecto vides quanto expressiora quantoque illustriora futura sint cum aliquantum ex provincia atque ex imperio laudis accesserit. quamquam te ita gerere volo quae per exercitum atque imperium gerenda sunt ut haec multo ante meditere, huc te pares, haec cogites, ad haec te exerceas, sentiasque, id quod quia semper sperasti non dubito quin adeptus intellegas, te facillime posse obtinere summum atque altissimum gradum civitatis. quae quidem mea cohortatio ne tibi inanis aut sine causa suscepta videatur, illa me ratio movit ut te ex nostris eventis communibus admonendum putarem ut considerares in omni re<li>qua vita quibus crederes, quos caveres.

10   Quod scribis te velle scire qui sit rei publicae status, summa dissensio est, sed contentio dispar; nam qui plus opibus, armis, potentia valent perfecisse tamen mihi videntur stultitia et inconstantia adversariorum ut etiam auctoritate iam plus valerent. itaque perpaucis adversanti-

---

4 I.e. the dominant coalition between Pompey, Caesar, and Crassus often called the First Triumvirate.

5 M. Cato and his friends: the optimates.

thanks to your noble self, I am not overmuch dissatisfied with *my* lot, for you saw to it that what I forfeited in worldly prosperity should appear more than made up to my future reputation and memory.

Your services to me and my affection for you alike prompt me to a word of admonition. Use all diligence and effort to win all the glory that has fired your imagination since you were a lad. Never let any man's injustice bend the greatness of spirit which I have always admired and loved in you. Yours is a great reputation, your liberality is loudly commended, your Consulship has left a fine memory. You cannot fail to see how much all this will gain in definition and brilliance by an access of credit from provincial office and command. All the same, while I want you to do what may properly be done by military means in the exercise of military authority, I also want you to plan well beforehand your future in Rome. Prepare for that, think of it, train for it. Realize—it is what you have always hoped for, so I do not doubt that you are aware now that you have achieved it—that without any difficulty you can hold the greatest and highest place in our society. I trust you will not think this exhortation on my part a piece of unnecessary verbiage. It was the reason why I felt I should advise you in the light of our common experience to consider whom to trust, and of whom to beware, throughout the rest of your natural life.

You enquire as to the political situation. There is bitter conflict but the two sides are unequally matched. The party[4] superior in resources, armed force, and power has actually contrived, so it seems to me, to gain moral ascendancy as well, thanks to the stupidity and irresolution of their adversaries.[5] Accordingly they have secured from the

bus omnia quae ne per populum quidem sine seditione se
⟨posse⟩³ adsequi arbitrabantur per senatum consecuti
sunt. nam et stipendium Caesari decretum est et decem
legati, et ne lege Sempronia succederetur facile perfectum
est. quod e[g]o ad te brevius scribo quia me status hic rei
publicae non delectat, scribo tamen ut te admoneam, quod
ipse litteris omnibus a pueritia deditus experiendo tamen
magis quam discendo cognovi, tu ut tuis rebus integris
discas: neque salutis nostrae rationem habendam nobis
esse sine dignitate neque dignitatis sine salute.

11   Quod mihi de filia et de Crassipede gratularis, agnosco
humanitatem tuam speroque et opto nobis hanc coniunctionem voluptati fore. Lentulum nostrum, eximia spe,
summa virtute adulescentem, cum ceteris artibus quibus
studuisti semper ipse tum in primis imitatione tui fac eru-
dias; nulla enim erit hac praestantior disciplina. quem nos
et quia tuus et quia te dignus est filius et quia nos diligit
semperque dilexit in primis amamus carumque habemus.

3 *(Lamb.)*

6 Now in process of conquering Gaul north of the Roman
provinces.

Senate with very few opposing voices all that they did not expect to obtain even through the People without civil disorder. Caesar[6] has been voted a grant to pay his troops and ten Legates; and the appointment of a successor under the lex Sempronia[7] has been blocked without difficulty. I tell you this rather briefly because the present political situation is little to my liking; but I tell it all the same, so that I can advise you to learn before you meet with any setback a lesson that I myself have learned from experience rather than books (devoted to every class of literature as I have been since childhood): we must not consider our security without regard to honour, nor honour without regard to security.

It is very kind of you to offer me your congratulations on my daughter's engagement to Crassipes. I hope and pray that this connection will bring us pleasure. Mind you instruct our dear Lentulus,[8] most promising and excellent young man that he is, in the accomplishments to which you have always applied yourself, but especially in the imitation of his father; he can have no finer education. I have a special regard and affection for him because he is your son and worthy to be yours, and because he is and always has been fond of me.

[7] Under this law of C. Sempronius Gracchus the Senate was bound to name two provinces for the Consuls of the following year (55) before their election. These they would take over in 54. Had one of the two Gauls been named, an extension of Caesar's command, which was due to expire that year, would have been precluded.

[8] P. Lentulus Spinther the Younger. So Cicero regularly refers to his own son as 'Cicero' (Marcus in this translation).

19 (I.8)

Scr. Romae fort. m. Febr. an. 55

‹M. CICERO S. D. P. LENTULO PRO COS.›

1   De omnibus rebus quae ad te pertinent, quid actum, quid constitutum sit, quid Pompeius susceperit, optime ex M. Plaetorio cognosces, qui non solum interfuit iis rebus sed etiam praefuit neque ullum officium erga te hominis amantissimi, prudentissimi, diligentissimi praetermisit. ex eodem de toto statu rerum communium cognosces; quae quales sint, non facile est scribere. sunt quidem certe in amicorum nostrorum potestate, atque ita ut nullam mutationem umquam hac hominum aetate habitura res esse videatur.

2   Ego quidem, ut debeo et ut tute mihi praecepisti et ut me pietas utilitasque cogit, me ad eius rationes adiungo quem tu in meis rationibus tibi esse adiungendum putasti. sed te non praeterit quam sit difficile sensum in re publica, praesertim rectum et confirmatum, deponere. verum tamen ipse me conformo ad eius voluntatem a quo honeste dissentire non possum, neque id facio, ut forsitan quibusdam videar, simulatione; tantum enim animi inductio et mehercule amor erga Pompeium apud me valet ut, quae illi utilia sunt et quae ille vult, ea mihi omnia iam et recta et vera videantur; neque, ut ego arbitror, errarent ne adversarii quidem eius si, cum pares esse non possent, pugnare desisterent.

---

[1] Its nature is unknown. Pompey and Crassus were now Consuls.

[2] The 'Triumvirs,' or perhaps only Pompey and Caesar.

19 (I.8)

CICERO TO LENTULUS SPINTHER

Rome, February (?) 55

From M. Cicero to P. Lentulus, Proconsul, greetings.

On all matters that concern you—proceedings, decisions, Pompey's undertaking[1]—you will have an excellent informant in M. Plaetorius, who has taken, not only part, but the leading part in them. He has performed on your behalf every friendly service that affection, sagacity, and industry could render. You will likewise learn from him the whole state of public affairs, which are not easy to explain in writing. They are at all events in our friends'[2] control, so firmly that no change in the position seems likely for a generation to come.

For my part I follow my prescribed course, the course which you advised and which gratitude and expediency dictate; that is to say, I attach myself to the interests of the personage[3] whom you thought proper to attach to yourself where my interests were concerned. But you realize how hard it is to put aside one's political views, especially when they are well and firmly founded. However, as I cannot honourably oppose him, I adapt myself to his wishes. Nor in so doing am I belying my real feelings, as some may perhaps imagine. My inclination, indeed my affection for Pompey is strong enough to make me now feel that whatever is to his advantage and whatever he wants is right and proper. Even his opponents would in my opinion make no mistake if they gave up fighting, since they cannot be a match for him.

[3] Pompey.

3   Me quidem etiam illa res consolatur quod ego is sum cui vel maxime concedant omnes ut vel ea defendam quae Pompeius velit vel taceam vel etiam, id quod mihi maxime libet, ad nostra m<e> studia referam litterarum; quod profecto faciam, si mihi per eiusdem amicitiam licebit. quae enim proposita fuerant nobis cum et honoribus amplissimis et laboribus maximis perfuncti essemus, dignitas in sententiis dicendis, libertas in re publica capessenda, ea sublata tota sunt,[1] nec mihi magis quam omnibus. nam aut adsentiendum est nulla cum gravitate paucis aut frustra dissentiendum.

4   Haec ego ad te ob eam causam maxime scribo ut iam de tua quoque ratione meditere. commutata tota ratio est senatus, iudiciorum, rei totius publicae. otium nobis exoptandum est, quod ii qui potiuntur rerum praestaturi videntur, si quidam homines patientius eorum potentiam ferre potuerint. dignitatem quidem illam consularem fortis et constantis senatoris nihil est quod cogitemus; amissa culpa est eorum qui a senatu et ordinem coniunctissimum et hominem clarissimum abalienarunt.

5   Sed ut ad ea quae coniunctiora rebus tuis sunt revertar, Pompeium tibi valde amicum esse cognovi. [ut] eo tu consule, quantum ego perspicio, omnia quae voles obtinebis. quibus in rebus me sibi ille adfixum habebit, neque a me ulla res quae ad te pertineat neglegetur; neque enim verebor ne sim ei molestus, cui iucundum erit etiam propter se[2] ipsum cum me esse gratum videbit.

---

[1] si (*Madvig*)   [2] te (*Graevius*)

---

[4] I.e. the Knights (cf. *Letters to Atticus* 21 (II.1).7) and Pompey, alienated by Cato and company.

I have another consolation. Everyone agrees that I of all people am entitled either to support Pompey's wishes or to hold my peace or simply (and this is my chief wish) to return to my literary studies. That, you may be sure, is what I shall do, if the claims of Pompey's friendship allow me. As for what I had promised myself after attaining the highest state dignities and passing through the most severe ordeals—a lofty platform in the Senate, a position of independence in public life—there is an end to all that, not for me in particular, but for all and sundry. The choice lies between undignified support for a clique and fruitless opposition.

I am writing all this to you chiefly because I want you now to give thought to your own position. The whole face of things has changed—the Senate, the courts, the whole body politic. Tranquillity is what we have to pray for, and this the present holders of power seem likely to provide, if certain persons can submit with a modicum of patience to their domination. The old concept of a Consular playing his firm and courageous part in the Senate must be dismissed from our minds. It has disappeared through the fault of those who lost the Senate the sympathies of a very friendly class and a very eminent individual.[4]

But to return to matters bearing more directly on your own position, I know that Pompey is very much your friend. While he is Consul, so far as I can judge, all you wish will be yours. In that connection he will have me close at his elbow, and I shall not neglect anything which may concern you. I have no fear of his finding me importunate—he will be glad even for his own sake to see that I know the meaning of gratitude.

6   Tu velim tibi ita persuadeas, nullam rem esse minimam
quae ad te pertineat quae mihi non carior sit quam meae
res omnes; idque cum sentiam, sedulitate mihime<t> ipse
satis facere non possim, re quidem ipsa ideo mihi non satis
facio quod nullam partem tuorum meritorum non modo
referenda sed ne cogitanda quidem gratia consequi possum.

7   Rem te valde bene gessisse rumor erat. exspectabantur
litterae tuae, de quibus eramus iam cum Pompeio locuti.
quae si erunt adlatae, nostrum studium exstabit in conveniendis magistratibus et senatoribus; ceteraque quae ad
te pertinebunt cum etiam plus contenderimus quam
possumus, minus tamen faciemus quam debemus.

20 (I.9)

Scr. Romae m. Dec. an. 54

M. CICERO S. D. LENTULO IMP.

1   Periucundae mihi fuerunt litterae tuae, quibus intellexi
te perspicere meam in te pietatem; quid enim dicam benevolentiam, cum illud ipsum gravissimum et sanctissimum
nomen pietatis levius mihi meritis erga me tuis esse videatur? quod autem tibi grata mea erga te studia scribis esse,
facis tu quidem abundantia quadam amoris ut etiam grata
sint ea quae praetermitti sine nefario scelere non possunt.
tibi autem multo notior atque illustrior meus in te animus

---

⁵ No doubt against the Free Cilicians of the Taurus or Amanus
mountains, at whose expense Cicero himself was to win laurels in
51.

I hope you will rest assured that the least of your concerns means more to me than all of mine put together. Such being my feelings, I could not be assiduous enough to satisfy my own mind; as for results, the reason why I fail to satisfy myself is that I cannot adequately repay, or even imagine myself repaying, any part of what I owe you.

There is a report that you have had a highly successful campaign.[5] We are waiting for a dispatch from you, as to which I have already had a talk with Pompey. Once it arrives, I shall be zealously to the fore in canvassing magistrates and members of the Senate;[6] and in other matters which concern you my efforts may go beyond my capacity, but they will fall short of my obligations.

20 (I.9)
CICERO TO LENTULUS SPINTHER

Rome, December 54

From M. Cicero to Lentulus, Imperator, greetings.

I am very glad to have your letter, which shows that you appreciate my *piety* towards you—I won't say my good will, for even this solemn, sacred word 'piety' seems to me inadequate for what I owe you. When you write that you are grateful for my efforts on your behalf, it must be out of the overflowing affection of your heart. *Grateful*, because I do what it would be rank villainy to leave undone? But you would have a much better and clearer impression of my sentiments towards you, if we had been together and in

---

[6] For a public Thanksgiving (Supplication) in honour of Lentulus' success. He finally celebrated his Triumph in 51.

esset si hoc tempore omni quo di⟨i⟩uncti[1] fuimus et una et
2 Romae fuissemus. nam in eo ipso quod te ostendis esse
facturum quodque et in primis potes et ego a te vehementer exspecto, in sententiis senatoriis et in omni actione
atque administratione rei publicae [floruissemus],[2] de qua
ostendam equidem paulo post qui sit meus sensus et status
et rescribam tibi ad ea quae quaeris—sed certe et ego te
auctore amicissimo ac sapientissimo et tu me consiliario
fortasse non imperitissimo, fideli quidem et benevolo
certe, usus esses. quamquam tua quidem causa te esse imperatorem provinciamque bene gestis rebus cum exercitu
victore obtinere, ut debeo, laetor; sed certe qui tibi ex me
fructus debentur eos uberiores et praesentiores praesens
capere potuisses, in iis vero ulciscendis quos tibi partim
inimicos esse intellegis propter tuam propugnationem
salutis meae, partim invidere propter illius actionis amplitudinem et gloriam, mirificum me tibi comitem praebuis-
sem. quamquam ille perennis inimicus amicorum suorum,
qui tuis maximis beneficiis ornatus in te potissimum frac-
tam illam et debilitatam vim suam contulit, nostram vicem
ultus est ipse sese. ea est enim conatus quibus patefactis
nullam sibi in posterum non modo dignitatis sed ne liber-
3 tatis quidem partem reliquit. te autem, etsi mallem in meis
rebus expertum quam etiam in tuis, tamen in molestia gaudeo eam fidem cognosse hominum non ita magna mercede
quam ego maximo dolore cognoram.

[1] *(Vict.)*
[2] *(SB)*

---

[1] L. Domitius Ahenobarbus, now Consul along with Ap. Claudius Pulcher (see my Commentary).

Rome all this time we have been separated. Take what you say you have in view (nobody can do it better than you, and I am eagerly looking forward to the prospect)—speeches in the Senate and general activity and conduct of public affairs, as to which I shall tell you my opinion and position presently and answer your enquiries—well, at least I should have found in you the wisest and most affectionate of guides, while you would have found in me an adviser of experience perhaps not altogether negligible, and of undeniable loyalty and good will. For your sake, it is true, I am duly delighted to think of you as Imperator, governing your province after a successful campaign at the head of a victorious army. But at least you could have enjoyed the due fruits of my gratitude fuller and fresher on the spot; and when it came to repaying certain people, some of them hostile to you, as you know, because you championed my restoration, others jealous of the grandeur and glory of the achievement—what a companion in arms I should have made you! To be sure, that inveterate enemy of his friends[1] who recompensed your signal favours by turning the feeble remnants of his violence against you[2] has done our work for us. The exposure of his recent operations[3] has robbed him of all independence in the future, let alone prestige. I could have wished that you had gained your experience in my case and not in your own as well, but I am glad in a bad business to think that you have not paid so very heavy a price for a lesson in the unreliability of mankind which *I* learned to my bitter sorrow.

[2] We do not know how Domitius had attacked Lentulus.

[3] The scandalous electoral compact revealed by C. Memmius in September 54; see *Letters to Atticus* 91 (IV.17).2.

4 De qua ratione tota iam videtur mihi exponendi tempus dari ut tibi rescribam ad ea quae quaeris. certiorem te per litteras scribis esse factum me cum Caesare et cum Appio esse in gratia teque id non reprehendere adscribis; Vatinium autem scire te velle ostendis quibus rebus adductus defenderim et laudarim. quod tibi ut planius exponam, altius paulo rationem consiliorum meorum repetam necesse est.

Ego me, Lentule, initio ‹beneficio›[3] rerum atque actionum tuarum non solum meis sed etiam rei publicae restitutum putabam et, quoniam tibi incredibilem quendam amorem et omnia in te ipsum summa ac singularia studia deberem, rei publicae, quae te in me restituendo multum adiuvisset, eum certe me animum merito ipsius debere arbitrabar quem antea tantum modo communi officio civium, non aliquo erga me singulari beneficio debitum praestitissem. hac me mente fuisse et senatus ex me te consule audivit et tu in nostris sermonibus collocutioni-
5 busque vidisti. etsi iam primis temporibus illis multis rebus meus offendebatur animus, cum te agente de reliqua nostra dignitate aut occulta non nullorum odia aut obscura in me studia cernebam. nam neque de monumentis meis ab iis adiutus es a quibus debuisti neque de vi nefaria qua cum fratre eram domo expulsus neque hercule in iis ipsis rebus quae, quamquam erant mihi propter rei familiaris naufragia necessariae, tamen a me minimi putabantur, in meis damnis ex auctoritate senatus sarciendis, eam volun-

---

[3] (*Sternkopf*)

---

[4] No doubt including the one referred to in Letter 20.15.
[5] See *Letters to Atticus* 75 (IV.3).2.

This seems a good opportunity for me to give an exposition of the whole topic by way of a reply to your enquiries. You write that you have heard by letter that I am in good relations with Caesar and Appius, and you add that you have nothing to say against that. But you intimate that you would like to know my reasons for defending Vatinius and speaking to his character. To give you a clear explanation I must trace the principles of my political conduct a little further back.

To begin with, thanks to your public endeavours, dear sir, I conceived myself as restored, not only to my family and friends, but to my country. I owed *you* an affection well-nigh transcending reason and the most complete and signal personal devotion. To our country, which had lent you no slight assistance in your campaign for my restoration, I felt myself to owe as a matter of gratitude at least the loyalty which I had formerly rendered only as the common duty of a Roman, and not as due in respect of any special favour to myself. The Senate heard these sentiments from my own lips during your Consulship, and you perceived them in the talks and discussions we had together. Yet even in those early days there was much to give me pause. I saw how your efforts to complete my rehabilitation met with covert ill will in some quarters and doubtful support in others. In the matter of my memorials[4] those who ought to have helped you did not; similarly with respect to the criminal violence with which I and my brother were driven out of our homes.[5] I must add that even in those items to which, necessary as they were to me after the ruin of my private fortune, I attached minimal importance, I mean the indemnification of my losses by authority of the

tatem quam exspectaram praestiterunt. quae cum viderem
(neque erant obscura), non tamen tam acerba mihi haec
accidebant quam erant illa grata quae fecerant.

6   Itaque, quamquam et Pompeio plurimum te quidem
ipso praedicatore ac teste debebam et eum non solum
beneficio sed amore etiam et perpetuo quodam iudicio
meo diligebam, tamen non reputans quid ille vellet in
omnibus meis sententiis de re publica pristinis per-
7   <ma>nebam. ego sedente Cn. Pompeio, cum ut laudaret P.
Sestium introisset in urbem dixissetque testis Vatinius me
fortuna et felicitate C. Caesaris commotum illi amicum
esse coepisse, dixi me M. Bibuli fortunam, quam ille adflictam putaret, omnium triumphis victoriisque anteferre,
dixique eodem teste alio loco eosdem esse qui Bibulum
exire domo prohibuissent et qui me coegissent. tota vero
interrogatio mea nihil habuit nisi reprehensionem illius
tribunatus. in qua omnia dicta sunt libertate animoque
maximo de vi, de auspiciis, de donatione regnorum, neque
vero hac in causa modo sed constanter saepe in senatu.
8   quin etiam Marcellino et Philippo consulibus Non. Apr.
mihi est senatus adsensus ut de agro Campano frequenti
senatu Id. Mai. referretur. num potui magis in arcem illius
causae invadere aut magis oblivisci temporum meorum,
meminisse actionum?

    Hac a me sententia dicta magnus animorum motus est

---

    6 Tried on charges of violence in February 56, Cicero defend-
ing. He was acquitted.

    7 As Consul in 59 Bibulus had spent most of the year shut up in
his house. The remarks quoted here do not in fact occur in the extant speech *In Vatinium.*

Senate, they showed a less forthcoming attitude than I had expected. I saw all this—it was plain enough; but any bitterness was outweighed by gratitude for what they had done.

And so, notwithstanding my regard for Pompey, to whom by your own declaration and testimony I owed a very great deal—a regard founded not only upon his goodness to me but on affection and what I might call lifelong predilection—I made no account of his wishes and held firmly by all my old political sentiments. When Pompey came into town to speak to character on behalf of P. Sestius[6] and Vatinius said in evidence that I had made friends with C. Caesar because of his success and good fortune, I said in Cn. Pompeius' presence that I thought M. Bibulus' sad plight (as Vatinius regarded it) preferable to any man's Triumphs and victories. At another point in Vatinius' evidence I said that the same people who had not allowed Bibulus to leave his home had forced me to leave mine.[7] My whole cross-examination was nothing but a condemnation of Vatinius' career as Tribune. In it I spoke throughout with the greatest frankness and spirit, dwelling on the use of violence, the auspices, and the grants of foreign kingdoms. And I did so not only at this trial but in the Senate, consistently and often. On the Nones of April in the Consulship of Marcellinus and Philippus the Senate actually adopted a proposal of mine that the question of the Campanian land should be referred to a full House on the Ides of May. Was not that invading the innermost citadel of the ruling clique with a vengeance? And could I have shown myself more oblivious of my past vicissitudes or more mindful of my political record?

That speech of mine caused a sensation, not only where

factus cum eorum quorum oportuit tum illorum etiam
9 quorum numquam putaram. nam hoc senatus consulto in
meam sententiam facto Pompeius, cum mihi nihil osten-
disset se esse offensum, in Sardiniam et in Africam profectus est eoque itinere Lucam ad Caesarem venit. ibi multa
de mea sententia questus est Caesar, quippe qui etiam
Ravennae Crassum ante vidisset ab eoque in me esset in-
census. sane moleste Pompeium id ferre constabat; quod
ego, cum audissem ex aliis, maxime ex meo fratre cognovi.
quem cum in Sardinia Pompeius paucis post diebus quam
Luca discesserat convenisset, 'te' inquit 'ipsum cupio; nihil
opportunius potuit accidere. nisi cum Marco fratre diligenter egeris, dependendum tibi est quod mihi pro illo
spopondisti.' quid multa? questus est graviter, sua merita
commemoravit, quid egisset saepissime de actis Caesaris
cum ipso meo fratre quidque sibi is de me recepisset in
memoriam redegit seque quae de mea salute egisset voluntate Caesaris egisse ipsum meum fratrem testatus est.
cuius causam dignitatemque mihi ut commendaret, roga-
vit ut eam ne oppugnarem, si nollem aut non possem tueri.
10   Haec cum ad me frater pertulisset et cum tamen Pompeius ad me cum mandatis Vibullium misisset ut integrum
mihi de causa Campana ad suum reditum reservarem,
collegi ipse me et cum ipsa quasi re publica collocutus
sum, ut mihi tam multa pro se perpesso atque perfuncto
concederet ut officium meum memoremque in bene meritos animum fidemque fratris mei praestarem, eumque

8 Probably Caesar and Pompey are respectively indicated.
9 Pompey spoke metaphorically, Q. Cicero having in 57 made
himself responsible for his brother's future political behaviour if
restored from exile.

I had intended but in quite unexpected quarters.[8] After the Senate had passed a decree in accordance with my motion, Pompey (without giving me any indication of displeasure) left for Sardinia and Africa, and joined Caesar at Luca on the way. Caesar there complained at length about my motion—he had been stirred up against me by Crassus, whom he had seen previously at Ravenna. Pompey by general admission was a good deal upset. I heard this from various sources, but my principal informant was my brother. Pompey met him in Sardinia a few days after laving Luca. 'You're the very man I want,' he told him. 'Most lucky our meeting just now. Unless you talk seriously to your brother Marcus, you are going to have to pay up on the guarantee[9] you gave me on his behalf.' In short, he remonstrated in strong terms, mentioning his services to me, recalling the many discussions he had had with my brother himself about Caesar's legislation and the pledges my brother had given him concerning my future conduct, appealing to my brother's personal knowledge of the fact that his own support for my restoration had been given with Caesar's blessing. He asked him to commend to me Caesar's cause and prestige, with the request that I should refrain from attacking them if I would not or could not defend them.

Though my brother conveyed all this to me, Pompey also sent Vibullius with an oral message, asking me not to commit myself on the Campanian question till his return. Then I took stock. It was like a dialogue between me and my country. Would she not allow me, after all I had suffered and gone through for her sake, to behave with propriety and gratitude towards my benefactors and to honour my brother's pledge? Would she not let her loyal

quem bonum civem semper habuisset bonum virum esse pateretur.

In illis autem meis actionibus sententiisque omnibus quae Pompeium videbantur offendere certorum hominum, quos iam debes suspicari, sermones referebantur ad me qui, cum illa sentirent in re publica quae ego agebam semperque sensissent, me tamen non satis facere Pompeio Caesaremque inimicissimum mihi futurum gaudere se aiebant. erat hoc mihi dolendum, sed multo illud magis, quod inimicum meum (meum autem? immo vero legum, iudiciorum, oti, patriae, bonorum omnium) sic amplexabantur, sic in manibus habebant, sic fovebant, sic me praesente osculabantur, non illi quidem ut mihi stomachum facerent, quem ego funditus perdidi, sed certe ut facere se arbitrarentur. hic ego, quantum humano consilio efficere potui, circumspectis rebus meis omnibus rationibusque subductis summam feci cogitationum mearum omnium; quam tibi, si potero, breviter exponam.

11   Ego, si ab improbis et perditis civibus rem publicam teneri viderem, sicut et Cinnanis[4] temporibus scimus et non nullis aliis accidisse, non modo praemiis, quae apud me minimum valent, sed ne periculis quidem compulsus ullis, quibus tamen moventur etiam fortissimi viri, ad eorum causam me adiungerem, ne si summa quidem eorum in me merita constarent. cum autem in re publica Cn. Pompeius princeps esset vir, is qui hanc potentiam et gloriam maximis in rem publicam meritis praestantissimisque re-

---

[4] Cinneis *(Graevius)*

---

[10] Optimates like Hortensius, Bibulus, and Domitius.

citizen, as I had always shown myself, be also a man of honour?

Now all the time I was acting and speaking in a manner liable to annoy Pompey, I received reports of how certain folk,[10] whose identity you should by now be able to guess, were talking. Fully as the course I was now following accorded with their past and present political sentiments, they were none the less expressing satisfaction at Pompey's disappointment with me and at the prospect that Caesar would be my sworn enemy in future. This was wounding enough; but much more so was their behaviour to my enemy[11]—the enemy, I should rather say, of law, justice, and tranquillity, of Rome and all honest men. This individual they chose to embrace and caress, petting and cosseting him before my very eyes. It was not enough to raise my spleen, because that organ has entirely disappeared, but enough at any rate to let them think they were raising it. At this point I surveyed the whole range of my affairs, so far as I could with only human wit to guide me, cast up my accounts in full, and arrived at the grand total of my cogitations. That is what I shall try to set out for you in brief.

If I had seen the state in the control of rascals and villains, as we know happened in Cinna's time and at some other periods of its history, no reward, or danger either (and while rewards count for little with me, even the bravest of us are influenced by dangers), would have driven me on to their side, no matter how much they might have done for me personally. But the leading man in Rome was Cn. Pompeius. The power and glory he enjoyed had been earned by state services of the highest importance and by

11 Clodius.

bus gestis esset consecutus cuiusque ego dignitatis ab adulescentia fautor, in praetura autem et in consulatu adiutor etiam exstitissem, cumque idem auctoritate et sententia per se, consiliis et studiis tecum me adiuvisset meumque inimicum unum in civitate haberet inimicum, non putavi famam inconstantiae mihi pertimescendam si quibusdam in sententiis paulum me immutassem meamque voluntatem ad summi viri de meque optime meriti dignitatem adgregassem.

12   In hac sententia complectendus erat mihi Caesar, ut vides, in coniuncta et causa et dignitate. hic multum valuit cum vetus amicitia, quam tu non ignoras mihi et Quinto fratri cum Caesare fuisse, tum humanitas eius ac liberalitas brevi tempore et litteris et officiis perspecta nobis et cognita. vehementer etiam res ipsa publica me movit, quae mihi videbatur contentionem, praesertim maximis rebus a Caesare gestis, cum illis viris nolle fieri et ne fieret vehementer recusare. gravissime autem me in hanc mentem impulit et Pompei fides, quam de me Caesari dederat, et fratris mei, quam Pompeio.

Erant praeterea haec animadvertenda in civitate quae sunt apud Platonem nostrum scripta divinitus, quales in re publica principes essent talis reliquos solere esse civis. tenebam memoria nobis consulibus ea fundamenta iacta iam[5] ex Kal. Ian. confirmandi senatus ut neminem mirari

---

5 iactatam *(Baiter)*

---

12 In the spring of 54 Q. Cicero left for Gaul to take up an appointment as Caesar's Legate.   13 Cf. *Laws* 711c. But Cicero's words are in fact an almost exact translation of a passage in Xenophon's *Education of Cyrus* (8.8.5).

the most signal military achievements. From early man-
hood I had rejoiced in his success, and as Praetor and Consul had come forward to promote it. On his side, he had
individually helped me with his influence and voice in the
Senate, and in conjunction with yourself by planned effort
in my cause. His only enemy in Rome was also mine. All
these points considered, I did not feel I need fear the reputation of inconsistency if in certain speeches I changed my
tack a little and rallied in sentiment to the support of this
great figure, my personal benefactor.

In this determination I could not but embrace Caesar,
as you will recognize, for his interest and prestige were
bound up with Pompey's. Here the old friendship which,
as you are aware, existed between Caesar and myself and
my brother Quintus counted for much, and no less Caesar's own gracious and generous attitude, which soon
became plainly apparent to us in his letters and friendly
acts.[12] Moreover, patriotic considerations had great weight
with me. It was not, I felt, the will of our country that there
should be a struggle with these men, especially after Caesar's great achievements; I felt she was keenly anxious to
avoid such a struggle. But the weightiest element in thus
persuading me was the pledge concerning myself which
Pompey had given to Caesar and which my brother gave to
Pompey.

I had besides to note in our community the phenomena
which our favourite Plato has characterized so wonder-
fully—the tendency for the members of a political society
to resemble its leaders.[13] I remembered that from the very
first day of my Consulship sure foundations were laid for
the strengthening of the Senate, so that no one ought to
have been surprised either at the courage or the moral

oporteret Non. Dec. tantum vel animi fuisse in illo ordine
vel auctoritatis; idemque memineram nobis privatis usque
ad Caesarem et Bibulum consules, cum sententiae nostrae
magnum in senatu pondus haberent, unum fere sensum
13 fuisse bonorum omnium. postea, cum tu Hispaniam cite-
riorem cum imperio obtineres neque res publica consules
haberet sed mercatores provinciarum et seditionum ser-
vos ac ministros, iecit quidam casus caput meum quasi cer-
taminis causa in mediam contentionem dissensionemque
civilem. quo in discrimine cum mirifica senatus, incredibilis Italiae totius, singularis omnium bonorum consensio in
me tuendo exstitisset, non dicam quid acciderit (multorum
est enim et varia culpa), tantum dicam brevi, non mihi
exercitum sed duces defuisse. in quo, ut iam sit in iis culpa
qui me non defenderunt, non minor est in iis qui reliquerunt; et si accusandi sunt si qui pertimuerunt, magis etiam
reprehendendi si qui se timere simularunt. illud quidem
certe nostrum consilium iure laudandum est, qui meos
civis et a me conservatos et me servare cupientis spoliatos
ducibus servis armatis obici noluerim declararique malue-
rim quanta vis esse potuisset in consensu bonorum, si iis
pro me stante pugnare licuisset, cum adflictum excitare
potuissent; quorum quidem animum tu non perspexisti

---

14 The day on which the Senate voted for the execution of the
Catilinarian conspirators.

15 According to Cicero's version of events, the Consuls of 58,
Piso and Gabinius, were bribed by Clodius with appointments to
the provincial governorships of Macedonia and Syria respectively.

16 Not the mass of the 'honest men' but Pompey; cf. *Letters to
Atticus* 171 (IX.5).2.

power of that Order as revealed on the Nones of December following.[14] Equally I remembered that after my retirement from office down to the Consulship of Caesar and Bibulus, when my views carried considerable weight in the Senate, all honest men were pretty much of one mind. Later, while you were governor of Hither Spain and the state had no Consuls, only traffickers in provinces[15] and servile instruments of sedition, accident may be said to have flung my person as a bone of contention into the midst of civil conflict and strife. At that crisis the consensus in my defence of the Senate, of all Italy, of all honest men was truly remarkable, a thing transcending belief. I will not say what happened—the blame is complex and many shared in it—only this briefly, that it was generals, not an army, that I lacked. Granted that those who failed to defend me[16] were to blame, no less so were those who left me in the lurch;[17] and if those who were afraid should be in the dock, those who only pretended to be afraid are yet more deserving of censure.[18] At any rate there must be applause for my refusal to let my countrymen, whom I had preserved and who were desirous of saving me, be thrown leaderless against armed slaves—for my decision to let the potential power of honest[19] men united (had they been allowed to fight for me before I fell) be demonstrated rather when the opportunity came to raise me from the dust. You saw their spirit when you took action on my be-

[17] The optimate leaders.

[18] In Cicero's obstinately held opinion the behaviour of certain of his friends (especially Hortensius) at the crisis of March 58 amounted to deliberate treachery; cf. *Letters to Atticus* 52 (III.7).2 etc.   [19] See Glossary.

solum, cum de me ageres, sed etiam confirmasti atque
14 tenuisti. qua in causa (non modo non negabo sed etiam
semper et meminero et praedicabo libenter) usus es quibusdam nobilissimis hominibus fortioribus in me restituendo quam fuerant idem in tenendo. qua in sententia si
constare voluissent, suam auctoritatem simul cum salute
mea reciperassent. recreati⟨s⟩ enim boni⟨s⟩ viri⟨s⟩ consulatu tuo et constantissimis atque optimis actionibus tuis
excitati(s), Cn. Pompeio praesertim ad causam adiuncto,
cum etiam Caesar rebus maximis gestis singularibus ornatus et novis honoribus ac iudiciis senatus ad auctoritatem
eius ordinis adiungeretur, nulli improbo civi locus ad rem
publicam violandam esse potuisset.
15 Sed attende, quaeso, quae sint consecuta. primum illa
furia,[6] ⟨ille fur⟩[7] muliebrium religionum, qui non pluris
fecerat Bonam Deam quam tris sorores, impunitatem est
illorum sententiis adsecutus qui, cum tribunus pl. poenas a
seditioso civi per bonos viros iudicio persequi vellet, exemplum praeclarissimum in posterum vindicandae seditionis
de re publica sustulerunt, idemque postea non meum
monumentum (non enim illae manubiae meae sed operis
locatio mea fuerat), monumentum vero senatus hostili
nomine et cruentis inustum litteris esse passi sunt. qui me

[6] illa furta (*Man.*: ille fur ⵦ)
[7] (*SB*)

---

[20] See *Letters to Atticus* 12 (I.12).3.
[21] Probably Racilius; cf. Letter 5 (II.1).3 of Cicero's letters to
Quintus.
[22] Cf. para. 5. It may have been a building started at the end
of Cicero's Consulship to commemorate the suppression of the

half; more, you confirmed and maintained it. In that campaign—so far from denying, I shall always remember and gladly proclaim it—you found certain very high-born personages more courageous in securing my reinstatement than they had shown themselves in preventing my exile. Had they chosen to hold to that policy, they would have recovered the respect of the community at the same time as they restored me to its membership. Your Consulship had put fresh heart into the honest men, roused from their apathy by your resolute and praiseworthy initiatives, especially when Cn. Pompeius joined the cause. Even Caesar, now that the Senate had recognized his splendid achievements by signal and unprecedented honours and marks of esteem, was moving towards a position of support for the authority of the Order. No bad citizen would have had a loophole through which to injure his country.

Now pray mark the sequel. That embodiment of mischief, that pilferer of the secrets of women's worship, who treated the Good Goddess[20] with as little respect as his three sisters, escaped scot-free. A Tribune[21] was ready to bring the agitator to trial and punishment at the hands of honest men. He was saved by the votes of those who thereby lost Rome what should have been a splendid example to posterity of the chastisement of sedition. Subsequently the same group allowed a memorial[22]—not *my* memorial, for the funds employed were not victory spoils of mine, I merely signed the contract for the work—allowed the *Senate's* memorial to be inscribed with the name of a public enemy in letters of blood. These people desired

Catilinarian conspiracy. Clodius seems to have effaced the inscription and substituted one bearing his own name.

homines quod salvum esse voluerunt est mihi gratissimum; sed vellem non solum salutis meae quem ad modum medici sed ut aliptae etiam virium et coloris rationem habere voluissent. nunc, ut Apelles Veneris caput et summa pectoris politissima arte perfecit, reliquam partem corporis incohatam reliquit, sic quidam homines in capite meo solum elaborarunt, reliquum corpus imperfectum ac rude reliquerunt.

16   In quo ego spem fefelli non modo invidorum sed etiam inimicorum meorum, qui de uno acerrimo et fortissimo viro meoque iudicio omnium magnitudine animi et constantia praestantissimo, Q. Metello L. f., quondam falsam opinionem acceperant,[8] quem post reditum dictitant fracto animo et demisso fuisse (est vero probandum, qui et summa voluntate cesserit et egregia animi alacritate afuerit neque sane redire curarit, eum ob id ipsum f<r>actum fuisse in quo cum omnis homines tum M. illum Scaurum, singularem virum, constantia et gravitate superasset!)—sed quod de illo acceperant aut etiam suspicabantur de me idem cogitabant, abiectiore animo me futurum, cum res publica maiorem etiam mihi animum quam umquam habuissem daret cum declarasset se non potuisse me uno civi carere, cumque Metellum unius tribuni pl. rogatio, me universa res publica duce senatu, comitante Italia, pro-

---

[8] acceperunt *(Ern.)*

---

[23] Cicero plays on two meanings of *caput:* head and status as a citizen.

[24] Numidicus. In 100 he had gone into exile rather than swear obedience to the agrarian law of the Tribune Saturninus. Scaurus took the oath.

my restoration, and for that I am deeply beholden. But I could have wished that they had not merely taken a doctor's interest in the life of the patient, but a trainer's in his strength and physical appearance. Certain persons in my case have followed the example of Apelles, who applied the utmost refinement of his art to perfecting the head and bust of his Venus, but left the rest of the body a mere sketch—they made a finished job of the capital[23] section only, leaving the rest unfinished and rough.

In this connection I disappointed the expectations of the jealous as well as the hostile. Once upon a time they were told, and believed, a false story about one of the boldest and most stout-hearted men who ever lived, whose equal in grandeur and resolution of spirit I do not know, Q. Metellus,[24] son of Lucius. He, so they like to say, was a broken man after his return from exile. A likely tale! Had he not gone quite readily into banishment, endured it with notable cheerfulness, and been at no great pains to return? Was he broken as the result of an episode in which he had emerged superior to all his contemporaries, even the eminent M. Scaurus, in resolution and integrity? Be that as it may, they formed the same notion about me as they had been given, or even surmised for themselves, about Metellus. They thought I should be a humbled man henceforth—whereas my country was making me actually prouder than I had ever been in my life! Had she not declared that she could not do without me—one single citizen? Metellus, after all, was brought back by the bill of a single Tribune, I by the whole state under the leadership of the Senate and with all Italy in attendance. The relevant

mulgantibus omnibus ⟨paene[9] magistratibus[10]⟩, te fe-
rente[11] consule, comitiis centuriatis, cunctis ordinibus
hominibus incumbentibus, omnibus denique suis viribus
reciperavisset.

17   Neque vero ego mihi postea quicquam adsumpsi neque
hodie adsumo quod quemquam malevolentissimum iure
possit offendere; tantum enitor ut neque amicis neque
etiam alienioribus opera, consilio, labore desim. hic meae
vitae cursus offendit eos fortasse qui splendorem et
speciem huius vitae intuentur, sollicitudinem autem et
laborem perspicere non possunt. illud vero non obscure
queruntur, in meis sententiis quibus ornem Caesarem
quasi desciscere m⟨e a⟩[12] pristina causa. ego autem cum
illa sequor quae paulo ante proposui tum hoc non in post-
remis de quo coeperam exponere: non offendes eundem
bonorum sensum, Lentule, quem reliquisti; qui confirma-
tus consulatu nostro, ⟨non⟩ numquam postea interruptus,
adflictus ante te consulem, recreatus abs te, totus est nunc
ab iis a quibus tuendus fuerat derelictus; idque non solum
fronte atque vultu, quibus simulatio facillime sustinetur,
declarant ii qui tum nostro illo statu optimates nominaban-
tur sed etiam sententiis[13] saepe iam tabellaque docuerunt.

18   Itaque tota iam sapientium civium, qualem me et esse
et numerari volo, et sententia et voluntas mutata esse debet. id enim iubet idem ille Plato, quo ego vehementer

9 *(SB)*
10 *(Lehmann)*
11 referent *(Lehmann)*
12 *(Schütz et Man.)*
13 sensu *(Goodyear:* sententia *Madvig:* -ia sua *SB olim)*

law was promulgated by almost[25] the entire body of magistrates, moved by yourself as Consul at the Assembly of the Centuries with the enthusiastic support of all classes and individuals. In a word, all the forces of the commonwealth were mobilized to that one end.

Not that after this experience I made any pretensions, or make any today, to which the most jaundiced critic could fairly take exception. I merely endeavour to serve my friends, or even my acquaintances, with time and counsel and hard work. My way of life perhaps irritates those who look at its outward show and glitter, but cannot see the care and toil behind. One stricture, of which they make no secret, is that in my speeches in favour of Caesar I am more or less deserting the good old cause. Well, I have just advanced my reasons, but to these I would add another, not the least important, which I had begun to explain. Dear sir, you will not find again among our honest men that league of sentiment which you left behind you. Established in my Consulship, thereafter disturbed from time to time, shattered before you became Consul, and then restored by you, it has now been forsaken in its entirety by those who should have been its champions. Their faces, though faces can easily play the hypocrite, declare as much; more, they have shown it to be so by many a vote in Senate and court-room—these men who in the world as we used to know it were called Optimates.

Accordingly, men of sense, of whom I hope I am and am considered to be one, have now completely to recast their views and sympathies. To cite Plato again, a very weighty

[25] See critical notes. One Praetor (Clodius' brother Appius) and two Tribunes stayed out.

auctore moveor, tantum[14] contendere in re publica quantum probare tuis civibus possis; vim neque parenti nec patriae adferre oportere. atque hanc quidem ille causam sibi ait non attingendae rei publicae fuisse, quod, cum offendisset populum Atheniensem prope iam desipientem senectute cumque eum nec persuadendo nec cogendo regi [posse][15] vidisset, cum persuaderi posse diffideret, cogi fas esse non arbitraretur. mea ratio fuit alia, quod neque desipiente populo nec integra re mihi ad consulendum capesseremne rem publicam implicatus tenebar; sed laetatus tamen sum quod mihi liceret in eadem causa et mihi utilia et cuivis bono recta defendere. huc accessit commemoranda quaedam et divina Caesaris in me fratremque meum liberalitas. qui mihi, quascumque res gere⟨re⟩t, tuendus esset; nunc in tanta felicitate tantisque victoriis, etiam si in nos non is esset qui est, tamen ornandus videretur. si⟨c⟩ enim te existimare velim, cum a vobis meae salutis auctoribus discesserim, neminem esse cuius officiis me tam esse devinctum non solum confitear sed etiam gaudeam.

19   Quod quoniam tibi exposui, facilia sunt ea quae a me de Vatinio et de Crasso requiris. nam de Appio quod scribis sicuti de Caesare te non reprehendere, gaudeo tibi consilium probari meum. de Vatinio autem, primum reditus intercesserat in gratiam per Pompeium, statim ut ille prae-

---

14 quod ego . . . auctoremque ortatum *(Mend.)*
15 *(Sternkopf)*

---

26 In *Crito* 51c.
27 Cf. Plato, *Epist.* 5.322a, b.

authority with me; he tells us to push our political efforts as
far as may be acceptable to our countrymen, but never to
use force against parent or fatherland.[26] He gives his reason for keeping out of public affairs as follows: finding the
people of Athens almost in its dotage, and seeing them
without government either of persuasion or compulsion,
he did not believe them amenable to persuasion and regarded compulsion as a sacrilege.[27] My situation was different. I was not dealing with a nation in its dotage, nor did
I have a free choice whether or not to engage in public life,
being inextricably involved. But I congratulated myself on
having a cause to champion both expedient to myself personally and commendable to any honest man.[28] An added
incentive was Caesar's quite remarkable, in fact amazing,
generosity towards my brother and myself. He would have
deserved my support whatever his accomplishments, but
in so brilliant a career of success and victory I should think
him worthy of honour even if he were not the good friend
to us that he is. For I would have you believe that, apart
from yourself and your fellow architects of my restoration,
there is no man to whose good offices I acknowledge myself so deeply beholden—and am glad to do so.

After this exposition your enquiries as to Vatinius and
Crassus are easily answered—about Appius, as about Caesar, you say you have no criticism to offer, and I am glad my
action has your approval. To take Vatinius then, Pompey
originally arranged a reconciliation between us immedi-

[28] The maintenance of Caesar in his command, championed
by Cicero in his speech *On the Consular Provinces* (summer of 56;
Caesar's personal generosity came later).

tor est factus, cum quidem ego eius petitionem gravissimis
in senatu sententiis oppugnassem, neque tam illius laeden-
di causa quam defendendi atque ornandi Catonis; post
autem Caesaris ut illum defenderem mira contentio est
consecuta. cur autem laudarim, peto a te ut id a me neve in
hoc reo neve in aliis requiras, ne tibi ego idem reponam
cum veneris. tametsi possum vel absenti; recordare enim
quibus laudationem ex ultimis terris miseris; nec hoc per-
timueris, nam a me ipso laudantur et laudabuntur idem.
sed tamen defendendi Vatini fuit etiam ille stimulus de
quo in iudicio, cum illum defenderem, dixi me facere
quiddam quod in 'Eunucho' parasitus suaderet militi:

> ubi nominabit Phaedriam, tu Pamphilam
> continuo. si quando illa dicet 'Phaedriam
> intro mittamus comissatum.' 'Pamphilam
> cantatum provocemus.' si laudabit haec
> illius formam, tu huius contra. denique
> par pro pari referto, quod eam mordeat.

sic petivi a iudicibus ut, quoniam quidam nobiles homines
et de me optime meriti nimis amarent inimicum meum
meque inspectante saepe eum in senatu modo severe se-
ducerent, modo familiariter atque hilare amplexarentur,
quoniamque illi haberent suum Publium, darent mihi ipsi
alium Publium in quo possem illorum animos mediocriter

---

29 Early in 55. M. Cato's candidature was defeated by bribery
and violence.

30 In 54, when Vatinius was accused of bribery. Cicero's witness to character seems to have been given in a second trial.

31 Terence, *The Eunuch* 440 ff. Phaedria is a male character,
Pamphila female.

ately after his election to the Praetorship,[29] although I had
made some very strong speeches in the Senate against his
candidature—not so much to damage *him* as in support
and compliment to Cato. Subsequently Caesar made a tre-
mendous point of my undertaking his defence.[30] As for
why I spoke for his character, I appeal to you not to ask me
that question about Vatinius or any other defendant, otherwise I shall ask you a similar question when you come
home. For that matter I can ask it while you are still
abroad. Just call to mind the men for whom you have sent
testimonials from the ends of the earth—don't be afraid, I
do the same myself for the same people and shall so continue. To resume, I had another incentive to defend
Vatinius, to which I referred in my speech at the trial. I said
I was doing what the Parasite in the *Eunuch* recommends
to the Captain:[31]

> When she says 'Phaedria,' you must straight away
> Say 'Pamphila.' Should she want Phaedria in
> To dinner, you must counter 'Why not ask
> Pamphila for a song?' If she commends
> His handsome looks, you praise the girl's. In short,
> Give tit, my friend, for tat. The pin will prick.

So I drew the parallel. Certain high-born gentlemen, to
whom I owed a debt of gratitude, were overfond of an
enemy of mine. In the Senate they would sometimes
take him aside for a serious talk, sometimes salute him
in hearty, hail-fellow-well-met style; this before my eyes.
Well then, since they had *their* Publius, I hoped the gentlemen of the jury would allow *me* another Publius, with
whom to sting those personages just a little in return for

lacessitus leviter repungere. neque solum dixi sed etiam
saepe facio dis hominibusque approbantibus.

20   Habes de Vatinio. cognosce de Crasso: ego, cum mihi
cum illo magna iam gratia esset, quod eius omnis gravissi-
mas iniurias communis concordiae causa voluntaria quadam oblivione cont<ri>eram, repentinam eius defensio-
nem Gabini, quem proximis superioribus diebus acerrime
oppugnasset, tamen, si sine ulla mea contumelia suscepisset, tulissem. sed cum me disputantem, non lacessentem,
laesisset, exarsi non solum praesenti, credo, iracundia
(nam ea tam vehemens fortasse non fuisset) sed cum inclu-
sum illud odium multarum eius in me iniuriarum, quod
ego effudisse me omne arbitrabar, residuum tamen insciente me fuisset, omne repente apparuit. quo quidem
tempore ipso quidam homines, et[16] idem illi quos saepe
signific[ati]o[17] neque appello, cum se maximum fructum
cepisse dicerent ex libertate mea meque tum denique sibi
esse visum rei publicae qualis fuissem restitutum, cumque
ea contentio mihi magnum etiam foris fructum tulisset,
gaudere se dicebant mihi et illum inimicum et eos qui in
eadem causa essent numquam amicos futuros. quorum
iniqui sermones cum ad me per homines honestissimos
perferrentur, cumque Pompeius ita contendisset ut nihil
umquam magis ut cum Crasso redirem in gratiam Cae-
sarque per litteras maxima se molestia ex illa contentione
adfectum ostenderet, habui non temporum solum ratio-

16 *del. coni. SB*   17 *(Madvig)*

---

32 When Gabinius restored Ptolemy the Piper to his throne in
55 Cicero attacked him in the Senate. According to Dio Cassius

the mild provocation I had received! Nor did I merely *say* this; I often do it, Gods and men approving.

So much for Vatinius. Now as to Crassus: I was on very good terms with him, having in the interests of general harmony expunged by what I might call a deliberate act of oblivion all the grave wrongs he had done me. I should have stomached his sudden defence of Gabinius,[32] whom he had attacked on the days immediately preceding, if he had gone to work without abusing me. But when I argued with him politely, he insulted me. I flared up. It was not, I think, just the irritation of the moment, which might not have carried me so far, but my suppressed resentment at the many injuries he had done me. I thought I had dissipated all that, but a residue was still there without my being aware of it, and now it all suddenly came to the surface. Here again certain persons, the same whom I so often indicate without naming names, expressed the greatest satisfaction at my plain speaking, and told me that now at last they felt I was restored to Rome the man I used to be; and outside the House too this fracas brought me many congratulations. And yet they went around saying how pleased they were to think that Crassus would be my enemy henceforward, and that his associates would never be my friends. These backbitings were brought to my knowledge by very worthy folk; and when Pompey pressed me as strongly as I have ever known him to do to make it up with Crassus, and Caesar wrote a letter making it plain that this quarrel greatly upset him, why, I took account of my circumstances

(39. 60.1) the Consuls, Pompey and Crassus, came to his defence, calling Cicero an exile, but no doubt the insult came from Crassus, not Pompey.

nem meorum sed etiam naturae, Crassusque, ut quasi
testata populo Romano esset nostra gratia, paene a meis
laribus in provinciam est profectus; nam, cum mihi
condixisset, cenavit apud ‹me› in mei generi Crassipedis
hortis. quam ob rem eius causam, quod te scribis audisse,
magna illius commendatione susceptam defendi in senatu,
sicut mea fides postulabat.

21   Accepisti quibus rebus adductus quamque rem causamque defenderim quique meus in re publica sit pro mea
parte capessenda status. de quo sic velim statuas, me haec
eadem sensurum fuisse si mihi integra omnia ac libera
fuissent. nam neque pugnandum arbitrarer contra tantas
opes neque delendum, etiam si id fieri posset, summorum
civium principatum ‹neque› permanendum in una sententia conversis rebus ac bonorum voluntatibus mutatis,
sed temporibus adsentiendum. numquam enim ‹in›[18]
praestantibus in re publica gubernanda viris laudata est in
una sententia perpetua permansio; sed ut in navigando
tempestati obsequi artis est etiam si portum tenere non
queas, cum vero id possis mutata velificatione adsequi stul-
tum est eum tenere cum periculo cursum quem coeperis
potius quam eo commutato quo velis tamen pervenire, sic,
cum omnibus nobis in administranda re publica propositum esse debeat, id quod a me saepissime dictum est, cum
dignitate otium, non idem semper dicere sed idem semper
spectare debemus.

Quam ob rem, ut paulo ante posui, si essent omnia mihi
solutissima, tamen in re publica non alius essem atque

18 *(Wes.)*

144

and of my heart as well. And Crassus, as though to make all Rome witness of our reconciliation, set out for his province virtually from my doorstep. He offered to dine with me, and did so at my son-in-law Crassipes' place in the suburbs. Accordingly I took up his cause at his urgent request and defended it in the Senate,[33] as you say you have heard. Good faith required no less.

You now know my reasons for defending each particular cause or case, and the general position from which I take such part in politics as I may. I should like it to be clear to you that my attitude would have been just the same if I had had a completely open and untrammelled choice. I should not be in favour of fighting such formidable power, nor of abolishing the preeminence of our greatest citizens, even if that were possible. Nor should I be for sticking fast to one set of opinions, when circumstances have changed and the sentiments of honest men are no longer the same. I believe in moving with the times. Unchanging consistency of standpoint has never been considered a virtue in great statesmen. At sea it is good sailing to run before the gale, even if the ship cannot make harbour; but if she *can* make harbour by changing tack, only a fool would risk shipwreck by holding to the original course rather than change and still reach his destination. Similarly, while all of us as statesmen should set before our eyes the goal of peace with honour to which I have so often pointed, it is our aim, not our language, which must always be the same.

Therefore, as I have just stated, my politics would be exactly what they now are, even if my hands were completely free. But since I am attracted to this standpoint by

[33] In January 54 (cf. Letter 25.1).

nunc sum. cum vero in hunc sensum et adliciar beneficiis hominum et compellar iniuriis, facile patior ea me de re publica sentire ac dicere quae maxime cum meis tum etiam rei publicae rationibus putem conducere. apertius autem haec ago ac saepius quod et Quintus, frater meus, legatus est Caesaris et nullum meum minimum dictum, non modo factum, pro Caesare intercessit quod ille non ita illustri gratia exceperit ut ego eum mihi devinctum putarem. itaque eius omni et gratia, quae summa est, et opibus, quas intellegis esse maximas, sic fruor ut meis; nec mihi aliter potuisse videor hominum perditorum de me consilia frangere nisi cum praesidiis iis quae semper habui nunc etiam potentium benevolentiam coniunxissem.

22   His ego consiliis, si te praesentem habuissem, ut opinio mea fert, essem usus isdem. novi enim temperantiam et moderationem naturae tuae, novi animum cum mihi amicissimum tum nulla in ceteros malevolentia suffusum contraque cum magnum et excelsum tum etiam apertum et simplicem. vidi ego quosdam in te talis qualis tu eosdem in me videre potuisti. quae me moverunt, movissent eadem te profecto. sed quocumque tempore mihi potestas praesentis tui fuerit, tu eris omnium moderator consiliorum meorum, tibi erit eidem, cui salus mea fuit, etiam dignitas curae. me quidem cérte tuarum actionum, sententiarum, voluntatum, rerum denique omnium socium comitemque habebis, neque mihi in omni vita res tam erit ulla proposita quam ut cottidie vehementius te de me optime meritum esse laetere.

23   Quod rogas ut mea tibi scripta mittam quae post discessum tuum scripserim, sunt orationes quaedam, quas Me-

favours from some quarters and pushed to it by injuries from others, I am by no means loath to take and express the political views which I deem most conducive to the public welfare as well as my own. I take this line the more openly and frequently because my brother Quintus is Caesar's Legate, and because Caesar has always received my slightest intervention, even purely verbal, on his behalf with such display of gratitude as to make me feel that he is deeply obliged to me. I use all his influence, which is very powerful, and his resources, which you know to be very large, as though they were my own. In fact, I do not think I could have foiled the designs of evil men against me in any other way than by now adding to the means of defence which have always been at my disposal the good will of the powers that be.

Had I had you with me here, my belief is that I should have followed this same course. I know your natural temperance and moderation. I know that your warm friendship towards myself has no cast of malice towards others, that on the contrary you are as frank and straightforward as you are high-minded and unselfish. I have seen certain persons behave to you as you could once see them behaving to me. Surely my motives would have been yours. But when eventually I can avail myself of your presence, you will be my director in all things, with the same care for my standing as you had for my existence as a citizen. As for me, you may be sure of finding in me a partner and companion in all things, in your every act, opinion, and desire. No object in all my life will be so precious to me as to make you happier every day in the services you have rendered me.

You ask me to send you the products of my pen since you left Rome. There are some speeches, which I shall give

nocrito dabo, neque ita multae, ne pertimescas. scripsi etiam (nam me iam[19] ab orationibus diiungo fere referoque ad mansuetiores Musas, quae me maxime sicut iam a prima adulescentia delectarunt)—scripsi igitur Aristotelio more, quem ad modum quidem volui, tris libros in disputatione ac dialogo *De Oratore,* quos arbitror Lentulo tuo fore non inutilis. abhorrent enim a communibus praeceptis atque omnem antiquorum et Aristoteliam et Isocratiam rationem oratoriam complectuntur. scripsi etiam versibus tris libros *De temporibus meis,* quos iam pridem ad te misissem si esse edendos putassem; sunt enim testes et erunt sempiterni meritorum erga me tuorum meaeque pietatis. sed quia verebar, non eos qui se laesos arbitrarentur (etenim id feci parce et molliter), sed eos quos erat infinitum bene de ‹me› meritos omnis nominare * * *[20] quos tamen ipsos libros, si quem cui recte committam invenero, curabo ad te perferendos. atque istam quidem partem vitae consuetudinisque nostrae totam ad te defero; quantum litteris, quantum studiis, veteribus nostris delectationibus, consequi poterimus, id omne ‹ad› arbitrium tuum, qui haec semper amasti, libentissime conferemus.

24 　Quae ad me de tuis rebus domesticis scribis quaeque mihi commendas ea tantae mihi curae sunt ut me nolim admoneri, rogari vero sine magno dolore vix possim. quod de Quinti fratris negotio scribis, te priore aestate, quod morbo impeditus in Ciliciam non transieris, conficere non

---

[19] nam etiam *(Or.)*
[20] non misi *suppl. Man.,* nolui divulgari *vel sim. Wes.*

---

[34] I.e. Cilicia proper, as distinct from the whole Roman province so called. It has been suggested that Quintus wanted to buy a

to Menocritus—don't be alarmed, there are not very many of them! I have also composed—I am now tending to get away from oratory and go back to the gentler Muses who please me best, as they always have from my youth—composed, as I was saying, three volumes in the form of an argument and dialogue *On the Orator,* in the manner (so at least I intended) of Aristotle. I think your son will find them of some use. They do not deal in the standard rules, but embrace the whole theory of oratory as the ancients knew it, both Aristotelian and Isocratic. I have also written a poem in three books *On My Vicissitudes.* I should have sent you this before, if I had thought right to publish it, for it is, and will be to all eternity, evidence of your services and of my gratitude. But I was inhibited by the thought, not so much of those who might feel themselves aspersed (*that* I have done sparingly and gently), but of my benefactors—if I had named them all, there would have been no end to it. All the same I shall see that you get these volumes too, if I can find a reliable bearer. All this part of my daily life I submit to you. Everything I may achieve in the way of literature and study, my old delights, I shall be most happy to bring to the bar of your judgement. You have always cared for these things.

What you say about your domestic concerns and the commissions you give me lie so close to my heart that I desire no reminder; a *request* I can scarcely take without real pain. You say you were unable to settle my brother Quintus' business, because sickness prevented you from crossing over to Cilicia[34] last summer, but that you will now

property adjoining one of his two estates near Arpinum, of which the owner was in Cilicia and so amenable to Lentulus' influence.

potuisse, nunc autem omnia facturum ut conficias, id scito esse eius modi ut frater meus vere existimet adiuncto isto fundo patrimonium fore suum per te constitutum. tu me de tuis rebus omnibus et de Lentuli tui nostrique studiis et exercitationibus velim quam familiarissime certiorem et quam saepissime facias existimesque neminem cuiquam neque cariorem neque iucundiorem umquam fuisse quam te mihi, idque me non modo ut tu sentias sed ut omnes gentes, etiam ut posteritas omnis intellegat esse facturum.

25   Appius[21] in sermonibus antea dictitabat, postea dixit etiam in senatu palam, sese, si licitum esset legem curiatam ferre, sortiturum esse cum collega provinciam;[22] si curiata lex non esset, se paraturum cum collega tibique successurum, legemque[23] curiatam consuli ferri opus esse, necesse non esse; se, quoniam ex senatus consulto provinciam haberet, lege Cornelia imperium habiturum quoad in urbem introisset. ego quid ad te tuorum quisque necessariorum scribat nescio; varias esse opiniones intellego. sunt qui putant posse te non decedere quod sine lege curiata tibi succedatur; sunt etiam qui, si decedas, a te relinqui posse qui provinciae praesit. mihi non tam de iure certum est, quamquam ne id quidem valde dubium est, quam illud, ad tuam summam amplitudinem, dignitatem, libertatem, qua te scio libentissime frui solere, pertinere te sine ulla mora provinciam successori concedere, praesertim cum sine suspicione tuae cupiditatis non possis illius cupiditatem refutare. ego utrumque meum puto esse, et quid

[21] *novam hic ep. incipiendam coni. SB*
[22] provincias *Wes.*
[23] legem *Man.*

use your best efforts to settle it. The fact is that my brother considers with good cause that once he has annexed this property his fortunes will have been placed on a firm foundation, thanks to you. I hope you will keep me abreast, as intimately and as often as you can, of all your own affairs and of your (and my) dear boy's studies and exercises. And I would have you believe that you are to me the dearest and most valued friend that ever a man had, and that I shall make it my business to prove this, not only to you, but to all mankind, indeed to all posterity.

Appius was in the habit of saying in private, and later said publicly in the Senate, that, if passage was given to a curiate law, he would draw lots for a province with his colleague; but if there was no curiate law, he would come to an arrangement with his colleague and supersede you. A curiate law, he contended, was something a Consul should have, but did not absolutely need. Since he had a province by decree of the Senate, he would hold military authority under the lex Cornelia until he reentered the city boundary. What your various friends may write to you I do not know—I understand that opinions differ. Some think you have the right to stay in your province because you are being superseded without a curiate law; others that, if you go, you are entitled to leave a governor in charge. For my part, I am less certain of the legal position (though even that is not so very dubious) than of the advisability of your handing over the province to your successor without delay. Your high standing and prestige, your independence, in which I know you take especial satisfaction, are involved, particularly as you cannot rebuff Appius' exorbitance without incurring some suspicion of a similar fault. I regard myself

sentiam ostendere et quod feceris defendere.

26   Scripta iam epistula superiore accepi tuas litteras de publicanis, ⟨in⟩[24] quibus aequitatem tuam non potui non probare, felicitate quadam[25] vellem consequi potuisses ne eius ordinis quem semper ornasti rem aut voluntatem offenderes. equidem non desinam tua decreta defendere; sed nosti consuetudinem hominum, scis quam graviter inimici ipsi illi Q. Scaevolae fuerint. tibi tamen sum auctor ut, si quibus rebus possis, eum tibi ordinem aut reconcilies aut mitiges. id etsi difficile est, tamen mihi videtur esse prudentiae tuae.

21 (I.10)

Scr. Romae fort. an. 54

M. CICERO S. D. L. VALERIO IURISCONSULTO (cur enim tibi hoc non gratificer nescio, praesertim cum his temporibus audacia pro sapientia liceat uti).

Lentulo nostro egi per litteras tuo nomine gratias diligenter. sed tu velim desinas iam nostris litteris uti et nos aliquando revisas et ibi malis esse ubi aliquo numero sis

---

[24] *(Ern.)*
[25] aquid *(Gron.*: quidem ⲥ)

---

[35] As governor of Asia he had defended the provincials against the tax farmers.

as no less bound to tell you my sentiments than to defend whatever course you adopt.

After writing the foregoing I received your letter about the tax farmers. I cannot but commend your sense of justice, but could have wished that you had had the good luck, as it were, to avoid offending the interests or sentiments of that class, which you have always favoured in the past. *I* shall steadily defend your rulings. But you know their way, you know how strongly hostile they were to the great Q. Scaevola himself.[35] Despite what has happened, I hope you will do everything in your power to reconcile, or at any rate mollify, their feelings towards you. That is difficult I grant, but I think it is what a wise man like yourself ought to do.

21 (I.10)
CICERO TO L. VALERIUS

Rome, 54 (?)

From M. Cicero to L. Valerius, Counsellor, greetings (I don't see why I should not make you a present of the title, especially in these days, when effrontery can stand substitute for good counsel).[1]

I have written to thank our friend Lentulus on your behalf in suitable terms. But I wish you would stop using my letters and revisit us after all this while, and elect to spend

---

[1] *Sapientia* (wisdom or good sense) has a special application to the science of the jurist with which Cicero likes to make play when writing to his legal friends Valerius and Trebatius.

quam istic ubi solus sapere videare. quamquam qui istinc
veniunt partim te superbum esse dicunt, quod nihil respondeas, partim contumeliosum, quod male respondeas.
sed iam cupio tecum coram iocari. qua re fac ut quam primum venias neque in Apuliam tuam accedas, ut possimus
salvum venisse gaudere. nam illo si veneris tam Ulixes,
cognosces tuorum neminem.

22 (V.12)

Scr. in Cumano, ut vid., c. prid. Id. Apr. an. 55

M. CICERO S. D. L. LUCCEIO Q. F.

1   Coram me tecum eadem haec agere saepe conantem
deterruit pudor quidam paene subrusticus quae nunc ex-
promam absens audacius; epistula enim non erubescit.

---

2 Literally 'where you will be in some number (account) . . .
where you seem to be the only man of sense' (legal learning; with a
play on *sapere*). Robbed of *doubles entendres* the sense amounts
to: better be in Rome, where jurists have their place, than in
Cilicia, where Roman law is unknown. For 'ken' as a term in Scot-
tish law (Valerius seems to have come from Apulia) see the *Oxford
English Dictionary*.

3 *Respondere* is technically used of a jurisconsult's opinions—
legal rulings given in response to questions. It is also used of
answering a question or a greeting. Not to answer such would be
the reverse of polite. Cicero is fond of playing on the various uses
of this verb (see note in my Cambridge edition of the *Letters to
Atticus*, Vol. II, p. 222).

4 *Male respondere* means reply insultingly or alternatively give

your time here, where you will be a *kent* man,[2] rather than over yonder, where I suppose nobody *kens* but you. To be sure some travellers tell that you are grown arrogant, because you don't 'respond';[3] others complain of your incivility, because you respond in bad form.[4] However, I hope I shall soon be cracking my joke with you face to face. So mind you come back as quickly as you can, and don't go to your beloved Apulia. We want some pleasure in your safe return.[5] If you go there after such an odyssey, you won't recognize any of your folk.[6]

22 (V.12)
CICERO TO LUCCEIUS

Cumae (?), ca. 12 April 55

From M. Cicero to L. Lucceius, son of Quintus, greetings.

Although I have more than once attempted to take up my present topic with you face to face, a sort of shyness, almost awkwardness, has held me back. Away from your presence, I shall set it out with less trepidation. A letter has no blushes.

---

bad (mistaken) legal advice. Cicero really seems to have had a poor opinion of Valerius professionally; see Letter 64.3.

[5] *Salvum venisse gaudere,* 'to be glad you have arrived safely,' is a polite formula (cf. *Letters to Atticus* 114 (V.21).1), to which Cicero here gives a special twist. Valerius' friends in Rome would *not* be glad if he buried himself down in Apulia.

[6] In the *Odyssey* (as Cicero may not have precisely remembered) the returning hero recognizes his family and friends but they do not recognize him.

155

Ardeo cupiditate incredibili neque, ut ego arbitror, reprehendenda nomen ut nostrum scriptis illustretur et celebretur tuis. quod etsi mihi saepe ostendis⟨ti⟩[1] te esse facturum, tamen ignoscas velim huic festinationi meae. genus enim scriptorum tuorum, etsi erat semper a me vehementer exspectatum, tamen vicit opinionem meam meque ita vel cepit vel incendit ut cuperem quam celerrime res nostras monumentis commendari tuis. neque enim me solum commemoratio posteritatis ac spes quaedam[2] immortalitatis rapit sed etiam illa cupiditas ut vel auctoritate testimoni tui vel indicio benevolentiae vel suavitate ingeni vivi perfruamur.

2 Neque tamen haec cum scribebam eram nescius quantis oneribus premerere susceptarum rerum et iam institutarum. sed quia videbam Italici belli et civilis historiam iam a te paene esse perfectam, dixeras autem mihi te reliquas res ordiri, deesse mihi nolui quin te admonerem ut cogitares coniunctene malles cum reliquis rebus nostra contexere an, ut multi Graeci fecerunt, Callisthenes Phocicum[3] bellum, Timaeus Pyrrhi, Polybius Numantinum, qui omnes a perpetuis suis historiis ea quae dixi bella separaverunt, tu quoque item civilem coniurationem ab hostilibus externisque bellis seiungeres. equidem ad nostram laudem non multum video interesse, sed ad properationem meam quiddam interest non te exspectare dum ad

[1] *(Ern.)*   [2] ad spem quandam *(Hofmann)*
[3] troicum *(Westermann)*

[1] I.e. from the beginning of the war between Rome and her Italian allies in 91 down to Sulla's final victory over the Marians in 81.

I have a burning desire, of a strength you will hardly credit but ought not, I think, to blame, that my name should gain lustre and celebrity through your works. You have often promised me, it is true, that you will comply with my wish; but I ask you to forgive my impatience. The quality of your literary performances, eagerly as I have always awaited them, has surpassed my expectation. I am captivated and enkindled. I want to see my achievements enshrined in your compositions with the minimum of delay. The thought that posterity will talk of me and the hope, one might say, of immortality hurries me on, but so too does the desire to enjoy in my lifetime the support of your weighty testimony, the evidence of your good will, and the charm of your literary talent.

As I write these words, I am not unaware of the heavy burden weighing upon you of projects undertaken and already commenced. But seeing that you have almost finished your account of the Italian War and the Civil War,[1] and remembering that you told me you were embarking on subsequent events, I feel I should be failing myself if I did not suggest two alternatives for your consideration. Would you prefer to weave my affairs along with those of the rest of the period into a single narrative, or might you not rather follow many Greek precedents, as Callisthenes with the Phocian War, Timaeus with the War of Pyrrhus, and Polybius with that of Numantia, all of whom detached their accounts of these particular wars from their continuous histories? Just so, you might deal with the domestic conspiracy apart from wars against external enemies. From my point of view there seems little to choose, so far as my credit is concerned. But there is my impatience to be considered; and here it does make a difference, if, instead

locum venias ac statim causam illam totam et tempus adri-
pere; et simul, si uno in argumento unaque in persona
mens tua tota versabitur, cerno iam animo quanto omnia
uberiora atque ornatiora futura sint.

Neque tamen ignoro quam impudenter faciam qui primum tibi tantum oneris imponam (potest enim mihi dene-
gare occupatio tua), deinde etiam ut ornes me postulem.
3 quid si illa tibi non tanto opere videntur ornanda? sed
tamen, qui semel verecundiae finis transierit, eum bene et
naviter oportet esse impudentem. itaque te plane etiam
atque etiam rogo ut et ornes ea vehementius etiam quam
fortasse sentis et in eo leges historiae neglegas gratiamque
illam de qua suavissime quodam in prohoemio scripsisti, a
qua te flecti[4] non magis potuisse demonstras quam Hercu-
lem Xenophontium illum a Voluptate, eam, si me tibi vehementius commendabit, ne aspernere amorique nostro
plusculum etiam quam concedet veritas largiare.

Quod si te adducemus ut hoc suscipias, erit, ut mihi
4 persuadeo, materies digna facultate et copia tua. a princi-
pio enim coniurationis usque ad reditum nostrum videtur
mihi modicum quoddam corpus confici posse, in quo et illa
poteris uti civilium commutationum scientia vel in expli-
candis causis rerum novarum vel in remediis[5] incommodo-
rum, cum et reprehendes ea quae vituperanda duces et

---

[4] te effecti (*Vict.*)   [5] in ⟨expromendis⟩ remediis *Pluygers*

---

[2] Prodicus the Sophist's allegory of the Choice of Hercules is
retailed by Xenophon in his *Memoirs of Socrates* (2.1.21). Cicero
refers to it in his treatise *On Duties* (1.118).

This passage ought not to be taken too literally. It is an exhibi-
tion of false modesty—Cicero did not really believe that the wine

of waiting until you reach the place, you immediately seize upon that entire subject and period. Furthermore, if your whole mind is directed upon a single theme and a single figure, I can already envisage the great gain in general richness and splendour.

Not that I am unconscious of the effrontery of what I am about, first in laying such a burden upon you (pressure of work may refuse me), and secondly in asking you to write about me eulogistically. What if the record does not appear to you so eminently deserving of eulogy? But the bounds of delicacy once passed, it is best to be frankly and thoroughly brazen. Therefore I ask you again, not mincing my words, to write of this theme more enthusiastically than perhaps you feel. Waive the laws of history for this once. Do not scorn personal bias, if it urge you strongly in my favour—that sentiment of which you wrote very charmingly in one of your prefaces, declaring that you could no more be swayed thereby than Xenophon's Hercules by Pleasure.[2] Concede to the affection between us just a little more even than the truth will license.

If I prevail upon you to undertake the task, I persuade myself that the material will be worthy of your ready and skilful pen. I fancy a work of moderate length could be made up, from the beginning of the plot down to my return from exile. In it you will also be able to make use of your special knowledge of political changes, in explaining the origins of the revolutionary movement and suggesting remedies for things awry. You will blame what you judge deserving of reproof and give reasons for commending

of his achievements needed any bush—and a compliment to Lucceius, as showing how much store Cicero set upon his praise.

quae placebunt exponendis rationibus comprobabis et, si liberius, ut consuesti, agendum putabis, multorum in nos perfidiam, insidias, proditionem notabis. multam etiam casus nostri varietatem tibi in scribendo suppeditabunt plenam cuiusdam voluptatis, quae vehementer animos hominum in legendo te scriptore tenere possit. nihil est enim aptius ad delectationem lectoris quam temporum varietates fortunaeque vicissitudines. quae etsi nobis optabiles in experiendo non fuerunt, in legendo tamen erunt iucundae; habet enim praeteriti doloris secura recordatio

5 delectationem; ceteris vero nulla perfunctis propria molestia, casus autem alienos sine ullo dolore intuentibus, etiam ipsa misericordia est iucunda. quem enim nostrum ille moriens apud Mantineam Epaminondas non cum quadam miseratione delectat? qui tum denique sibi evelli[6] iubet spiculum postea quam ei percontanti dictum est clipeum esse salvum, ut etiam in vulneris dolore aequo animo cum laude moreretur. cuius studium in legendo non erectum Themistocli fuga †redituque†[7] retinetur? etenim ordo ipse annalium mediocriter nos retinet quasi enumeratione fastorum; at viri saepe excellentis ancipites variique casus habent admirationem, exspectationem, laetitiam, molestiam, spem, timorem; si vero exitu notabili concluduntur, expletur animus iucundissima lectionis voluptate.

6 Quo mihi acciderit optatius si in hac sententia fueris,

---

[6] avelli *(Kayser)*   [7] interituque *Ferrarius*

---

[3] Cf. Virgil's *forsan et haec olim meminisse iuvabit.*

[4] The manuscripts say 'and return.' But Themistocles never returned from his exile.

what you approve; and if, according to your usual practice, you think proper to deal pretty freely, you will hold up to censure the perfidy, artifice, and betrayal of which many were guilty towards me. Moreover, my experiences will give plenty of variety to your narrative, full of a certain kind of delectation to enthrall the minds of those who read, when you are the writer. Nothing tends more to the reader's enjoyment than varieties of circumstance and vicissitudes of fortune. For myself, though far from desirable in the living, they will be pleasant in the reading; for there is something agreeable in the secure recollection of bygone unhappiness.[3] For others, who went through no personal distress and painlessly survey misfortunes not their own, even the emotion of pity is enjoyable. Which of us is not affected pleasurably, along with a sentiment of compassion, at the story of the dying Epaminondas on the field of Mantinea, ordering the javelin to be plucked from his body only after he had been told in answer to his question that his shield was safe, so that even in the agony of his wound he could meet an honourable death with mind at ease? Whose sympathies are not aroused and held as he reads of Themistocles' flight and death?[4] The actual chronological record of events exercises no very powerful fascination upon us; it is like the recital of an almanac. But in the doubtful and various fortunes of an outstanding individual we often find surprise and suspense, joy and distress, hope and fear; and if they are rounded off by a notable conclusion, our minds as we read are filled with the liveliest gratification.

So I shall be especially delighted if you find it best to set

ut a continentibus tuis scriptis, in quibus perpetuam rerum gestarum historiam complecteris, secernas hanc quasi fabulam rerum eventorumque nostrorum. habet enim
varios actus multasque ⟨mut⟩ationes[8] et consiliorum et
temporum. ac non vereor ne adsentatiuncula quadam au-
cupari tuam gratiam videar cum hoc demonstrem, me a te
potissimum ornari celebrarique velle. neque enim tu is es
qui quid sis nescias et qui non eos magis qui te non admi-
rentur invidos quam eos qui laudent adsentatores arbitrere; neque autem ego sum ita demens ut me sempiternae
gloriae per eum commendari velim qui non ipse quoque in
me commendando propriam ingeni gloriam consequatur.

7   neque enim Alexander ille gratiae causa ab Apelle potissimum pingi et a Lysippo fingi volebat, sed quod illorum
artem cum ipsis tum etiam sibi gloriae fore putabat. atque[9]
illi artifices corporis simulacra ignotis nota faciebant, quae
vel si nulla sint, nihilo sint tamen obscuriores clari viri. nec
minus est Spa⟨r⟩tiates Agesilaus †ille[10] perhibendus†, qui
neque pictam neque fictam [tam] imaginem suam passus
est esse, quam qui in eo genere laborarunt. unus enim
Xenophontis libellus in eo rege laudando facile omnis
imagines omnium statuasque superavit.

Atque hoc praestantius mihi fuerit et ad laetitiam animi
et ad memoriae dignitatem si in tua scripta pervenero
quam si in ceterorum quod non ingenium mihi solum sup-
peditatum fuerit tuum, sicut Timoleonti a Timaeo aut ab
Herodoto Themistocli, sed etiam auctoritas clarissimi et
spectatissimi viri et in rei publicae maximis gravissimisque

---

[8] actiones *(SB)*
[9] atqui *Lamb.*
[10] mihi *coni. SB*

my story apart from the main stream of your work, in which you embrace events in their historical sequence—this drama, one may call it, of what I did and experienced; for it contains various 'acts,' and many changes of plan and circumstance. Nor am I apprehensive of appearing to angle for your favour with the bait of a little flattery when I declare that you of all others are the writer by whom I desire my praises to be sung. After all, you are not ignorant of your own worth; a man like you knows better than to see sycophancy in admiration rather than jealousy in its absence. Nor am I myself so foolish as to ask any author to immortalize my name in glory but one who in so doing will gain glory for his own genius. Alexander the Great did not ask Apelles to paint his portrait and Lysippus to sculpt his statue in order to curry favour with these artists, but because he believed the work would redound to his own fame as well as theirs. Those artists, however, only made a physical likeness known to people unacquainted with the original; and even in default of such memorials famous men would lose none of their celebrity. Agesilaus of Sparta, who would not allow representations of himself in paintings or sculpture, is no less pertinent to my case (?) than those who took pains over the matter. Xenophon's one little volume in eulogy of that king has achieved far more than all the portraits and statues under the sun.

There is a further reason why a place in your works as compared with those of other writers will bring my mind a more lively satisfaction and my memory more signal honour. You will confer upon me the benefit not only of your literary skill, as Timaeus did upon Timoleon or Herodotus upon Themistocles, but of your authority as a famed and admired public man, tried and notably approved in public

causis cogniti atque in primis probati, ut mihi non solum praeconium, quod, cum in Sigeum venisset, Alexander ab Homero Achilli tributum esse dixit, sed etiam grave testimonium impertitum clari hominis magnique videatur. placet enim Hector ille mihi Naevianus, qui non tantum 'laudari' se laetatur sed addit etiam 'a laudato viro.'

8   Quod si a te non impetro, hoc est, si quae te res impedierit (neque enim fas esse arbitror quicquam me rogantem abs te non impetrare), cogar fortasse facere quod non nulli saepe reprehendunt: scribam ipse de me, multorum tamen exemplo et clarorum virorum. sed, quod te non fugit, haec sunt in hoc genere vitia: et verecundius ipsi de sese scribant necesse est si quid est laudandum et praetereant si quid reprehendendum est. accedit etiam ut minor sit fides, minor auctoritas, multi denique reprehendant et dicant verecundiores esse praecones ludorum gymnicorum, qui, cum ceteris coronas imposuerint victoribus eorumque nomina magna voce pronuntiarint, cum ipsi ante ludorum missionem corona donentur, alium praeconem adhibeant, ne sua voce se ipsi victores esse praedicent.

9   haec nos vitare cupimus et, si recipis causam nostram, vitabimus idque ut facias rogamus.

Ac ne forte mirere cur, cum mihi saepe ostenderis te accuratissime nostrorum temporum consilia atque eventus litteris mandaturum, a te id nunc tanto opere et tam multis verbis petamus, illa nos cupiditas incendit de qua initio scripsi, festinationis, quod alacres animo sumus ut et ceteri viventibus nobis ex libris tuis nos cognoscant et nosmet ipsi vivi gloriola nostra perfruamur.

---

5 Cf. Letter 112.1. The verse is from Naevius' (lost) play *Hector's Departure*.

affairs of the greatest moment. Not only shall I gain a herald, such as Alexander when he visited Sigeum said Homer was to Achilles, but a witness—the weighty testimony of a great and famous man. For I am of one mind with Naevius' Hector, who delights, not in praise merely, but, he adds, 'from one that praisèd is.'[5]

Suppose, however, I am refused; that is to say, suppose something hinders you (for I feel it would be against nature for you to *refuse* any request of mine), I shall perhaps be driven to a course often censured by some, namely to write about myself—and yet I shall have many illustrious precedents. But I need not point out to you that this *genre* has certain disadvantages. An autobiographer must needs write over modestly where praise is due and pass over anything that calls for censure. Moreover, his credit and authority are less, and many will blame him and say that heralds at athletic contests show more delicacy, in that after placing garlands on the heads of the winners and loudly proclaiming their names, they call in another herald when it is *their* turn to be crowned at the end of the games, in order to avoid announcing their own victory with their own lips. I am anxious to escape these drawbacks, as I shall, if you take my case. I beg you so to do.

In case it may surprise you that I urge you so earnestly and at such length *now*, when you have repeatedly promised me that you will compose the record of my public career, its policies and events, and spare no pains, my motive is, as I wrote in the first place, impatience. I cannot wait to see the world learning about me in my lifetime from your books and to enjoy my modicum of glory myself before I die.

10   His de rebus quid acturus sis, si tibi non est molestum,
rescribas mihi velim. si enim suscipis causam, conficiam
commentarios rerum omnium; sin autem differs me in
tempus aliud, coram tecum loquar. tu interea non cessabis
et ea quae habes instituta perpolies nosque diliges.

23 (V.17)

Scr. Romae an., ut vid., 56

M. CICERO S. D. P. SITTIO P. F.

1   Non oblivione amicitiae nostrae neque intermissione
consuetudinis meae superioribus temporibus ad te nullas
litteras misi, sed quod priora tempora in ruinis rei publicae
nostrisque iacuerunt, posteriora autem me a scribendo
tuis iniustissimis atque acerbissimis incommodis retarda-
runt. cum vero et intervallum iam satis longum fuisset et
tuam virtutem animique magnitudinem diligentius essem
mecum recordatus, non putavi esse alienum institutis meis
haec ad te scribere.

2   Ego te, P. Sitti, et primis temporibus illis quibus in invidiam absens et in crimen vocabare defendi et, cum in tui
familiarissimi iudicio ac periculo tuum crimen coniunge-
retur, ut potui accuratissime te tuamque causam tutatus
sum et proxime recenti adventu meo, cum rem aliter insti-
tutam offendissem ac mihi placuisset si adfuissem, tamen
nulla re saluti tuae defui; cumque eo tempore invidia an-

---

6 I.e. factual statements for Lucceius to embellish.
1 P. Cornelius Sulla, successfully defended by Cicero in an
extant speech.

If it is not troubling you too much, please write back and tell me what you intend to do. If you undertake the case, I will prepare notes on all points.[6] If you put me off to a later date, I shall talk to you personally. Meanwhile, do not be idle: Give a thorough polish to the work you have in hand. And love me well.

23 (V.17)
CICERO TO P. SITTIUS

Rome, 56 (?)

From M. Cicero to P. Sittius, son of Publius, greetings.

It is not from unmindfulness of our friendship, or any interruption in my normal habit, that I have not sent you a letter at an earlier time. A period of prostrating calamity for our country and for myself was followed by one in which your own misfortunes, as painful as they were undeserved, made me reluctant to write. But the interval has now grown long enough; and recalling more closely your manly and lofty spirit, I thought it would be consonant with my general practice to write you these lines.

My dear Sittius, in the days when you first became the object of a slanderous attack in your absence, I defended you; and when your closest friend[1] was brought to trial and his ordeal was conjoined with the charge against yourself, I championed you and your cause as diligently as I was able. Then latterly, shortly after my return to Rome, finding the matter had been handled otherwise than I should have wished if I had been on the spot, I none the less did everything I could to save you. But the public prejudice due to

167

nonae, inimici non solum tui verum etiam amicorum tuorum, iniquitas totius iudici multaque alia rei publicae vitia plus quam causa ipsa veritasque valuissent, Publio tuo neque opera neque consilio neque labore neque gratia neque testimonio defui.

3   Quam ob rem omnibus officiis amicitiae diligenter a me sancteque servatis ne hoc quidem praetermittendum esse duxi, te ut hortarer rogaremque ut et hominem te et virum esse meminisses, id est, ut et communem incertumque casum, quem neque vitare quisquam nostrum nec praestare ullo pacto potest, sapienter ferres et dolori fortiter ac Fortunae resisteres cogitaresque et in nostra civitate et in ceteris quae rerum potitae sunt multis fortissimis atque optimis viris iniustis iudiciis talis casus incidisse. illud utinam ne ve⟨re⟩ scriberem, ea te re publica carere in qua neminem prudentem hominem res ulla delectet!

4   De tuo autem filio vereor ne, si nihil ad te scripserim, debitum eius virtuti videar testimonium non dedisse,[1] sin autem omnia quae sentio perscripserim, ne refricem meis litteris desiderium ac dolorem tuum. sed tamen prudentissime facies si illius pietatem, virtutem, industriam, ubicumque eris, tuam esse, tecum esse duces. nec enim minus nostra sunt quae animo complectimur quam quae
5 oculis intuemur. quam ob rem et illius eximia virtus summusque in te amor magnae tibi consolationi debet esse et

---

[1] cepisse (*Man.*)

---

[2] Evidently a reference to the grain crisis in September 57, just after Cicero's return from exile, when Pompey was given charge of supplies for five years. Why Sittius was blamed is unknown.

the grain shortage,[2] enemies—your friends' enemies as well as your own—the unfairness of the whole court proceedings, and many other disorders in the body politic proved more powerful than truth and the merits of the case. Then I did not fail your son Publius; my time, my advice, my trouble, my testimony were at his disposal.

Thus I may claim to have observed faithfully and strictly all the obligations of friendship; and these include another which I do not deem it right to leave unfulfilled, and that is to urge and beg you to remember that you are both a human being and a man: as the former, to bear with philosophy the working of chance, universal and unpredictable, which none of us can avoid and which none can by any means guarantee; and, as the latter, to offer stout resistance to pain and misfortune, and to bear in mind that such misadventures as a result of unjust trials have befallen many gallant and excellent men in our own and in other imperial states. I wish it were not true to add that you are deprived of a commonwealth in which no man of sense finds anything to give him pleasure.

As for your son, I am afraid that if I say nothing you may feel that I have withheld the tribute due to his merit; whereas if I write down all I feel, my letter may exacerbate the pain of your separation. Your wisest course, however, is to deem that wherever you may be, his filial affection, manliness, and diligence belong to you and are beside you. What we envisage in our minds is no less our own than what we see with our eyes. So his exemplary character and profound affection should be a great source of comfort to

nos ceterique qui te non ex fortuna sed ex virtute tua
pendimus semperque pendemus et maxime animi[2] tui
conscientia,[3] cum tibi nihil merito accidisse reputabis et
illud adiunges, homines sapientis turpitudine, non casu, et
delicto suo, non aliorum iniuria, commoveri.

Ego et memoria nostrae veteris amicitiae et virtute
atque observantia fili tui monitus nullo loco deero neque
ad consolandam neque ad levandam fortunam tuam. tu si
quid ad me forte scripseris, perficiam ne te frustra scripsisse arbitrere.

24 (VII.1)

Scr. Romae c. m. Sept. an. 55

M. CICERO S. D. M. MARIO

1   Si te dolor aliqui corporis aut infirmitas valetudinis tuae
tenuit quo minus ad ludos venires, Fortunae magis tribuo
quam sapientiae tuae; sin haec quae ceteri mirantur
contemnenda duxisti et, cum per valetudinem posses,
venire tamen noluisti, utrumque laetor, et sine dolore corporis te fuisse et animo valuisse, cum ea quae sine causa
mirantur alii neglexeris, modo ut tibi constiterit fructus oti
tui; quo quidem tibi perfrui mirifice licuit cum esses in ista

2 amici *(Man.)*
3 conscienti(a)e *(Rut.)*

---

[1] Given by Pompey in his second Consulship to inaugurate his
stone theatre (the first built in Rome) and the temple of Venus
Victrix. Pliny the Elder and Cassius Dio write of its magnificence.

170

you; so too should be the thought of myself and those others who value you, and always shall, by your character, not your worldly fortune; and so above all should be your own conscience. You will reflect that you have deserved nothing of what has happened, and you will add the thought that wise men are troubled by dishonour, not by chance, and by their own fault, not by others' ill usage.

Prompted by the memory of our old friendship and the merit and attention of your son. I shall ever be ready both to comfort and to alleviate your plight. If you care to write me a few words, I shall not let you feel that you have written them for nothing.

24 (VII.1)
CICERO TO M. MARIUS

Rome, ca. September (?) 55

From M. Cicero to M. Marius greetings.

If some bodily distress or the frailty of your health has kept you from coming to the show,[1] I give credit to Fortune rather than to your own good sense. On the other hand, if you thought these objects of public wonderment unworthy of your notice, and chose not to come though your health would have permitted, why, I rejoice both at your freedom from physical distress and at your health of mind, in that you have disregarded these spectacles at which others idly marvel—always provided that you have reaped the fruits of your leisure. You have had a wonderful opportunity to

amoenitate paene solus relictus. neque tamen dubito quin
tu in[1] illo cubiculo tuo, ex quo tibi Stabianum perforando[2]
patefecisti sinum, per eos dies matutina tempora lectiun-
culis consumpseris, cum illi interea qui te istic reliquerunt
spectarent communis[3] mimos semisomni. reliquas vero
partis diei tu consumebas iis delectationibus quas tibi ipse
ad arbitrium tuum compararas; nobis autem erant ea per-
petienda quae Sp. Maecius probavisset.

2   Omnino, si quaeris, ludi apparatissimi, sed non tui sto-
machi; coniecturam enim facio de meo. nam primum honoris causa in scaenam redierant ii quos ego honoris causa
de scaena decessisse arbitrabar. deliciae vero tuae, noster
Aesopus, eius modi fuit ut ei desinere per omnis homines
liceret. is iurare cum coepisset, vox eum defecit in illo loco,
'si sciens fallo.' quid tibi ego alia narrem? nosti enim reliquos ludos; qui ne id quidem leporis habuerunt quod
solent mediocres ludi. apparatus enim spectatio tollebat
omnem hilaritatem; quo quidem apparatu non dubito quin
animo aequissimo carueris. quid enim delectationis habent sescenti muli in 'Clytaemestra' aut in 'Equo Troiano'

---

¹ ex *(Lallemand)*   ² perforasti et *(Reid)*   ³ *suspectum*

---

² Elsewhere Cicero writes of Marius as his neighbour at Pompeii. But Marius' villa may have been two or three miles to the
south above modern Castellammare di Stabia.

³ The weather in high summer was naturally oppressive.
Valerius Maximus (2.4.6) says that streams of running water were
channelled through the theatre to mitigate the heat.

⁴ Spurius Maecius Tarpa selected the plays to be produced at
the show. He may have been Chairman *(magister)* of the Guild of
Poets established in the third century: cf. Horace, *Satires* 1.10.38
and *Art of Poetry* 386.

enjoy it, left almost on your own in that delightful spot.[2]
And after all, I don't doubt that throughout the period of
the show you have spent the mornings browsing over your
books in that bedroom of yours with its window that you let
into the wall to overlook the bay of Stabiae. Meanwhile
those who left you there were watching the public panto-
mimes half-asleep.[3] As for the rest of the day, you have
been spending it in such diversions as you have provided to
suit your own taste while we have had to endure what Sp.
Maecius[4] presumably thought proper.

To be sure, the show (if you are interested) was on the
most lavish scale; but it would have been little to your taste,
to judge by my own. To begin with, certain performers
honoured the occasion by returning to the boards, from
which I thought they had honoured their reputation by retiring.[5] Your favourite, our friend Aesopus, gave a display
which everyone was willing should be his finale. When
he came to take an oath[6] and got as far as 'if I knowingly
swear false,' he lost his voice! I need not give you further
details—you know the other shows.[7] They did not even
have the sprightliness which one mostly finds in ordinary
shows—one lost all sense of gaiety in watching the elaborate productions. These I don't doubt you are very well
content to have missed. What pleasure is there in getting a
Clytemnestra with six hundred mules or a *Trojan Horse*

[5] The common phrase *honoris causa*, 'by way of compliment,'
is echoed in another sense, 'for the sake of (their) repute.'

[6] Perhaps as part of his role. Others suppose that actors had to
take an oath before starting their performance (but why?).

[7] I.e. comedies and mimes.

creterrarum tria milia aut armatura varia peditatus et equi-
tatus in aliqua pugna? quae popularem admirationem
3 habuerunt, delectationem tibi nullam attulissent. quod si
tu per eos dies operam dedisti Protogeni tuo, dum modo is
tibi quidvis potius quam orationes meas legerit, ne tu haud
paulo plus quam quisquam nostrum delectationis habuisti.
non enim te puto Graecos aut Oscos ludos desiderasse,
praesertim cum Oscos vel in senatu vestro spectare possis,
Graecos ita non ames ut ne ad villam quidem tuam via
Graecos ire soleas. nam quid ego te athletas putem deside-
rare, qui gladiatores contempseris? in quibus ipse Pompeius confitetur se et operam et oleum perdidisse. reliquae
sunt venationes binae per dies quinque, magnificae, nemo
negat; sed quae potest homini esse polito delectatio cum
aut homo imbecillus a valentissima bestia laniatur aut
praeclara bestia venabulo transverberatur? quae tamen,
si videnda sunt, saepe vidisti, neque nos qui haec specta-
ta<vi>mus quicquam novi vidimus. extremus elephanto-
rum dies fuit. in quo admiratio magna vulgi atque turbae,
delectatio nulla exstitit; quin etiam misericordia quaedam
consecuta est atque opinio eius modi, esse quandam illi

---

8 The first of these two tragedies was by Accius. Grammarians
ascribe a *Trojan Horse* both to Livius Andronicus and to Naevius.
The bowls are thought to have figured as part of the spoils of Troy.

9 No doubt a reader *(anagnostes)*.

10 Probably Greek plays performed in Greek, as distinct from
Latin adaptations of Greek originals; cf. *Letters to Atticus* 410
(XVI.5).1.

11 I.e. *Fabulae Atellanae*, a type of coarse farce with stock
characters, like a Punch and Judy show.

174

with three thousand mixing bowls[8] or a variegated display
of cavalry and infantry equipment in some battle or other?
The public gaped at all this; it would not have amused you
at all. If you were listening to your man Protogenes[9] during
those days (so long as he read you anything in the world except my speeches), you have certainly had a good deal
better time of it than any of us. As for the Greek[10] and
Oscan[11] shows, I don't imagine you were sorry to miss
them—especially as you can see an Oscan turn on your
town council,[12] and you care so little for Greeks that you
don't even take Greek Street to get to your house! Or perhaps, having scorned gladiators,[13] you are sorry not to have
seen the athletes! Pompey himself admits that they were a
waste of time and midday oil![14] That leaves the hunts, two
every day for five days, magnificent—nobody says otherwise. But what pleasure can a cultivated man get out of
seeing a weak human being torn to pieces by a powerful
animal or a splendid animal transfixed by a hunting spear?
Anyhow, if these sights are worth seeing, you have seen
them often; and we spectators saw nothing new. The last
day was for the elephants. The groundlings showed much
astonishment thereat, but no enjoyment. There was even
an impulse of compassion, a feeling that the monsters had

[12] Oscan here standing for Campanian. Graffiti found in Pompeii show that an M. Marius stood for election as Aedile.

[13] Part of Pompey's show rather than a private allusion. The
explanation that Marius had defied Clodius' gangs does not suit
what is known of him.   [14] *Operam et oleum perdere* was a
proverbial expression for a waste of time and money, *oleum* referring to 'midnight oil.' Here it is humorously applied to the oil used
by athletes in anointing themselves.

beluae cum genere humano societatem.

4   His ego tamen diebus, ludis scaenicis, ne forte videar tibi non modo beatus sed liber omnino fuisse, dirupi me paene in iudicio Galli Canini, familiaris tui. quod si tam facilem populum haberem quam Aesopus habuit, libenter mehercule artem desinerem tecumque et cum similibus nostri viverem. nam me cum antea taedebat, cum et aetas et a‹m›bitio me hortabatur et licebat denique quem nolebam non defendere, tum vero hoc tempore vita nulla est. neque enim fructum ullum laboris exspecto et cogor non numquam homines non optime de me meritos rogatu eorum qui bene meriti sunt defendere.

5   Itaque quaero causas omnis aliquando vivendi arbitratu meo teque et istam rationem oti tui et laudo vehementer et probo, quodque nos minus intervisis, hoc fero animo aequiore quod, si Romae esses, tamen neque nos lepore tuo neque te, si qui est in me, meo frui liceret propter molestissimas occupationes meas. quibus si me relaxaro (nam ut plane exsolvam non postulo), te ipsum, qui[4] multos annos nihil aliud commentaris, docebo profecto quid sit humaniter vivere. tu modo istam imbecillitatem valetudinis tuae sustenta et tuere, ut facis, ut nostras villas obire et mecum

---

4 et ipsum quid *(Rut.)*

---

something human about them.[15]

As for me, these past days, during the plays (in case you picture me as a free man, if not a happy one), I pretty well ruptured my lungs defending your friend Gallus Caninius.[16] If only my public were as accommodating as Aesopus', upon my word I should be glad to give up my profession and spend my time with you and other congenial spirits. I was weary of it even in the days when youth and ambition spurred me forward, and when moreover I was at liberty to refuse a case I did not care for. But now life is simply not worth living. I have no reward to expect for my labours, and sometimes I am obliged to defend persons who have deserved none too well of me at the behest of those who *have* deserved well.

Accordingly, I am looking for any excuse to live as I please at long last; and you and your leisured manner of existence have my hearty commendation and approval. I resign myself to the rarity of your visits more easily than I otherwise should, because, even if you were in Rome, I am so confoundedly busy that I should not be able to enjoy the entertainment of your company, nor you of mine (if any entertainment it holds). When and if I slacken my chains (for to be loose of them entirely is more than I can ask), then, no question about it, I shall teach you the art of civilized living, to which you have been giving your undivided attention for years! Only you must go on propping up that frail health of yours and looking after yourself, so that you can visit my places[17] in the country and run around with

[17] Possibly 'our places;' Marius too may have had more than one villa in the area. Cicero at this period had one at Pompeii and one at Cumae.

simul lecticula concursare possis.

6   Haec ad te pluribus verbis scripsi quam soleo non oti abundantia sed amoris erga te, quod me quadam epistula subinvitaras, si memoria tenes, ut ad te aliquid eius modi scriberem quo minus te praetermisisse ludos paeniteret. quod si adsecutus sum, gaudeo; sin minus, hoc me tamen consolor, quod posthac ad ludos venies nosque vises neque [in][5] epistulis relinques meis spem aliquam delectationis tuae.

25 (V.8)

Scr. Romae m. Ian., ut vid., an. 54

M. CICERO M. LICINIO P. F. CRASSO

1   Quantum †ad†[1] meum studium exstiterit dignitatis tuae vel tuendae vel etiam augendae, non dubito quin ad te omnes tui scripserint. non enim fuit aut mediocre aut obscurum aut eius modi quod silentio posset praeteriri. nam et cum consulibus et cum multis consularibus tanta contentione decertavi quanta numquam antea ulla in causa suscepique mihi perpetuam propugnationem pro omnibus ornamentis tuis veterique nostrae necessitudini iam diu debitum sed multa varietate temporum interruptum officium cumulate reddidi.

[5] *(SB post Mend.; vide comm.)*
[1] a.d. *lac. sequente R. Klotz:* Id. *Ellis*

---

[1] Of January (but the reading is conjectural). The debate in

me in my little litter.

I have written at unusual length, out of an abundance, not of spare time, but of affection for you, because in one of your letters you threw out a hint, if you remember, that I might write something to prevent you feeling sorry to have missed the show. If I have succeeded in that, so much the better; but if not, I console myself with the thought that henceforth you will come to the shows and visit us, and that you won't forgo any prospect of pleasure to yourself on account of my letters.

25 (V.8)
CICERO TO CRASSUS

Rome, January (?) 54

From M. Cicero to M. Licinius Crassus, son of Publius, greetings.

I do not doubt that all your friends have apprised you in their letters of the zeal which I put forward on the Ides (?)[1] for the defence, or even enhancement, of your position. It was too ardent and too conspicuous to go unrecorded. Against the Consuls and many of the Consulars I joined issue with a vehemence which I have never before displayed in any cause, thus taking upon myself the standing role of protagonist on behalf of all that tends to your honour, and discharging more than amply the service which has long been owing to our old friendship, but which the many variations of circumstance had caused me to intermit.

the Senate concerned the allocation of funds etc. to Crassus as governor of Syria.

2   Neque mehercule umquam mihi tui aut colendi aut ornandi voluntas defuit. sed quaedam pestes hominum laude
aliena dolentium et te non numquam a me alienarunt et
me aliquando immutarunt tibi. sed exstitit tempus optatum mihi magis quam speratum, ut florentissimis tuis
rebus mea perspici posset et memoria nostrae voluntatis et
amicitiae fides. sum enim consecutus non modo ut domus
tua tota sed ut cuncta civitas me tibi amicissimum esse
cognosceret. itaque et praestantissima omnium femina-
rum, uxor tua, et eximia pietate, virtute, gratia tui Crassi
meis consiliis, monitis, studiis actionibusque nituntur et
senatus populusque Romanus intellegit tibi absenti nihil
esse tam promptum aut tam paratum quam in omnibus
rebus quae ad te pertineant operam, curam, diligentiam,
auctoritatem meam.

3   Quae sint acta quaeque agantur, domesticorum tibi litteris declarari puto. de me sic existimes ac tibi persuadeas
vehementer velim, non me repentina aliqua voluntate aut
fortuito ad tuam amplitudinem meis officiis amplecten-
dam incidisse[2] sed, ut primum forum attigerim, spectasse
semper ut tibi possem quam maxime esse coniunctus. quo
quidem ex tempore memoria teneo neque meam tibi
observantiam neque mihi tuam summam benevolentiam
ac liberalitatem defuisse. si quae inciderunt[3] non tam re
quam suspicione violata, ea, cum fuerint et falsa et inania,
sint evulsa ex omni memoria vitaque nostra. is enim tu vir
es et eum me esse cupio ut, quoniam in eadem rei publicae

[2] incubuisse *coni. SB*
[3] interciderunt *(Crat.)*

But indeed I never lacked will to cultivate your friendship and contribute to your advancement. Only certain pestilent fellows, whom it hurts to hear others well spoken of, estranged you from me more than once, and at times changed my attitude to you. But now the occasion has arisen which I prayed for, but scarcely hoped to see: in the full tide of your prosperity I have had the chance to show myself mindful of our mutual sentiments and loyal to our friendship. Yes, I have succeeded in making plain, not only to your entire domestic circle but to the community at large, that I am your very good friend. Your wife, the paragon of her sex, and your two sons, whose filial affection, high character, and popularity do them honour, rely on my counsels and promptings and active support. And the Senate and People of Rome now know that in all matters affecting you during your absence my devoted and indefatigable service and the influence I command are absolutely and unreservedly at your disposal.

Day-to-day events, past and current, are presumably conveyed to you by your domestic correspondents. As for me personally, I very much hope you will thoroughly persuade yourself that I have not *happened* to embrace your cause and work for your greatness through any accident or sudden whim, but have always made it my aim ever since my entry into public life to be on the closest terms with you. Since those days I recall no failure of attention on my part or of good will and generosity in the highest measure on yours. If certain infringements, surmised rather than real, have occurred so as to affect our relations, these are mere figments of the imagination; let them be utterly eradicated from our memories and our lives. Between two men such as you are and I desire to be, whose lot has fallen

tempora incidimus, coniunctionem amicitiamque nostram
utrique nostrum laudi sperem fore.

4 Quam ob rem tu, quantum tuo iudicio tribuendum esse
nobis putes, statues ipse et, ut spero, statues ex nostra dignitate. ego vero tibi profiteor atque polliceor eximium et
singulare meum studium in omni genere offici quod ad honestatem et gloriam tuam spectet. in quo etiam si multi
mecum contendent, tamen cum reliquis omnibus tum
Crassis tuis iudicibus omnis facile superabo; quos quidem
ego ambo unice diligo, sed in [Marco][4] benevolentia pari
hoc magis sum Publio deditus quod me, quamquam a pueritia sua semper, tamen hoc tempore maxime sicut alterum
parentem et observat et diligit.

5 Has litteras velim existimes foederis habituras esse vim,
non epistulae, meque ea quae tibi promitto ac recipio
sanctissime esse observaturum diligentissimeque esse facturum. quae a me suscepta defensio est te absente dignitatis tuae, in ea iam ego non solum amicitiae nostrae sed
etiam constantiae meae causa permanebo. quam ob rem
satis esse hoc tempore arbitratus sum hoc ad te scribere,
me, si quid ipse intellegerem aut ad voluntatem aut ad
commodum aut ad amplitudinem tuam pertinere, mea
sponte id esse facturum; sin autem quippiam aut a te essem admonitus aut a tuis, effecturum ut intellegeres nihil
neque te scripsisse neque quemquam tuorum frustra ad
me detulisse. quam ob rem velim ita et ipse ad me scribas
de omnibus minimis, maximis, mediocribus rebus ut ad
hominem amicissimum et tuis praecipias ut opera, consilio, auctoritate, gratia mea sic utantur in omnibus publicis
privatis, forensibus domesticis, tuis, amicorum, hospitum,

[4] *(Mend.)*

on the same political ground, I would hope that alliance and friendship will conduce to the credit of both.

You yourself, therefore, will decide the place in your esteem which you think appropriate for me, and I trust your decision will take account of my standing in the world. On my side, I profess and promise you my signal and exemplary devotion in every kind of service tending to your dignity and glory. Many may be my rivals, but by the verdict of every beholder, and of your sons above all, I shall comfortably win the race. For both young men I have a particular regard, but, while both have my good will equally, I am the more attached to Publius because ever since he was a boy, but especially at the present time, he pays me attention and regard as though to a second father.

Please believe that this is no ordinary letter; it will have the force of a covenant. Be sure that the promises and undertakings I give you will be religiously respected and carried out to the letter. Having taken up the defence of your standing while you are abroad, I shall persevere therein, not only for our friendship's sake but to maintain my own reputation for consistency. Accordingly, I have thought it enough at present to assure you of my unsolicited activity wherever I myself see an opportunity to promote your wish, your interest, or your dignity; and to add that, should any suggestion reach me from you or yours, I shall take care you do not suppose any written word of your own or any representations from your folk to have been lost upon me. So please write to me yourself on all matters, large, small, or in between, as to a most sincere friend, and advise your people to make use of my service and counsel, my public and personal influence, in all concerns—no matter whether public or private, business or

clientium tuorum negotiis ut, quod eius fieri possit, prae-
sentiae tuae desiderium meo labore minuatur.

26 (VII.5)

Scr. Romae m. Apr. an. 54

CICERO CAESARI IMP. S. D.

1   Vide quam mihi persuaserim te me esse alterum, non
modo in iis rebus quae ad me ipsum sed etiam in iis quae
ad meos pertinent. C. Trebatium cogitaram, quocumque
exirem, mecum ducere, ut eum meis omnibus studiis
beneficiis quam ornatissimum domum reducerem. sed
postea quam et Pompei commoratio diuturnior erat quam
putaram et mea quaedam tibi non ignota dubitatio aut impedire profectionem meam videbatur aut certe tardare,
vide quid mihi sumpserim: coepi velle ea Trebatium exspectare a te quae sperasset a me, neque mehercule minus
ei prolixe de tua voluntate promisi quam eram solitus de
mea polliceri.

2   Casus vero mirificus quidam intervenit quasi vel testis
opinionis meae vel sponsor humanitatis tuae. nam cum de
hoc ipso Trebatio cum Balbo nostro loquerer accuratius
domi meae, litterae mihi dantur a te, quibus in extremis

---

[1] In 55 Pompey received a five-year command in Spain and in
the autumn of 54 he appointed Cicero as his Legate; cf. *Letters to
Quintus* 21 (III.1).18, *Letters to Atticus* 93 (IV.19).2. But neither
he nor Cicero went there. The 'hesitation' is usually understood as
referring to apprehensions about Clodius' designs.

[2] *M. Curti filium,* conjectured for *M. itfiuium* in the manuscripts. The person referred to is clearly the M. Curtius whom

domestic, your own or your friends' or your guests' or your clients'. My labour shall go to fill, so far as may be, the void created by your absence.

26 (VII.5)
CICERO TO CAESAR

Rome, April 54

From Cicero to Caesar, Imperator, greetings.

Please observe how fully I am persuaded that you are my *alter ego,* not only in my own concerns but in those of my friends also. I had intended to take C. Trebatius with me wherever I might go, in order to bring him home again the richer by any and every benefit and mark of good will in my power to bestow. But Pompey has stayed on longer than I expected, and my own departure seems prevented, or at any rate delayed, by a certain hesitation on my part of which you are not uninformed.[1] So observe my presumption: I now want Trebatius to look to you for everything he would have hoped for from me, and I have assured him of your friendly disposition in terms really no less ample than I had previously been wont to use respecting my own.

But a remarkable coincidence has supervened, as though in evidence of the correctness of my opinion and in guarantee of your kindness. Just as I was talking rather seriously to our friend Balbus at my house on the subject of this very Trebatius, a letter comes in from you concluding as follows: 'I shall make M. Curtius' son,[2] whom you

Cicero had asked Caesar to appoint Military Tribune in the following year (*Letters to Quintus* 18 (II.14).3).

scriptum erat: 'M. ⟨Cur⟩ti filium,[1] quem mihi commendas, vel regem Galliae faciam; vel hunc Leptae delega, si vis, tu ad me alium mitte quem ornem.' sustulimus manus et ego et Balbus. tanta fuit opportunitas ut illud nescio quid non fortuitum sed divinum videretur.

Mitto igitur ad te Trebatium atque ita mitto ut initio mea sponte, post autem invitatu tuo mittendum duxerim.

3 hunc, mi Caesar, sic velim omni tua comitate complectare ut omnia quae per me possis adduci ut in meos conferre velis in unum hunc conferas. de quo tibi homine haec spondeo, non illo vetere verbo meo quod, cum ad te de Milone scripsissem, iure lusisti sed more Romano quomodo homines non inepti loquuntur, probiorem hominem, meliorem virum, pudentiorem esse neminem. accedit etiam quod familiam ducit in iure civili, singulari memoria, summa scientia.

Huic ego neque tribunatum neque praefecturam neque ullius benefici certum nomen peto; benevolentiam tuam et liberalitatem peto, neque impedio quo minus, si tibi ita placuerit, etiam hisce eum ornes gloriolae insignibus. totum denique hominem tibi ita trado, de manu, ut aiunt, in manum tuam istam et victoria et fide praestantem. simus enim putidiusculi, quam⟨quam⟩[2] per te vix licet; verum, ut video, licebit.

1 itfiuium *(SB)*
2 *(Ern.:* quod *H. Stephanus)*

---

3 See Index under Paconius. This is his first appearance in the Letters and Caesar's reason for mentioning him is unknown.

4 Or 'old saw.' What this was, or why Cicero wrote to Caesar about Milo, we do not know.

recommend to me, king of Gaul. Or, if you please, make him over to Lepta,[3] and send me somebody else on whom to bestow my favours.' Balbus and I both raised our hands to heaven. It came so pat as to seem no accident, but divine intervention.

I send you Trebatius accordingly. I thought it right to do so of my own accord in the first instance, but at your invitation in the second. In embracing his acquaintance with all your usual graciousness, my dear Caesar, I should wish you to confer upon his single person all the kindnesses which I could induce you to wish to confer upon my friends. As for him, I will answer that you will find him—I won't use that old-fashioned expression[4] of which you rightly made fun when I wrote to you about Milo, I'll say it in plain Latin, in the language of sensible men: there is no better fellow, no more honest and honourable gentleman alive. Add to which, he is a leading light in Civil Law; his memory is extraordinary, his learning profound.

I do not ask on his behalf for a Tribunate or Prefecture or any other specific favour. It is your good will and generosity I bespeak; though if in addition you have a mind to decorate him with such ambitious trinkets, I say nothing to deter you. In fine, I put him altogether, as the phrase goes, out of my hand into yours—the hand of a great conqueror and a great gentleman,[5] if I may become a trifle fulsome, though that's hardly permissible with you. But you will let it pass, I see you will.[6]

[5] Literally 'preeminent both in victory' (i.e. with the sword) 'and loyalty' (to its pledges).   [6] The good nature apparent in Caesar's letter will tolerate even flattery of himself.

Cura ut valeas, et me, ut amas, ama.

27 (VII.6)

Scr. in Cumano aut Pompeiano m. Mai. post. parte an. 54
CICERO S. D. TREBATIO

1   In omnibus meis epistulis quas ad Caesarem aut ad Balbum mitto legitima quaedam est accessio commendationis
tuae, nec ea vulgaris sed cum aliquo insigni indicio meae
erga te benevolentiae. tu modo ineptias istas et desideria
urbis et urbanitatis depone et, quo consilio profectus es, id
adsiduitate et virtute consequere. hoc tibi tam ignoscemus
nos amici quam ignoverunt Medeae

> quae Corinthum arcem altam habebant matronae
>   opulentae, optimates,

quibus illa 'manibus gypsatissimis' persuasit ne sibi vitio
illae verterent quod abesset a patria. nam

> multi suam rem bene gessere et publicam patria
>   procul;
> multi, qui domi aetatem agerent, propterea sunt
>   improbati.

quo in numero tu certe fuisses nisi te extrusissemus.

2   Sed plura scribemus alias. tu, qui ceteris cavere didi-

---

1 The quotations are from a Latin version by Ennius of Euripi-
des' *Medea.*

2 Gypsum, used as a cosmetic for whitening. Whether these
words are Cicero's or Pompe the play is uncertain.

Take care of your health and keep that warm corner in your heart for me.

27 (VII.6)
CICERO TO TREBATIUS

Cumae or Pompeii, latter May 54

From Cicero to Trebatius greetings.

Every letter I write to Caesar or to Balbus carries as a kind of statutory bonus a recommendation of yourself, and not the standard sort but phrased with some special indication of my regard for you. Now what you have to do is to put aside this foolish hankering after Rome and city ways, and by dint of perseverance and energy achieve the purpose with which you set out. I and your other friends will excuse you, as the 'rich and noble dames that dwelt in Corinth, lofty citadel'[1] excused Medea. She persuaded them 'hands thick in plaster'[2] not to censure her for living abroad:

> Helping self and helping country many a rover wide
> doth roam.
> Naught accounted in his staying sitteth many a stay-
> at-home.

This latter case would certainly have been yours, if I had not thrust you forth.

But I shall be writing more anon. Now you, who have learned how to enter caveats[3] for others, enter one for

---

[3] *Cavere* (beware, look out for) was also used in a legal sense, of a jurisconsult advising a client or prescribing a form of procedure. I have had to resort to paraphrase.

cisti, in Britannia ne ab essedariis decipiaris caveto et (quoniam Medeam coepi agere) illud semper memento:

qui ipse sibi sapiens prodesse non quit, nequiquam sapit.

Cura ut valeas.

28 (VII.7)

Scr. Romae fort. ex. m. Iun. an. 54

CICERO TREBATIO

1 Ego te commendare non desisto, sed quid proficiam ex te scire cupio. spem maximam habeo in Balbo, ad quem de te diligentissime et saepissime scribo. illud soleo mirari, non me totiens accipere tuas litteras quotiens a Quinto mihi fratre adferantur. in Britannia nihil esse audio neque auri neque argenti; id si ita est, essedum aliquod capias 2 suadeo et ad nos quam primum recurras. sin autem sine Britannia tamen adsequi quod volumus possumus, perfice ut sis in familiaribus Caesaris. multum te in eo frater adiuvabit meus, multum Balbus, sed, mihi crede, tuus pudor et labor plurimum. imperatorem ⟨habes⟩[1] liberalissimum, aetatem opportunissimam, commendationem certe singularem, ut tibi unum timendum sit ne ipse tibi defuisse videare.

[1] *(hic Baiter, alii alibi)*

---

[4] Caesar's second expedition to Britain was now in preparation. He describes how the Britons used their war chariots in *Gallic War* 4.33.

yourself against the tricks of those charioteers in Britain.[4]
And since I have started to play Medea, always remember
what she says: 'He who cannot help his own case, be he
wise, his *wisdom's* vain.'[5]

Take care of your health.

28 (VII.7)
CICERO TO TREBATIUS

Rome, end of June (?) 54

From Cicero to Trebatius.

I am continually putting in a word for you, but with
what effect I am anxious to hear from yourself. My greatest hope is in Balbus, to whom I write about you very
earnestly and often. What surprises me is that I don't get a
letter from you whenever one comes in from my brother
Quintus. I hear there is not an ounce of either gold or silver
in Britain. If that is true, my advice is to lay hold of a char-
iot and hurry back to us at full speed! But if we can gain our
end even without Britain, contrive to make yourself one of
Caesar's intimates. My brother will give you valuable assistance, and so will Balbus; but your greatest asset, believe
me, is your own honourable character and hard work. You
are serving under a very generous chief, your age is just
right, your recommendation is certainly out of the ordinary. So the one thing you have to be afraid of is seeming to
do yourself less than justice.

[5] The Euripidean original may be the line quoted in Letter
317, which is not in our text of the Greek play. On 'wisdom' see
Letter 21, n. 1.

29 (VII.8)

Scr. Romae post. parte m. Sext., ut vid.

CICERO TREBATIO

1   Scripsit ad me Caesar perhumaniter nondum te sibi
satis esse familiarem propter occupationes suas, sed certe
fore. cui quidem ego rescripsi quam mihi gratum esset
futurum si quam plurimum in te studi, offici, liberalitatis
suae contulisset. sed ex tuis litteris cognovi praeproperam
quandam festinationem tuam et simul sum admiratus cur
tribunatus commoda, dempto praesertim labore militiae,

2   contempseris. querar cum Vacerra et Manilio; nam Cornelio nihil audeo dicere, cuius tu periculo stultus es, quoniam
te ab eo sapere didicisse profiteris. quin tu urges istam oc-
casionem et facultatem, qua melior numquam reperietur?

Quod scribis de illo Preciano iureconsulto, ego te ei
non desino commendare; scribit enim[1] ipse mihi te sibi
gratias agere debere. de eo quid sit, cura ut sciam. ego vestras Britannicas litteras exspecto.

---

[1] etiam ⲥ: autem *coni. SB*

29 (VII.8)
CICERO TO TREBATIUS

Rome, (late August?) 54

From Cicero to Trebatius.

Caesar has written to me very civilly, regretting that he has so far been too busy to get to know you very well, but assuring me that this will come. I told him in my reply how greatly he would oblige me by conferring upon you all he could in the way of good will, friendly offices, and liberality. But your letter gave me an impression of undue impatience; also it surprised me that you make so little account of the advantages of a Tribunate, especially one involving no military service. I shall complain to Vacerra and Manilius.[1] I dare not say a word to Cornelius.[2] He is responsible if you play the fool, since you give out that it was from him you learned your *wisdom*. Now why don't you press this opportunity, this chance? You'll never find a better.

As for what you say about that Counsellor Precianus,[3] I go on commending you to him, for he writes himself that he has given you reason to be grateful. Let me know how that matter stands. I am looking forward to Britannic letters from you all.

[1] Two of Trebatius' fellow jurisconsults.

[2] Q. Cornelius Maximus is mentioned in the *Digest* as Trebatius' teacher in law.

[3] Unknown. Possibly *Preciano* means 'in the Precius business.'

30 (VII.9)

Scr. Romae post. parte m. Oct., ut vid., an. 54

CICERO TREBATIO

1 Iam diu ignoro quid agas; nihil enim scribis, neque ego ad te his duobus mensibus scripseram. quod cum Quinto fratre meo non eras, quo mitterem aut cui darem nesciebam. cupio scire quid agas et ubi sis hiematurus. equidem velim cum Caesare, sed ad eum propter eius ⟨luctum⟩[1]

2 nihil sum ausus scribere; ad Balbum tamen scripsi. tu tibi deesse noli; serius potius ad nos, dum plenior. quod huc properes nihil est, praesertim Battara mortuo. sed tibi consilium non deest. quid constitueris cupio scire.

Cn. Octavius est (an Cn. Cornelius?)[2] quidam,[3] tuus familiaris, summo genere natus, terrae filius. is me, quia scit tuum familiarem esse, crebro ad cenam invitat. adhuc non potuit perducere, sed mihi tamen gratum est.

[1] *(Vict.)*
[2] *dist. SB*
[3] quidem *(Ern.)*

30 (VII.9)
CICERO TO TREBATIUS

Rome, middle or late October (?) 54

From Cicero to Trebatius.

It's a long time since I had news of you. You don't write, and the last two months I have not written to you myself. As you were not with my brother Quintus, I could not tell where to send a letter or whom to give it to. I am anxious to know what you are doing and where you will be spending the winter—with Caesar, I hope; but I have not ventured to write anything to him on account of his recent loss.[1] I did write to Balbus though. Mind you don't let yourself down. Better later back to us, so you come fatter! There is no occasion for you to hurry, especially now that Battara[2] is no more. But you are well able to make your own plans. I am anxious to know what you have decided.

There is a certain friend of yours called Cn. Octavius (or is it Cn. Cornelius?), 'mother Earth's son, a fine old family.'[3] Knowing me to be a friend of yours, he showers me with invitations to dinner. So far he has not succeeded in getting me all the way, but I am obliged just the same.

[1] Julia, Caesar's only child and Pompey's wife, died in September 54.

[2] Who he was and what Cicero means is unknown. The suggestion that Battara was a nickname for Vacerra (see previous letter) does not seem very likely.

[3] Perhaps quoted from a play, though this is not certain. 'Son of Earth' *(terrae filius)* means a nobody. The name which Cicero was, or pretended to be, unable to remember was in fact Octavius; Letter 32.2.

31 (VII.17)

Scr. Romae m. Oct. vel Nov. an. 54

CICERO TREBATIO S.

1   Ex tuis litteris et Quinto fratri gratias egi et te aliquando collaudare possum quod iam videris certa aliqua in sententia constitisse. nam primorum mensum litteris tuis vehementer commovebar, quod mihi interdum (pace tua dixerim) levis in urbis urbanitatisque desiderio, interdum piger, interdum timidus in labore militari, saepe autem etiam, quod a te alienissimum est, subimpudens videbare. tamquam enim syngrapham ad imperatorem, non epistulam, attulisses, sic pecunia ablata domum redire properabas, nec tibi in mentem veniebat eos ipsos qui cum syngraphis venissent Alexandream nummum adhuc <n>ullum auferre potuisse.

2   Ego, si mei commodi rationem ducerem, te mecum esse maxime vellem. non enim mediocri adficiebar vel voluptate ex consuetudine nostra vel utilitate ex consilio atque opera tua. sed cum te ex adulescentia tua in amicitiam et fidem meam contulisses, semper te non modo tuendum mihi sed etiam augendum atque ornandum putavi. itaque, quoad opinatus sum me in provinciam exiturum, quae ad te ultro detulerim,[1] meminisse te credo.

---

[1] attulerim *(Lamb.)*

---

[1] Ptolemy the Piper had borrowed large sums with which to bribe Roman politicians to further his restoration to his throne; that achieved, he was in no hurry to pay his debts. Cicero's de-

31 (VII.17)
CICERO TO TREBATIUS

Rome, October or November 54

From Cicero to Trebatius greetings.

On the strength of your letter I gave thanks to my brother Quintus, and can at last commend yourself in that you now seem to have fairly made up your mind. Your letters in the first few months disturbed me not a little, for they gave me an impression (if you will forgive me for saying so) at times of irresponsibility in your hankering for Rome and city ways, at times of indolence, at times of timidity in face of the labours of army life, and often too, most uncharacteristically, of something not unlike presumption. You seemed to think you had brought a note of hand to the Commander-in-Chief instead of a letter—such a hurry you were in to take your money and get back home! It did not seem to occur to you that people who *did* go with notes of hand to Alexandria have thus far been unable to get a penny![1]

Were I thinking in terms of my own convenience, I should wish you to be with me of all things, for I gained no small pleasure from our intercourse and no small profit from your advice and services. But since from youth upwards you have confided yourself to my friendship and patronage, I have always felt a responsibility not only for your protection but for your promotion and betterment. Accordingly, as long as I expected to go myself on a provincial assignment, I made you certain unsolicited offers,

fence of C. Rabirius Postumus in the following winter had to do with this matter.

postea quam ea[2] mutata ratio est, cum viderem me a Caesare honorificentissime tractari et unice diligi hominisque liberalitatem incredibilem et singularem fidem nossem, sic ei te commendavi et tradidi ut gravissime diligentissimeque potui. quod ille ita et accepit et mihi saepe litteris significavit et tibi et verbis et re ostendit mea commendatione sese valde esse commotum. hunc tu virum nactus, si me aut sapere aliquid aut velle tua causa putas, ne dimiseris et, ⟨si⟩ quae te forte res aliquando offenderit, cum ille aut occupatione aut difficultate tardior tibi erit visus, perferto et ultima exspectato; quae ego tibi iucunda et honesta praestabo.

3   Pluribus te hortari non debeo. tantum moneo, neque amicitiae confirmandae clarissimi ac liberalissimi viri neque uberioris provinciae neque aetatis magis idoneum tempus, si hoc amiseris, te esse ullum umquam reperturum. hoc, quem ad modum vos scribere soletis in vestris libris, idem Q. Cornelio videbatur.

In Britanniam te profectum non esse gaudeo, quod et labore caruisti et ego te de rebus illis non audiam. ubi sis hibernaturus et qua spe aut condicione perscribas ad me velim.

[2] mea R

which you doubtless remember. When that plan changed, I hit on another. Observing that Caesar extended to me the most flattering courtesies and held me in particular regard, knowing too his extraordinary generosity and punctilious loyalty to his engagements, I commended you to his care in the fullest and most emphatic terms I could find. He took my words in the same spirit, and has often intimated to me by letter and made clear to you by word of mouth and by act that he has been greatly impressed by my recommendation. Now that you have come by such a patron, if you credit me with any good sense or good will towards you, don't let him go. Should anything occur to ruffle you, should you find him less prompt than you expected through pressure of affairs or some untoward circumstance, be patient and wait for the final outcome. That it will be agreeable to yourself I will guarantee.

I must not urge you at greater length. I will only point out that if you let slip this opportunity of securing the friendship of a most eminent and generous personage in a wealthy province at just the right time of your life, you will never find a better. In this opinion, as you jurists say in your books, Q. Cornelius concurs.

I am glad that you have not gone to Britain. You are quit of the fatigues, and I shall not be listening to your accounts of it all! Please send me full details as to where you will be spending the winter, in what expectations or under what conditions.

32 (VII.16)

Scr. Romae ex. m. Nov. an. 54

M. CICERO S. D. TREBATIO

1   In 'Equo Troiano' scis esse in extremo 'sero sapiunt.' tu
tamen, mi vetule, non sero. primas illas rabiosulas sat fa-
tuas dedisti. deinde quod in Britannia non nimis[1] ψιλο-
θέωρον te praebuisti, plane non reprehendo. nunc vero in
hibernis [in]tectus[2] mihi videris; itaque te commovere
non curas. 'usquequaque sapere oportet; id erit telum
acerrimum.'

2   Ego, si foris cenitarem, Cn. Octavio, familiari tuo, non
defuissem. cui tamen dixi, cum me aliquotiens invitaret,
'oro te, quis tu es?' sed mehercules, extra iocum, homo
bellus est; vellem eum tecum abduxisses.

3   Quid agatis et ecquid in Italiam venturi sitis hac hieme,
fac plane sciam. Balbus mihi confirmavit te divitem futurum. id utrum Romano more locutus sit, bene nummatum
te futurum, an quo modo Stoici dicunt omnis esse divites
qui caelo et terra frui possint, postea videro. qui istinc
veniunt superbiam tuam accusant quod negent te percon-
tantibus respondere. sed tamen est quod gaudeas; constat
enim inter omnis neminem te uno Samarobrivae iuris
peritiorem esse.

> 1 minus *(Rut.)*
> 2 iniectus *(SB*: bene t- *coni. idem)*

---

1 Cf. Letter 24, n. 8.
2 From an unknown play.

32 (VII.16)
CICERO TO TREBATIUS

Rome, late November 54

From M. Cicero to Trebatius greetings.

You remember the words at the end of the *Trojan Horse:*[1] 'Their wisdom comes too late.' But yours, you old fox, does not come too late. First you sent those snappish letters, which were silly enough. Then you showed yourself none too keen a sightseer in the matter of Britain, for which I frankly don't blame you. Now you seem to be snug in winter quarters, and so you have no mind to stir. '*Wisdom* everywhere befitteth; that shall be thy sharpest arm.'[2]

If I were by way of dining out, I should not have disappointed your friend Cn. Octavius; though I did say to him after several invitations 'Do please tell me, who *are* you?' But really, in all seriousness, he is a pretty fellow. A pity you did not take him with you!

Let me know plainly what all of you are about and whether you will be coming to Italy this winter. Balbus has assured me that you are going to be a rich man. Whether he uses the word in plain Roman style, meaning that you will have plenty of cash, or after the manner of the Stoics when they say that all are rich who can enjoy the sky and the earth, remains to be seen. Travellers from Gaul complain of your arrogance—they say you don't *respond*[3] to enquiries. Still you have one satisfaction; everybody agrees that there is no greater legal pundit than yourself in all Samarobriva.[4]

---

[3] Cf. Letter 21, n. 3.

[4] Caesar's winter headquarters, modern Amiens.

Scr. Romae m. Dec. an. 54

M. CICERO S. D. TREBATIO

1   Legi tuas litteras, ex quibus intellexi te Caesari nostro
valde iure consultum videri. est quod gaudeas te in ista
loca venisse, ubi aliquid sapere viderere. quod si in Britanniam quoque profectus esses, profecto nemo in illa tanta
insula peritior te fuisset. verum tamen (rideamus licet;
sum enim a te invitatus) subinvideo tibi ultro etiam accer-
situm ab eo ad quem ceteri, non propter superbiam eius
sed propter occupationem, adspirare non possunt.

2   Sed tu in ista epistula nihil mihi scripsisti de tuis rebus,
quae mehercule mihi non minori curae sunt quam meae.
valde metuo ne frigeas in hibernis. quam ob rem camino
luculento utendum censeo (idem Mucio et Manilio placebat), praesertim qui sagis non abundares. quamquam vos
nunc istic satis calere audio, quo quidem nuntio valde
mehercule de te timueram. sed tu in re militari multo es
cautior quam in advocationibus, qui neque in Oceano na-

---

1 With innuendo. *Frigere*, to be cold, often means have nothing to do or be coldly received ('a frost').

2 Famous lawyers of the past bore these names, M'. Manilius
(Consul in 149) and (along with other members of his family) Q.
Mucius Scaevola the Pontifex. Trebatius of course would catch the
echo. But primarily Cicero must be referring to contemporaries
(cf. Letter 31.3 'Q. Cornelius concurs'). Manilius is obviously the
lawyer mentioned in Letter 29.2. For a contemporary Mucius
Scaevola see Index. If he was, as may be presumed, a friend of
Trebatius, Cicero might bring him in for the sake of the legal associations of his name even though he was not himself a jurist.

33 (VII.10)
CICERO TO TREBATIUS

Rome, December 54

From M. Cicero to Trebatius greetings.

I have read your letter, from which I understand that our friend Caesar is much impressed with you as a jurist. You may congratulate yourself on having got to your present part of the world, where you can pass for a man of some *wisdom*! Had you gone to Britain as well, I daresay there would have been no greater expert than you in the whole vast island. But really (you won't mind my jokes—after all, you challenged me), I am half inclined to be jealous of you, actually sent for by a personage whom affairs, not arrogance, make inaccessible to the rest of mankind.

But you say nothing in your letter about *your* activities, which I assure you interest me no less than my own. I am terribly afraid you may have a chilly time of it[1] in winter quarters. So I advise you to install a good stove. Mucius and Manilius[2] concur. After all, you are not too well supplied with army greatcoats![3] To be sure, I hear that things are warm enough for you all out there just now,[4] and truly that intelligence made me very nervous about you. However, you are a much safer campaigner than counsel. Keen swimmer[5] as you are, you had no mind for a dip in the

---

[3] *Saga.* Cicero pretends to assume that the unsoldierly Trebatius would be short of them.

[4] The tribe of the Eburones in northeast Gaul rose against the Romans and destroyed two legions in the winter of 54–53.

[5] Horace in his *Satires* (2.1.8) alludes to Trebatius' partiality for swimming, as well as for wine.

203

tare volueris studiosissimus homo natandi neque spectare essedarios, quem antea ne andabata quidem defraudare poteramus. sed iam satis iocati sumus.

3   Ego de te ad Caesarem quam diligenter scripserim, tute scis; quam saepe, ego. sed mehercule iam intermiseram, ne viderer liberalissimi hominis meique amantissimi voluntati erga me diffidere. sed tamen iis litteris quas proxime dedi putavi esse hominem commonendum. id feci. quid profecerim, facias me velim certiorem et simul de toto statu tuo consiliisque omnibus. scire enim cupio quid agas, quid exspectes, quam longum istum tuum discessum a nobis futurum putes. sic enim tibi persuadeas

4   velim, unum mihi esse solacium qua re facilius possim[1] pati te esse sine nobis si tibi esse id emolumento sciam. sin autem id non est, nihil duobus nobis est stultius, me qui te non Romam attraham, te qui non huc advoles. una mehercule nostra vel severa vel iocosa congressio pluris erit quam non modo hostes sed etiam fratres nostri Haedui. qua re omnibus de rebus fac ut quam primum sciam.

aut consolando aut consilio aut re iuvero.

---

[1] possem (*Man.*)

ocean and you didn't care to watch those charioteers,[6] though in the old days we could never do you out of a blindfold gladiator. But enough of badinage.

How pressingly I have written to Caesar on your behalf, you know; how often, I know. But to tell the truth, I had temporarily given it up, because in dealing with so generous a man and so warm a friend of mine I did not want to risk appearing to lack confidence in his good will. All the same, in my last letter I thought it time for a reminder, and wrote accordingly. Please let me know the result, and inform me at the same time of your whole situation and all your plans. I am anxious to learn of your present doings and future prospects. How long do you think this absence of yours will continue? For I do assure you that the only thing that consoles me and makes our separation easier to bear is the knowledge (if it be so) that you are the gainer thereby. If that is *not* the case, we are arrant fools, both of us—I for not hauling you back to Rome, you for not hastening hither. I'll be bound that a single meeting of ours, serious or jocose, will be worth more than all our Aeduan brethren,[7] to say nothing of the enemy. So please inform me on all points as soon as possible.

By comfort or by counsel or by act I'll help.[8]

6 See Letter 27, n. 4.
7 As the first Gaulish tribe to form an alliance with Rome the Aedui had been addressed by the Senate as 'brothers and kinsmen' (Caesar, *Gallic War* 1.33.2; cf. *Letters to Atticus* 19 (I.19).2).
8 From Terence's *Self-Tormentor* (86).

34 (VII.11)

Scr. fort. in Tusculano m. Ian., ut vid., an. 53

CICERO TREBATIO

1   Nisi ante Roma profectus esses, nunc eam certe relinqueres. quis enim tot interregnis iureconsultum desiderat? ego omnibus unde petitur hoc consili dederim, ut a singulis interregibus binas advocationes postulent. satisne tibi videor abs te ius civile didicisse?

2   Sed heus tu! quid agis? ecquid fit? video enim te iam iocari per litteras. haec signa meliora sunt quam in meo Tusculano. sed quid sit, scire cupio. consuli quidem te a Caesare scribis, sed ego tibi ab illo consuli mallem. quod si aut fit aut futurum putas, perfer istam militiam et permane; ego enim desiderium tui spe tuorum commodorum consolabor. sin autem ista sunt inaniora, recipe te ad nos. nam aut erit hic aliquid aliquando aut, si minus, una mehercule collocutio nostra pluris erit quam omnes Samarobrivae. denique, si cito te rettuleris, sermo nullus erit; si diutius frustra afueris, non modo Laberium sed etiam sodalem nostrum Valerium pertimesco. mira enim persona

3   induci potest Britannici iure consulti. haec ego non rideo, quamvis tu rideas, sed de re severissima tecum, ut soleo,

---

1 See Glossary. The year 53 opened with no curule magistrates, disorders in Rome having made it impossible to elect them. Consuls were finally elected in July.

2 This would mean that the hearing would be postponed until a new Interrex came into office, and the process could be repeated indefinitely.

3 A play on two senses of *signum:* sign and statue.

34 (VII.11)
CICERO TO TREBATIUS

Tusculum (?), January 53 (?)

From Cicero to Trebatius.

If you had not already left Rome, you would surely be leaving now. Who wants a lawyer with all these *interregna*?[1] The advice I should give to all defendants in civil suits is to ask every Interrex for two adjournments.[2] Aren't you proud of your pupil in Civil Law?

But look here, what are you up to? Is anything happening? I notice that you now crack jokes in your letters. That looks good, better than the statues[3] in my place at Tusculum! But I want to know what it means. You say that Caesar is consulting you. I had rather he consulted your interests! If that is happening, or you think it is going to happen, put up with your soldiering and stay right on. While missing you, I shall comfort myself with the hope of your advancement. But if all that is in the nature of moonshine, then rejoin us. Something will turn up here one of these days, and even if it doesn't, I'll be bound that a single conversation of ours will be worth more than all the Samarobrivas in Gaul. Furthermore, if you come back soon, there won't be any talk; whereas if you are away for a long while to no purpose, I am afraid of Laberius, even of our friend Valerius.[4] A Britannic counsellor would make a marvellous figure of fun! I am not laughing at all this, though maybe you are, but cracking jokes with you in my

---

[4] See Index. Not impossibly this Valerius is to be identified with an author of mimes called Catullus, mentioned by Martial and others.

iocor. remoto ioco, tibi hoc amicissimo animo praeci⟨pi⟩o,
ut, si istic mea commendatione tuam dignitatem obtinebis,
perferas nostri desiderium, honestatem et facultates tuas
augeas; sin autem ista frigebunt, recipias te ad nos. omnia
tamen quae vis et tua virtute profecto et nostro summo
erga te studio consequere.

35 (VII.12)

Scr. Romae m. Febr. an. 53

CICERO TREBATIO

1   Mirabar quid esset quod tu mihi litteras mittere inter-
misisses: indicavit mihi Pansa meus Epicureum te esse factum. o castra praeclara! quid tu fecisses si te Tarentum et
non Samarobrivam misissem? iam tum mihi non placebas

2   cum idem [in]tuebare¹ quod †zeius†,² familiaris meus. sed
quonam modo ius civile defendes cum omnia tua causa
facias, non civium? ubi porro illa erit formula fiduciae, 'ut
inter bonos bene agier oportet'? quis enim ⟨bonus⟩³ est
qui facit nihil nisi sua causa? quod ius statues communi
dividundo cum commune nihil possit esse apud eos qui

---

¹ *(Lamb.)*   ² Seius *Vict.*: Velleius *Préchac*: Saufeius *coni.*
SB   ³ *(Wes.*: est b- *iam Man.)*

---

¹ A notorious centre of luxury and pleasure.

² C. Velleius is the Epicurean spokesman in Cicero's dialogue
On the Nature of the Gods, but the reading is doubtful. There is
probably an allusion to some litigation in which Trebatius had
been involved as legal adviser.   ³ In this passage Cicero face-

usual style about an extremely serious matter. Joking aside,
my advice to you as a most sincere well-wisher is this: if as
a result of my recommendation you are likely to receive
in Gaul the recognition that is your due, then bear your
homesickness and advance your standing and means; but if
the outlook there is bleak, come back to us. You will doubtless achieve all your aims even so by your own energies and
my wholehearted zeal for your welfare.

35 (VII.12)
CICERO TO TREBATIUS

Rome, February 53

From Cicero to Trebatius.

I was wondering why you had stopped sending me letters. Now my friend Pansa intimates that you have turned
Epicurean. A remarkable camp yours must be! What
would you have done if I had sent you to Tarentum[1] instead
of Samarobriva? I was uneasy about you even in the days
when you were maintaining the same position as my crony
Velleius (?).[2] But how are you going to be a champion of
Civil Law if everything you do is done for your own sweet
sake and not for the community?[3] And what becomes of
the trust formula 'in accordance with honest practice
proper between honest men'? Who is honest that does
nothing except for his own interest? What rule will you lay
down for division of goods held jointly, seeing that nothing
can be joint among people whose only yardstick is their

tiously sets out to prove that Epicurean dogmas are incompatible
with the vocabulary of Roman civil law.

omnia voluptate sua metiuntur? quo modo autem tibi pla-
cebit Iovem lapidem iurare cum scias Iovem iratum esse
nemini posse? quid fiet porro populo Ulubrano si tu statueris πολιτεύεσθαι non oportere?

Qua re si plane a nobis deficis, moleste fero; sin Pansae
adsentari commodum est, ignosco. modo scribe aliquando
ad nos quid agas et a nobis quid fieri aut curari velis.

36 (VII.13)

Scr. Romae IV *Non. Mart. an. 53*

M. CICERO S. D. TREBATIO

1   Adeone me iniustum esse existimasti ut tibi irascerer
quod parum mihi constans et nimium cupidus decedendi
viderere ob eamque causam me arbitrabare[1] litteras ad te
iam diu non misisse? mihi perturbatio animi tui quam primis litteris perspiciebam molestiam, ‹non iram›,[2] attulit;
neque alia ulla fuit causa intermissionis epistularum nisi
quod ubi esses plane nesciebam. hic tu me etiam insimulas
nec satisfactionem meam accipis? audi, Testa mi: utrum
superbiorem te pecunia facit an quod te imperator consu-
lit? moriar ni, quae tua gloria est, puto te malle a Caesare

---

[1] arbitrarere (*SB*: -trare *Madvig*)   [2] (*SB*)

---

[4] The man swearing this most solemn of Roman oaths flung a
stone, praying that if guilty of deliberate perjury he should be cast
out like the stone.

[5] A small place near the Pontine Marshes (see Letter 37.3).
Trebatius had become its patron, no doubt by legal services.

own pleasure? How will you think it proper to swear by Jupiter Stone,[4] when you know that Jupiter can't get angry with anybody? And what is to become of the good folk of Ulubrae,[5] if you decide that it is wrong to take part in public affairs?[6]

Well, if you are really forsaking us, I'm put out. But if it suits your book to humour Pansa, you have my forgiveness. Only write me at long last, and tell me what you are doing and what you want me to do or see to on your behalf.

36 (VII.13)
CICERO TO TREBATIUS

Rome, 4 March 53

From M. Cicero to Trebatius greetings.

Did you really suppose me so unreasonable as to be angry with you because I thought you lacking in perseverance and too eager to leave Gaul? And did you imagine that this was the reason why I have not sent you a letter for some considerable time? The agitation visible in your first letters caused me distress, not annoyance; and there was no reason whatsoever for the intermission of mine other than my complete ignorance of your whereabouts. And now do you still persist in making false charges against me and refuse to accept my explanation? Hark ye, my good Testa: is it money that is swelling your head or the fact that you are consulted by the Commander-in-Chief? Upon my soul, you are such a coxcomb that I believe you would rather be consulted by Caesar than covered in gold! But if

---

[6] As held by Epicurus.

consuli quam inaurari! si vero utrumque est, quis te feret
praeter me, qui omnia <tua>[3] ferre possum?

2   Sed ut ad rem redeam, te istic invitum non esse vehementer gaudeo et, ut illud erat molestum, sic hoc est
iucundum. tantum metuo ne artificium tuum tibi parum
prosit. nam, ut audio, istic

> non ex iure manum consertum, sed magis ferro
>   rem repetunt.

et tu soles ad vim faciundam adhiberi. neque est quod
illam exceptionem in interdicto pertimescas, 'quod[4] tu
prior vi hominibus armatis non veneris'; scio enim te non
esse procacem in lacessendo. sed ut ego quoque te aliquid
admoneam de vestris cautionibus, Treviros vites censeo.
audio capitalis esse; mallem aere argento auro[5] essent. sed
alias iocabimur. tu ad me de istis rebus omnibus scribas
velim quam diligentissime.

D. IIII Non. Mart.

[3] (coni. SB: a te Pluygers)*
[4] quo Beier
[5] auro (a)ere argento (sc. ex a. a. a.) (Mend.)

---

[1] From Ennius' Annals (Vahlen[2], 272).
[2] The joke, implying that Trebatius was not a man to risk his
skin if he could help it, is based on procedural technicalities
arising under Roman law of property. For details see my Commentary.

it's both together, I wonder who is going to put up with you except myself, who can put up with anything from you.

But to come back to the point, I am heartily glad that you are tolerably content to be out there. That gives me as much pleasure as the other gave me distress. My only apprehension is that your professional skill may stand you in poor stead, for out there, as I hear,

> No claim in form of laws lay they; with steel
> Their due they seek.[1]

You yourself are used to being called in for 'a using of force.' But you don't have to worry about that limiting clause in the injunction, 'provided you have not been the first to enter by armed force'—I know you are no ruffling blade to start a quarrel![2] However, to give you a caveat from your own legal arsenal, I advise you to keep clear of the Treviri—I hear they are *capital* customers, like their Roman namesakes. If you want a Board of Three, better try the Masters of the Mint![3] But we'll have our joke some other time. Please write to me in full detail about everything over there.

Dispatched 4 March.

[3] Another complex joke with a pun on Treviri, a Gaulish tribe, and *tres viri* (probably pronounced identically), Board of Three. Two Roman Boards of Three are involved, *tres viri capitales,* who were police functionaries (but in general usage *capitalis* means dangerous, deadly), and *tres viri monetales,* in charge of the Roman mint.

37 (VII.18)

Scr. in Pomptino VI *Id. Apr. an. 53*

CICERO TREBATIO S.

1   Accepi a te aliquot epistulas uno tempore, quas tu diversis temporibus dederas. in quibus me cetera delectarunt; significabant enim te istam militiam iam firmo animo ferre et esse fortem virum et constantem. quae ego paulisper in te ita desideravi ⟨ut⟩[1] non imbecillitate animi tui sed magis ut desiderio nostri te aestuare putarem. qua re perge ut coepisti; forti animo istam tolera militiam. multa, mihi crede, adsequere; ego enim renovabo commendationem, sed tempore. sic habeto, non tibi maiori esse curae ut iste tuus a me discessus quam[2] fructuosissimus tibi sit quam mihi. itaque, quoniam vestrae cautiones infirmae sunt, Graeculam tibi misi cautionem chirographi mei. tu me velim de ratione Gallici belli certiorem facias; ego enim ignavissimo cuique maximam fidem habeo.

2   Sed ut ad epistulas tuas redeam, cetera belle; illud miror: quis solet eodem exemplo pluris dare qui sua manu scribit? nam quod in palimpsesto, laudo equidem parsimo-

---

[1] *(Benedict)*
[2] tam *(Vict.)*

---

[1] What this was is doubtful. Some think a letter of advice on how to behave to Caesar, written in Greek for greater security. Rather perhaps an epigram or other literary *jeu d'esprit*.

[2] Important letters were sometimes dispatched in two or more copies by separate messengers to ensure delivery. The sender would naturally use an amanuensis for such copies, though other-

37 (VII.18)
CICERO TO TREBATIUS

The Pomptine Marshes, 8 April 53

From Cicero to Trebatius greetings.

I have received several letters from you in a batch, dispatched at different times. In every respect but one they made pleasant reading. They show that you are now bearing your army life with a stout heart, and that you are a man of fortitude and resolution. For a little while I missed these qualities in you, not however putting down your restlessness to weakness of spirit but to your pain at being parted from us. So carry on as you have begun. Tolerate your service with a stout heart. Depend upon it, you will be well rewarded. I shall follow up my recommendation, but at the right time. Rest assured that I am as anxious as yourself for you to derive the maximum of advantage from this separation of ours. And since the caveats you legal gentlemen enter are none too dependable, I am sending you a little caveat in Greek under my own hand.[1] On your side, please give me an account of the war in Gaul—the less adventurous my informant, the more I trust the information.

However, to get back to your letters: all very nice, except for one feature, which surprises me. Is it not unusual to send several identical letters in one's own handwriting?[2] As for the palimpsest, I applaud your thrift. But I won-

wise it was considered polite to write in one's own hand. Cicero jestingly implies that Trebatius' letters were so similar to one another as to be virtually copies. The quaint notion that Roman etiquette required letters sent as aforesaid *not* to be verbally identical is baseless.

niam, sed miror quid in illa chartula fuerit quod delere
malueris quam haec ‹non›[3] scribere, nisi forte tuas formu-
las; non enim puto te meas epistulas delere ut reponas
tuas. an hoc significas, nihil fieri, frigere te, ne chartam
quidem tibi suppeditare? iam ista tua culpa est qui vere-
cundiam tecum extuleris et non hic nobiscum reliqueris.

3   Ego te Balbo, cum ad vos proficiscetur, more Romano
commendabo. tu, si intervallum longius erit mearum litterarum, ne sis admiratus; eram enim afuturus mense Aprili.
has litteras scripsi in Pomptino, cum ad villam M. Aemili[4]
Philemonis devertissem, ex qua iam audieram fremitum
clientium meorum, quos quidem tu mihi conciliasti. nam
Ulubris honoris mei causa vim maximam ranunculorum se
commosse constabat.

Cura ut valeas.

vi Id. Apr. de Pomptino.

4   Epistulam tuam, quam accepi ab L. Arruntio, conscidi
innocentem; nihil enim habebat quod non vel in contione
recte legi posset. sed et Arruntius ita te mandasse aiebat et
tu adscripseras. verum illud esto. nihil te ad me postea
scripsisse demiror, praesertim tam novis rebus.

---

[3] *(Rut.)*
[4] villametrilii *(Man.)*

---

[3] With the usual implication that Trebatius did not know his
legal business. Forms of procedure *(formulae)* drawn up by him
would be expendable.

der what could have been on that scrap of paper which you thought proper to erase rather than not write these screeds. Your forms of procedure perhaps?[3] I scarcely suppose that you rub out my letters in order to substitute your own. Or do you mean to imply that nothing is happening, that you are neglected, without even a supply of paper? Well, that is your own fault for taking your modesty away with you instead of leaving it behind with us.

When Balbus sets out to join you, I shall commend you to him in plain Roman style. If you get no further letter from me for some time, don't be astonished. I am going to be away through April. I am writing this in the Pomptine country, having turned in for the night at M. Aemilius Philemo's[4] house, from which I have already heard the hubbub created by my clients, those, that is, whom you have procured for me—it is common knowledge that a vast crowd of frogs in Ulubrae[5] have bestirred themselves to pay me their respects.

Take care of your health.

8 April, Pomptine Marshes.

P.S. I have torn up a letter of yours received from L. Arruntius—which did not deserve it, for it contained nothing that could not properly have been read out at a public meeting. However, Arruntius said that you had so requested, and you had added a note to the same effect. Well, no matter. I am much surprised that you have not written since then, especially in view of the startling developments.[6]

[4] A freedman of Lepidus', the future Triumvir.
[5] See Letter 35, n. 5.
[6] In Gaul (revolts in north and northeast).

Scr. Romae m. Mai. vel Iun., ut vid., an. 53

CICERO TREBATIO

1   Chrysippus Vettius, Cyri architecti libertus, fecit ut te
non immemorem putarem mei; salutem enim verbis tuis
mihi nuntiarat. valde iam lautus es qui gravere litteras ad
me dare, homini praesertim prope domestico. quod si scribere oblitus es, minus multi iam te advocato causa cadent;
si nostri oblitus es, dabo operam ut istuc veniam ante quam
plane ex animo tuo effluo. sin aestivorum timor te debilitat, aliquid excogita, ut fecisti de Britannia.

2   Illud quidem perlibenter audivi ex eodem Chrysippo,
te esse Caesari familiarem. sed mehercule mallem, id
quod erat aequius, de tuis rebus ex tuis litteris quam saepissime cognoscerem. quod certe ita fieret si tu maluisses
benevolentiae quam litium iura perdiscere.

Sed haec iocati sumus et tuo more et non nihil etiam
nostro. te valde amamus nosque a te amari cum volumus
tum etiam confidimus.

38 (VII.14)
CICERO TO TREBATIUS

Rome, May or June (?) 53

Cicero to Trebatius.

Chrysippus Vettius, Cyrus the architect's freedman, has made me think that you have some recollection of my existence; he has given me your kind regards. Very grand we have become! Was it too much trouble to give him a letter for me, and him practically one of my own household? If, however, you have forgotten how to put pen to paper, you will have fewer clients in future to lose their cases! If I have slipped your mind, I'll make shift to come to Gaul myself before I fade out of it completely. But if it is apprehension of the summer campaign that is sapping your energies, you must think up an excuse, as you did in the matter of Britain.

One thing I was greatly pleased to hear from the same Chrysippus, that you are on close terms with Caesar. But I must say, I would rather have learned how you are getting on from your own letters as often as possible; it would have been more fitting. No doubt that is the way it would be if you had cared to study the rules of friendship as thoroughly as those of court procedure.

But all this is badinage in your own style—and a little in mine too. I am very fond of you, and not only want you to be fond of me but am confident that you are.

39 (VII.15)

Scr. Romae m. Iun., ut vid., an. 53

CICERO TREBATIO

1   'Quam sint morosi qui amant' vel ex hoc intellegi potest: moleste ferebam antea te invitum istic esse; pungit
me rursus quod scribis esse te istic libenter. neque enim
mea commendatione te non delectari facile patiebar et
nunc angor quicquam tibi sine me esse iucundum. sed hoc
tamen malo ferre nos desiderium quam te non ea quae
spero consequi.

2   Cum vero in C. Mati, suavissimi doctissimique hominis, familiaritatem venisti, non dici potest quam valde gaudeam. qui fac ut te quam maxime diligat. mihi crede, nihil
ex ista provincia potes quod iucundius sit deportare.

Cura ut valeas.

40 (XVI.13)

Scr. in Cumano IV Id. Apr. an. 53

TULLIUS TIRONI S.

Omnia a te data mihi putabo si te valentem videro.
summa cura exspectabam adventum [men]Andri<ci>,[1]

---

[1] menandri *(Man.)*

39 (VII.15)
CICERO TO TREBATIUS

Rome, June (?) 53

From Cicero to Trebatius.

'Lovers are contrary folk.'[1] How true that is may be seen from the fact that I used to be distressed because you were unhappy in Gaul, whereas now I feel a prick when you write that you are well-content with life there. I used to be vexed that you were not pleased with the result of my recommendation, and now it hurts me to find that you can enjoy anything without me. However, I prefer that we put up with your absence than that you miss the advantages which I hope for on your account.

I cannot tell you how pleased I am to hear that you have struck up a friendship with C. Matius. He is a very charming, cultivated person. Make him as fond of you as possible. Take my word for it, nothing you can bring back from this province of yours will give you more pleasure.

Take care of your health.

40 (XVI.13)
CICERO TO TIRO

Cumae, 10 April 53

From Tullius to Tiro greetings.

I shall feel you have given me all I could ask, once I see you fit and well. I am waiting in great anxiety for Andricus,

---

[1] Probably from a comedy.

quem ad te miseram. cura, si me diligis, ut valeas et, cum te bene confirmaris, ad nos venias.

Vale.

IIII Id. Apr.

41 (XVI.14)

Scr. in Cumano III Id. Apr. an. 53

TULLIUS TIRONI S.

1 Andricus postridie ad me venit quam exspectaram; itaque habui noctem plenam timoris ac miseriae. tuis litteris nihilo sum factus certior quo modo te haberes, sed tamen sum recreatus. ego omni delectatione litterisque omnibus careo, quas ante quam te videro attingere non possum.

Medico mercedis quantum poscet promitti iubeto. id 2 scripsi ad Ummium. audio te animo angi et medicum dicere ex eo te laborare. si me diligis, excita ex somno tuas litteras humanitatemque, propter quam mihi es carissimus. nunc opus est te animo valere ut corpore possis. id cum tua tum mea causa facias a te peto. Acastum retine, quo commodius tibi ministretur. conserva te mihi. dies promissorum adest, quem[1] etiam repraesentabo si adveneris.

Etiam atque etiam vale.

III Id. h. VI.

[1] quae *Man.*

whom I sent to you, to arrive. If you care for me, see that you get well and join us when you are thoroughly strong again.

Good-bye.

10 April.

41 (XVI.14)
CICERO TO TIRO

Cumae, 11 April 53

From Tullius to Tiro greetings.

Andricus arrived a day later than I expected him, so I had a miserable, apprehensive night. I am none the wiser from your letters as to how you are, but still it made me feel better. I have nothing to amuse me, no literary work—I cannot touch it before I see you.

Give orders for the doctor to be promised whatever fee he asks. I have written to Ummius to that effect. I hear you are in distress of mind, and that the doctor says your sickness is due to this. If you care for me, rouse your dormant love of literary work and the things of the spirit, which makes you very dear to me. Now you need health of mind to recover health of body, and I ask you to gain it for my sake as well as your own. Keep Acastus, so that you are better looked after. Preserve yourself for me. My promise[1] is almost due now. If you come, I will even settle up right away.

Again, good-bye.

11, noon.

[1] To give Tiro his freedom.

42 (XVI.15)

Scr. in Cumano prid. Id. Apr. an. 53

TULLIUS TIRONI S.

1   Aegypta ad me venit prid. Id. Apr. is, etsi mihi nuntiavit
te plane febri carere et belle habere, tamen, quod negavit
te potuisse ad me scribere, curam mi attulit, et eo magis
quod Hermia, quem eodem die venire oportuerat, non ve-
nerat. incredibili sum sollicitudine de tua valetudine; qua
si me liberaris, ego te omni cura liberabo. plura scriberem
si iam putarem libenter te legere posse. ingenium tuum,
quod ego maximi facio, confer ad te mihi tibique conservandum. cura te etiam atque etiam diligenter.
        Vale.

2   Scripta iam epistula Hermia venit. accepi tuam epistulam, vacillantibus litterulis, nec mirum tam gravi morbo.
ego ad te Aegyptam misi, quod nec inhumanus est et te visus est mihi diligere, ut is tecum esset, et cum eo cocum
quo uterere.
        Vale.

43 (XVI.10)

Scr. in Cumano XIV Kal. Mai. an. 53

TULLIUS TIRONI S.

1   Ego vero cupio te ad me venire, sed viam timeo. gravissime aegrotasti, inedia et purgationibus et vi ipsius morbi

42 (XVI.15)
CICERO TO TIRO

Cumae, 12 April 53

From Tullius to Tiro greetings.

Aegypta arrived today, 12 April. He told me that you are quite free of fever and in pretty good shape, but said you had not been able to write to me. That made me anxious, all the more so because Hermia, who ought also to have arrived today, has not come. You cannot imagine how anxious I feel about your health. If you relieve my mind on this score, I shall relieve yours of every worry. I should write more if I thought you could read with any pleasure at the present time. Put your clever brain, which I value so highly, to the job of preserving yourself for us both. Look after yourself carefully, I repeat.

Good-bye.

P.S. Hermia has arrived and I have received your letter, shakily written, poor fellow—no wonder, when you are so seriously ill. I have sent you Aegypta to be with you. He is not uncivilized and I think he is fond of you. Also a cook for your use.

Good-bye.

43 (XVI.10)
CICERO TO TIRO

Cumae, 17 April 53

From Tullius to Tiro greetings.

Indeed I want you to join me, but I am afraid of the journey. You have been very seriously ill, you are worn out,

consumptus es. graves solent offensiones esse ex gravibus morbis si quae culpa commissa est. iam ad id biduum quod fueris in via, dum in Cumanum venis, accedent continuo ad reditum dies quinque. ego in Formiano a. d. III Kal. esse volo. ibi te ut firmum offendam, mi Tiro, effice.

2   Litterulae meae sive nostrae tui desiderio oblangue-runt; hac tamen epistula quam Acastus attulit oculos pau-lum sustulerunt. Pomponius[1] erat apud me cum haec scribebam, hilare et libenter. ei cupienti audire nostra dixi sine te omnia mea muta esse. tu Musis nostris para ut operas reddas. nostra ad diem dicta⟨m⟩ fient; docui enim te fides ἔτυμον quod haberet. fac plane ut valeas. nos adsumus.

Vale.

XIIII Kal.

44 (XVI.16)

Scr. in Gallia Transalpina ex. m. Mai. vel in. m. Iun. an. 53
QUINTUS MARCO FRATRI S.

1   De Tirone, mi Marce, ita te meumque Ciceronem et meam[1] Tulliolam tuumque filium videam ut mihi gratissi-

---

1 Pompeius *(Rut.)**
1 tuam *Wes.*

---

1 I. e. Atticus, substituted by an old conjecture for traditional 'Pompeius.' Pompey seems miscast as a casual visitor with an interest in Cicero's literary work. For the error see my *Onamasticon to Cicero's Speeches* under Pomponius.

what with lack of food and purges and the disease itself. Serious illnesses often have serious repercussions, if there is any imprudence. And then, right on top of the two days you will have on the road travelling to Cumae, there will be five days for the return journey. I want to be at Formiae on the 28th. Let me find you there, my dear Tiro, well and strong.

My (or our) literary brain children have been drooping their heads missing you, but they looked up a little at the letter which Acastus brought. Pomponius[1] is staying with me as I write, enjoying himself in cheerful mood. He wanted to hear my compositions, but I told him that in your absence my tongue of authorship is tied completely. You must get ready to restore your services to my Muses. My promise will be performed on the appointed day (I have taught you the derivation of 'faith').[2] Now mind you get thoroughly well. I shall be with you soon.

Good-bye.

17th.

44 (XVI.16)

Q. CICERO TO M. CICERO

Transalpine Gaul, May (end) or June (beginning) 53

From Quintus to his brother Marcus greetings.

My dear Marcus, as I hope to see you again and my boy and my[1] Tulliola and your son, I am truly delighted with what you have done about Tiro, in judging his former con-

---

[2] *Fides*, supposed to be derived from *fit* ('is done').
[1] Perhaps a scribal mistake for 'your.'

mum fecisti cum eum indignum illa fortuna ac nobis amicum quam servum esse maluisti. mihi crede, tuis et illius
litteris perlectis exsilui gaudio, et tibi et ago gratias et
2 gratulor. si enim mihi Stati fidelitas est tantae voluptati,
quanti esse in isto haec eadem bona debent additis litteris
et sermonibus humanitateque, quae sunt his ipsis commodis potiora! amo te omnibus equidem de maximis causis
verum etiam propter hanc, vel quod mihi sic ut debuisti
nuntiasti. te totum in litteris vidi.

Sabini pueris et promisi omnia et faciam.

45 (II.1)

Scr. Romae parte priore an. 53, ut vid.

M. CICERO S. D. CURIONI

1 Quamquam me nomine neglegentiae suspectum tibi
esse doleo, tamen non tam mihi molestum fuit accusari abs
te officium meum quam iucundum requiri, praesertim
cum, in quo accusabar, culpa vacarem, in quo autem desi-
derare te significabas meas litteras, prae te ferres perspectum mihi quidem sed tamen dulcem et optatum amorem
tuum. equidem neminem praetermisi, quem quidem ad te
perventurum putarem, cui litteras non dederim; etenim

---

2 Quintus will not have forgotten his brother's annoyance
when Statius was freed; cf. *Letters to Atticus* 38 (II.18).4, 39
(II.19).1.

3 Sabinus is very likely Titurius Sabinus, one of Caesar's
Legates who had lost his life and his army in the revolt of the

dition to be below his deserts and preferring us to have him
as a friend rather than a slave. Believe me, I jumped for joy
when I read your letter and his. Thank you, and congratulations! If Statius' loyalty gives me so much pleasure,[2] how
highly you must value the same qualities in Tiro, with the
addition of literary accomplishments and conversation and
culture, gifts worth even more than they! I have all manner
of great reasons to love you, but this is a reason—the very
fact that you so properly announced the event to me is a
reason. I saw all that is you in your letter.

I have promised Sabinus'[3] boys all assistance, and shall
be as good as my word.

45 (II.1)
CICERO TO CURIO[1]

Rome, 53 (first half)

From M. Cicero to Curio greetings.

I am sorry to be under suspicion of neglecting a friendly
duty, but I am not so much put out by your accusation as I
am pleased by your exigency—especially as I am innocent
of the offence alleged against me, whereas when you show
that you miss my letters, you demonstrate your affection
for me. I am well aware of it to be sure, but it is delightful
and gratifying to me none the less. Now *I* have let nobody
set out without a letter whom I thought likely to reach you.

Eburones. 'Boys' could mean either children or slaves, but the
former is more likely.

[1] In 53 the younger Curio was serving as Proquaestor under
the governor of the province of Asia, C. Claudius Pulcher.

quis est tam in scribendo impiger quam ego? a te vero bis terve summum et eas perbrevis accepi. qua re, si iniquus es in me iudex, condemnabo eodem ego te crimine; sin me id facere noles, te mihi aequum praebere debebis.

Sed de litteris hactenus; non enim vereor ne non scribendo te expleam, praesertim si in eo genere studium meum non aspernabere. ego te afuisse tam diu a nobis et dolui, quod carui fructu iucundissimae consuetudinis, et laetor, quod absens omnia cum maxima dignitate es consecutus quodque in omnibus tuis rebus meis optatis Fortuna respondit. breve est quod me tibi praecipere meus incredibilis in te amor cogit: tanta est exspectatio vel animi vel ingeni tui ut ego te obsecrare obtestarique non dubitem sic ad nos conformatus revertare ut, quam exspectationem tui concitasti, hanc sustinere ac tueri possis. et quoniam meam tuorum erga me meritorum memoriam nulla umquam delebit oblivio, te rogo ut memineris, quantaecumque tibi accessiones fient et fortunae et dignitatis, eas te non potuisse consequi ni meis puer olim fidelissimis atque amantissimis consiliis paruisses. qua re hoc animo in nos esse debebis ut aetas nostra iam ingravescens in amore atque in adulescentia tua conquiescat.

After all, I can challenge all comers as an active correspondent. From *you*, on the other hand, I have heard only two or three times at most, and very short letters at that. So if you are a hanging judge to me, I shall convict you on the same charge. Unless you want that to happen, you should take a lenient view of my case.

But there's enough about letters; I don't doubt I can give you your fill of them, especially if you are going to appreciate my efforts in that direction. I have been sorry that you have been so long away from us, because I have missed your most delectable company; but at the same time I am glad, because in your absence you have attained all your objectives with the greatest *éclat* and because in all your affairs Fortune has seconded my prayers. One short admonition, which my transcendent affection for you compels me to offer: your spirit and talents are so eagerly expected that I don't scruple to beg and adjure you to shape yourself, before you come back to us, into one capable of matching and living up to the expectation you have aroused. No forgetfulness will ever wipe out the memory of your services[2] to me, and so I ask you to remember, whatever further success and honour may come your way, that you would never have attained them, if in the days of your boyhood you had not listened to my sincere and affectionate advice. So your feelings towards me should be such that my now declining years may rest happily upon your affection and your youth.

[2] Rendered no doubt during Cicero's exile; cf. Letter 50.2.

46 (II.2)

Scr. Romae parte priore an. 53.

M. CICERO S. D. CURIONI

Gravi teste privatus sum amoris summi erga te mei
patre tuo, clarissimo viro; qui cum suis laudibus tum vero
te filio superasset omnium fortunam si ei contigisset ut te
ante videret quam a vita discederet. sed spero nostram
amicitiam non egere testibus. tibi patrimonium di fortu-
nent! me certe habebis cui et carus aeque sis et iucundus
ac fuisti patri.

47 (II.3)

Scr. Romae parte priore an. 53, ut vid.

M. CICERO S. D. C. CURIONI

1   Rupae studium non defuit declarandorum munerum
tuo nomine, sed nec mihi placuit nec cuiquam tuorum
quicquam te absente fieri quod[1] tibi, cum venisses, non
esset integrum. equidem ⟨quid⟩ sentiam aut scribam ad te
postea pluribus aut, ne ad ea meditere, imparatum te
offendam coramque contra istam rationem meam dicam,
ut aut te in meam sententiam adducam aut certe testatum

[1] quo *coni.* SB

---

[1] Curio the Elder, Consul in 76. Cicero's relations with him
had been chequered and never warmly friendly.

46 (II.2)
CICERO TO CURIO

Rome, 53 (first half)

From M. Cicero to C. Curio greetings.

I have lost a weighty witness to the great affection I bear you in your illustrious father;[1] with his own fine record and with you for a son, he would have been the most fortunate of men had it been granted him to see you before he passed away. However, I hope our friendship needs no testimony. May the Gods prosper you in your inheritance! In me you may be sure of having one to whom you are as dear and as delightful as you were to your father.

47 (II.3)
CICERO TO CURIO

Rome, 53 (first half)

From M. Cicero to C. Curio greetings.

Rupa[1] was ready and willing to announce a show in your name, but I and all your friends thought that no step should be taken in your absence by which you would be committed on your return. I shall write to you later at greater length to give my views, or else, since you might then think of arguments to counter them, I shall take you unprepared and advance my opinion against yours face to face. In that way, if I do not convert you, I shall at least leave my sentiments on record in your mind; so that if the

---

[1] An agent (not necessarily freedman) of Curio's. When an eminent man died his son(s) sometimes gave a show in his honour.

apud animum tuum relinquam quid senserim, ut, si quando, quod nolim, displicere tibi tuum consilium coeperit, possis meum recordari. brevi tamen sic habeto, in eum statum temporum tuum reditum incidere ut iis bonis quae tibi natura, studio, fortuna data sunt facilius omnia quae sunt amplissima in re publica consequi possis quam muneribus. quorum neque facultatem quisquam admiratur (est enim copiarum, non virtutis) neque quisquam est quin satietate iam defessus sit.

2   Sed aliter atque ostenderam facio qui ingrediar ad explicandam rationem sententiae meae; qua re omnem hanc disputationem in adventum tuum differo. summa ⟨te⟩[2] scito in exspectatione esse eaque a te exspectari quae a summa virtute summoque ingenio exspectanda sunt. ad quae si es, ut debes, paratus, quod ita esse confido, plurimis maximisque muneribus et nos amicos et civis tuos universos et rem publicam adficies. illud cognosces profecto, mihi te neque cariorem neque iucundiorem esse quemquam.

48 (II.4)

Scr. Romae parte priore an. 53

CICERO S. D. C. CURIONI

1   Epistularum genera multa esse non ignoras sed unum illud certissimum, cuius causa inventa res ipsa est, ut cer-

2 *(hic Crat., alii alibi)*

time comes (as I hope it never will) when you begin to repent your own counsel, you may remember mine. All the same, to put it in a few words, do realize that you are returning at a juncture in which your gifts of nature, application, and fortune will count for more in winning you the highest political prizes than will shows. Nobody admires the capacity to give shows, which is a matter of means, not personal qualities; and everybody is sick and tired of them.[2]

But I am doing what I said I was not going to do, starting to explain my reasons. So I defer the whole argument till your return. Be sure that the highest anticipations have been formed—all is expected of you that may be expected of the highest qualities and talents. If you are prepared to meet those hopes worthily, and I am confident you are, you will give us, your friends, and all your countrymen, and your country, the greatest of shows[3]—and many of them. One thing you will surely find, that no one is dearer or more delightful to me than yourself.

48 (II.4)
CICERO TO CURIO

Rome, 53 (first half)

From Cicero to C. Curio greetings.

That there are many different categories of letters you are aware. But the most authentic, the purpose in fact for

---

[2] Curio did not take this advice, but gave a show of memorable splendour.

[3] The Latin word for show also means gift (*munus*).

tiores faceremus absentis si quid esset quod eos scire aut nostra aut ipsorum interesset. huius generis litteras a me profecto non exspectas. tuarum enim rerum domesticos[1] habes et scriptores et nuntios, in meis autem rebus nihil est sane novi. reliqua sunt epistularum genera duo, quae me magno opere delectant, unum familiare et iocosum, alterum severum et grave. utro me minus deceat uti non intellego. iocerne tecum per litteras? civem mehercule non puto esse, qui temporibus his ridere possit. an gravius aliquid scribam? quid est quod possit graviter a Cicerone scribi ad Curionem nisi de re publica? atqui[2] in hoc genere haec mea causa est ut neque ea ⟨quae sentio audeam neque ea⟩[3] quae non sentio velim scribere.

2   Quam ob rem, quoniam mihi nullum scribendi argumentum relictum est, utar ea clausula qua soleo teque ad studium summae laudis cohortabor. est enim tibi gravis adversaria constituta et parata incredibilis quaedam exspectatio; quam tu una re facillime vinces, si hoc statueris, quarum laudum gloriam adamaris, quibus artibus eae laudes comparantur, in iis esse laborandum. in hanc sententiam scriberem plura, nisi te tua sponte satis incitatum esse confiderem. et hoc, quicquid attigi, non feci inflammandi tui causa sed testificandi amoris mei.

[1] domesticarum (*fragm. Feierianum, Ursinus*)
[2] atque (*Calderius*)
[3] *Madvig, similia priores*

which letter-writing was invented, is to inform the absent of what it is desirable for them to know, whether in our interest or their own. Letters of this kind I suppose you do not expect from me, since you have your domestic correspondents and messengers to tell you about your affairs, and there is nothing very new to report about mine. That leaves two categories which give me great pleasure; one familiar and jocular, the other serious and grave. Which would be the less fitting for me to use I don't know. How can I joke with you by letter in these times, when upon my word I don't think a Roman who can laugh deserves the name? As for something in more serious vein, what is there for Cicero to write seriously about to Curio except public affairs? But on that subject my predicament is that I dare not write what I think and do not care to write what I don't think.

Well then, having no topic left, I shall resort to my usual conclusion and urge you to strive for highest glory. You have a formidable adversary ready and waiting—public expectation, which is really amazingly high. This you will easily overcome, but in one way only, and that is by determining to work hard at those pursuits[1] which bring the kind of credit you have set your heart on. I should write more in this strain, if I were not sure that you are your own sufficient spur. Even this little I have said, not to kindle your enthusiasm, but to demonstrate my affection.

[1] Oratory seems to be meant.

49 (II.5)

Scr. Romae parte priore an. 53

CICERO S. D. C. CURIONI

1   Haec negotia quo modo se habeant, epistula ne ‹ad te›[1] quidem narrare audeo. tibi, etsi ubicumque es, ut scripsi ad te ante, in eadem es navi, tamen quod abes gratulor, vel quia non vides ea quae nos vel quod excelso et illustri loco sita est laus tua in plurimorum et sociorum et civium conspectu; quae ad nos nec obscuro nec vario sermone sed et clarissima et una omnium voce perfertur.

2   Unum illud nescio gratulerne tibi an timeam, quod mirabilis est exspectatio reditus tui; non quo verear ne tua virtus opinioni hominum non respondeat, sed mehercule ne, cum veneris, non habeas iam quod cures; ita sunt omnia debilitata iam ‹et›[2] prope exstincta. sed haec ipsa nescio rectene sint litteris commissa. quare cetera cognosces ex aliis. tu tamen, sive habes aliquam spem de re publica sive desperas, ea para, meditare, cogita quae esse in eo civi ac viro debent qui sit rem publicam adflictam et oppressam miseris temporibus ac perditis moribus in veterem dignitatem et libertatem vindicaturus.

[1] ne epistula *(SB)*
[2] *(Lamb.)*

49 (II.5)
CICERO TO CURIO

Rome, 53 (first half)

From Cicero to C. Curio greetings.

The state of things here I dare not tell even to you in a letter. As I wrote once before, wherever you are, you are in the same boat; but all the same I congratulate you on your absence. On the one hand, you do not see what we are seeing; on the other, you are in a place where your merit shines high before the eyes of a multitude, Roman citizens and natives. The report of it comes to us, not by doubtful and various gossip, but in a single loud, concerted voice.

On one point I hardly know whether to congratulate you or to take alarm—the extraordinary eagerness with which your return is awaited. It is not that I doubt your capacity to live up to public expectation, but I am seriously afraid that when you do come home, you may no longer have anything to work for. Such is the decay, almost to extinction, of all our institutions. But perhaps even such remarks as this ought not to be entrusted to a letter, so I leave others to tell you the rest. But whether you see any ray of hope for the commonwealth or none, you must prepare and train and plan as befits a man and a Roman whose mission it is in sad times and evil manners to raise his country from the depth of affliction to her ancient dignity and freedom.

Scr. Romae fort. m. Quint. an. 53

M. CICERO S. D. C. CURIONI

1   Nondum erat auditum te ad Italiam adventare cum
Sex. Villium, Milonis mei familiarem, cum his ad te litteris
misi. sed tamen, cum appropinquare tuus adventus puta-
retur et te iam ex Asia Romam versus profectum esse con-
staret, magnitudo rei fecit ut non vereremur ne nimis cito
mitteremus, cum has quam primum ad te perferri litteras
magno opere vellemus.

    Ego, si mea in te essent officia solum, Curio, tanta
quanta magis a te ipso praedicari quam a me ponderari
solent, verecundius a te, si quae magna res mihi petenda
esset, contenderem. grave est enim homini pudenti petere
aliquid magnum ab eo de quo se bene meritum putet, ne id
quod petat exigere magis quam rogare et in mercedis
2 potius quam benefici loco numerare videatur. sed quia tua
in me [vel][1] nota omnibus vel ipsa novitate meorum temporum clarissima et maxima beneficia exstiterunt estque
animi ingenui, cui multum debeas, eidem plurimum velle
debere, non dubitavi id a te per litteras petere quod mihi
omnium esset maximum maximeque necessarium. neque
enim sum veritus ne sustinere tua in me vel innumerabilia
⟨officia⟩[2] non possem, cum praesertim confiderem nullam

    [1] *(SB)*   [2] *(SB)*

---

    1 His full name seems to have been Sex. Villius Annalis and he
can be identified with the Villius mentioned by Horace (*Satires*
1.2.64) as a lover of Milo's wife Fausta.

50 (II.6)
CICERO TO CURIO

Rome, July (?) 53

From M. Cicero to C. Curio greetings.

As I dispatch this letter by the hand of my dear Milo's friend, Sex. Villius,[1] no news has yet come in of your approaching Italy. But your arrival is thought not to be far off, and reports agree that you have set out from Asia on your way to Rome. So, considering the importance of the matter in hand, I feel no scruples on the score of undue haste, for I am very anxious that you should get this letter at the earliest possible moment.

If obligations between us were all on your side, and my services to you had been such as you are apt to proclaim them rather than as I myself appraise them, I should approach you with some diffidence if I had to beg you for an important favour. It is not easy for a man of sensibility to ask a great deal of someone who he thinks has reason to be grateful to him. He will be afraid of presenting the appearance of a creditor demanding payment rather than of a petitioner seeking a kindness. But in fact your benefactions to me are great and notorious, rendered the more conspicuous by the strange turns of fortune through which I have passed. And it is the mark of a liberal spirit to wish to owe more where one already owes much. Therefore I do not hesitate to write to you with a request of the highest consequence, one that lies very near to my heart. After all, I am not afraid of succumbing under the load of your good offices, past number though they may be. Whatever favour

esse gratiam tuam quam non vel capere animus meus in accipiendo vel in remunerando cumulare atque illustrare posset.

3 Ego omnia mea studia, omnem operam, curam, industriam, cogitationem, mentem denique omnem in Milonis consulatu fixi et locavi statuique in eo me non offici solum fructum sed etiam pietatis laudem debere quaerere. neque vero cuiquam salutem ac fortunas suas tantae curae fuisse umquam puto quantae mihi sit honos eius, in quo omnia mea posita esse decrevi. huic te unum tanto adiumento esse, si volueris, posse intellego ut nihil sit praeterea nobis requirendum. habemus haec omnia, bonorum studium conciliatum ex tribunatu propter nostram, ut spero te intellegere, causam, vulgi ac multitudinis propter magnificentiam munerum liberalitatemque naturae, iuventutis et gratiosorum in suffragiis studia propter ipsius excellentem in eo genere vel gratiam vel diligentiam, nostram suffragationem, si minus potentem, at probatam tamen et iustam et debitam et propterea fortasse etiam 4 gratiosam. dux nobis et auctor opus est et eorum ventorum quos proposui moderator quidam et quasi gubernator. qui si ex omnibus unus optandus esset, quem tecum conferre possemus non haberemus.

Quam ob rem, si me memorem, si gratum, si bonum virum vel ex hoc ipso quod tam vehementer de Milone laborem existimare potes, si dignum denique tuis beneficiis

---

2 Explained in *American Journal of Ancient History* 14 (1998): 72 as the six *suffragia* (centuries) of *equites* in the Assembly of Centuries, consisting of young aristocrats and distinguished members of the Order; cf. Letter 434, n. 2.

you may confer upon me, I feel confident that my mind has the capacity to accept it and the power to make a generous return, such as will add lustre to your gift.

Well then, I have firmly concentrated all my efforts, all my time, care, diligence, and thought, my whole mind in short, on winning the Consulship for Milo. In so doing, as I see it, I have to look not only for the reward of friendly service but for the credit of gratitude displayed to a benefactor. I do not believe any man's life and fortune ever meant as much to himself as Milo's success means to me. On this, I have decided, everything for me now depends. It is evident to me that your single self, if you will, can lend such effectual assistance to our campaign that we shall need nothing else. We have so much on our side—the good will of the honest men, acquired from his Tribunate through his championship of my cause, as I expect you appreciate; that of the common people, through the magnificence of his shows and the generosity of his nature; that of the younger generation and those influential in the Centuries,[2] through his own outstanding influence and activity in that sphere; and my own interest on his behalf, which may not be powerful, but is at any rate approved and right and due, and therefore perhaps not without some influence. What we need is a leader and a counsellor, one to govern and harness, as it were, the favourable currents of which I have spoken; and if we could choose from all the world, we should find no one comparable to you.

You may judge from the very depth of my concern on Milo's behalf whether I am a man who does not forget, a man of gratitude and honour. If so, if in short you consider me worthy of your kindness, then I appeal to you to come

iudicas, hoc a te peto, ut subvenias huic meae sollicitudini et huic meae laudi vel, ut verius dicam, prope saluti tuum studium dices. de ipso T. Annio tantum tibi polliceor, te maioris animi, gravitatis, constantiae benevolentiaeque erga te, si complecti hominem volueris, habiturum esse neminem. mihi vero tantum decoris, tantum dignitatis adiunxeris ut eundem te facile agnoscam fuisse in laude mea qui fueris in salute.

5   Ego, ni te videre scirem qua mente[3] haec scriberem, quantum offici sustinerem, quanto opere mihi esset in hac petitione Milonis omni non modo contentione sed etiam dimicatione elaborandum, plura scriberem. nunc tibi omnem rem atque causam meque totum commendo atque trado. unum hoc sic habeto, si a te hanc rem impetraro, me paene plus tibi quam ipsi Miloni debiturum. non enim mihi tam mea salus cara fuit, in qua praecipue sum ab illo adiutus, quam pietas erit in referenda gratia iucunda. eam autem unius tuo studio me adsequi posse confido.

51 (V.18)

Scr. Romae post fin. m. Mart. an. 52

M. CICERO S. D. T. FADIO

1   Etsi egomet, qui te consolari cupio, consolandus ipse sum, propterea quod nullam rem gravius iam diu tuli

---

[3] quaminte (*Boot*)

---

[3] Milo's full name was T. Annius Milo or T. Annius Milo Papianus.

to my help at this anxious time, and to dedicate your efforts to a cause in which my credit, indeed I might more properly say my virtual existence, is involved. As for T. Annius[3] himself, I promise you that if you will take him to your heart you will have no bolder, steadier, more resolute, or more sincere friend. As for me, you will add lustre and prestige to my name; and I shall readily recognize the same concern for my credit as you once showed for my existence as a citizen.

I should continue further, if I did not know how well you see my mind as I write this letter, that you realize what a load of obligation I carry and how in this candidature of Milo's I must needs labour and strive, and even fight my hardest. Knowing that, I put the whole matter in your hands; Milo's cause and I myself are all yours to do with as you will. Only understand that, if you do as I ask, I shall owe you more almost than I owe Milo himself; for my restoration, in which he was my chief helper, meant less to me than the satisfaction I shall take in repaying a sacred debt of gratitude. That I am sure your single support will enable me to attain.

51 (V.18)
CICERO TO T. FADIUS

Rome, 52 (after end of March)

From M. Cicero to T. Fadius greetings.

I, your would-be comforter, stand in need of comfort myself; for nothing this long while past has distressed me

quam incommodum tuum, tamen te magno opere non hortor solum sed etiam pro amore nostro rogo atque oro te colligas virumque praebeas et qua condicione omnes homines et quibus temporibus no<s> nati[1] simus cogites. plus tibi virtus tua dedit quam Fortuna abstulit, propterea quod adeptus es quod non multi homines novi, amisisti quae plurimi homines nobilissimi. ea denique videtur condicio impendere legum, iudiciorum, temporum ut optime actum cum eo videatur esse qui quam levissima poena ab

2 hac re publica discesserit. tu vero, qui et fortunas et liberos habeas et nos ceterosque necessitudine et benevolentia tecum coniunctissimos, quique[2] magnam facultatem sis habiturus nobiscum et cum omnibus tuis vivendi, et cuius[3] unum sit iudicium ex tam multis quod reprehendatur, ut quod una sententia eaque dubia potentiae alicuius condonatum existimetur, omnibus his de causis debes istam molestiam quam lenissime ferre. meus animus erit in te liberosque tuos semper quem tu esse vis et qui esse debet.

[1] notati *(Man.)*
[2] quamque
[3] cum *(SB)*

so deeply as your mishap.[1] However, I not only urge but earnestly beg and entreat you in the name of our mutual affection to take a firm hold of yourself and play the man. Remember the lot of mankind in general and the times in which we have been born. Your merit has given you more than Fortune has taken from you. Few self-made men have attained what you have attained, whereas many of the highest birth have lost what you have lost. Moreover, the future of our laws, law courts, and political conditions in general is likely to be such that whoever makes his exit from this commonwealth under the lightest penalty may be accounted highly fortunate. You have your property and your children. You also have me and others closely attached to you in friendship and good will. You will have ample opportunity to spend your time with me and all those dear to you. Yours is the only trial out of so many in which the verdict is criticized, as depending on a single dubious vote[2] and given, it is thought, to please a powerful personage.[3] For all these reasons you should take this trouble as easily as may be. My disposition towards you and your children will ever remain what you wish and what is right and proper.

[1] Fadius had been found guilty on a bribery charge, probably in connection with his election to the Praetorship.

[2] Or possibly 'wavering.' The circumstances of Fadius' conviction are known only from this letter.

[3] Presumably Pompey.

52 (VII.2)

Scr. Romae fort. m. Ian. an. 51

M. CICERO S. D. M. MARIO

1   Mandatum tuum curabo diligenter. sed homo acutus ei mandasti potissimum cui expediret illud venire quam plurimo. sed eo vidisti multum quod praefinisti quo ne pluris emerem. quod si mihi permisisses, qui meus amor in te est, confecissem cum coheredibus. nunc, quoniam tuum pretium novi, illicitatorem potius ponam quam illud minoris

2   veneat. sed de ioco satis est. tuum negotium agam, sicuti debeo, diligenter.

De Bursa te gaudere certo scio, sed nimis verecunde mihi gratularis. putas enim, ut scribis, propter hominis sordis minus me magnam illam laetitiam putare. credas mihi velim magis me iudicio hoc quam morte inimici laetatum. primum enim iudicio malo quam gladio, deinde gloria potius amici quam calamitate; in primisque me delectavit tantum studium bonorum in me exstitisse contra incredi-

3   bilem contentionem clarissimi et potentissimi viri. postremo (vix veri simile fortasse videatur) oderam multo peius hunc quam illum ipsum Clodium. illum enim op-

---

[1] Marius had asked Cicero to buy on his account something (perhaps an article of *virtu*) at the auction of an estate to which Cicero was one of the heirs.

[2] I.e. his condemnation on a charge of violence brought by Cicero himself (whose role as prosecutor in this case was for him most unusual).

[3] Clodius, of whom Bursa had been a leading supporter. He was killed by Milo on 18 January 52.

52 (VII.2)
CICERO TO M. MARIUS

Rome, January (?) 51

From M. Cicero to M. Marius greetings.

I shall execute your commission[1] with care. But shrewd business man that you are, you have selected the very person whose interest it is that the article should sell for as high a price as possible! Very wise of you, though, to set a limit on what I am to pay! Now if you had left me a free hand, my regard for you being what it is, I should have come to an arrangement with my co-heirs. As matters stand, now that I know your price, I'll put up a dummy bidder rather than see the thing go for less! But joking apart, I'll do your business with all proper care.

I am sure you are pleased about Bursa,[2] but you need not have been so diffident in your congratulations. You say you suppose I don't rate the triumph very high, because he's such a low creature. Well, I ask you to believe that this trial gave me more satisfaction than the death of my enemy.[3] To begin with, I prefer to get my revenge in a court of law than at sword point. Secondly, I prefer my friend to come out of it with credit rather than with ruin.[4] I was especially pleased at the display of good will towards me on the part of the honest men in the face of an astonishing amount of pressure from a very grand and powerful personage.[5] Lastly, and this may seem hard to credit, I detested this fellow far more than Clodius himself. I had

---

[4] Apparently the meaning is that Milo, who was in banishment for Clodius' murder, had been vindicated by Bursa's conviction.

[5] Pompey.

pugnaram, hunc defenderam; et ille, cum omnis res publica in meo capite discrimen esset habitura, magnum quiddam spectavit, nec sua sponte sed eorum auxilio qui me
stante stare non poterant, hic simiolus animi causa me in
quem inveheretur delegerat persuaseratque non nullis
invidis meis se in me emissarium semper fore. quam ob
rem valde iubeo gaudere te. magna res gesta est. numquam ulli fortiores cives fuerunt quam qui ausi sunt eum
contra tantas opes eius a quo ipsi lecti iudices erant con-
demnare. quod fecissent numquam nisi iis dolori meus
fuisset dolor.

4   Nos hic in multitudine et celebritate iudiciorum et
novis legibus ita distinemur ut cottidie vota faciamus ne
intercaletur, ut quam primum te videre possimus.

53 (XIII.42)

Scr. Romae an. 61 vel 60

M. CICERO S. D. L. CULLEOLO[1] PRO COS.

1   L. Lucceius, meus familiaris, homo omnium gratissimus, mirificas tibi apud me gratias egit, cum diceret omnia
te cumulatissime et liberalissime procuratoribus suis polli-
citum esse. cum oratio tua tam ei grata fuerit, quam gratam
rem ipsam existimas fore, cum, ut spero, quae pollicitus es

[1] Luc(c)eio

---

[6] Nothing more is known about this.

[7] The 'Triumvirs.' It suits Cicero's argument here to ignore
Clodius' personal reasons for attacking him in 58.

been Clodius' adversary, whereas I had defended the other in court.[6] Clodius had a great object in view—he knew that the entire state would be jeopardized in my person; and he acted, not all on his own, but with the assistance of those whose power depended on my downfall.[7] Whereas this little ape selected me for attack just because he felt like it, giving certain ill-wishers of mine to understand that he was ready to be set on me at any time. Therefore I tell you to rejoice and be glad. It is a great victory. No braver Romans ever lived than those jurymen who dared to find him guilty in spite of all the power of the very personage who had empanelled them. They would never have done that if they had not felt my grievance as their own.

What with the multitude of *causes célèbres* and the new legislation I am kept so busy here that I offer up a prayer against intercalation every day, so that I may be able to see you as soon as possible.

53 (XIII.42)
CICERO TO CULLEOLUS

Rome, 61 or 60

From M. Cicero to L. Culleolus, Proconsul, greetings.

My friend L. Lucceius, who is the last man in the world to fail in appreciation of a kindness, has expressed to me the most profuse gratitude to yourself for your most handsome and liberal promises to his agents. Since your words have so deeply obliged him, you can imagine how beholden he will feel when you have actually performed what you have promised, as I look forward to your doing. To be

feceris? omnino ostenderunt Bulliones sese Lucceio Pom-
2 pei arbitratu satis facturos, sed vehementer opus est nobis
et voluntatem et auctoritatem et imperium tuum accedere; quod ut facias te etiam atque etiam rogo. illudque
mihi gratissimum est quod ita sciunt Luccei procuratores
et ita Lucceius ipse ex litteris tuis quas ad eum misisti intel-
lexit, hominis nullius apud te auctoritatem aut gratiam valere plus quam meam. id ut re experiatur iterum et saepius
te rogo.

54 (XIII.41)

Scr. Romae an. 61 vel 60

CICERO CULLEOLO S.

1   Quae fecisti L. Luccei causa scire te plane volo te homini gratissimo commodasse; et cum ipsi quae fecisti pergra-
ta sunt, tum Pompeius, quotienscumque me vidit (videt
autem saepe), gratias tibi agit singularis. addo etiam illud,
quod tibi iucundissimum esse certo scio, me ipsum ex tua
2 erga Lucceium benignitate maxima voluptate adfici. quod
superest, quamquam mihi non est dubium quin, cum antea nostra causa, nunc iam etiam tuae constantiae gratia
mansurus sis in eadem ista liberalitate, tamen abs te vehementer etiam atque etiam peto ut ea quae initio ostendisti,
deinceps fecisti, ad exitum augeri et cumulari per te velis.
id et Lucceio et Pompeio valde gratum fore teque apud eos
praeclare positurum confirmo et spondeo.

sure the people of Byllis have expressed their readiness to meet Lucceius' claims at Pompey's discretion. But we urgently need your good will, influence, and official authority in addition. Let me again request of you that they be forthcoming. I am particularly gratified that Lucceius' agents are aware, and Lucceius himself has gathered from the letter you sent him, that no man's word and influence counts for more with you than mine. Allow me to beg you yet again to let him find by experience that this is really so.

54 (XIII.41)
CICERO TO CULLEOLUS

Rome, 61 or 60

Cicero to Culleolus greetings.

I want you to feel thoroughly assured that in doing what you have for L. Lucceius you have accommodated one who never forgets a favour. He is very much beholden to you for it, and Pompey expresses his gratitude in the warmest terms whenever we meet, as we often do. I will add what I feel sure will be highly agreeable to you, that I have personally been deeply gratified by your kindness to Lucceius. As for the future, I have no doubt that you will continue in your generosity, your earlier concern for our sakes being now supported by regard for your own consistency. However, let me again entreat you to be so good as to add at the conclusion some enhancing, crowning touches to your original promise and subsequent performance. You have my solemn guarantee that both Lucceius and Pompey will be deeply obliged and that your favour will be excellently placed.

De re publica deque his negotiis cogitationibusque nostris perscripseram ad te diligenter paucis ante diebus easque litteras dederam pueris tuis.

Vale.

55 (XIII.60)

Scr. Romae post m. Sept. an. 57

M. CICERO C. MUNATIO C. F. S.

1   L. Livineius Trypho est omnino L. Reguli, familiarissimi mei, libertus; cuius calamitas etiam officiosiorem me facit in illum; nam benevolentior quam semper fui esse non possum. sed ego libertum eius per se ipsum diligo. summa enim eius erga me officia exstiterunt iis nostris temporibus quibus facillime [bonam][1] benevolentiam ho-

2 minum et fidem perspicere potui. eum tibi ita commendo ut homines grati et memores bene meritos de se commendare debent. pergratum mihi feceris si ille intellexerit se, quod pro salute mea multa pericula adierit, saepe hieme summa navigarit, pro tua erga me benevolentia gratum etiam tibi fecisse.

[1] *ante* fidem *Lamb.*

I wrote to you a few days ago at some length about the political situation and about what is afoot here and my thoughts thereupon. I gave the letter to your boys.

Good-bye.

55 (XIII.60)
CICERO TO C. MUNATIUS[1]

Rome, after September 57

From Cicero to C. Munatius, son of Gaius, greetings.

L. Livincius Trypho is to be sure a freedman of my close friend L. Regulus, whose misfortune[2] has made me even more anxious to serve him—*feel* more kindly than I always did I cannot. But I am fond of his freedman for his own sake. He rendered me great service at that crisis of my life in which it was easiest for me to discern the good will and loyalty of my fellows.[3] I recommend him to you as men who gratefully remember what is done for them ought to recommend their benefactors. You will oblige me greatly if Trypho finds that, when he exposed himself to many dangers in the cause of my restoration (frequently taking ship in the depth of winter), he earned *your* gratitude as well as mine in virtue of your kindly disposition towards me.

[1] Nothing known.
[2] Exile.
[3] Cf. *Letters to Atticus* 62 (III.17).1.

56 (I.3)

Scr. Romae fort. m. Ian. an. 56

‹ M. CICERO S. D. P. LENTULO PRO COS. ›

1   A. Trebonio, qui in tua provincia magna negotia et ampla et expedita habet, multos annos utor valde familiariter.
is cum antea semper et suo splendore et nostra cetero-
rumque amicorum commendatione grati‹osi›ssimus[1] in
provincia fuit, tum hoc tempore propter tuum in me amorem nostramque necessitudinem vehementer confidit his
2   meis litteris se apud te gratiosum fore. quae ne spes eum
fallat vehementer rogo te commendoque tibi eius omnia
negotia, libertos, procuratores, familiam, in primisque ut,
quae T. Ampius de eius re decrevit, ea comprobes omni-
busque rebus eum ita tractes ut intellegat meam commendationem non vulgarem fuisse.

57 (XIII.6)

Scr. Romae an. 56 vel 55

M. CICERO Q. VALERIO Q. F. ORCAE PRO COS.

1   S. v. b.; e. v.
Credo te memoria tenere me et coram P.[1] Cuspio te-

1 *(Lamb.)*   1 ‹de› P. *Lamb.*

---

1 Distinct from Caesar's assassin, C. Trebonius.
2 Cilicia.
3 Lentulus' predecessor.

56 (I.3)
CICERO TO LENTULUS SPINTHER

Rome, January (?) 56

From M. Cicero to P. Lentulus, Proconsul, greetings.

For many years I have been on friendly terms with A. Trebonius,[1] who has important business concerns, both extensive and in good order, in your province.[2] In the past he has always been very well regarded in the province on account of his personal distinction and of recommendations from myself and his other friends; and he now trusts that this letter from me will put him in your good graces in view of your affection for me and the close relations between us. May I earnestly request you not to disappoint him, and commend to you all his business affairs, his freedmen, agents, and household? May I ask you in particular to confirm T. Ampius'[3] decisions with respect to his property, and to treat him in all matters in such a way as to let him understand that my recommendation has been more than routine?

57 (XIII.6)
CICERO TO VALERIUS ORCA[1]

Rome, late 56 or 55

From M. Cicero to Q. Valerius Orca, son of Quintus, Proconsul, greetings.

I trust you are well, as I am.

I expect you have not forgotten that I spoke to you in P.

---

[1] Governor of the province of Africa.

cum locutum esse cum te prosequerer paludatum et item postea pluribus verbis tecum egisse ut, quoscumque tibi eius necessarios commendarem, haberes eos in numero meorum necessariorum. id tu pro tua summa erga me benevolentia perpetuaque observantia mihi liberalissime atque humanissime recepisti.

2 Cuspius, homo in omnis suos officiosissimus, mirifice quosdam homines ex ista provincia tuetur et diligit propterea quod fuit in Africa bis, cum maximis societatis negotiis praeesset. itaque hoc eius officium quod adhibetur erga illos ego mea facultate et gratia soleo quantum possum adiuvare. qua re Cuspianorum omnium commendationis causam hac tibi epistula exponendam putavi, reliquis epistulis tantum faciam ut notam apponam eam quae mihi tecum convenit, et simul significem de numero esse Cuspi amicorum.

3 Sed hanc commendationem quam his litteris consignare volui scito esse omnium gravissimam. nam P. Cuspius singulari studio contendit a me ut tibi quam diligentissime L. Iulium commendarem. eius ego studio vix videor mihi satis facere posse si utar verbis iis quibus, cum diligentissime quid agimus, uti solemus. nova quaedam postulat et putat me eius generis artificium quoddam tenere. ei ego pollicitus sum me ex intima nostra arte deprompturum mirificum genus commendationis. id quoniam adsequi non possum, tu re velim efficias ut ille genere mearum
4 litterarum incredibile quiddam perfectum arbitretur. id

---

2 Perhaps L. Julius Calidus, a friend of Atticus and in his day a celebrated poet.

Cuspius' presence when I accompanied you as you were leaving Rome in uniform for your province, and likewise that I subsequently asked you at considerable length to regard any friends of his whom I recommended to you as friends of mine. With the great friendship and courtesy you always show me, you gave me your promise in the kindest and most handsome fashion.

Cuspius, who makes a point of serving all his friends, takes a remarkably close and benevolent interest in certain individuals from your province—the reason being that he was twice in Africa in charge of important company business. It is my habit to second his friendly endeavours on their behalf with such means and influence as I can command. I have therefore deemed it proper in this letter to set before you the general position as regards my recommendation of Cuspius' people. In future letters I shall simply affix the symbol on which you and I agreed, along with an intimation that the person concerned is one of Cuspius' friends.

Let me, however, assure you that the recommendation which I desire to put on record in this letter is of the most serious character. P. Cuspius has been extraordinarily urgent to have me give L. Julius[2] a most particular recommendation to you. He is so earnest in the matter that I hardly think it will be enough for me to use the phrases which we normally employ when we are making a very pressing request. He demands novelties, and supposes me to possess a special skill in this genre. I have promised him to produce from the secret stores of my art something quite amazing in the way of a recommendation. As I am unable to keep my word, I hope that you will use practical means to make him think that the style of my letter has

facies si omne genus liberalitatis quod et ab humanitate et potestate tua proficisci poterit non modo re sed etiam verbis, vultu denique, exprompseris; quae quantum in provincia valeant, vellem expertus essem,[2] sed tamen suspicor.

Ipsum hominem quem tibi commendo perdignum esse tua amicitia non solum quia mihi Cuspius dicit credo, tametsi id satis esse debebat, sed quia novi eius iudicium in hominibus et amicis deligendis.

5   Harum litterarum vis quanta fuerit propediem iudicabo tibique, ut confido, gratias agam. ego quae te velle quaeque ad te pertinere arbitrabor omnia studiose diligenterque curabo.

Cura ut valeas.

58 (XIII.6a)

Scr. Romae aliquanto post superiorem

⟨ M. CICERO Q. VALERIO Q.F. ORCAE PRO COS. ⟩

P. Cornelius, qui tibi litteras dedit, est mihi a P. Cuspio commendatus; cuius causa quanto opere cuperem deberemque profecto ex me facile cognosti. vehementer te rogo ut cures ut ex hac commendatione mihi Cuspius quam maximas, quam primum, quam saepissime gratias agat.

Vale.

[2] esses (*Or.*)

---

[3] At this time Cicero's experience of provincial government was confined to the subordinate office of Quaestor, which he had held in Sicily in 75.

worked wonders. To effect this you have only to bring out for the occasion all the manifold generosity that it lies within your good nature and your present power to provide, not only in a practical way but in words and even in looks. How much these things can do in a province I can guess, though unfortunately without experience.[3]

That the person whom I am recommending is very worthy to be your friend I believe not only because Cuspius tells me so, though that ought to be enough, but because I know his good judgement in choosing men and friends.

I shall soon be assessing the efficacy of this letter and, I feel sure, expressing my thanks to you. On my side I shall zealously and conscientiously attend to whatever I suppose to be relevant to your wishes and interests.

Take care of your health.

58 (XIII.6a)
CICERO TO VALERIUS ORCA

Rome, some time after the preceding

From M. Cicero to Q. Valerius, son of Quintus, Proconsul, greetings.

P. Cornelius, the bearer of this letter, has been recommended to me by P. Cuspius. Doubtless you have readily gathered from what I have told you how anxious I am, and ought to be, to serve Cuspius. Let me particularly ask you to ensure that as a result of this recommendation he thanks me as warmly, as soon, and as often as circumstances admit.

Good-bye.

59 (XIII.40)

Scr. Romae ex. an. 55 vel 54

M. CICERO S. D. Q. ANCHARIO Q. F. PRO COS.

L. et C. Aurelios L. filios, quibus et ipsis et patre eorum, viro optimo, familiarissime utor, commendo tibi maiorem in modum, adulescentis omnibus optimis artibus ornatos, meos pernecessarios, tua amicitia dignissimos. si ulla mea apud te commendatio valuit, quod scio multas plurimum valuisse, haec ut valeat rogo. quod si eos honorifice liberaliterque tractaris, et tibi gratissimos optimosque adulescentis adiunxeris et mihi gratissimum feceris.

60 (XIII.75)

Scr. Romae ex. an. 52 vel in. an. 51

M. CICERO T. TITIO T. F. LEG. S. D.

1   Etsi non dubito quin apud te mea commendatio prima satis valeat, tamen obsequor homini familiarissimo, C. Avianio Flacco, cuius causa omnia cum cupio tum mehercule etiam debeo. de quo et praesens tecum egi diligenter, cum tu mihi humanissime respondisti, et scripsi ad te accurate antea; sed putat interesse sua me ad te quam saepis-

---

1 L. Piso's successor as governor of Macedonia.

1 Evidently serving in a grain-exporting province, probably Sicily, and perhaps identical with the recipient of Letter 187.

59 (XIII.40)
CICERO TO Q. ANCHARIUS[1]

Rome, 55 (late) or 54

From M. Cicero to Q. Ancharius, son of Quintus, Proconsul, greetings.

Let me warmly recommend to you L. and C. Aurelius, sons of Lucius, with whom and with that very worthy gentleman their father I am on the most familiar terms. They are highly accomplished young men, very close to me, and thoroughly deserving of your friendship. If any recommendation of mine has carried weight with you (and I know that many have carried a great deal), please accord it to this. If you deal with them in handsome and complimentary style, you will attach two excellent and most appreciative young men to yourself and greatly oblige me.

60 (XIII.75)
CICERO TO T. TITIUS

Rome, 52 (end) or 51 (beginning)

From M. Cicero to T. Titius, son of Titus, Legate,[1] greetings.

Although I do not doubt that my original recommendation carries sufficient weight with you, I am none the less complying with the request of my very good friend C. Avianius Flaccus, whose well-wisher in all things I not only am but assuredly ought to be. I spoke of him to you in person at some length, and you answered me in the kindest way; also I have already written to you about him in detail. However, he thinks it is to his advantage that I should write

263

sime scribere. qua re velim mihi ignoscas si illius voluntati
obtemperans minus videbor meminisse constantiae tuae.

2   A te idem illud peto, ut de loco quo deportet frumen-
tum et de tempore Avianio commodes, quorum utrumque
per eundem me obtinuit triennium, dum Pompeius isti
negotio praefuit. summa est ⟨haec: est⟩[1] in quo mihi gratissimum facere possis, si curaris ut Avianius, quoniam se a
me amari putat, me a te amari sciat. erit id mihi pergratum.

61 (XIII.51)

Scr. Romae an. incerto

CICERO P. CAESIO S. D.

P. Messienum, equitem Romanum omnibus rebus ornatum meumque perfamiliarem, tibi commendo ea commendatione quae potest esse diligentissima. peto a te et
pro nostra et pro paterna amicitia ut eum in tuam fidem
recipias eiusque rem famamque tueare. virum bonum
tuaque amicitia dignum tibi adiunxeris mihique gratissimum feceris.

[1] (*SB*: est: ⟨est⟩ *Tyrrell*)

---

[2] Pompey's five-year term as High Commissioner for grain
supplies expired in the autumn of 52. The concessions to Avianius
appear to have come into operation in 55.

to you as often as I can. So please forgive me if, in deferring to his wishes, I may seem less mindful than I should be of your dependability.

My request is the same as ever. I want you to accommodate Avianius with regard to his shipments of grain, both as to place and time of disembarcation. In both respects his wishes were met, likewise at my intercession, for the three years during which Pompey presided over the business.[2] The long and short of it is that you have the opportunity to oblige me greatly, if you will let Avianius, since he thinks that I am his good friend, know that you are mine. That will oblige me very much indeed.

61 (XIII.51)
CICERO TO P. CAESIUS[1]

Rome, date uncertain

From Cicero to P. Caesius greetings.

May I most particularly recommend to you a Roman Knight, a man of quality in every sense of the word, and a very good friend of mine, P. Messienus, and request you in the name of my friendship with yourself and your father to take him under your patronage and protect his interests and reputation? You will attach to yourself an honourable man, worthy to be your friend, and you will greatly oblige me.

---

[1] Nothing is known about him or Messienus. There may be a connection with the Caesii of Arpinum.

62 (XIII.76)

Scr. Romae an. incerto

M. CICERO IIII VIRIS ET DECURIONIBUS S. D.

1   Tantae mihi cum Q. Hippio causae necessitudinis sunt
ut nihil possit esse coniunctius quam nos inter nos sumus.
quod nisi ita esset, uterer mea consuetudine, ut vobis nulla
in re molestus essem. etenim vos mihi optimi testes estis,
cum[1] mihi persuasum esset nihil esse quod a vobis impetrare non possem, numquam me tamen gravem vobis esse

2   voluisse. vehementer igitur vos etiam atque etiam rogo ut
honoris mei causa quam liberalissime C. Valgium Hippia-
num tractetis remque cum eo conficiatis ut, quam possessionem habet in agro Fregellano <a> vobis emptam, eam
liberam et immunem habere possit. id si a vobis impetraro,
summo me beneficio vestro adfectum arbitrabor.

63 (XIII.1)

Scr. Athenis ex. m. Iun. vel in. m. Quint. an. 51

M. CICERO S. D. C. MEMMIO

1   Etsi non satis mihi constiterat cum aliquane animi mei

1 quam *(Man.)*

---

1 The town of Fregellae, not far from Arpinum, was destroyed
after its revolt in 125 and Fabrateria Nova founded in its place.
But the latter was governed by two magistrates *(duoviri)*. This

62 (XIII.76)

CICERO TO THE MAGISTRATES AND TOWN COUNCIL OF FABRATERIA VETUS (?)

Rome, date uncertain

From M. Cicero to the Board of Four and Councillors greetings.

I am attached to Q. Hippius by so many bonds that no relationship could be closer than ours. Otherwise I should not be departing from my practice of never troubling your worships. You yourselves can best testify that, although persuaded of your readiness to grant any request I might make, I have never cared to impose upon you. Therefore let me beg of you most earnestly, as a compliment to myself, to give C. Valgius Hippianus the handsomest of treatment, and to come to a settlement with him so that he can hold his property purchased from your corporation in the district of Fregellae[1] free of all dues and charges. If you grant me this request, I shall feel myself beholden to your worships for a most important favour.

63 (XIII.1)

CICERO TO C. MEMMIUS

Athens, June (end) or July (beginning) 51

From M. Cicero to C. Memmius greetings.

I was not quite sure whether it would have been in a

letter may therefore have been addressed to the governing body of the old town, Fabrateria Vetus, which had four magistrates and may have been granted some of the Fregellane territory.

molestia an potius libenter te Athenis visurus essem, quod
iniuria quam accepisti dolore me adficeret, sapientia tua
qua fers iniuriam laetitia, tamen vidisse te mallem; nam
quod est molestiae non sane multo levius est cum te non
video, quod esse potuit voluptatis certe, si vidissem te, plus
fuisset. itaque non dubitabo dare operam ut te videam,
cum id satis commode facere potero. interea quod per litteras et agi tecum et, ut arbitror, confici potest, agam nunc.
2 ac te illud primum rogabo, ne quid invitus mea causa
facias, sed id quod mea intelleges multum,[1] tua nullam in
partem interesse ita mihi des si tibi ut id libenter facias
ante persuaseris.

Cum Patrone Epicurio mihi omnia sunt, nisi quod in
philosophia vehementer ab eo dissentio. sed et initio
Romae, cum te quoque et tuos omnis observabat, me
coluit in primis et nuper, cum ea quae voluit de suis commodis et praemiis consecutus est, me habuit suorum de-
fensorum et amicorum fere principem et iam a Phaedro,
qui nobis cum pueri essemus, ante quam Philonem cogno-
vimus, valde ut philosophus, postea tamen ut vir bonus et
suavis et officiosus probabatur, traditus mihi commenda-
tusque est.

3 Is igitur Patro cum ad me Romam litteras misisset, uti
te sibi placarem peteremque ut nescio quid illud Epicuri
parietinarum sibi concederes, nihil scripsi ad te ob eam

---

[1] multum *post* partem *(Man.)*

---

[1] On his way to his province of Cilicia in 51 Cicero stopped in
Athens from 24 June to 6 July. With this letter cf. *Letters to Atticus*
104 (V.11).6.

[2] Condemnation for electoral bribery in 52.

way distressing to me to see you in Athens[1] or a pleasure. I should have felt pain at the injustice[2] of which you are the victim, but happiness in the philosophy with which you bear it. However, I would rather I *had* seen you. The measure of distress is not very much diminished when you are out of my sight, and, had I seen you, the pleasure I might have had would assuredly have been greater. So I shall not hesitate to try to see you as soon as I can fairly conveniently do so. In the meanwhile, allow me to raise with you now a matter which can be raised, and I imagine, settled, in correspondence. And first I would ask you not to do anything on my account which you would rather not. I hope you will grant me a favour which, as you will see, matters a good deal to me and not at all to you, but only if you are satisfied beforehand that you will do it gladly.

I have all manner of ties with Patro the Epicurean, except that in philosophy I strongly disagree with him. But in the early days in Rome I was one of those whose acquaintance he particularly cultivated (that was when he was also paying attentions to you and all connected with you). Recently too he gained what he wanted in the way of personal advantages and honoraria with myself as pretty well the chief among his protectors and friends. He was originally recommended to my care and regard by Phaedrus, of whom as a philosopher I had a great opinion when I was a boy, before I knew Philo, and whom ever afterwards I respected as a man, honourable, amiable, and obliging.

Well, this Patro wrote to me in Rome, asking me to make his peace with you and to beg you to let him have those ruins (or whatever they are) of Epicurus' house. I did not write to you, not wanting your building plans to be

rem quod aedificationis tuae consilium commendatione
mea nolebam impediri. idem, ut veni Athenas, cum idem
ut ad te scriberem rogasset, ob eam causam impetravit
quod te abiecisse illam aedificationem constabat inter
4 omnis amicos tuos. quod si ita est et si iam tua plane nihil
interest, velim, si qua offensiuncula facta est animi tui per-
versitate aliquorum (novi enim gentem illam), des te ad
lenitatem vel propter summam ⟨tuam⟩[2] humanitatem vel
etiam honoris mei causa. equidem, si quid ipse sentiam
quaeris, nec cur ille tanto opere contendat video nec cur
tu repugnes, nisi tamen multo minus tibi concedi potest
quam illi laborare sine causa. quamquam Patronis et orationem et causam tibi cognitam esse certo scio; honorem,
officium, testamentorum ius, Epicuri auctoritatem, Phae-
dri obtestationem, sedem, domicilium, vestigia summorum hominum sibi tuenda esse dicit. totam hominis vitam
rationemque quam sequitur in philosophia derideamus
licet si hanc eius contentionem volumus reprehendere.
sed mehercules, quoniam illi ceterisque quos illa delectant
non valde inimici sumus, nescio an ignoscendum sit huic si
tanto opere laborat; in quo etiam si peccat, magis ineptiis
quam improbitate peccat.

5 Sed ne plura (dicendum enim aliquando est), Pomponium Atticum sic amo ut alterum fratrem. nihil est illo
mihi nec carius nec iucundius. is (non quo sit ex istis; est
enim omni liberali doctrina politissimus, sed valde diligit

2 (*R. Klotz*: *ante* summam *Man.*)

---

3 A notable statement. Atticus' Epicurean leanings were not
taken very seriously by those who knew him.

interfered with by a vicarious request of mine. When I arrived in Athens he again asked me to write to you to the same effect. This time I consented, because all your friends were agreed that you had given up your building. If that is so, and your interests are now quite unaffected, I hope you will take a lenient view of any little vexation which the untowardness of certain people may have caused you (I know the breed!), out of the great goodness of your heart or even by way of compliment to me. For my part, if you wish to know my personal sentiments, I don't see why he should make such a point of it nor why you should object—except that, after all, it is much less allowable in *you* to make a fuss about nothing than in him. However, I am sure you know Patro's case and how he puts it. He pleads that he owes a responsibility to his office and duty, to the sanctity of testaments, to the prestige of Epicurus' name, to Phaedrus' adjuration, to the abode, domicile, and memorials of great men. If we wish to find fault with his insistence in this matter, we are at liberty to deride his whole life and philosophical principles. But really, since we have no deadly enmity towards him and others who find these doctrines to their taste, perhaps we ought not to be hard on him for taking it so much to heart. Even if he is wrong, it is silliness rather than wickedness that is leading him astray.

However, to make an end (I must come to it some time), I love Pomponius Atticus like a second brother. Nothing is more precious and delightful to me than to have him as a friend. Nobody is less of a busybody, less inclined to importune, but I have never known him request anything of me more pressingly than this—not that he is one of the sect,[3] for he is a person of the most comprehensive and

271

Patronem, valde Phaedrum amavit) sic a me hoc contendit, homo minime ambitiosus, minime in rogando molestus, ut nihil umquam magis, nec dubitat quin ego a te nutu
hoc consequi possem etiam si aedificaturus esses. nunc
vero, si audierit te aedificationem deposuisse neque tamen
me a te impetrasse, non te in me illiberalem sed me in se
neglegentem putabit. quam ob rem peto a te ut scribas ad
tuos posse tua voluntate decretum illud Areopagitarum,
quem ὑπομνηματισμὸν illi vocant, tolli.

6   Sed redeo ad prima. prius velim tibi persuadeas ut hoc
mea causa libenter facias quam ut[3] facias. sic tamen habeto, si feceris quod rogo, fore mihi gratissimum.
      Vale.

64 (III.1)

Scr., ut vid., Romae ex. an. 53 vel in. an. 52

CICERO APPIO IMP. S. D.

1   Si ipsa res publica tibi narrare posset quo modo sese haberet, non facilius ex ea cognoscere posses quam ex liberto
tuo Phania; ita est homo non modo prudens verum etiam,
quod iuvet, curiosus. quapropter ille tibi omnia explanabit;
id enim mihi et ad brevitatem est aptius et ad reliquas res
providentius. de mea autem benevolentia erga te, etsi po-

---

[3] *del. coni. SB*

---

[4] The Epicureans by their own profession were not, and
Cicero often jeers at their supposed ignorance and stupidity.

[5] The ancient Athenian court and council.

refined culture,[4] but he has a great regard for Patro, and had a deep affection for Phaedrus. He is confident that I should only have to signify a wish for you to grant the point, even if you intended to build. But now, if he hears that you have put aside your building project and that I have still not obtained the favour, he is going to think, not that you have been disobliging to me, but that I have not troubled to oblige *him*. May I therefore ask you to write to your people and tell them that the relevant decree of the Areopagus[5] (*hypomnematismos* as they call it) may be rescinded with your blessing?

However, I go back to where I started. Before you decide to comply with my request I want you to be satisfied that you will do so gladly for my sake. None the less, you may be sure that I shall be extremely grateful if you do what I ask.

Good-bye.

64 (III.1)
CICERO TO APPIUS PULCHER

Rome, 53 (end) or 52 (beginning)

From Cicero to Appius, Imperator,[1] greetings.

If our country could tell you for herself how she does, you would find her no better a source of information than your freedman Phanias. He is so sensible and, what is more, so inquisitive, in a good sense of the word. So he will make all plain to you. That will help me to be brief, and will be wiser from other standpoints. As to my good will to-

---

[1] As governor of Cilicia Appius had concluded a successful campaign.

tes ex eodem Phania cognoscere, tamen videntur etiam aliquae meae partes. sic enim tibi persuade, carissimum te mihi esse cum propter multas suavitates ingeni, offici, humanitatis tuae tum quod ex tuis litteris et ex multorum sermonibus intellego omnia quae a me profecta sunt in te tibi accidisse gratissima. quod cum ita sit, perficiam profecto ut longi temporis usuram, qua caruimus intermissa nostra consuetudine, et gratia et crebritate et magnitudine officiorum meorum sarciam, idque me, quoniam tu ita vis, puto non invita Minerva esse facturum. quam quidem ego si forte de tuis sumpsero, non solum Πολιάδα[1] sed etiam Ἀππιάδα nominabo.

2 Cilix, libertus tuus, antea mihi minus fuit notus; sed ut mihi reddidit a te litteras plenas et amoris et offici, mirifice ipse suo sermone subsecutus est humanitatem litterarum tuarum. iucunda mihi eius oratio fuit cum de animo tuo, de sermonibus quos de me haberes cottidie, mihi narraret. quid quaeris? biduo factus est mihi familiaris, ita tamen ut Phaniam valde sim desideraturus. quem cum Romam remittes, quod, ut putabamus, celeriter eras facturus, omnibus ei de rebus quas agi, quas curari a me voles mandata des velim.

[1] πολλάδα (?) (SB)

---

2 More literally 'with Minerva's good will' (*non invita Minerva*), i.e. 'not against the grain.' Minerva (Athene) represents intellect and natural aptitude. But Cicero uses the expression here for the sake of the following allusion to a statue of the goddess which he was apparently hoping to acquire from Appius (a famous art collector).   3 Or 'your people.'

4 Polias (of the city) and Poliouchos (guarding the city) were

wards you, there too Phanias can be your informant, but I think that I also have a word to say. Please assure yourself that you are very dear to me. Your natural gifts, your obliging and kindly disposition, attract me in many ways; furthermore, from what you write and others say, I know that you are very appreciative of anything I have been able to do for you. Since that is so, I must evidently contrive to make up for what has been sacrificed in the long period of suspension of our intercourse by the acceptability, the frequency, and the magnitude of the services I render you; and since you so wish, I flatter myself that I shall succeed—by grace of Minerva.[2] If by any chance I obtain the Goddess from your collection,[3] I shall style her not Polias only, but Appias.[4]

I was not previously very well acquainted with your freedman Cilix, but after handing me your affectionate and friendly letter, he followed up its kind expressions with words of his own to quite remarkable effect. I enjoyed listening to his account of your disposition towards me and of what you say about me from day to day. In fact within a couple of days he has become my friend—but not so much so that I shall not miss Phanias sorely. When you send him back to Rome, as I imagine you will shortly be doing, please give him your commissions on all matters on which you would like action or attention from me.

cult titles of Athene; *Minerva custos urbis* is the Latin equivalent. The statue, whether or not the one dedicated by Cicero in the Capitol on the eve of his exile (see Letter 373.1), represented the goddess in this guise (the vulgate 'Pallas' here is not supported by our only valid manuscript). 'Appias' is, of course, a title invented by Cicero on the spur of the moment to make a pleasantry.

3   L. Valerium iureconsultum valde tibi commendo, sed
ita etiam si non est iure consultus; melius enim ei cavere
volo quam ipse aliis solet. valde hominem diligo; est ex
meis domesticis atque intimis familiaribus. omnino tibi
agit gratias, sed idem scribit meas litteras maximum apud
te pondus habituras. id eum ne fallat etiam atque etiam
rogo.

65 (III.2)

Scr. ad urbem m. Febr. vel Mart. an. 51

M. CICERO PRO COS. S. D. APPIO PULCHRO IMP.

1   Cum et contra voluntatem meam et praeter opinionem
accidisset ut mihi cum imperio in provinciam proficisci necesse esset, in multis et variis molestiis cogitationibusque
meis haec una consolatio occurrebat, quod neque tibi amicior quam ego sum quisquam posset succedere neque ego
ab ullo provinciam accipere qui mallet eam quam maxime
mihi aptam explicatamque tradere. quod si tu quoque
eandem de mea voluntate erga te spem habes, ea te profecto numquam fallet. a te maximo opere pro nostra summa coniunctione tuaque singulari humanitate etiam atque
etiam quaeso et peto ut quibuscumque rebus poteris

---

5 See Letter 21.

6 See Letter 27, n. 3.

1 A law passed during Pompey's third Consulship (52) en-
joined a five-year interval between the holding of a Consulship or
Praetorship and the consequent governorship of a province. To fill
the resulting gap the Senate called upon former Consuls and

Allow me to recommend to you warmly Counsellor L. Valerius,[5] but with the proviso that the quality of his counsel is not guaranteed—I want to make a better caveat[6] for him than he generally drafts for his clients. I have a strong regard for him; he is one of my inner circle of familiar friends. He expressed gratitude to you, it is true, but he also writes that a letter from me will carry great weight with you. May I particularly request that he be not disappointed therein?

65 (III.2)
CICERO TO APPIUS PULCHER

Neighbourhood of Rome, February or March 51

From M. Cicero, Proconsul, to Appius Pulcher, Imperator, greetings.

Contrary to my own inclination and quite unexpectedly, I find myself under the necessity of setting out to govern a province.[1] My only consolation in a multitude of various annoyances and preoccupations lies in the reflection that you could not have a more friendly successor than me, and that I could not take over the province from anyone more anxious to consign it to me in as orderly and unembarrassed a state as possible. If you on your side expect the same of my disposition towards yourself, you may be sure you will never be disappointed. Let me particularly pray and request you, bearing in mind the close bond between

Praetors who had not previously held provincial command, of whom Cicero was one. Cilicia was assigned to him for a term of one year. His reluctance seems to have been entirely sincere.

2 (poteris autem pluribus) prospicias et consulas rationibus
meis. vides ex senatus consulto provinciam esse habendam. si eam, quod eius facere potueris, quam expeditissi-
mam mihi tradideris, facilior erit mihi quasi decursus mei
temporis. quid in eo genere efficere possis, tui consili est;
ego te quod tibi veniet in mentem mea interesse ‹ut
facias›[1] valde rogo.

Pluribus verbis ad te scriberem si aut tua humanitas
longiorem orationem exspectaret aut id fieri nostra amicitia pateretur aut res verba desideraret ac non pro se ipsa
loqueretur. hoc velim tibi persuadeas, si rationibus meis
provisum a te esse intellexero, magnam te ex eo et perpetuam voluptatem esse capturum.

66 (III.3)

Scr. Brundisii paulo post XI *Kal. Iun. an.* 51

CICERO S. D. APPIO PULCHRO

1 A. d. XI Kal. Iun. Brundisium cum venissem, Q. Fa-
bi‹us Vergili›anus,[1] legatus tuus, mihi praesto fuit eaque
me ex tuis mandatis monuit quae non ‹modo›[2] mihi, ad
quem pertinebant, sed universo senatui venerant in mentem, praesidio firmiore opus esse ad istam provinciam;
censebant enim omnes fere ut in Italia supplementum
meis et Bibuli legionibus scriberetur. id cum Sulpicius

[1] *(coni. SB*)*
[1] *(Bengel)*
[2] *(Crat.)*

278

us and your characteristic consideration for others, to watch and provide for my interests in every way you can—and there will be many ways. You see that I am obliged under a senatorial decree to take the province. If you hand it over to me free from all embarrassments, so far as you find that possible, I shall run my lap (so to speak) of tenure the more easily. It is for you to decide what you can do in this way, but you have my urgent request to take any steps which may occur to you as helpful.

I will not use more words. Your kindness will not expect a lengthy discourse, our friendship does not permit it; nor does the case call for words, it speaks for itself. I should only like you to feel assured that, if I find you have been thoughtful for what concerns me, it will bring you deep and lasting satisfaction.

66 (III.3)
CICERO TO APPIUS PULCHER

Brundisium, shortly after 22 May 51

From Cicero to Appius Pulcher greetings.

On my arrival at Brundisium on 22 May your Legate Q. Fabius Vergilianus was there to meet me. He conveyed to me your admonition to the effect that a larger military force is needed for the defence of this province. The considerations you raise had occurred not only to me, whom they especially concern, but to the whole Senate, which declared almost without exception in favour of a levy in Italy to reinforce my troops and those of Bibulus.[1] How-

[1] Consul in 59, now appointed governor of Syria.

consul passurum se negaret, multa nos quidem questi sumus, sed tantus consensus senatus fuit ut mature proficisceremur parendum ut fuerit, itaque fecimus.

Nunc, quod a te petii litteris iis quas Romae tabellariis tuis dedi, velim tibi curae sit ut, quae successori coniunctissimo et amicissimo commodare potest is qui provinciam tradit, ut ea pro nostra consociatissima voluntate cura ac diligentia tua complectare, ut omnes intellegant nec me benevolentiori cuiquam succedere nec te amiciori potuisse provinciam tradere.

2   Ex iis litteris quarum ad me exemplum misisti, quas in senatu recitari voluisti, sic intellexeram, permultos a te milites esse dimissos; sed mihi Fabius idem demonstravit te id cogitasse facere, sed, cum ipse a te discederet, integrum militum numerum fuisse. id si ita est, pergratum mihi feceris si istas exiguas copias quas habuisti quam minime imminueris. qua de re senatus consulta quae facta sunt ad te missa esse arbitror. equidem pro eo quanti te facio quicquid feceris approbabo, sed te quoque confido ea facturum quae mihi intelleges maxime esse accommodata.

Ego C. Pomptinum, legatum meum, Brundisi exspectabam eumque ante Kal. Iun. Brundisium venturum arbitrabar.[3] quo cum venerit, quae primum navigandi nobis facultas data erit, utemur.

[3] arbitrabor *(Ern.)*

ever, Consul Sulpicius said he would not allow it. I pro-
tested at length, but in face of the Senate's unanimous desire for me to leave without delay I had no choice but to
comply, as I have done.

Let me now repeat the request I made in the letter
which I gave your couriers in Rome. I hope you will do
whatever can be done by an outgoing governor to ease
matters for a successor to whom he is bound by close ties
of friendship. Bearing in mind the perfect harmony of
sentiment which exists between us, employ your care and
diligence in this regard, so that all may understand that I
could have had no more benevolent predecessor and that
you could not have handed over your province to a better
friend.

I understood from the dispatch which you desired to be
read aloud in the Senate, of which you sent me a copy, that
you had given large numbers of soldiers their discharge.
Fabius, however, has explained that you had proposed to
do this, but that at the time he left you numbers were still
up to complement. If that is so, I shall be very grateful if
you make the minimum of reductions in the meagre forces
under your command. I think the decrees passed by the
Senate on this subject have been sent to you. For my part,
my regard for you is such that whatever you do will have
my approval, but I feel sure that you on your side will take
such measures as you see to be most convenient for me.

I am waiting for my Legate C. Pomptinus at Brundisium, and expect him to arrive before the beginning of
June. When he does, we shall sail at the first opportunity.

67 (III.4)

Scr. Brundisii prid. Non. Iun. vel paulo post, an. 51

‹CICERO S. D. APPIO PULCHRO›

1   Prid. Non. Iun., cum essem Brundisi, litteras tuas accepi, quibus erat scriptum te L. Clodio mandasse quae illum
mecum loqui velles. eum sane exspectabam, ut ea quae a te
adferret quam primum cognoscerem. meum studium erga
te et officium, tametsi multis iam rebus spero tibi esse
cognitum, tamen in iis maxime declarabo quibus plurimum significare potuero tuam mihi existimationem et dignitatem carissimam esse. mihi et Q. Fabius Vergilianus et
C. Flaccus L. f. et diligentissime M. Octavius Cn. f. demonstravit me a te plurimi fieri. quod egomet multis argu-
mentis iam antea iudicaram maximeque illo libro augurali,
quem ad me amantissime scriptum suavissimum misisti.

2   Mea in te omnia summa necessitudinis officia consta-
bunt. nam cum te ipsum, ex quo tempore tu me diligere
coepisti, cottidie pluris feci, tum accesserunt etiam con-
iunctiones necessariorum tuorum (duo enim duarum ae-
tatum plurimi facio, Cn. Pompeium, filiae tuae socerum,
et M. Brutum, generum tuum), collegique coniunctio
praesertim tam honorifice a te approbata non mediocre
vinculum mihi quidem attulisse videtur ad voluntates nostras copulandas.

Sed et, si Clodium convenero, ex illius sermone ad te

---

¹ Appius' Prefect of Engineers (see Glossary).

² The first two certainly, and the third presumably, were on
Appius' staff.   ³ Cicero had been elected to the College of
Augurs, of which Appius was a member, in 53 or 52.

67 (III.4)
CICERO TO APPIUS PULCHER

Brundisium, 4 June, or shortly after, 51

From Cicero to Appius Pulcher, greetings.

On 4 June I received a letter from you at Brundisium in which you write that you have commissioned L. Clodius[1] to discuss certain matters with me. I am eagerly expecting him, so as to learn as soon as possible what word he brings from you. You have, I hope, already had evidence in plenty of my good will and desire to serve you, but I shall demonstrate it most conspicuously where I can most clearly show how precious to me are your good name and dignity. Your warm regard for myself had been made plain to me by Q. Fabius Vergilianus, by C. Flaccus, son of Lucius, and especially by M. Octavius, son of Gnaeus.[2] I had previously deduced it from many indications, above all the charming gift of your volume on Augury[3] with its affectionate dedication to me.

All that I can do for you to the uttermost limits of friendly service shall be done. My esteem for you has increased from day to day ever since you began to have a regard for me. To that has accrued my associations with connections of yours, for two of whom, belonging to different generations, I have the greatest esteem, namely Cn. Pompeius, your daughter's father-in-law, and your son-in-law, M. Brutus; further our association in the same College, especially now that you have approved it in so flattering a fashion, has in my eyes added a tie of no small importance to the linking of our sentiments.

Well, when I have met Clodius, I shall write to you

scribam plura et ipse operam dabo ut te quam primum videam. quod scribis tibi manendi causam eam fuisse ut me convenires, id mihi, ne mentiar, est gratum.

68 (III.5)

Scr. Trallibus a. d. VI vel V Kal. Sext. an. 51

CICERO S. D. APPIO PULCHRO

1   Trallis veni a. d. VI Kal. Sext. ibi mihi praesto fuit L. Lucilius cum litteris mandatisque tuis; quo quidem hominem neminem potuisti nec mihi amiciorem nec, ut arbitror, ad ea cognoscenda quae scire volebam aptiorem prudentioremve mittere. ego autem et tuas litteras legi libenter et audivi Lucilium diligenter. nunc, quoniam et tu ita sentis (scribis enim quae <de> nostris officiis ego ad te scripseram, etsi tibi iucunda fuerint, tamen, quoniam ex alto repetita sint, non necessaria te putasse) et re vera confirmata amicitia et perspecta fide commemoratio officiorum supervacanea est, eam partem orationis praetermittam, tibi tamen agam, ut debeo, gratias. animadverti enim et didici ex tuis litteris te omnibus in rebus habuisse rationem ut mihi consuleres statueresque[1] et parares quodam modo

2   omnia quo mea ratio facilior et solutior esse posset. hoc tuum officium cum mihi gratissimum esse dicam, sequitur illud, ut te existimare velim mihi magnae curae fore atque esse iam, primum ut ipse tu tuique omnes, deinde ut etiam reliqui, scire possint me tibi esse amicissimum. quod qui-

---

[1] restit- (*Gul.*: praestit- *Or.*)

further in the light of what he has to say, and I shall do my best to see you as soon as possible. Your statement that you are staying on in order to meet me gives me pleasure, I won't deny it.

68 (III.5)
CICERO TO APPIUS PULCHER

Tralles, 27 or 28 July 51

From Cicero to Appius Pulcher greetings.

I arrived at Tralles on 27 July. There to meet me was L. Lucilius with your letter and messages. You could not have sent me any friendlier or, as I suppose, better qualified or more sensible informant to tell me what I want to know. I was glad to read your letter, and I have listened carefully to Lucilius. Well, since you feel as you do (you write that, while the remarks in my letter about our services to one another gave you pleasure, you saw no need to go back so far into the past), and since reminders of services rendered are in truth superfluous between firm and tried friends, I shall leave that topic on one side. Nevertheless I shall thank you as I ought. From my own observation and from your letter I find that in all matters you have been studiously thoughtful of me, and that you have, as it were, predetermined and prepared everything so as to give me an easier and freer run. When I tell you that I am most grateful for this friendly behaviour on your part, it follows that I wish you to believe that I shall be, and now am, most sedulous for you yourself and all connected with you in the first place, and for the rest of the world in the second, to know how sincerely I am attached to you. Those who are still not

285

bus adhuc non satis est perspectum ii mihi nolle magis nos hoc animo esse quam non intellegere videntur. sed profecto intellegent; neque enim obscuris personis nec parvis in causis res agetur. sed haec fieri melius quam dici aut scribi volo.

3   Quod itinerum meorum ratio te non nullam in dubitationem videtur adducere, visurusne me sis in provincia, ea res se sic habet: Brundisi cum loquerer cum Phania, liberto tuo, veni in eum sermonem ut dicerem me libenter ad eam partem provinciae primum esse venturum quo te maxime velle arbitrarer. tunc mihi ille dixit, quod classe tu velles decedere, per fore accommodatum tibi si ad Sidam[2] [maritimam partem provinciae][3] navibus accessissem. dixi me esse facturum itaque fecissem nisi mi L. Clodius noster Corcyrae dixisset minime id esse faciendum; te Laodiceae fore ad meum adventum. erat id mihi multo brevius multoque commodius, cum praesertim te ita malle arbitrarer. tua ratio postea est commutata. nunc quid fieri possit, tu facillime statues; ego tibi meum consilium exponam. prid.[4] Kal. Sext. puto me Laodiceae fore. perpaucos dies, dum pecunia accipitur quae mihi ex publica permutatione debetur, commorabor. deinde iter faciam ad exercitum, ut circiter Id. Sext. putem me ad Iconium fore. sed si quid nunc me fallit in scribendo (procul enim aberam ab re ipsa et a locis), simul ac progredi coepero, quam celerrime potero et quam creberrimis litteris faciam ut tibi nota sit omnis ratio dierum atque itinerum meorum. oneris tibi imponere nec audeo quicquam rec debeo; sed, quod commodo tuo fieri possit, utriusque rostrum magni inte⟨resse

4

---

    2 illam *(Rut.)*   3 *(Gul. pro glossemate)*
    4 propter *(Man.)*

altogether convinced on this point must, I think, be unwilling rather than unable to perceive our sentiments. But perceive them they surely will, for the persons involved are not obscure, nor are the issues trivial. But I want all this to come out better in the doing than in the saying or writing.

My itineraries seem to have raised some doubt in your mind as to whether you will be seeing me in the province. This is how the matter stands: When I spoke with your freedman Phanias at Brundisium, I told him in the course of conversation that I should be glad to go first to whatever part of the province I thought you preferred. Then he told me that you wished to leave by boat, and that it would therefore be very much to your convenience if I made my approach by sea and landed at Side. I said I would do so, and so I should have done, if our friend L. Clodius had not told me at Corcyra that this would not answer at all, and that you would be at Laodicea awaiting my arrival. That was a much shorter and more convenient route for me, especially as I supposed you preferred it. Later your plans changed. It will be easiest for you to decide what can be done now; I shall simply explain my own intentions. I expect to reach Laodicea on 31 July. I shall stay only a very few days, to collect the sum due on my Treasury draft. Then I shall proceed to join the army, so that I should expect to be in the neighbourhood of Iconium about the Ides of August. But if at such a distance from the places and circumstances I am at all out in what I write now, as soon as I start making progress I shall send you by letter, as quickly and as often as possible, full details of my dates and routes. I dare not and ought not to impose upon you, but I do think it important for both of us that we should meet before your

puto ut te videam ante >[5] quam decedas. quam facultatem
si quis casus eripuerit, mea tamen in te omnia officia con-
stabunt non secus ac si te vidissem. tibi de nostris rebus
nihil sum ante mandaturus per litteras quam desperaro
coram me tecum agere posse.

5   Quod te a Scaevola petisse dicis ut, dum tu abesses,
ante adventum meum provinciae praeesset, eum ego
Ephesi vidi fuitque mecum familiariter triduum illud
quod ego Ephesi commoratus sum nec ex eo quicquam
audivi quod sibi a te mandatum diceret. ac[6] sane vellem
potuisset obsequi voluntati tuae; non enim arbitror no-
luisse.

69 (III.6)

Scr. in castris ad Iconium prid. Kal. Sept. an. 51

M. CICERO S. D. APPIO PULCHRO

1   Cum meum factum cum tuo comparo, etsi non magis
mihi faveo in nostra amicitia tuenda quam tibi, tamen multo magis meo facto delector quam tuo. ego enim Brundisi
quaesivi ex Phania, cuius mihi videbar et fidelitatem erga
te perspexisse et nosse locum quem apud te is teneret,
quam in partem provinciae maxime putaret te velle ut in
succedendo primum venirem. cum ille mihi respondisset
nihil me tibi gratius facere posse quam si ad Sidam navi-
gassem, etsi minus dignitatis habebat ille adventus et ad
multas res mihi minus erat aptus, tamen ita me dixi esse

    [5] *(SB, auct.* ⊊*)*
    [6] an *(Benedict)*

288

departure, if you can conveniently manage it. If chance robs us of the opportunity, I shall still try to serve you in every way just as though I had seen you. On my own affairs I shall not send you any commissions by letter until I have given up hope of being able to discuss them with you personally.

You say you asked Scaevola[1] to take charge of the province in your absence pending my arrival. I saw him at Ephesus and he was on a familiar footing with me during the three days I spent in the city; but I heard nothing from him about any instructions from you. I certainly regret that he was unable to comply with your wish—for I do not believe him to have been unwilling.

69 (III.6)
CICERO TO APPIUS PULCHER

Camp near Iconium, 29 August 51

From M. Cicero to Appius Pulcher greetings.

When I compare my conduct with yours, for all my desire to give you no less credit than myself in the maintenance of our friendship, I feel much more satisfied with the former. At Brundisium I enquired of Phanias, of whose loyalty to you and place in your confidence I thought I had good evidence and knowledge, what part of the province he thought you would wish me to enter first as your successor. He replied that I could do nothing more agreeable to you than if I came by ship to Side. Although this mode of arrival was less dignified and in many ways less convenient

---

[1] Probably another of Appius' Legates.

2 facturum. idem ego, cum L. Clodium Corcyrae convenissem, hominem ita tibi coniunctum ut mihi cum illo cum loquerer tecum loqui viderer, dixi ei me ita facturum esse ut in eam partem quam Phania rogasset primum venirem. tunc ille, mihi cum gratias egisset, magno opere a me petivit ut Laodiceam protinus irem; te in prima provincia velle esse ut quam primum decederes; quin, nisi ego successor essem quem tu cuperes videre, te antea quam tibi successum esset decessurum fuisse. quod quidem erat consentaneum cum iis litteris quas ego Romae acceperam, ex quibus perspexisse mihi videbar quam festinares decedere. respondi Clodio me ita esse facturum, ac multo quidem libentius quam si illud esset faciendum quod promiseram Phaniae. itaque et consilium mutavi et ad te statim mea manu scriptas litteras misi, quas quidem ex tuis litteris intellexi satis mature ad te esse perlatas.

3 Hoc ego meo facto valde delector; nihil enim potuit fieri amantius. considera nunc vicissim tuum. non modo ibi non fuisti ubi me quam primum videre posses sed eo discessisti quo ego te ne persequi quidem possem triginta diebus qui tibi ad ‹de›cedendum[1] lege, ut opinor, Cornelia constituti essent; ut tuum factum ‹iis›[2] qui quo animo inter nos simus ignorent alieni hominis, ut levissime[3] dicam, et fugientis congressum, meum vero coniunctissimi

4 et amicissimi esse videatur. ac mihi tamen, ante quam in provinciam veni, redditae sunt a te litterae quibus, etsi te Tarsum proficisci demonstrabas, tamen mihi non dubiam spem mei conveniendi adferebas; cum interea, credo equidem, malevoli homines (late enim patet hoc vitium et est in multis), sed tamen probabilem materiem nacti sermo-

   1 *(Rut.)* 2 *(Or.)* 3 lenissime *Mart.*

290

to me, I promised so to do. Then, when I met L. Clodius in Corcyra, a person so close to you that in talking to him I felt I was talking to yourself, I told him that I should be sure to enter the province where Phanias had asked. He thanked me, but requested me emphatically to go straight to Laodicea, saying that you wanted to be on the borders of the province, so as to leave as quickly as possible; in fact, he said, if your successor were someone whom you were less desirous to see, you would have left before he arrived. That fitted in with the letter I had received in Rome, from which it seemed to me evident that you were in a hurry to leave. I replied to Clodius that I should do as he suggested, and should in fact be much better pleased than if I had had to do what I promised Phanias. Accordingly I altered my plan, and immediately dispatched a letter to you in my own hand. From your letter I see that it reached you in quite good time.

With my conduct, as described, I am well satisfied; nothing could have been more friendly. Now consider yours. Not only did you fail to be where you could see me soonest, you withdrew where I could not even follow you within thirty days, that being, I believe, the period prescribed for your departure by the lex Cornelia. Those who do not know our mutual sentiments might well regard your conduct as that of a person indifferent (to use no harsher word), avoiding his successor, whereas mine would appear that of the closest of friends. And yet before I entered the province a letter from you was delivered to me in which you held out assured hope of meeting me, although you intimated that you were leaving for Tarsus. Meanwhile malicious persons, as I believe (a widespread human failing, many have it), finding, however, a plausible theme for

nis, ignari meae constantiae conabantur alienare a te voluntatem meam; qui te forum Tarsi agere, statuere multa, decernere, iudicare dicerent, cum posses iam suspicari tibi esse successum, quae ne ab iis quidem fieri solerent qui brevi tempore sibi succedi putarent.

5 Horum ego sermone non movebar. quin etiam, credas mi velim, si quid tu ageres, levari me putabam molestia et ex annua provincia, quae mihi longa videretur, prope iam undecim mensuum provinciam factam esse gaudebam, si absenti mihi unius mensis labor detractus esset. illud, vere dicam, me movet, in tanta militum paucitate abesse tris cohortis, quae sint plenissimae, nec me scire ubi sint. molestissime autem fero quod te ubi visurus sim nescio; eoque ad te tardius scripsi quod cottidie te ipsum exspectabam, cum interea ne litteras quidem ullas accepi quae me docerent quid ageres aut ubi te visurus essem. itaque virum fortem mihique in primis probatum, D. Antonium, praefectum evocatorum, misi ad te, cui si tibi videretur, cohortis traderes, ut, dum tempus anni esset idoneum, aliquid negoti gerere possem. in quo tuo consilio ut me sperarem esse usurum et amicitia nostra et litterae tuae fecerant, quod ne nunc quidem despero. sed plane quando aut ubi te visurus sim, nisi ad me scripseris, ne suspicari quidem possum.

6 Ego ut me tibi amicissimum esse et aequi et iniqui intellegant curabo. de tuo in me animo iniquis secus existimandi videris non nihil loci dedisse. id si correxeris, mihi

---

[1] *Evocati,* an elite body of veterans, retained or reenlisted after completing their service.

talk, tried to influence my mind in your disfavour, unaware how firmly it is anchored. They said you were holding assizes in Tarsus, making many decisions both administrative and judicial, although you already had reason to think that your successor had arrived—unusual procedure even when a governor expects to be superseded within a short time.

Their talk had no effect upon me. Indeed I can assure you that I considered any such action on your part as relieving me of trouble. My year of office seems all too long, and I am glad it has been reduced almost to eleven months, if a month's work has been taken off my hands in my absence. But I must candidly own that I am disturbed to find three cohorts missing from my exiguous force, and those the most nearly up to strength, and to be ignorant of their whereabouts. What vexes me most, however, is not to know where I shall see you. That is why I have been slow in writing, since I have been expecting you in person from day to day. Meanwhile I have not even had a letter to tell me what you are doing or where I am to see you. I am therefore sending to you Prefect of Reserves[1] D. Antonius, a gallant officer, one of the best I have, to take over the cohorts, if you have no objection, so that I can get something done before the season is over. Our friendship and your letter had led me to hope that I should have the benefit of your advice in that connection, nor have I given up hoping even now. But unless you write to me when and where I am to see you, I am quite unable even to make a guess.

I shall take good care to make it clear that I am your very good friend to well-wishers and ill-wishers alike. You appear to have given some handle to the latter for misconstruction of your attitude towards myself. I shall be grate-

valde gratum erit. et ut habere rationem possis quo loco
me salva lege Cornelia convenias, ego in provinciam veni
prid. Kal. Sext., iter in Ciliciam facio per Cappadociam,
castra movi ab Iconio prid. Kal. Sept. nunc tu et ex diebus
et ex ratione itineris, si putabis me esse conveniendum,
constitues quo loco id commodissime fieri possit et quo
die.

70 (III.8)

Scr. in castris in agro Mopsuhestiae a. d. VIII Id. Oct. an. 51

CICERO S. D. APPIO PULCHRO

1   Etsi, quantum ex tuis litteris intellegere potui, videbam
te hanc epistulam cum ad urbem esses esse lecturum refri-
gerato iam levissimo sermone hominum provincialium,
tamen, cum tu tam multis verbis ad me de improborum
oratione scripsisses, faciendum mihi putavi ut tuis litteris
brevi responderem.

2   Sed prima duo capita epistulae tuae tacita mihi quodam
modo relinquenda sunt. nihil enim habent quod definitum
sit aut certum, nisi me vultu et taciturnitate significasse tibi
non esse amicum, idque pro tribunali cum aliquid ageretur
et non nullis in conviviis intellegi potuisse. hoc totum nihil
esse possum intellegere, sed, cum sit nihil, ne quid dicatur
quidem intellego. illud quidem scio, meos multos et illustris et ex superiore et ex aequo loco sermones habitos cum
tua summa laude et cum magna [sollicitudine] significa-
tione nostrae familiaritatis ad te vere potuisse deferri.

Nam quod ad legatos attinet, quid a me fieri potuit aut
elegantius aut iustius quam ut sumptus egentissimarum

ful if you will put this straight. And to enable you to judge
where you can meet me without breach of the lex Cornelia,
I entered the province on 31 July, am travelling to Cilicia
through Cappadocia, and am breaking camp near Iconium
on 29 August. You will now decide on the basis of dates and
route where and on what day you can most conveniently
meet me, if you think a meeting with me is called for.

70 (III.8)
CICERO TO APPIUS PULCHER

In camp near Mopsuhestia, 8 October 51

From Cicero to Appius Pulcher greetings.

So far as I can gather from your letter you will read this
of mine after you get to Rome, when provincial tittle-tattle
will have grown stale. None the less, as you have written to
me at such length about what evil-minded folk have been
saying, I feel I ought to reply briefly to your letter.

Its first two paragraphs, however, I must in a sense
leave unanswered, since they contain nothing precise or
positive, except that I am supposed to have indicated by
looks and silences that I was no friend of yours, and that
this was perceptible in proceedings before my Tribunal
and at certain dinner parties. That this is all nothing I can
see; but since it *is* nothing, I cannot even make out what is
being said. This I do know, that you might truthfully have
been told of many notorious utterances of mine, both official and private, in which I praised you highly and implied
the close relations between us in unmistakable terms.

As for the matter of delegates, how could I have acted
with greater propriety or fairness than by reducing the out-

civitatum minuerem sine ulla imminutione dignitatis tuae,
praesertim ipsis civitatibus postulantibus? nam mihi totum
genus legationum tuo nomine proficiscentium notum non
erat. Apameae cum essem, multarum civitatum principes
ad me detulerunt sumptus decerni legatis nimis magnos,
3 cum solvendo civitates non essent. hic ego multa simul
cogitavi. primum te, hominem non solum sapientem verum etiam, ut nunc loquimur, urbanum, non arbitrabar genere isto legationum delectari, idque me arbitror Synnadis
pro tribunali multis verbis disputavisse: primum Ap. Clau-
dium senatui populoque Romano non Midaensium[1] testimonio (in ea enim civitate mentio facta est) sed sua sponte
esse laudatum; deinde me i[s]ta vidisse accidere multis ut
eorum causa legationes Romam venirent, sed iis legationibus non meminisse ullum tempus laudandi aut locum dari;
studia mihi eorum placere, quod in te bene merito grati
essent, consilium totum videri minime necessarium; si
autem vellent declarare in eo officium suum, laudaturum
me si qui suo sumptu functus esset officio, concessurum si
legitimo, non permissurum si infinito.

Quid enim[2] reprehendi potest? nisi quod addis visum
esse quibusdam edictum meum quasi consulto ad istas legationes impediendas esse accommodatum. iam non tantum mihi videntur iniuriam facere ii qui haec disputant
4 quam si cuius aures ad hanc disputationem patent. Romae
composui edictum; nihil addidi nisi quod publicani me

[1] Mideaes- (*Quartier*)
[2] in me *Or.*: horum *vel* eorum *Mend.*: in hoc *coni. SB*

lays of penurious communes, at their own request more-over, without any derogation to your dignity? This whole matter of deputations travelling on your behalf lay outside my ken. When I was at Apamea, the leading men in a num-ber of communes submitted to me that excessive sums were being voted for delegates, although the communes concerned were in a state of bankruptcy. I had many fac-tors here to consider. First, I did not suppose that so intelli-gent and furthermore (to use the fashionable expression) so urbane a man as yourself would take any pleasure in such deputations. I made this point at considerable length from my Tribunal, at Synnada I think it was. I said that in the first place the Senate and People of Rome did not need a testimonial from the townsfolk of Midaium (the commu-nity concerned) in praise of Appius Claudius; his praises sang themselves. I further remarked that I had often seen deputations coming to Rome on this or that person's ac-count, but did not remember them ever being given a time or place to deliver their encomia. While approving their zeal and gratitude to you for what you had done for them, I said that the whole plan seemed to me very far from neces-sary. If, however, they desired to manifest their loyalty in that way, those who travelled at their own expense would have my commendation, and those who claimed expenses authorized by law would have my permission; unlimited expenses I should not allow.

What is there to censure? To be sure, you add that cer-tain persons thought my edict was framed as though on purpose to stop these deputations. At this point, I do not consider myself so much wronged by those who so contend as by those whose ears are open to such a contention. I drew up my edict in Rome, and made no addition except

rogarunt, cum Samum ad me venissent, ut de tuo edicto totidem verbis transferrem in meum. diligentissime scriptum caput est quod pertinet ad minuendos sumptus civitatum. quo in capite sunt quaedam nova, salutaria civitatibus, quibus ego magno opere delector; hoc vero ex quo suspicio nata est me exquisisse aliquid in quo te offenderem tralaticium est. neque enim eram tam desipiens ut privatae rei causa legari putarem qui et tibi non privato et pro re non privata sua sed publica, non in privato sed in publico orbis terrae consilio, id est in senatu, ut gratias agerent mittebantur; neque, cum edixi ne quis iniussu meo proficisceretur, exclusi eos qui me in castra et qui trans Taurum persequi non possent—nam id est maxime in tuis litteris irridendum. quid enim erat quod me persequerentur in castra Taurumve transirent, cum ego Laodicea usque ad Iconium iter ita fecerim ut me omnium illarum dioecesium quae cis Taurum sunt omniumque earum civitatum magistratus legationesque convenirent? nisi forte postea coeperunt legare quam ego Taurum transgressus sum; quod certe non ita est. cum enim Laodiceae, cum Apameae, cum Synnadis, cum Philomeli, cum Iconi essem, quibus in oppidis omnibus commoratus sum, omnes iam istius generis legationes erant constitutae. atque hoc tamen te scire volo, me de isto sumptu legationum aut minuendo aut remittendo decrevisse nil nisi quod principes civitatum a me postulassent, ne in venditionem tributorum et illam acerbissimam exactionem, quam tu non ignoras, capitum atque ostiorum inducerent[ur][3] sumptus

5

<hr>

[3] *(Watt)*

what the tax farmers asked me to transfer verbatim from your edict into mine, when they waited upon me at Samos. The section directed to reducing the expenses of the communes was very carefully worded. It contains some novelties beneficial to the communes, in which I take much satisfaction, but the passage which has given rise to the suspicion that I went out of my way to cross you is common form. I was not so irrational as to suppose that these deputations were in a private interest, sent as they were to express gratitude to you, no private individual, for a matter not private to themselves but public, and in no private conclave but before the parliament of the world; that is to say, the Senate. And when I laid down that no one should leave without my authority, I did *not* eliminate persons unable to follow me to my camps or to the other side of the Taurus—this is the most ludicrous point in your letter. Why should they have to follow me to my camps or to cross the Taurus, when I so managed my journey from Laodicea to Iconium that the magistrates and deputations of all districts our side of the Taurus and of their appertaining communes could meet me? Or did they start appointing deputations after I had crossed the mountains? Certainly they did not. When I was at Laodicea, and at Apamea, and at Synnada, and at Philomelium, and at Iconium (I spent time in all these towns), all deputations of this sort had already been nominated. All the same, I wish you to know that I made no ruling for the reduction or cancellation of such expenditure on deputations except at the request of the leading men of the communes, lest expenditures of a far from necessary kind lead them into the sale of taxes and those very harsh imposts (you will know to what I refer), the poll tax

minime necessarii. ego autem, cum hoc suscepissem non solum iustitia sed etiam misericordia adductus ut levarem miseriis perditas civitates et perditas maxime per magistratus suos, non potui in illo sumptu non necessario neglegens esse.

Tu, ⟨si⟩[4] istius modi sermones ad te delati de me sunt, non debuisti credere; si autem hoc genere delectaris, ut quae tibi in mentem veniant aliis attribuas, genus sermonis inducis in amicitiam minime liberale. ego, si in provincia de tua fama detrahere umquam cogitassem, non generum tuum * * *[5] libertum Brundisi neque ad praefectum fabrum Corcyrae quem in locum me venire velles rettulissem. qua re potes doctissimis hominibus auctoribus, quorum sunt de amicitia gerenda praeclarissime scripti libri, genus hoc totum orationis tollere, 'disputabant, ego contra disserebam; dicebant, ego negabam.'

6   An mihi de te nihil esse dictum umquam putas? ne hoc quidem quod, cum me Laodiceam venire voluisses, Taurum ipse transisti? quod isdem diebus meus conventus erat Apameae, Synnade, Philomeli, tuus Tarsi? non dicam plura, ne in quo te obiurgem id ipsum videar imitari; illud dicam ut sentio: si ista quae alios loqui dicis ipse sentis, tua summa culpa est; sin autem alii tecum haec loquuntur, tua tamen, quod audis, culpa non nulla est. mea ratio in tota amicitia nostra constans et gravis reperietur. quod si qui me astutiorem fingit, quid potest esse callidius quam, cum te absentem semper defenderim, cum praesertim mihi usu

[4] *(Or.)*
[5] *lac. agnovit Vict.*

---

[1] See *Letters to Atticus* 109 (V.16).2.

and the door tax.[1] As for me, having undertaken not only in justice but in mercy to relieve the miseries of these ruined communes, ruined in the main by their own magistrates, I could not turn a blind eye to this unnecessary expenditure.

If such talk about me has been carried to you by others, you should not have believed them. If, on the other hand, you favour the practice of attributing to others the thoughts that enter your own mind, you introduce into friendship a far from gentlemanly mode of conversation. Had I ever had it in mind to derogate from your good name in the province, I should not * * * your son-in-law, nor should I have consulted your freedman at Brundisium or your Prefect of Engineers at Corcyra as to where you wished me to go. So, following the advice of learned men who have written excellent books on the conduct of friendship, you can dismiss this whole line of language—'they contended . . . *I* argued to the contrary,' 'they said . . . *I* denied it.'

Perhaps you suppose that nothing has ever been said to *me* about *you*? For example, that after desiring me to go to Laodicea you yourself crossed the Taurus? That at one and the same time I held assizes at Apamea, Synnada, and Philomelium, and you at Tarsus? I will not continue, or I might seem to be following your example in the very point on which I am reproaching you. One thing I *will* say as I think: if the sayings you attribute to others are your own sentiments, you are very much to blame; but if others do talk to you in this strain, you are still in some degree to blame for listening. My attitude throughout our friendship will be found consistent and responsible. If I am credited with cunning, may I point out that I always upheld your interests in your absence, even though I had no thought

venturum non arbitrarer ut ego quoque a te absens defen-
dendus essem, nunc committere[6] ut tu iure optimo me absentem deserere posses?

7 Unum genus excipio sermonis in quo persaepe aliquid
dicitur quod te putem nolle dici, si aut legatorum tuorum
cuipiam aut praefectorum aut tribunorum militum male
dicitur; quod tamen ipsum non mehercule adhuc accidit
me audiente ut aut gravius diceretur aut in pluris quam
mecum Corcyrae Clodius est locutus, cum in eo genere
maxime quereretur te aliorum improbitate minus felicem
fuisse. hos ego sermones, quod et multi sunt et tuam existimationem, ut ego sentio, non offendunt, lacessivi numquam, sed non valde repressi.

Si quis est qui neminem bona fide in gratiam putet redire posse, non nostram is perfidiam coarguit sed indicat
suam, simulque non de me is peius quam de te existimat;
sin autem quem mea instituta in provincia non delectant et
quadam dissimilitudine institutorum meorum ac tuorum
laedi se putat, cum uterque nostrum recte fecerit sed non
idem uterque secutus sit, hunc ego amicum habere non
8 curo. liberalitas tua ut hominis nobilissimi latius in provincia patuit. nostra si angustior (etsi de tua prolixa bene-
ficaque natura limavit aliquid posterior annus propter
quandam tristitiam temporum), non debent mirari homines, cum et natura semper ad largiendum ex alieno fuerim

6 committerem (*Man.*)

that I should one day stand in need of your support in similar circumstances? Would I now give you an excellent justification for deserting my absent self? That would be artful dodging indeed!

One sort of talk, in which things are very frequently said which I imagine you would prefer unsaid, I put in a special category, I mean unfavourable comment on one or other of your Legates or Prefects or Military Tribunes. Even so, I can assure you that no such criticism has so far been uttered in my hearing in more severe terms or reflecting upon a larger number of persons than what Clodius said to me on the subject at Corcyra, when he spoke with especial emphasis of his regret that you should have been so unfortunate in the rascality of others. Since such talk is frequent and does not in my opinion damage *your* reputation, I have not repressed it very vigorously, though I have never encouraged it.

Anyone who believes that bona fide reconciliations are impossible does not convict my bad faith, but exposes his own; and he thinks as badly of you as of me. Whereas anyone who is dissatisfied with my administration here and considers himself injured by a certain dissimilarity between my administration and yours, the fact being that both of us have acted properly but on different principles, why, I do not care to have him as a friend. You, as a great nobleman, were more open-handed here than I have been. I may have kept a rather tight hand on the purse strings—though your own bountiful and kindly instincts were a little cramped in your second year by something unpropitious in the times. I have always been naturally rather conservative in generosity at other people's expense and am influenced by the same temporary conditions as influence others. So

303

restrictior et temporibus, quibus alii moventur, isdem ego movear,

me‹d›[7] esse acerbum sibi ut‹i›[8] sim dulcis mihi.

9   De rebus urbanis quod me certiorem fecisti, cum per se mihi gratum fuit, tum quod significasti tibi omnia mea mandata curae fore. in quibus unum illud te praecipue rogo, ut cures ne quid mihi ad hoc negoti aut oneris accedat aut temporis, Hortensiumque, nostrum collegam et familiarem, roges ut, si umquam mea causa quicquam aut sensit aut fecit, de hac quoque sententia bima decedat, qua mihi nihil potest esse inimicius.

10   De nostris rebus quod scire vis, Tarso Non. Oct. Amanum versus profecti sumus. haec scripsi postridie eius diei, cum castra haberem in agro Mo‹p›s‹u›hestiae.[9] si quid egero, scribam ad te neque domum umquam ad me litteras mittam quin adiungam eas quas tibi reddi velim. de Parthis quod quaeris, fuisse nullos puto. Arabes qui fuerunt admixto Parthico ornatu dicuntur omnes revertisse. hostem esse in Syria negant ullum.

Tu velim ad me quam saepissime et de tuis rebus scribas et de meis et de omni rei publicae statu. de quo sum sollicitus eo magis quod ex tuis litteris cognovi Pompeium nostrum in Hispaniam iturum.

[7] *(Mart.)*
[8] *(Ribbeck)*
[9] *(Man.)*

folk ought not to be surprised that to be 'sweet to myself, I must be sour to them.'[2]

I am obliged for your information about affairs in Rome for its own sake, and also because you intimate that you will attend to all my commissions. On one of them I make a special request; please see that this charge of mine is not increased or its period extended, and please ask our friend and colleague[3] Hortensius, if he has ever voted or acted for my sake, to give up this two-year proposal. Nothing could be more hostile to me.

You ask my news. I left Tarsus for the Amanus on the Nones of October, and am writing this the following day from camp in the territory of Mopsuhestia. If I do anything, I shall write to you, and I shall never send a letter to my home without adding one to be forwarded to you. As for your question about the Parthians, I do not think there *were* any Parthians. There were Arabs,[4] some of them with Parthian equipment, and they are said to have all withdrawn. We are told that there is not a single enemy in Syria.

I hope you will write to me as often as you can about your affairs and my own and about the whole state of the commonwealth, as to which your information that our friend Pompey is to go to Spain has aggravated my concern.

---

[2] From an unknown Latin play.
[3] As Augur.
[4] See Letter 87.2.

71 (III.7)

Scr. Laodiceae paulo post a.d. III Febr. an. 50

CICERO S. D. APPIO PULCHRO

1   Pluribus verbis ad te scribam cum plus oti nactus ero.
haec scripsi subito, cum Bruti pueri Laodiceae me con-
venissent et se Romam properare dixissent. itaque nullas
iis praeterquam ad te et ad Brutum dedi litteras.

2   Legati Appiani mihi volumen a te plenum querelae ini-
quissimae reddiderunt, quod eorum aedificationem litteris meis impedissem. eadem autem epistula petebas ut eos
quam primum, ne in hiemem inciderent, ad facultatem
aedificandi liberarem, et simul peracute querebare quod
eos tributa exigere vetarem prius quam ego re cognita per-
misissem. genus enim quoddam fuisse impediendi, cum
ego cognoscere non <possem> nisi cum ad hiemem me ex
Cilicia recepissem.

3   Ad omnia accipe et cognosce aequitatem expostulatio-
nis tuae. primum, cum ad me aditum esset ab iis qui dicerent a se intolerabilia tributa exigi, quid habuit iniquitatis
me scribere ne facerent ante quam ego rem causamque
cognossem? non poteram, credo, ante hiemem; sic enim
scribis. quasi vero ad cognoscendum ego ad illos, non illi ad
me venire debuerint! 'tam longe?' inquis. quid? cum dabas
iis litteras per quas mecum agebas ne eos impedirem quo
minus ante hiemem aedificarent, non eos ad me venturos

71 (III.7)
CICERO TO APPIUS PULCHER

Laodicea, soon after 11 February 50

From Cicero to Appius Pulcher greetings.

I shall be writing to you at greater length when I get more time. I am writing this in haste, Brutus' boys having met me at Laodicea and told me that they are in a hurry to get back to Rome. So I have given them no letters except to you and to Brutus.

Envoys from Appia have handed me a roll from you full of highly unreasonable complaints concerning their building, which is said to have been stopped by a letter of mine. In the same missive you ask me to set them free to proceed with the building as soon as possible before they run into winter, and at the same time you complain with much asperity of my having forbidden them to levy special taxes until I had examined the case and given permission. That, you say, was one way of stopping them, since I could not make any examination until I returned from Cilicia for the winter.

Allow me to answer all these points, and observe the justice of your expostulation. To start with, I had been approached by persons who claimed that they were being subjected to taxation on an intolerable scale. Was it so unfair that I should write instructing them not to proceed until I had investigated the facts of the case? Oh, but I could not do this before winter—that's what you say in your letter. As though it was for me to go to them to investigate, and not for them to come to me! 'At such a distance?' you ask. Come, when you gave them your letter asking me not to stop them building before winter, did you not sup-

arbitrabare? tametsi id quidem fecerunt ridicule; quas enim litteras adferebant ut opus aestate facere possent, eas mihi post brumam reddiderunt. sed scito et multo pluris esse qui de tributis recusent quam qui exigi velint et me tamen quod te velle existimem esse facturum. de Appianis hactenus.

4   A Pausania, Lentuli liberto, accenso meo, audivi cum diceret te secum esse questum quod tibi obviam non prodissem. scilicet contempsi te, nec potest fieri me quicquam superbius! cum puer tuus ad me secunda fere vigilia venisset isque te ante lucem Iconium mihi venturum nuntiasset incertumque utra via, cum essent duae, altera ⟨A.⟩[1] Varronem, tuum familiarissimum, altera Q. Leptam, praefectum fabrum meum, tibi obviam misi. mandavi utrique eorum ut ante ad me recurrerent[2] ut tibi obviam prodire possem. currens Lepta venit mihique nuntiavit te iam castra praetergressum esse. confestim Iconium veni. cetera iam tibi nota sunt. an ego tibi obviam non prodirem, primum Ap. Claudio, deinde imperatori, deinde more maiorum, deinde, quod caput est, amico, ⟨qui⟩[3] in isto genere multo etiam ambitiosius facere soleam quam honos meus

5   et dignitas postulat? sed haec hactenus. illud idem Pausania dicebat te dixisse: 'quidni? Appius Lentulo, Lentulus Ampio[4] processit obviam, Cicero Appio noluit.' quaeso, etiamne tu has ineptias, homo mea sententia summa prudentia, multa etiam doctrina, plurimo rerum usu, addo

---

[1] *(Purser)*   [2] excurrerent *(Ern.)*
[3] *(Wes.:* cum GR)   [4] appio *(C.F.Hermann)*

---

[1] About 9 p.m.   [2] We do not. But it seems unlikely that a meeting took place.   [3] See Letter 56, n. 3.

pose they would come to me? To be sure they managed this absurdly enough—they did not bring me the letter, which was meant to enable them to do the job during the summer, until after midwinter. But you must understand that the objectors to the taxes are in a large majority over those who want them levied—and that none the less I shall do what I think you wish. So much for the good folk of Appia.

I have heard from my marshal Pausanias, Lentulus' freedman, that you complained to him about my not having gone to meet you. I treated you with contempt, it seems, and my arrogance is quite monstrous! The facts are that your boy arrived about the second watch[1] with a message that you would join me before daybreak in Iconium. As there were two roads and he said it was uncertain which of them you were taking, I sent A. Varro, a close friend of yours, by one and my Prefect of Engineers, Q. Lepta, by the other to meet you, instructing both to hasten back from you to me so that I could go to meet you. Lepta came hurrying back to tell me that you had already passed the camp. I went to Iconium immediately. The rest you already know.[2] Was it likely that I should not turn out to meet you—Appius Claudius, Commander-in-Chief, entitled by traditional practice to the courtesy, and, what is most to the purpose, my friend—I who am in the habit of carrying my desire to please in many such matters much further even than my own rank and dignity require? But I say no more. Pausanias also told me of the following remark of yours: 'Well, of course! Appius went to meet Lentulus, Lentulus went to meet Ampius;[3] but Cicero go to meet Appius, oh no!' Really! These absurdities from you—a man of excellent sound sense, as I judge, much learning also, great knowledge of the world, and, let me add, urbanity, which

urbanitatem, quae est virtus, ut Stoici rectissime putant? ullam Appietatem aut Lentulitatem valere apud me plus quam ornamenta virtutis existimas? cum ea consecutus nondum eram quae sunt hominum opinionibus amplissima, tamen ista vestra nomina numquam sum admiratus; viros eos qui ea vobis reliquissent magnos arbitrabar. postea vero quam ita et cepi et gessi maxima imperia ut mihi nihil neque ad honorem neque ad gloriam acquirendum putarem, superiorem quidem numquam, sed parem vobis me speravi esse factum. nec mehercule aliter vidi existimare vel Cn. Pompeium, quem omnibus qui umquam fuerunt, vel P. Lentulum, quem mihi ipsi antepono. tu si aliter existimas, nihil errabis si paulo diligentius, ut quid sit εὐγένεια [quid sit nobilitas] intellegas, Athenodorus, Sandonis filius, quid de his rebus dicat attenderis.

6   Sed ut ad rem redeam, me tibi non amicum modo verum etiam amicissimum existimes velim. profecto omnibus meis officiis efficiam ut ita esse vere possis iudicare. tu autem si id agis ut minus mea causa, dum ego absim, debere videaris quam ego tua laborarim, libero te ista cura:

> παρ᾽ ἔμοιγε καὶ ἄλλοι
> οἵ κέ με τιμήσουσι, μάλιστα δέ μητίετα Ζεύς.

si autem natura es φιλαίτιος, illud non perficies, quo minus tua causa velim; hoc adsequere ut, quam in partem tu accipias, minus laborem.

Haec ad te scripsi liberius fretus conscientia offici mei

---

4 I.e. nobility, as though Appius was the name of a family. In fact it was a personal name *(praenomen)*, but one almost exclusive to the patrician Claudii, and often used instead of *gentilicium* or *cognomen*. Both nouns are, of course, coined by Cicero.

the Stoics very rightly rank as a virtue! Do you suppose that any Appiety or Lentulity⁴ counts more with me than the ornaments of merit? Even before I gained the distinctions which the world holds highest, I was never dazzled by aristocratic names; it was the men who bequeathed them to you that I admired. But after I won and filled positions of the highest authority in such a fashion as to let me feel no need of additional rank or fame, I hoped to have become the equal (never the superior) of you and your peers. And I may add that I have never observed a different way of thinking in Cn. Pompeius or P. Lentulus, one of whom I judge the greatest man that ever lived, the other greater than myself. If *you* think otherwise, you might do worse than pay rather particular attention to what Athenodorus, son of Sandon, has to say on these points—in order to understand the true meaning of *noblesse*.

But to come back to the point. I want you to believe that I am not only your friend, but your very good friend. Naturally I shall do all I can in a practical way to enable you to decide that this is really so. As for yourself, if your object is not to appear bound to work for my interests while I am away as heartily as I worked for yours, why, I hereby relieve you of that preoccupation—

> Others stand by me
> to do me grace, and before all wise Zeus.⁵

But if you are a fault-finder by nature, you will not make me any the less your well-wisher; all you will achieve is to leave me less concerned about your reactions.

I have written rather frankly, in the consciousness of my

⁵ *Iliad*, 1.174 f. 'Wise Zeus' seems to indicate Pompey.

benevolentiaeque, quam a me certo iudicio susceptam, quoad tu voles, conservabo.

72 (III.9)

Scr. Laodiceae paulo post x *Kal. Mart. an. 50*

CICERO APPIO PULCHRO S.

1   Vix tandem legi litteras dignas Ap. Claudio, plenas humanitatis, offici, diligentiae. aspectus videlicet urbis tibi tuam pristinam urbanitatem reddidit. nam quas ex itinere ante quam ex Asia egressus es ad me litteras misisti, unas de legatis a me prohibitis proficisci, alteras de Appi⟨an⟩orum[1] aedificatione impedita, legi perinvitus. itaque conscientia meae[2] constantis erga te voluntatis rescripsi tibi subiratus. iis vero litteris lectis quas Philotimo, liberto meo, dedisti cognovi intellexique in provincia multos fuisse qui nos quo animo inter nos sumus esse nollent, ad urbem vero ut accesseris, vel potius ut primum tuos videris, cognosse te ex iis qua in te absentem fide, qua in omnibus officiis tuendis erga te observantia et constantia fuissem. itaque quanti illud me aestimare putas quod est in tuis litteris scriptum, si quid inciderit quod ad meam dignitatem pertineat, etsi vix fieri possit, tamen te parem mihi gratiam relaturum? tu vero facile facies; nihil est enim

1 (*Vict.*)
2 mea (*Man.*)

---

1 A sort of play on words: *urbis* (= Rome), *urbanitatem.*

own friendly conduct and good will, an attitude which, as I have adopted it of deliberate choice, I shall maintain so long as *you* wish.

72 (III.9)
CICERO TO APPIUS PULCHER

Laodicea, shortly after 20 February 50

Cicero to Appius Pulcher greetings.

Well, at long last I have read a letter worthy of Appius Claudius, full of courtesy, friendliness, and consideration! It would seem that the sight of Rome has given you back your old urbanity.[1] For I was very sorry to read the letters you sent me en route before you left Asia, one concerning my alleged orders to stop deputations leaving, the other about my holding up the building in Appia; and so, in the consciousness of my unswerving good will towards you, I wrote back in some irritation. But having read the letter you gave to my freedman[2] Philotimus, I find and understand that, whereas there are many in this province who would sooner we did not feel towards one another as we do, you had only to approach Rome, or rather to see your friends there, to learn from their lips how loyal I was to you during your absence, how attentive and steadfast in fulfilling all friendly offices towards you. So you can imagine how much I appreciate the promise you make in your letter to repay me in kind, should anything arise involving my own position—though you say such repayment is hardly possible. On the contrary, you will do it easily enough; for

[2] In fact, Terentia's.

quod studio[3] et benevolentia, vel amore potius, effici non possit.

2   Ego, etsi et ipse ita iudicabam et fiebam crebro a meis per litteras certior, tamen maximam laetitiam cepi ex tuis litteris de spe minime dubia et plane explorata triumphi tui, neque vero ob eam causam, quo ipse facilius consequerer (nam id quidem Ἐπικούρειον est), sed mehercule quod tua dignitas atque amplitudo mihi est ipsa cara per se. qua re, quoniam pluris tu habes quam ceteri quos scias in hanc provinciam proficisci, quod te adeunt fere omnes, si quid velis, gratissimum mihi feceris si ad me, simul atque adeptus eris quod et tu confidis et ego opto, litteras miseris. longi subselli, ut noster Pompeius appellat, iudicatio et mora si quem[4] tibi item unum alterumve diem abstulerit (quid enim potest amplius?), tua tamen dignitas suum locum obtinebit. sed si me diligis, si a me diligi vis, ad me litteras, ut quam primum laetitia adficiar, mittito.

3   Et velim, reliquum quod est promissi ac muneris tui, mihi persolvas. cum ipsam cognitionem iuris auguri consequi cupio tum mehercule tuis incredibiliter studiis erga me muneribusque delector. quod autem a me tale quiddam desideras, sane mihi considerandum est quonam te remunerer potissimum genere. nam profecto non est meum, qui in scribendo, ut soles admirari, tantum industriae ponam, committere ut neglegens ⟨non⟩[5] scriben-

---

3 studio ⟨tuo⟩ *coni. SB*   4 iam *coni. SB*   5 *(SB)*

---

3 Friendship according to Epicurus (and Cicero himself in his younger days; cf. *Pro Roscio Amerino* 111) was founded on self-interest.

4 This probably means the Board of Tribunes.

there is nothing beyond the power of zeal and good will, or rather affection.

The confident, in fact assured, hope of a Triumph expressed in your letter, although it only conforms to my own judgement and the frequent intimations of my correspondents, has given me the greatest happiness. That was not because I may find it the easier to gain one myself (an Epicurean point of view!),[3] but because your dignity and greatness are, I do assure you, intrinsically dear to me. Now you are better placed than others to know of persons setting out for this province, because practically all of them call on you for your commissions; so I shall be deeply obliged if you will send me a letter as soon as you have won the prize which you expect and for which I pray. If the dilatory deliberations of the 'long bench,'[4] to use Pompey's expression, cost you too a day or so (surely no more), your dignity will take no harm. But, if you care for me and wish me to care for you, send me a letter, so that I may rejoice at the earliest possible moment.

I hope too that you will discharge what remains of your promised gift[5] to me. I am anxious to instruct myself in augural law for its own sake, and am marvellously delighted, believe me, with your friendly gestures and gifts. I note that you would like something of the kind from me, and certainly must consider in what form I can best reciprocate your favour. It would hardly be in character in so industrious a writer as I am (to your amazement, as you often say) to let myself appear negligent through failure to

[5] The work on Augury. Evidently Cicero had received only the first section.

do fuisse videar, praesertim cum id non modo neglegentis
sed etiam ingrati animi crimen futurum sit.

4   Verum haec videbimus. illud quod polliceris velim pro
tua fide diligentiaque et pro nostra non instituta sed iam
inveterata amicitia cures ⟨et⟩[6] enitare, ut supplicatio nobis
quam honorificentissime quam primumque decernatur.
omnino serius misi litteras quam vellem (in quo cum dif-
ficultas navigandi fuit odiosa tum ⟨in⟩ ipsum discessum senatus incidisse credo meas litteras), sed id feci adductus
auctoritate et consilio tuo, idque a me recte factum puto
quod non statim ut appellatus imperator sim sed aliis rebus
additis aestivisque confectis litteras miserim. haec igitur
tibi erunt curae, quem ad modum ostendis, meque totum
et mea et meos commendatos habebis.

73 (III.10)

Scr. Laodiceae parte priore m. Apr. an. 50
CICERO APPIO PULCHRO S.

1   Cum est ad nos adlatum de temeritate eorum qui tibi
negotium facesserent, etsi graviter primo nuntio commotus sum, quod nihil tam praeter opinionem meam accidere
potuit, tamen, ut me collegi, cetera mi facillima videban-

---

[6] *(Kayser)*

---

[6] The Senate often rose for a vacation in April.
[1] A charge of lèse-majesté (see Glossary) had been laid against

write, especially where the charge of negligence would be aggravated by one of ingratitude.

But that we shall see. Now as to this other promise of yours, look to it, I beg you, as a man of your word and as our friendship (I won't say 'now established,' for it is already inveterate) claims; do all you can to have me decreed a Supplication in terms as complimentary, and with as little delay, as possible. I sent my dispatch later than I should have wished (there were tiresome difficulties of navigation, and I believe it will arrive just as the Senate goes into recess),[6] but I did so on your authority and advice. And after all, I think I was right not to send it as soon as I was saluted Imperator, but to wait for further achievements and the end of the season's campaigning. This then will be your concern, as you promise; and please regard me and all things and persons that are mine as entirely commended to your care.

73 (III.10)
CICERO TO APPIUS PULCHER

Laodicea, April (first half) 50

Cicero to Appius Pulcher greetings.

The first news of the reckless behaviour of the trouble-makers[1] gave me a severe shock, for nothing could have happened more against my expectations. But having had time to take stock, I believe that, except in one respect, everything will be plain sailing. I set my hopes chiefly upon

Appius by P. Cornelius Dolabella, of whose engagement to Tullia Cicero was informed three months later.

tur, quod et in te ipso maximum spem et in tuis magnam habebam, multaque mihi veniebant in mentem quam ob rem istum laborem tibi etiam honori putarem fore. illud plane moleste tuli, quod certissimum et iustissimum triumphum hoc invidorum consilio esse tibi ereptum videbam. quod tu si tanti facies quanti ego semper iudicavi faciendum esse, facies sapienter et ages victor ex inimicorum dolore triumphum iustissimum. ego enim plane video fore nervis, opibus, sapientia tua, vehementer ut inimicos tuos paeniteat intemperantiae suae. de me tibi si⟨c⟩ contestans omnis deos promitto atque confirmo, me pro tua dignitate (malo enim dicere quam pro salute) in hac provincia cui tu praefuisti rogando deprecatoris, laborando propinqui, auctoritate cari hominis, ut spero, apud civitates, gravitate imperatoris suscepturum officia atque partis. omnia volo a me et postules et ⟨ex⟩spectes. vincam meis officiis cogitationes tuas.

2   Q. Servilius perbrevis mihi a te litteras reddidit, quae mihi tamen nimis longae visae sunt; iniuriam enim mihi fieri putabam cum rogabar. nollem accidisset tempus in quo perspicere posses quanti te, quanti Pompeium, quem unum ex omnibus facio, ut debeo, plurimi, quanti Brutum facerem; quamquam in consuetudine cottidiana perspexisses, sicuti perspicies. sed quoniam accidit, si quid a me praetermissum erit, commissum facinus et admissum dedecus confitebor.

3   Pomptinus, qui a te tractatus est praestanti ac singulari

---

2 In order to answer the charge Appius had to cross the ancient city boundary and thereby give up his *imperium;* having given up his *imperium* he could not be decreed a Triumph.

yourself, but in no small measure upon your family and friends; and many reasons occur to persuade me that this ordeal will actually enhance your reputation. But I certainly am disheartened to see that this piece of malice has robbed you of a perfectly secure and thoroughly well-earned Triumph.[2] If you estimate that at what I have always judged to be its proper importance, you will do wisely; and you will celebrate a well-earned Triumph in virtue of the chagrin of your defeated enemies. For it is abundantly clear to me that your energy, resources, and sagacity will give them good cause to repent their insolence. As for me, I call all the Gods to witness this my solemn pledge, that in this province of which you were governor I shall do what in me lies for your honour (I prefer to say 'honour' rather than 'safety'). On your behalf I shall solicit like an intercessor, and work like a blood relation. My influence with the communes, which I flatter myself hold me in affection, and my authority as Commander-in-Chief shall be at your service. I want you to demand all things of me, and to expect no less. My good offices shall surpass anything you can imagine.

Q. Servilius gave me a very short letter from you. To me, however, it appeared too long, for I felt it an injury to be *asked*. Sorry I am that a time should have come in which you will be able to perceive the extent of my regard for yourself, and for Pompey (whom I esteem, as I ought, more than any man alive), and for Brutus—not that you would not have seen it in our day-to-day intercourse, as see it you will; but since such a time *has* come, I shall acknowledge any omission on my part as an offence against others and against my own honour.

Pomptinus, to whom you behaved with such truly re-

fide, cuius tui benefici sum ego testis, praestat tibi memoriam benevolentiamque quam debet. qui cum maximis suis rebus coactus a me invitissimo decessisset, tamen, ut vidit interesse tua, conscendens iam navem Epheso Laodiceam revertit. talia te cum studia videam habiturum esse innumerabilia, plane dubitare non possum quin tibi amplitudo ista sollicitudo futura sit. si vero efficis ut censores creentur et si ita gesseris censuram ut et debes et potes, non tibi solum sed tuis omnibus video in perpetuum summo te praesidio futurum. illud pugna et enitere, ne quid nobis temporis prorogetur, ut, cum hic tibi satis fecerimus, istic quoque nostram in te benevolentiam navare possimus.

4   Quae de hominum atque ordinum omnium erga te studiis scribis ad me minime mihi miranda et maxime iucunda acciderunt, eademque ad me perscripta sunt a familiaribus meis. itaque capio magnam voluptatem, cum tibi, cuius mihi amicitia non solum [etiam] ampla sed etiam iucunda est, ea tribui quae debeantur, tum vero remanere etiam nunc in civitate nostra studia prope omnium consensu erga fortis et industrios viros, quae mihi ipsi una semper tributa merces est laborum et vigiliarum mearum.

5   Illud vero mihi permirum accidit, tantam temeritatem fuisse in eo adulescente, cuius ego salutem duobus capitis iudiciis summa contentione defendi, ut tuis inimicitiis suscipiendis obliviceretur [pro][1] omnium fortunarum ac

[1] *(Bayet)*

---

[3] Cf. *Letters to Atticus* 92 (IV.18).4.

markable loyalty and kindness,[3] as I myself am witness, does not fail to remember you with the regard that is your due. Important private business obliged him to leave me, greatly to my regret. He was at Ephesus, just taking ship, when he heard that your interests were at stake, and at once returned to Laodicea. Such is the zeal which you can command in countless quarters. With that before my eyes, I simply cannot doubt that your present anxiety will bring you greater honour. And if further you secure the election of Censors, and discharge that office as you should and can,[4] you will clearly be a tower of enduring strength, not only to yourself, but to all connected with you. Only strive with might and main to prevent any extension of my tenure, so that, when I have done what is fitting for you here, I may have the opportunity to serve you as I wish in Rome.

What you write to me about the backing you get from all persons and classes gives me no surprise at all and a great deal of pleasure. My friends tell me the same story in their letters. I am truly happy to see that one whose friendship is to me no less a pleasure than an honour should receive what is his due; happy also to find that brave and active men still inspire in our community that almost universal good will which has always been vouchsafed to myself as the only reward of my toils and vigils.

I am, however, very much astonished to find a young man whom I have twice most strenuously defended on capital charges[5] so foolhardy and so wholly oblivious of his own fortunes and interests as to provoke your enmity. It is

[4] Cicero politely assumes that if Censors are elected Appius will be one of them (as in fact happened).
[5] Their nature is unknown.

rationum suarum, praesertim cum tu omnibus vel ornamentis vel praesidiis redundares, ‹ipsi›,[2] ut levissime dicam, multa deessent. cuius sermo stultus et puerilis erat
iam ante ad me a M. Caelio, familiari nostro, perscriptus;
de quo item sermone multa scripta sunt abs te. ego autem
citius cum eo qui tuas inimicitias suscepisset veterem
coniunctionem diremissem quam novam conciliassem;
neque enim de meo erga te studio dubitare debes neque id
est obscurum cuiquam in provincia nec Romae fuit.

6   Sed tamen significatur in tuis litteris suspicio quaedam
et dubitatio tua, de qua alienum tempus est mihi tecum
expostulandi, purgandi autem mei necessarium. ubi enim
ego cuiquam legationi fui impedimento quo minus Romam ad laudem tuam mitteretur? aut in quo potui, si te palam odissem, minus quod tibi obesset facere, si clam,[3]
magis aperte inimicus esse? quod si essem ea perfidia qua
sunt ii qui in nos haec conferunt, tamen ea stultitia certe
non fuissem ut aut in obscuro odio apertas inimicitias aut
in quo tibi nihil nocerem summam ostenderem voluntatem nocendi. ad me adire quosdam memini, nimirum ex
Epicteto, qui dicerent nimis magnos sumptus legatis decerni. quibus ego non tam imperavi quam censui sumptus
legatis quam maxime ad legem Corneliam decernendos;
atque in eo ipso me non perseverasse testes sunt rationes

---

[2] (*Or.*)
[3] siciam (*Man., auct. Danesio*)

---

[6] Clearly with reference to a marriage with Tullia. Caelius' letter has not survived.

especially surprising when one considers the superabundance of assets and resources on your side and the many deficiencies (to put it mildly) on his. My friend M. Caelius had previously informed me of his silly, childish talk;[6] and you too wrote to me about it at some length. I should have been more likely to break off an old tie with a self-constituted enemy of yours than to form a new one. And indeed you ought not to have any doubts about my sentiments towards you; they are plain to everyone in the province, and were no less so in Rome.

And yet your letter *does* imply a certain suspicion, a doubt in your mind. Present circumstances make it inopportune for me to reproach you on that account, but necessary to exculpate myself. Now when did I ever stop the dispatch of a deputation to Rome to sing your praises? If I hated you openly, could I have taken any step which would have harmed you less? If secretly, could I have done anything to make hostility more obvious? Suppose I were as treacherous as those who tell such tales against me, I surely should not have been so stupid as to make a parade of enmity if I wished to hide my malice, or to show the utmost will to hurt you in a fashion which did not hurt you at all. I do remember being approached by certain folk, from the Annexed Territory[7] if I am not mistaken, who alleged that excessive sums were being voted for deputations. I did not so much order as advise them to vote such sums as far as possible in accordance with the lex Cornelia. But that I did not insist even on that point can be proved from the public accounts of the communes, in which each one

---

[7] A district of Phrygia adjoining Bithynia, annexed by the king of Pergamum about 184. Hence the name Phrygia Epiktetos.

civitatum, in quibus quantum quaeque voluit legatis tuis
datum induxit.

7   Te autem quibus mendaciis homines levissimi onera-
runt! non modo sublatos sumptus sed etiam a procuratoribus eorum qui iam profecti essent repetitos et ablatos
eamque causam multis omnino non eundi fuisse. quererer
tecum atque expostularem ni, ut supra scripsi, purgare me
tibi hoc tuo tempore quam accusare te mallem idque putarem esse rectius. itaque nihil de te, quod credideris, de
me, quam ob rem non debueris credere, pauca dicam. nam
si me virum bonum, si dignum iis studiis eaque doctrina
cui me a pueritia dedi, si satis magni animi, non minimi
consili, in maximis rebus perspectum habes, nihil in me
non modo perfidiosum et insidiosum et fallax in amicitia
8   sed ne humile quidem aut ieiunum debes agnoscere. sin
autem me astutum et occultum libet fingere, quid est quod
minus cadere in eius modi naturam possit quam aut floren-
tissimi hominis aspernari benevolentiam aut eius existimationem oppugnare in provincia cuius laudem domi defen-
deris aut in ea re animum ostendere inimicum in qua nihil
obsis aut id eligere ad perfidiam quod ad indicandum
odium apertissimum sit, ad nocendum levissimum? quid
erat autem cur ego in te tam implacabilis essem, cum te ex
fratre meo ne tunc quidem cum tibi prope necesse esset
eas agere partis inimicum mihi fuisse cognossem? cum
vero reditum nostrum in gratiam uterque expetisset, quid
in consulatu tuo frustra mecum egisti quod me aut facere

---

8 During the conflict between Cicero and Appius' brother P.
Clodius.

entered whatever amount it desired as a grant to your delegates.

But what lies these irresponsibles have foisted upon
you! Not only were these expenses ruled out for the future,
they say, but refunds were demanded and exacted from the
agents of those who had already left, and many did not go
at all for this reason. I should complain and remonstrate
with you, if I did not prefer and think more proper, as I
have said above, to exculpate myself to you rather than to
arraign you in your present circumstances. So of you and
your belief in these tales I shall say nothing; but a little I
shall say about myself, to show why you ought not to have
believed them. If you know me as an honourable man,
worthy of the studies and culture to which I have devoted
myself since childhood, as one who in matters of great moment has shown no petty spirit and no contemptible intelligence, then you ought not to suppose me capable of
meanness or paltriness in friendship, much less of treachery, guile, and falsehood. But suppose you choose to think
of me as a crafty dissembler, how do these allegations
square with such a character? Would a person of this stamp
spurn the good will of one so prosperous? Would he attack
in a province the reputation of a man whose credit he defended at home? Would he display hostility just where he
could inflict no hurt? Would he elect to practise bad faith
in a form at once blatantly declaratory of his spite and quite
innocuous to its object? And then, why should I have borne
you so implacable a grudge, knowing as I did from my
brother that you were no enemy of mine even when circumstances almost compelled you to act like one?[8] After
the reconciliation which we mutually sought, did you once
during your Consulate solicit an action or a vote from me

aut sentire voluisses? quid mihi mandasti, cum te Puteo-
los[4] prosequerer, in quo non exspectationem tuam diligentia mea vicerim?

9   Quod si id est maxime astuti, omnia ad suam utilitatem
referre, quid mihi tandem erat utilius, quid commodis
meis aptius, quam hominis nobilissimi atque honoratissimi
coniunctio, cuius opes, ingenium, liberi, adfines, propinqui mihi magno vel ornamento vel praesidio esse possent?
quae tamen ego omnia in expetenda amicitia tua non astu-
tia quadam sed aliqua potius sapientia secutus sum. quid?
illa vincula, quibus quidem libentissime astringor, quanta
sunt, studiorum similitudo, suavitas consuetudinis, delectatio vitae atque victus, sermonis societas, litterae interio-
res! atque haec domestica; quid illa tandem popularia,
reditus illustris in gratiam, in quo ne per imprudentiam
quidem errari potest sine suspicione perfidiae, amplissimi
sacerdoti collegium, in quo non modo amicitiam violari
apud maiores nostros fas non erat sed ne cooptari quidem
sacerdotem licebat qui cuiquam ex collegio esset inimicus?

10   Quae ut omittam tam multa atque tanta, quis umquam
tanti quemquam fecit aut facere potuit aut debuit quanti
ego Cn. Pompeium, socerum tuae filiae? etenim, si merita
valent, patriam, liberos, salutem, dignitatem, memet ip-

4 Puteolis *(Or.)*

unsuccessfully? When I accompanied you on your outward journey as far as Puteoli, you gave me certain commissions. Was there one in which my assiduity did not
surpass your expectation?

If it is especially characteristic of a crafty fellow to measure all things by the yardstick of his own interest, what,
may I ask, could be more in mine, more advantageous and
convenient to me than connection with a personage of the
highest birth and rank, whose riches, talents, children,
and relations by blood and marriage would be a source of
pride and strength to me? Yet it was no craftiness which led
me to seek those advantages in soliciting your friendship,
rather I might call it sound judgement. And then there are
other bonds whose constraint I am most happy to feel—
similarity of pursuits, the charm of personal intercourse,
the enjoyment of a way of life, the give-and-take of conversation, the more recondite studies we share. These are
bonds! I speak of our private lives. But let us not forget that
some things between us interest the world at large. Our
reconciliation was so publicized that any slip, however
accidental, cannot but create a suspicion of bad faith. We
are colleagues in an exalted priestly office. Remember that
any violation of friendship between such was held a sacrilege in the good old days; indeed no priest could be co-
opted who was on terms of enmity with any member of the
College.

Reasons in plenty, and of no light weight! But suppose I
leave them aside, and only ask whether one man ever
thought, ever could or should think, more of another than I
think of your daughter's father-in-law, Cn. Pompeius? And
well I may. If services count, it was through him that I consider I regained country, children, citizenship, rank, my

sum mihi per illum restitutum puto; si consuetudinis
iucunditas, quae fuit umquam amicitia consularium in
nostra civitate coniunctior? si illa amoris atque offici signa,
quid mihi ille non commisit, quid non mecum communica-
vit, quid de se in senatu, cum ipse abesset, per quemquam
agi maluit, quibus ille me rebus non ornat[issim]um voluit
amplissime? qua denique ille facilitate, qua humanitate tulit contentionem meam pro Milone adversantem interdum
actionibus suis! quo studio providit ne quae me illius temporis invidia attingeret, cum me consilio, cum auctoritate,
cum armis denique texit suis! quibus quidem temporibus
haec in eo gravitas, haec animi altitudo fuit non modo ut
Phrygi alicui aut Lycaoni, quod tu in legatis fecisti, sed ne
summorum quidem hominum malevolis de me sermonibus crederet. huius igitur filius cum sit gener tuus cumque
praeter hanc coniunctionem adfinitatis quam sis Cn. Pompeio carus quamque iucundus intellegam, quo tandem
animo in te esse debeo? cum praesertim eas ad me is litteras miserit quibus, etiam si tibi, cui sum amicissimus, hostis essem, placarer tamen totumque me ad eius viri ita de
me meriti voluntatem nutumque converterem.

11   Sed haec hactenus; pluribus enim etiam fortasse verbis
quam necesse fuit scripta sunt. nunc ea quae a me profecta
quaeque instituta sunt cognosce.* * *[5]

Atque haec agimus et agemus magis pro dignitate

[5] *lac. statuit Rut.*

---

[9] According to existing accounts, Cicero was intimidated
rather than protected by Pompey's troops at Milo's trial. But *Letters to Atticus* 174B (IX.7B).2 shows that he asked Pompey for a
bodyguard and presumably obtained it.

very being; if the pleasures of private intercourse count,
were two Roman Consulars ever faster friends? If the tokens of affection and regard count, has he not made me the
confidant of all his secrets and projects? Has he not chosen
me of all others to represent his interests in the Senate
during his absences? Has he not desired for me all manner
of high distinctions? Can I forget how readily and gra-
ciously he accepted my efforts on Milo's behalf, which
sometimes ran counter to his own policies, how anxious he
was to ensure that I was not touched by the public feeling
aroused at that time? How he protected me by his dispositions, his authority, even his armed forces?[9] His firm and
lofty mind in those days would not let him lend credence to
ill-natured talk about me even from the highest quarters,
let alone some denizen of Phrygia or Lycaonia, as you did
in the matter of the delegates. Well, Pompey's son[10] is your
son-in-law; and apart from that connection I am well aware
how dear and delightful a friend you are to him. What then
should be my feelings towards you? Add that he has sent
me a letter, which, even if I had been your enemy, as I am
so sincerely your friend, would have disarmed my resentment and rendered me obedient to the wishes, the very
nod, of the man to whom I owe so much.

But that will do. Perhaps I have already used more
words than were needed. Now let me tell you what I have
arranged and set in motion[11] * * *.

All this I am doing and shall continue to do, more for

[10] Cn. Pompeius the Younger.
[11] The details that followed may have been omitted in the copy
of the letter preserved by Cicero.

quam pro periculo tuo. te enim, ut spero, propediem censorem audiemus, cuius magistratus officia, quae sunt maximi animi summique consili, tibi diligentius et accuratius quam haec quae nos de te agimus cogitanda esse censeo.

74 (III.11)

Scr. in castris ad Pyramum fort. v Kal. Quint. an. 50

CICERO APPIO PULCHRO, UT SPERO, CENSORI S. D.

1 Cum essem in castris ad fluvium Pyramum, redditae mihi sunt uno tempore a te epistulae duae, quas ad me Q. Servilius Tarso miserat. earum in altera dies erat adscripta Non. Apr., in altera, quae mihi recentior videbatur, dies non erat. respondebo igitur superiori prius, in qua scribis ad me de absolutione maiestatis. de qua etsi permulto a⟨n⟩te certior factus eram litteris, nuntiis, fama denique ipsa (nihil enim fuit clarius, non quo quisquam aliter putasset, sed nihil de insignibus ad laudem viris obscure nuntiari solet), tamen eadem illa laetiora fecerunt mihi tuae litterae, non solum quia planius loquebantur et uberius quam vulgi sermo sed etiam quia magis videbar tibi gratulari cum de te ex te ipso audiebam. complexus igitur sum 2 cogitatione te absentem, epistulam vero osculatus etiam ipse mihi gratulatus sum. quae enim ⟨a⟩ cuncto populo, a senatu, a iudicibus ingenio, industriae, virtuti tribuuntur, quia mihi ipse adsentor fortasse cum ea esse in me fingo, mihi quoque ipsi tribui puto.

your honour than for your protection. For shortly, I hope, we shall hear of you as Censor. I think the duties of that office, calling as they do for courage and policy of the highest order, more deserve your careful and diligent consideration than these steps I am taking on your behalf.

74 (III.11)
CICERO TO APPIUS PULCHER

Camp on the Pyramus, 26 June (?) 50

From Cicero to Appius Pulcher, Censor (I hope), greetings.

Two letters from you were delivered to me in camp on the river Pyramus at the same time, sent on to me from Tarsus by Q. Servilius. One of them was dated the Nones of April; the other seemed to me more recent, but bore no date. I shall therefore reply first to the former, in which you write of your acquittal on the charge of lèse-majesté. I had been informed of this long before by letters and oral messages and general report—it was in all mouths; not that anyone expected a different result, but tidings concerning distinguished reputations seldom lack advertisement. Your letter, however, added to my pleasure in the event. It spoke more distinctly and fully than the common talk, and I had a more vivid sense of congratulating you as I heard your news from yourself. So in my mind I embraced you from afar and kissed the letter, congratulating myself as well as you. For I feel the tribute paid by the whole people and the Senate and the jury to talent, energy, and virtue as paid also to me, flattering myself perhaps in fancying that I possess these qualities.

Nec tam gloriosum exitum tui iudici exstitisse sed tam pravam inimicorum tuorum mentem fuisse mirabar. 'de ambitu vero quid interest' inquies 'an de maiestate?' ad rem, nihil; alterum enim non attigisti, alteram auxisti. verum tamen est maiestas, etsi Sulla voluit ne in quemvis impune declamari liceret, ⟨ambigua⟩;[1] ambitus vero ita apertam vim habet ut aut accusetur improbe aut defendatur. quid enim? facta necne facta largitio ignorari potest? tuorum autem honorum cursus cui suspectus umquam fuit? me miserum, qui non adfuerim! quos ego risus excitassem!

3   Sed de maiestatis iudicio duo mihi illa ex tuis litteris iucundissima fuerunt: unum, quod te ab ipsa re publica defensum scribis, quae quidem etiam in summa bonorum et fortium civium copia tueri talis viros deberet, nunc vero eo magis quod tanta penuria est in omni vel honoris vel aetatis gradu ut tam⟨quam⟩[2] orba civitas talis tutores complecti debeat; alterum, quod Pompei et Bruti fidem benevolentiamque mirifice laudas. laetor virtute et officio cum tuorum necessariorum, meorum amicissimorum, tum alterius omnium saeculorum et gentium principis, alterius iam pridem iuventutis, celeriter, ut spero, civitatis. de

1 *(Lehmann, alii alia)*
2 tam *(coni. SB,* qui scripsit* iam)

---

[1] It is to be inferred from what follows that Dolabella had threatened to prosecute Appius for electoral corruption if he failed to get a conviction on the lèse-majesté charge; and he was as good as his word. The alleged corruption probably had to do with Appius' election as Censor.

What surprises me is not that your trial should have ended so gloriously, but that your enemies should have shown such perverseness.[1] You may ask what difference it makes—corruption or lèse-majesté. None at all, as to the substance. Corruption you have not touched, and as for the majesty of the state, you have enhanced it. Still there is something indeterminate about a lèse-majesté charge, in spite of Sulla's ordinance penalizing random declamation against individuals, whereas corruption is clearly defined—there must be rascality on one side of the case or on the other. For obviously the fact, whether improper disbursements have or have not taken place, cannot be unknown. And what suspicion has ever attached to *your* rise up the official ladder? How I regret that I was not there! The laughs I should have raised!

However, two points in your letter about the lèse-majesté proceedings have given me a great deal of pleasure. One is your remark that Rome herself was your advocate. To be sure, the country ought to protect men like yourself, no matter how plentiful the supply of brave and honest citizens. But as matters stand now, when at every grade of rank and age there is so sore a scarcity, our orphaned (so to speak) community could ill afford not to cling to such guardians. The other point is your enthusiastic praise for the staunchness and good will shown by Pompey and Brutus. I am delighted to learn of this sterling loyalty on their part—not only as they are connections of yours and very good friends of mine, but because one of them stands as the greatest man that any century or people has produced, while the other has for some time past been a leading figure among his contemporaries and is shortly, I hope, to become so in the community at large. As to the

mercennariis testibus a suis civitatibus notandis, nisi iam
factum aliquid est per Flaccum, fiet a me cum per Asiam
decedam.

4   Nunc ad alteram epistulam venio. quod ad me quasi
formam communium temporum et totius rei publicae misisti expressam, prudentia litterarum tuarum valde mihi
est grata; video enim et pericula leviora quam timebam et
maiora praesidia, si quidem, ut scribis, omnes vires civitatis se ad Pompei ductum applicaverunt, tuumque simul
promptum animum et alacrem perspexi ad defendendam
rem publicam mirificamque cepi voluptatem ex hac tua diligentia, quod in summis tuis occupationibus mihi tamen
rei publicae statum per te notum esse voluisti. nam augu-
ralis libros ad commune utriusque nostrum otium serva.
ego enim a te cum tua promissa per litteras flagitabam,
ad urbem te otiosissimum esse arbitrabar. nunc tamen,
ut ipse polliceris, pro auguralibus libris orationes tuas
confectas omnis exspectabo.

5   D. Tullius, cui mandata ad me dedisti, non convenerat
me, nec erat iam quisquam mecum tuorum praeter omnis
meos, qui sunt omnes tui. stomachosiores meas litteras
quas dicas esse non intellego. bis ad te scripsi me purgans
diligenter, te leviter[3] accusans in eo quod de me cito credi-
disses. quod genus querelae mihi quidem videbatur esse
amici; sin tibi displicet, non utar eo posthac. sed si, ut scribis, eae litterae non fuerunt disertae, scito meas non
fuisse. ut enim Aristarchus Homeri versum negat quem

---

3 leniter *Crat.*

censures to be passed upon venal witnesses by the communities to which they belong, if steps have not already been taken through Flaccus, they will be taken by me on my way home through Asia.

Now I come to the other letter. Your detailed survey, marked by so much good sense, of the crisis which affects us all and the whole political situation is most welcome. The dangers, it appears, are less serious than I feared, and the resources to deal with them greater, since, as you tell me, the entire forces of the state have rallied to Pompey's leadership. At the same time I well see your ready and forward spirit in the defence of the constitution, and am most sincerely gratified by your attention, in that in the middle of such grave preoccupations of your own you wished me none the less to learn the state of the commonwealth from *your* pen. As for the work on Augury, keep it until both of us have time to spare—when I wrote demanding the fulfilment of your pledge, I imagined you at the capital without a care in the world. As it is, I shall none the less expect the edition of your complete speeches in lieu of the work on Augury, as you yourself promise.

D. Tullius, to whom you gave a message for me, has not come my way. In fact none of your people is with me at the moment—except for all *my* people, who are all yours! I am at a loss to know which letter of mine you have in mind when you refer to 'a rather irritable letter.' I wrote to you twice exculpating myself in detail and mildly reproaching you because you had been quick to believe what you heard about me—a friendly sort of expostulation, so *I* thought; but if it displeases you, I shall eschew it in future. But if the letter was, as you say, not well expressed, you may be sure I did not write it. Just as Aristarchus denies the authenticity

non probat, sic tu (libet enim mihi iocari), quod disertum
non erit, ne putaris meum.

Vale, et in censura, si iam es censor, ut spero, de proavo
multum cogitato tuo.

75 (III.12)

Scr. Sidae III *aut prid. Non. Sext. an. 50*

CICERO APPIO PULCHRO S.

1   Gratulabor tibi prius (ita enim rerum ordo postulat),
deinde ad me convertar.

Ego vero vehementer gratulor de iudicio ambitus,
neque id quod nemini dubium fuit, absolutum esse te, sed
illud quod, quo melior civis, quo vir clarior, quo fortior
amicus es quoque plura virtutis ⟨ingeni⟩[1] industriae ornamenta in te sunt, eo mirandum est magis nullam ne in ta-
bellae quidem latebra fuisse absconditam malevolentiam
quae te impugnare auderet. non horum temporum, non
horum hominum atque morum negotium. nihil iam sum
pridem admiratus magis.

2   De me autem, suscipe paulisper meas partis et eum te
esse finge qui sum ego: si facile inveneris quid dicas, noli
ignoscere haesitationi meae. ego vero velim mihi Tulliae-
que meae, sicut tu amicissime et suavissime optas, pro-

[1] *(Wes.)**

---

[2] Ap. Claudius Caecus ('the Blind'), whose famous Censorship
beginning in 312, produced the Appian Way and the Claudian
Aqueduct.

of any Homeric line which he does not like, so I would request you (being in jocular vein), if you find any piece of writing not well-expressed, not to believe I wrote it.

Good-bye—and in your Censorship, if Censor, as I hope, you now are, keep your ancestor[2] much in mind.

75 (III.12)
CICERO TO APPIUS PULCHER

Side, 3 or 4 August 50

From Cicero to Appius Pulcher greetings.

I shall begin by offering you my congratulations, putting first things first, and then turn to myself.

Indeed I do congratulate you heartily on the corruption trial—not on your acquittal, which was a foregone conclusion, but on the circumstance that even behind the screen of a secret ballot no lurking malice dared to assail you. The better citizen you are, the greater public figure, the braver friend, the more distinguished for virtue, intellect, and energy, the more remarkable the fact. A thing quite out of tune with modern times and men and manners! Nothing for a long while past has so amazed me.

As for me, please for a moment put yourself in my shoes, imagine you are I; and if you have no difficulty in finding what to say, I won't ask you to forgive my embarrassment! I should indeed wish that the arrangement[1] made by my family without my knowledge may turn out well for my dear Tullia and myself, as you are charming and

---

[1] Tullia's engagement to Dolabella.

spere evenire ea quae me insciente facta sunt a meis. sed
ita cecidisse ut agerentur eo tempore, spero omnino cum
aliqua felicitate et opto—verum tamen plus me in hac spe
tua sapientia et humanitas consolatur quam opportunitas
temporis. itaque quem ad modum expediam exitum huius
institutae orationis non reperio. neque enim tristius dicere
quicquam debeo ea de re quam tu ipse om⟨i⟩nibus optimis
prosequeris neque non me tamen mordet aliquid. in quo
unum non vereor, ne tu parum perspicias ea quae gesta
sint ab aliis esse gesta; quibus ego ita mandaram ut, cum
tam longe afuturus essem, ad me ne referrent, agerent
3 quod probassent. in hoc autem mihi illud occurrit: 'quid tu
igitur si adfuisses?' rem probassem, de tempore nihil te
invito, nihil sine consilio egissem tuo.

Vides sudare me iam dudum laborantem quo modo
⟨et⟩[2] ea tuear quae mihi tuenda sunt et te non offendam.
leva me igitur hoc onere; numquam enim mihi videor trac-
tasse causam difficiliorem. sic habeto tamen: nisi iam tunc
omnia negotia cum summa tua dignitate diligentissime
confecissem, tametsi nihil videbatur ad meum erga te pris-
tinum studium addi posse, tamen hac mihi adfinitate nuntiata non maiore equidem studio sed acrius, apertius, sig-
4 nificantius dignitatem tuam defendissem. decedenti mihi
et iam imperio annuo terminato a. d. III Non. Sext., cum ad
Sidam navi accederem et mecum Q. Servilius esset, litterae a meis sunt redditae. dixi statim Servilio (etenim
videbatur esse commotus) ut omnia a me maiora exspectaret. quid multa? benevolentior tibi quam fui nilo sum fac-

2 *(Pluygers)*

338

kind enough to desire. But that the thing should have come about just when it did—well, I hope and pray some happiness may come of it, but in so hoping I take more comfort in the thought of your good sense and kind heart than in the timeliness of the proceeding! And so how to get out of the wood and finish what I have begun to say I cannot tell. I must not take a gloomy tone about an event to which you yourself wish all good luck; but at the same time I can't but feel a rub. On one point, though, my mind is easy—you will not fail to realize that what has been done has been done by others. I had told them not to consult me since I should be so far away, but to act as they thought best. But as I write, the question obtrudes itself: What should I have done if I had been on the spot? Well, I should have approved in principle; but as for the timing, I should have taken no step against your wishes or without consulting you.

You perceive what a pother I am in all this while, at my wits' end to know how to defend what defend I must without offending you. Lift the load from my back. I don't think I have ever pleaded a more awkward case. But of this you may be sure: though my longstanding zeal to serve you appears to admit of no enhancement, yet, had I not already settled all matters with the utmost regard for your honour, I should have championed it after the announcement of this connection, not indeed more zealously, but more ardently, openly, and emphatically. Letters from my people reached me on my voyage home after the end of my year of office, on 3 August, when I put into Side. Q. Servilius was with me. I told him then and there (he seemed upset) that he might expect more from me on all fronts. In a phrase, I am no whit the friendlier disposed towards you than I was

tus, diligentior ad declarandam benevolentiam multo. nam ut vetus nostra simultas antea stimulabat me ut caverem ne cui suspicionem ficte reconciliatae gratiae darem, sic adfinitas nova curam mihi adfert cavendi ne quid de summo meo erga te amore detractum esse videatur.

76 (III.13)

Scr. fort. Rhodi m. Sext. an. 50

CICERO APPIO PULCHRO S.

1   Quasi divinarem tali in officio fore mihi aliquando expetendum studium tuum, sic, cum de tuis rebus gestis agebatur, inserviebam honori tuo. dicam tamen vere, plus quam acceperas reddidisti. quis enim ad me non perscripsit te non solum auctoritate, oratione,[1] sententia tua, quibus ego a tali viro contentus eram, sed etiam opera, consilio, domum veniendo, conveniendis meis nullum onus[2] offici cuiquam reliquum fecisse? haec mihi ampliora multo sunt quam illa ipsa propter quae haec laborantur. insignia enim virtutis multi etiam sine virtute adsecuti sunt, talium virorum tanta studia adsequi sola virtus potest.

2   Itaque mihi propono fructum amicitiae nostrae ipsam amicitiam, quo[3] nihil est uberius, praesertim in iis studiis quibus uterque nostrum devinctus est. nam tibi me pro-

[1] orationis *(Gron.)*
[2] munus G
[3] qua *(SB)*

---

[1] A *supplicatio,* such as the Senate had just voted Cicero.

before, but I *am* much more anxious to show my friendly disposition to the world. Our old variance used to be a stimulus, leading me to guard against any suspicion that the reconciliation was not sincere on my side. Now my new connection makes me sedulous to avoid any semblance of a falling off in the profound regard I entertain for you.

76 (III.13)
CICERO TO APPIUS PULCHER

Rhodes (?), August 50

From Cicero to Appius Pulcher greetings.

In the days when your achievements were under discussion I worked for your distinction[1] as though I had a presentiment that in time to come I should need your support in similar circumstances. But in all candour, you have more than repaid me. From every quarter letters have come telling me how you took upon yourself the load of service, leaving nothing for others to do. From a man like yourself I should have been well content with the support of your moral influence and speech and vote; but in addition to these you contributed your trouble and advice, visiting my house and meeting my domestic circle. To me these efforts mean far more than the prize for which they are undertaken. The badges of merit have often been obtained without the thing itself, but merit alone can enlist such zealous support from men like you.

The gain I promise myself from our friendship is— friendship itself. Nothing rewards more richly, especially in the context of those pursuits to which both of us are dedicated. For I profess myself both your ally in public affairs,

fiteor et in re publica socium, de qua idem sentimus, et in
cottidiana vita coniunctum, quam his⁴ artibus studiisque
colimus. vellem ita Fortuna tulisset ut, quanti ego omnis
tuos facio, ⟨ta⟩nti tu meos facere posses; quod tamen ipsum nescio qua permotus animi divinatione non ⟨de⟩spe-
ro. sed hoc nihil ad te; nostrum est onus. illud velim sic habeas, quod ⟨iam⟩⁵ intelleges, hac re novata additum potius
aliquid ad meum erga te studium, quo nihil videbatur addi
posse, quam quicquam esse detractum.

Cum haec scribebam, censorem iam te esse sperabam.
eo brevior est epistula et ut adversus magistrum morum
modestior.

77 (VIII.1)

Scr. Romae c. VII Kal. Iun. an. 51

CAELIUS CICERONI S.

1   Quod tibi decedens¹ pollicitus sum me omnis res urba-
nas diligentissime tibi perscripturum, data opera paravi
qui sic omnia persequeretur ut verear ne tibi nimium arguta haec sedulitas videatur; tametsi tu² scio quam sis curiosus et quam omnibus peregrinantibus gratum sit minima-
rum quoque rerum quae domi gerantur fieri certiores.

⁴ iis⟨dem⟩ *J. Ross*
⁵ *(Watt)*
¹ discedens *Gron.*: -denti *R. Klotz*
² te *van den Es*

---

¹ The letters from M. Caelius Rufus, which constitute the

on which our views are identical, and your comrade in daily life, which we live in these accomplishments and pursuits. I wish matters had so fallen out that you could feel as much regard for my connections as I feel for all of yours—and yet some presentiment tells me not to despair even of that. But this is no concern of yours, the onus lies on me. I should only like you to believe what you will find to be the fact, that this unexpected development has rather added something to the warmth of my sentiments towards you, which seemed to admit of no addition, than in any degree diminished it.

As I write these words I trust you are already Censor. My letter is the shorter on that account and the more sober, as addressed to a director of public morals.

77 (VIII.1)
CAELIUS RUFUS TO CICER0

Rome, ca. 26 May 51

From Caelius to Cicero greetings.[1]

Redeeming the promise I made as I took my leave of you to write you all the news of Rome in the fullest detail, I have been at pains to find a person to cover the whole ground so meticulously that I am afraid you may find the result too wordy. However, I know how curious you are and how much everybody abroad likes to be told of even the most trifling happenings at home. But I do hope you won't find me guilty of uppishness in my performance of

eighth Book of the *Letters to Friends,* abound in problems of reading and interpretation.

tamen in hoc te deprecor ne meum hoc officium adro-
gantiae condemnes quod hunc laborem alteri delegavi,
non quin mihi suavissimum sit et occupato et ad litteras
scribendas, ut tu nosti, pigerrimo tuae memoriae dare
operam, sed ipsum volumen quod tibi misi facile, ut ego
arbitror, me excusat. nescio cuius oti esset non modo per-
scribere haec sed omnino animadvertere; omnia enim sunt
ibi senatus consulta, <e>dicta, fabulae, rumores. quod
exemplum si forte minus te delectarit, ne molestiam tibi
2   cum impensa mea exhibeam, fac me certiorem. si quid in
re publica maius actum erit, quod isti operarii minus commode persequi possint, et quem ad modum actum sit et
quae existimatio secuta quaeque de eo spes sit diligenter
tibi perscribemus.

Ut nunc est, nulla magno opere exspectatio est. nam et
illi rumores de comitiis Transpadanorum Cumarum tenus
caluerunt; Romam cum venissem, ne tenuissimam quidem auditionem de ea re accepi. praeterea Marcellus,
quod adhuc nihil rettulit de successione provinciarum
Galliarum et in Kal. Iun., ut mihi ipse dixit, eam distulit
relationem, sane quam eos sermones expressit qui de eo
tum fuerant cum Romae nos essemus.

3   Tu si Pompeium, ut volebas, offendisti, qui tibi visus sit
et quam orationem habuerit tecum quamque ostenderit
voluntatem (solet enim aliud sentire et loqui neque tan-

---

2 I.e. roll of papyrus.   3 Cf. *Letters to Atticus* 95 (V.2).4.

4 Caelius seems to have accompanied Cicero on his outward
journey as far as Pompeii, and is referring to his own return journey to Rome.   5 M. Claudius Marcellus, Consul this year. The
date on which Caesar should hand over his province was a main
issue in Roman politics during the two years preceding the Civil

this office because I have delegated the work to someone else. It is not that I shouldn't be charmed to give time to remembering you, busy though I am and, as you know, the laziest of letter writers. But I imagine the volume[2] I am sending you makes my excuses easily enough. I don't know how anyone could have so much time on his hands as to observe all these items, let alone record them. It's all here—the Senate's decrees, the edicts, the gossip, the rumours. If this specimen does not happen to appeal to you, please let me know, so that I don't spend money merely to bore you. If there is any major political event which these hirelings could not cover satisfactorily, I shall be careful to write you a full account of the manner of it and of consequent views and expectations.

At the moment we are not looking ahead to anything in particular. Those rumours about elections in Transpadane Gaul[3] were rife only as far as Cumae;[4] when I got back to Rome, I did not hear so much as a whisper on the subject. Moreover, Marcellus[5] has so far not referred the question of appointing new governors in the Gallic provinces to the Senate, and has put it off, so he told me himself, till the Kalends of June. That to be sure has elicited the same sort of talk as was going round about him when we were in Rome.[6]

If you found Pompey, as you wanted to do, be sure to write and tell me what you thought of him, how he talked to you, and what disposition he showed.[7] He is apt to say

War. After a vast amount of scholarly debate it is still doubtful when his command legally ended.

[6] Perhaps that he was slow and inefficient; cf. Letter 87.3.

[7] Cf. *Letters to Atticus* 100 (V.7).

tum valere ingenio ut non appareat quid cupiat), fac mihi
perscribas.

4   Quod ad Caesarem, crebri et non belli de eo rumores,
sed susurratores dumtaxat, veniunt. alius equitem perdidisse, quod, opinor, certe fictum[3] est, alius septimam
legionem vapulasse, ipsum apud Bel‹lo›vacos circumse-
deri interclusum ab reliquo exercitu. neque adhuc certi
quicquam est, neque haec incerta tamen vulgo iactantur,
sed inter paucos, quos tu nosti, palam secreto narrantur; at
Domitius cum manus ad os apposuit.

Te a.d. VIIII Kal. Iun. subrostrani (quod illorum capiti
sit!) dissiparant perisse. urbe[4] ac foro toto maximus rumor
fuit te a Q.[5] Pompeio in itinere occisum. ego, qui scirem Q.
Pompeium Baulis embaeneticam facere et usque eo ut ego
miserer eius esurire, non sum commotus et hoc men-
dacio, si qua pericula tibi impenderent, ut defungeremur
optavi. Plancus quidem tuus Ravennae est et magno con-
giario donatus a Caesare nec beatus nec bene instructus
est.

Tui politici libri omnibus vigent.

3 factum *(H. Stephanus)*
4 ur deurbe *(Wes.)*
5 fuit atque *(Man.)*

---

8 Now contending with the aftermath of the great Gallic revolt
of 52.

one thing and think another, but is usually not clever enough to keep his real aims out of view.

As regards Caesar,[8] rumours arrive in plenty about him and they are not pretty—but only of the whispering sort. One says he has lost his cavalry (which I think is certainly a fabrication), another that the Seventh Legion has taken a beating and that Caesar himself is under siege in the country of the Bellovaci, cut off from the rest of his army. But nothing is confirmed as yet, and even these unconfirmed reports are not bandied about generally but retailed as an open secret among a small coterie—you know who. But Domitius claps hand to mouth before he speaks.

On 24 May our pavement gossips[9] had spread it around that you were dead (their funeral, I hope!). All over town and in the Forum there was a great rumour that Q. Pompeius had murdered you on your road. Knowing that Q. Pompeius is operating boats at Bauli with so little to eat that my heart bleeds for him, I was unperturbed, and prayed that if any dangers *are* hanging over you we may be quit of them for the price of this lie. Your friend Plancus[10] is at Ravenna. Despite a massive largesse from Caesar, he is the same dismal vulgarian.[11]

Your work on politics[12] is all the rage.

[9] More literally 'loungers around the Rostra (in the Forum).'

[10] Bursa. Ravenna was in Caesar's province.

[11] The word play is untranslatable. After Caesar's liberality Plancus might be rich *(beatus)* and well provided *(bene instructus);* but he was not happy *(beatus)* and well educated *(bene instructus)*. The latter deficiency is ridiculed in Letter 217.2.

[12] The six Books *On the Republic*.

78 (VIII.2)

Scr. Romae in. m. Iun. an. 51

CAELIUS CICERONI S.

1   Certe, inquam, absolutus est (me ⟨in⟩ re praesent⟨i st⟩ante[1] pronuntiatum est), et quidem omnibus ordinibus, sed singulis in uno quoque ordine sententiis. '⟨ga⟩ude[2] modo,' inquis. non hercules; nihil umquam enim tam praeter opinionem, tam quod videretur omnibus indignum, accidit. quin ego, cum pro amicitia validissime faverem ei et me iam ad dolendum praeparassem, postquam factum est, obstipui et mihi visus sum captus esse. quid alios putas? clamoribus scilicet maximis iudices corripuerunt et ostenderunt plane esse quod ferri non posset. itaque relictus legi Liciniae[3] maior⟨e⟩ esse periculo videtur. accessit huc quod postridie eius absolutionem in theatrum Curionis Hortensius introi⟨i⟩t, u⟨t⟩[4] puto, ut suum gaudium gauderemus. hic tibi

strepitus, fremitus, clamor tonitruum et rudentum
     sibilus.

hoc magis animadversum est quod intactus ab sibilo perve-

---

1 me repraesentare (*SB, praecedentibus Purser et C.F.W. Mueller nisi quod illi* a(d)stante)

2 vide (*SB:* ride *Wes.*)

3 lege Licinia (*Man.*)

4 introitu (*Constans* (-oit))

---

1 M. Valerius Messalla Rufus, Consul in 53, and a friend of Cicero. His uncle Hortensius had just successfully defended him

78 (VIII.2)

CAELIUS RUFUS TO CICERO

Rome, early June 51

From Caelius to Cicero greetings.

Yes, I tell you, it's true. He[1] has been acquitted (I was there when the verdict was announced), and that by all three categories—but by one vote in each.[2] Just be thankful, say you. No, really; nothing so contrary to expectation, no such universal scandal, has ever been seen. Even I, who as a friend was wholeheartedly on his side and had prepared myself for the sad event, was dumbfounded when this happened, and felt as though I had been cheated. You can imagine how others reacted. Naturally they howled abuse at the jury and made it plain that *this* was going beyond all patience. So now he's left in what looks like a more perilous predicament than ever, to face the lex Licinia.[3] On top of this, Hortensius walked into Curio's theatre[4] the day after the acquittal, presumably to let us share in his jubilation. You should have heard the 'din and hubbub, roar of thunder, tackle whistling in the gale.'[5] It was all the more

on a charge of electoral malpractice; cf. *Letters to Atticus* 105 (V.12).2.

[2] At this period Roman juries were made up of equal numbers of Senators, Knights, and Paymaster Tribunes. The votes of each category were counted separately, but the verdict went by a majority of the whole jury.

[3] A recently passed measure concerned with illegal associations. Messalla was in fact prosecuted and found guilty under it.

[4] A wooden theatre of remarkable construction built by Curio in 53 for the show in honour of his dead father.

[5] From the *Teucer* of Pacuvius.

nerat Hortensius ad senectutem. sed tum tam[5] bene ut in
totam vitam cuivis satis esset et paeniteret eum iam vicisse.

2   De re publica quod tibi scribam nihil habeo. Marcelli
impetus resederunt, non inertia sed, ut mihi videbantur,
consilio. de comitiis consularibus incertissima est existimatio. ego incidi in competitorem nobilem et nobilem
agentem; nam M. Octavius Cn. f. et C. Hirrus mecum pe-
tit.[6] hoc ideo scripsi quod scio te acriter propter Hirrum
nuntium nostrorum comitiorum exspectaturum. tu tamen
simul ac me designatum audieris, ut tibi curae sit quod
<ad> pantheras attinet rogo. syngrapham Sittianam tibi
commendo. commentarium rerum urbanarum primum
dedi L. Castrinio[7] Paeto, secundum ei qui has litteras tibi
dedit.

79 (VIII.3)

Scr. Romae c. Id. Iun. an. 51

CAELIUS CICERONI S.

1   Estne? vici? et tibi saepe, quod negaras discedens curaturum tibi, litteras mitto? est, si quidem perferuntur quas
do. atque hoc e[g]o diligentius facio quod, cum otiosus
sum, plane ubi delectem otium meum non habeo. tu cum

----

5 sed tota (*Benedict*: sed tum ita *Man.*)
6 petunt *Wes.*   7 Castronio *Corr.* (*cf. 280 (XIII.13)*)

----

6 Literally 'playing the nobleman.' Hirrus' family was senatorial but not noble.   7 Hirrus had earned Cicero's displeasure
by standing against him for the Augurate.

noticed because Hortensius had come to old age without a single experience of the bird. But he had enough of it then to last anyone a lifetime, and rued his victory.

About politics I have nothing to tell you. Marcellus' initiatives have subsided, not from lack of energy, but, in my opinion, from policy. The consular elections are anybody's guess. *I* have got one nobleman to contend with and one acting-nobleman[6]—M. Octavius, son of Gnaeus, and C. Hirrus are standing with me. I am telling you this because I know how eagerly you will wait for the result of our elections on Hirrus' account.[7] As soon as you hear I am designate, please see to the matter of the panthers.[8] I recommend Sittius' bond to your kind attention.[9] I gave my first Abstract of Affairs in Rome to L. Castrinius Paetus, my second to the bearer of this letter.

79 (VIII.3)
CAELIUS RUFUS TO CICERO

Rome, ca. 13 June 51

From Caelius to Cicero greetings.

Well? Have I won? Am I sending you letters often, which as you were leaving you told me I should never bother to do for you? Yes—if those I dispatch get to their destination. I am all the more punctilious about it, because when I have no work on hand there is simply nowhere for

[8] For the games which Caelius would have to give as Aedile.

[9] Money was owing to Sittius (probably not the addressee of Letter 23, possibly his son) in Cicero's province. Perhaps Caelius was his creditor.

Romae eras, hoc mihi certum ac iucundissimum vacanti
negotium erat, tecum id oti tempus consumere; idque non
mediocriter desidero, ut mihi non modo solus esse sed
Romae te profecto solitudo videatur facta, et qui, quae
mea neglegentia est, multos saepe dies ad te cum hic eras
non accedebam, nunc cottidie non esse te ad quem cursi-
tem discrucior.

Maxime vero ut te dies noctesque quaeram competitor
Hirrus curat. quo modo illum putas auguratus tuum competitorem dolere et dissimulare me certiorem quam se
candidatum? de quo ut quem optas quam primum nuntium accipias, tua me dius fidius magis quam mea causa
cupio. nam mea, si fio, fi⟨eri⟩[1] forsitan cum locupletiore
referat;[2] sed hoc usque eo suave est ut, si acciderit, tota vita
risus nobis deesse non possit. est[3] tanti. sed mehercules
non multum M. Octavium eorum odia quae Hirrum pre-
munt, quae permulta sunt, subleva⟨n⟩t.[4]

2   Quod ad Philotimi liberti officium et bona Milonis
attinet, dedimus operam ut et Philotimus quam honestissime Miloni absenti eiusque necessariis satis faceret et
secundum eius fidem et sedulitatem existimatio tua con-
servaretur.

[1] si *(SB)*   [2] referam *(Reid)*
[3] sed *(Lamb.)*   [4] Octavius . . . sublevat *(Man.)*

---

[1] Hirrus, a very wealthy man. A poor Aedile might draw credit
from the outlay of a richer colleague, and Caelius had hoped to
share expenses (Letter 82.3).

[2] People could vote for as many candidates as there were
places to fill (two in this instance) but were probably not obliged to

me to amuse my leisure. When you were in Rome and I had any free time, I was sure of employment the most agreeable in the world—to pass it in your company. I miss that not a little. It is not merely that I feel lonely; Rome seems turned to desert now that you are gone. I am a careless dog, and when you were here I often used to let day after day go by without coming near you. Now it's a misery not to have you to run to all the time.

Above all else my fellow candidate Hirrus sees to it that I miss you day and night. Just imagine his chagrin—this competitor of yours, this would-be Augur—at finding my prospects of election better than his own, imagine his efforts to pretend it's otherwise! Upon my word, it's for your sake rather than my own that I want you to get the news you are praying for concerning him as soon as may be. As for *my* sake, if I do get elected, it might suit my book to be in company with the richer of the pair.[1] But *this* would be too delicious! If it happens, we shall never be short of a laugh for the rest of our days. Yes, it's worth a sacrifice. But it is a fact that the mislikes which a good many people feel for Hirrus keep him down without notably buoying M. Octavius up.[2]

With regard to the freedman Philotimus' duty and Milo's property,[3] I have been at pains to ensure that Philotimus behaves with complete propriety to the satisfaction of the absent Milo and of those close to him, and that with good faith and care on his part no harm comes to your reputation.

vote for more than one. In that case a refusal to vote for Hirrus would not automatically be a vote for Octavius.

[3] See *Letters to Atticus* 101 (V.8).2.

3   Illud nunc a te peto, si eris, ut spero, otiosus, aliquod ad
nos, ut intellegamus nos tibi curae esse, σύνταγμα con-
scribas. 'qui[5] tibi istuc' inquis 'in mentem venit, homini
non inepto?' <cupio>[6] aliquod[7] ex tam multis tuis monumentis exstare quod nostrae amicitiae memoriam po<s>te-
ris quoque prodat. cuius modi velim, puto, quaeris. tu citius, qui omnem nosti disciplinam, quod maxime convenit
excogitabis, genere tamen quod et ad nos pertineat et δι-
δασκαλίαν quandam, ut versetur inter manus, habeat.

80 (II.8)

Scr. Athenis prid. Non. Quint. an. 51

M. CICERO PRO COS. S. D. M. CAELIO

1   Quid? tu me hoc tibi mandasse existimas ut mihi gladia-
torum compositiones, ut vadimonia dilata et Chresti com-
pilationem mitteres et ea quae nobis cum Romae sumus
narrare nemo audeat? vide quantum tibi meo iudicio tri-
buam (nec mehercule iniuria; πολιτικώτερον enim te adhuc neminem cognovi): ne illa quidem curo mihi scribas
quae maximis in rebus rei publicae geruntur cottidie, nisi
quid ad me ipsum pertinebit. scribent alii, multi nuntia-
bunt, perferet multa etiam ipse rumor. qua re ego nec
praeterita nec praesentia abs te sed, ut ab homine longe in

---

⁵ quid *(Man.)*   ⁶ *(Ern.:* volo *Wes.)*
⁷ aliquid *(Man.)*

---

¹ Unknown. Chrestus is a common slave name.

Now I have a favour to ask. If you are going to have time on your hands, as I expect you will, won't you write a tract on something or other and dedicate it to me, as a token of your regard? You may ask what put that into my tolerably sensible head. Well, I have a desire that among the many works that will keep your name alive there should be one which will hand down to posterity the memory of our friendship. I suppose you will want to know what sort of book I have in mind. With your command of the whole range of knowledge you will think out the most appropriate subject quicker than I; but in general terms, let it be something of relevance to me, with a didactic character so as to have a steady circulation.

80 (II.8)
CICERO TO CAELIUS

Athens, 6 July 51

From M. Cicero, Proconsul, to M. Caelius greetings.

Really! Is this what you think I asked you to do—to send me pairings of gladiators, court adjournments, Chrestus'[1] pilfering, all the trivia which nobody would dare tell me when I am in Rome? Let me show you how highly I value your judgement—and right I am, for I have never known a better *politique* than you! I do not even particularly want you to tell me day-to-day political developments in matters of major consequence, unless I am affected personally. Others will be writing, I shall have plenty of oral informants, even common report will transmit a good deal. So I do not expect things past or present from *your* pen. What I want from so far-sighted a fellow as yourself is the future.

posterum prospiciente, futura exspecto, ut ex tuis litteris,
cum formam rei publicae viderim, quale aedificium futu-
2 rum sit scire possim. neque tamen adhuc habeo quod te
accusem; neque enim fuit quod tu plus providere posses
quam quivis nostrum in primisque ego, qui cum Pompeio
compluris dies nullis in aliis nisi de re publica sermonibus
versatus sum. quae nec possunt scribi nec scribenda sunt;
tantum habeto, civem egregium esse Pompeium et ad omnia quae providenda sunt in re publica et animo et consilio
paratum. qua re da te homini; complectetur, mihi crede.
iam idem illi et boni et mali cives videntur qui nobis videri
solent.

3   Ego, cum Athenis decem ipsos dies fuissem multumque mecum Gallus noster Caninius, proficiscebar inde
prid. Non. Quint., cum hoc ad te litterarum dedi. tibi cum
omnia mea commendatissima esse cupio tum nihil magis
quam ne tempus nobis provinciae prorogetur. in eo mihi
sunt omnia. quod quando et quo modo et per quos agendum sit, tu optime constitues.

81 (VIII.4)

Scr. Romae Kal. Sext. an. 51

CAELIUS CICERONI S.

1   Invideo tibi. tam multa cottidie quae mirer⟨is⟩ istoc
perferuntur. primum illud, absolutum Messallam, deinde
eundem condemnatum; C. Marcellum consulem factum,
M. Calidium ab repulsa postulatum a Galli⟨i⟩s duobus, P.

From your letters, having seen, as it were, an architect's drawing of the political situation, I shall hope to know what kind of building is to come. Not that I have any complaint so far. There has been nothing which you could foresee any better than the rest of us—myself especially, after spending several days with Pompey discussing nothing but public affairs. Of what passed between us I cannot and should not write, but of this much you may be sure: Pompey is a very good patriot, ready in spirit and plan for every political contingency against which we have to provide. So court him; believe me, you will be welcomed. He now sees good citizens and bad exactly where we are wont to see them.

I have spent ten clear days in Athens, much in the company of our friend Gallus Caninius.[2] I leave today, 6 July, after dispatching these few lines. I hope you will take all my interests under your special care, none more than the matter of my tenure here, which I do not want extended. This means everything to me. As to when, how, and through whom to proceed, you will be the best judge.

81 (VIII.4)
CAELIUS RUFUS TO CICERO

Rome, 1 August 51

From Caelius to Cicero greetings.

I really envy you. So many surprises landing on your doorstep every day! First Messalla acquitted; then convicted. C. Marcellus elected Consul. M. Calidius defeated, and prosecuted by the two Gallii. P. Dolabella a Quin-

---

[2] Perhaps in exile.

Dolabellam XV virum factum. hoc tibi non invideo, caruisse te pulcherrimo spectaculo et Lentuli Cruris repulsi vultum non vidisse. at qua spe, quam certa opinione descenderat, quam ipso diffidente Dolabella! et hercules, nisi nostri <oculi Curioni>sque[1] acutius vidissent, paene concedente adversario superasset.

2   Illud te non arbitror miratum, Servaeum,[2] designatum tribunum pl., condemnatum; cuius <in>[3] locum C. Curio petiit. sane quam incutit multis qui eum facilitatemque eius non norunt magnum metum. sed, ut spero et volo et ut se fert ipse, bonos et senatum malet; totus, ut nunc est, hoc scaturit. huius autem voluntatis initium et causa est quod eum non mediocriter Caesar, qui solet infimorum hominum amicitiam sibi qualibet impensa adiungere, valde contempsit. qua in re mihi videtur illud perquam venuste cecidisse, quod ab reliquis quoque usque eo est animadversum ut Curio, qui nihil consilio facit, ratione et insidiis[4] usus videretur in evitandis iis consiliis qui se intenderant adversarios in eius tribunatum, †laelios†[5] et Antonios et id genus valentis dico.

3   Has ego tibi litteras eo maiore misi intervallo quod comitiorum dilationes occupatiorem me habebant et

---

[1] *(coni. SB*)*   [2] serva eum *(Wes.)*
[3] *(Markland: ante* cuius *Or.)*
[4] consilio usus . . . iis insidiis *Man.*
[5] Lollios *Man.*

---

[1] The Quindecimviri (Board of Fifteen) were official custodians of the Sibylline prophecies.

[2] As I have interpreted this difficult passage, Curio was given credit for countering the plans of his pro-Caesarian opponents by

decimvir.[1] One thing I *don't* envy you—you missed a really beautiful sight, Lentulus Crus' face when he heard his defeat. He had gone down to the hustings in the highest fettle, thought to be a certainty. Even Dolabella had little opinion of his own chances. In fact I may say that but for the sharper eyes of your humble servant and Curio, Lentulus would have carried the day with his opponent practically conceding victory.

One thing I expect will *not* have surprised you, the conviction of Tribune-Elect Servaeus. C. Curio has announced himself as a candidate for the vacancy, much to the alarm of folk who don't know him and his easy ways. But as I expect and hope and as he himself declares, he will be for the Senate and the honest men. At the moment he is absolutely frothing with this sentiment. Its origin and cause is that Caesar, who doesn't usually care how much money he spends to get the friendship of any guttersnipe, has shown his indifference to Curio in no uncertain manner. A propos of which I feel this is a highly amusing coincidence, and others have noticed it—so much so that Curio, who does nothing except on impulse, is credited with deep cunning in evading the designs of certain persons who had set themselves to oppose him as Tribune, I mean Lollius (?), Antony, and other sturdy fellows of the same stamp.[2]

The interval between this letter and its predecessor has been the wider because the postponements of the elections kept me rather busy and made me wait for the out-

standing at a by-election instead of waiting till the following year. Lollius was a former satellite of Clodius. The manuscript reading *laelios* would presumably refer to D. Laelius, Tribune in 54, who is inappropriate.

‹ex›spectare in dies exitum cogebant, ut confectis omnibus te facerem certiorem. ad Kal. Sext. usque exspectavi. praetoriis morae quaedam inciderunt. mea porro comitia quem eventum sint habitura nescio; opinionem quidem, quod ad Hirrum attinet, incredibilem aedilium pl. comitiis nacta sunt. nam M. Coelium Vinicianum[6] mentio illa fatua, quam de‹ri›seramus olim, et promulgatio de dictatore subito deiecit et deiectum magno clamore insecuta est.[7] inde Hirrum cuncti ‹i›am non faciendum flagitare. spero te celeriter et de nobis quod sperasti et de illo quod vix sperare ausus es auditurum.

4   De re publica iam novi quicquam exspectare desieramus; sed cum senatus habitus esset ad Apollinis a. d. XI Kal. Sext. et referretur de stipendio Cn. Pompei, mentio facta est de legione ea quam expensam tulit C. Caesari Pompeius, quo numero esset, quoad pateretur[8] eam Pompeius esse in Gallia. coactus est dicere Pompeius se legionem abducturum, sed non statim sub mentionem et convicium obtrectatorum. inde interrogatum[9] de successione C. Caesaris; de qua, hoc est de provinciis, placitum est ut quam primum ad urbem reverteretur Cn. Pompeius, ut coram eo de successione provinciarum ageretur. nam Ari-

6 vicinianum *(Lamb.)*
7 magni clamores insecuti sunt *Boot*
8 quo appeteretur *(C.F.Hermann)*
9 interrogatus *(Kierdorf)*

3 As Tribune in 53 Hirrus had called for Pompey to be made Dictator. From this passage it is inferred that Coelius did likewise, and that his rout in the elections to the Plebeian Aedileship was now taken as a bad sign for Hirrus. How something that happened

come from day to day, in order to inform you when everything was over. I have waited until the Kalends of August.
The Praetorian elections have been held up by various ac-
cidents. What is going to happen in my own I don't know.
As regards Hirrus, the election of the Plebeian Aediles
has produced an amazing current of opinion. M. Coelius
Vinicianus was suddenly brought down (with loud shouts
to follow as he lay) by that silly statement of his which we
laughed at together at the time and the notice of legislation
about a Dictator.[3] After that came a universal hue and cry
that *now* Hirrus must not be elected. I trust that it won't be
long before you hear the news you have been hoping for
about me and the news for which you have hardly dared to
hope about him.

In the political arena we had stopped expecting anything fresh. But when the Senate met in the Temple of
Apollo[4] on 22 July, and was asked to consider the matter of
pay for Pompey's troops, a question was raised about the
legion which Pompey lent to C. Caesar[5]—whose was it,
and how long would Pompey let it remain in Gaul. Pompey
was forced to say that he *would* withdraw the legion, but
not immediately under prompting and clamour from his
critics. Then there was a question about the replacement
of C. Caesar, as to which (i.e. on the provinces generally) it
was determined that Pompey should return to Rome as
soon as possible in order that a debate be held on the re-

two years previously could 'suddenly' bring Coelius down is anybody's guess.

[4] In the Campus Martius, outside the ancient city boundary,
which Pompey, as holding *imperium,* could not enter except by
special dispensation.

[5] At the beginning of 53 (cf. Caesar, *Gallic War* 6.1).

minum ad exercitum Pompeius erat iturus et statim iit.
puto Id. Sext. de ea re actum[10] iri. profecto aut transigetur
aliquid aut turpiter intercedetur; nam in disputando co-
iecit illam vocem Cn. Pompeius,[11] omnis oportere senatui
dicto audientis esse. ego tamen sic nihil exspecto quo
modo Paullum, consulem designatum, primum sententiam dicentem.

5 Saepius te admoneo de syngrapha Sittiana (cupio enim
te intellegere eam rem ad me valde pertinere); item de
pantheris, ut Cibyratas accersas curesque ut mi vehantur;
praeterea (nuntiatum[12] nobis et pro certo iam habetur
regem Alexandrinum mortuum) quid mihi suadeas, quo
modo regnum illud se habeat, quis procuret, diligenter
mihi perscribas.

Kal. Sext.

82 (VIII.9)

Scr. Romae IV *Non. Sept. an.* 51

CAELIUS CICERONI S.

1 'Sic tu' inquis 'Hirrum tractasti?' immo, si scias quam
facile, quam ne contentionis quidem minimae fuerit,

---

10 factum *(Lamb.)*   11 Pompeio
12 nuntiatur ⟨enim⟩ *C.F.W.Mueller*

---

6 Consuls-Elect spoke first. Paullus, a friend of Cicero, had
previously been regarded as a firm optimate. In office he took a
passive line, allegedly bribed by Caesar. Caelius seems to have
had some inkling of his change of front.

placement of provincial governors in his presence (Pompey was about to go to Ariminum to visit his army and went immediately). I think the debate will be on the Ides of August. Presumably something will be decided, or there will be a scandalous veto. For in the course of the discussion Pompey threw out the remark that everyone ought to obey the Senate. For my own part though, I am looking forward to nothing in the world so much as to Consul-Elect Paullus making the first speech.[6]

I am reminding you about Sittius' bond, not for the first time, because I am anxious to make you realize my strong personal concern in that matter. Likewise about panthers—please send for some from Cibyra and have them shipped to me. Another thing, we have had word of the death of the king of Egypt,[7] and it is now taken as certain. Please write to me at length, advising me how to act and telling me of the state of the kingdom and who is in charge of it.

Kalends of August.

82 (VIII.9)
CAELIUS RUFUS TO CICERO

Rome, 2 September 51

From Caelius to Cicero greetings.

'So that's how you handled Hirrus, is it?' I hear you saying. My dear sir, if you only knew how easy it was, how

[7] Ptolemy the Piper. His successors, Ptolemy XIII and Cleopatra, being too young to rule, a regency was established. Caelius was presumably one of the late king's creditors.

pudeat te ausum illum umquam esse incedere tamquam tuum competitorem. post repulsam vero risus facit; civem bonum ludit et contra Caesarem sententias dicit, exspectationem corripit, <consules> [curionem] prorsus [curionem][1] non mediocriter obiurgat, <tot>us[2] <h>ac[3] repulsa se mutavit. praeterea, qui numquam in foro apparuerit, non multum in iudiciis versatus sit, agit causas liberalis, sed raro post meridiem.

2   De provinciis quod tibi scripseram Id. Sext. actum iri, interpellat[4] iudicium Marcelli, consulis designati. in Kal. <res>[5] reiecta est. ne frequentiam quidem efficere potuerant. has litteras a. d. IIII Non. Sept. dedi, cum ad eam diem ne profligatum quidem quicquam erat. ut video, causa haec integra in proximum annum transferetur et, quantum divino, relinquendum tibi erit qui provinciam obtineat. nam non expeditur successio, quoniam Galliae, quae habent intercessorem, in eandem condicionem quam ceterae provinciae vocantur. hoc mihi non est dubium; quo tibi magis scripsi ut ad hunc eventum te parares.

3   Fere litteris omnibus tibi de pantheris scripsi. turpe tibi erit Patiscum Curioni decem pantheras misisse, te[6] non

---

[1] *(SB)*   [2] obiurgatus *(Lünemann)*   [3] ac
[4] interpellavit *Wes.*: -larat *T.–P.*   [5] *(Or.)*
[6] te <mihi> *coni. SB*

---

[1] For their dilatory handling of the question of Caesar's command.   [2] Cases to determine whether a person was free or slave. A man of Hirrus' rank might gain popularity by appearing on behalf of such humble folk.

completely effortless, you would be ashamed to remember that he ever dared to parade as your competitor. After the defeat he's making us all laugh, playing the good citizen and delivering anti-Caesarian speeches in the Senate, denouncing the waiting game, and taking the Consuls to task in no uncertain terms.[1] This defeat has made a completely different man of him. On top of this, he that never showed his face in the Forum and has little experience of law courts has taken to appearing in freedom suits[2]—but not often after midday.

I told you earlier that there would be a debate on the provinces on the Ides of August, but Consul-Elect Marcellus' trial[3] has upset this timetable. The matter was put off to the Kalends. They had not even been able to get a quorum. I am dispatching this letter on 2 September, and up to that date nothing has been even in main part accomplished. It looks to me as though the entire question will be relegated to next year, and, as far as I can prophesy, you will have to leave a deputy governor behind you. There is no way clear to the appointment of a successor, because the Gauls, for which a veto is in readiness, are being linked with the other provinces. I am sure of this. That is another reason why I am writing to you, so that you prepare yourself for this outcome.

In almost every letter I have written to you I have mentioned the subject of panthers. It will be little to your credit that Patiscus has sent ten panthers for Curio and you not

[3] C. Marcellus, Consul in 50, was prosecuted by his unsuccessful competitor M. Calidius for electoral malpractice after the elections, but was acquitted.

multis partibus pluris; quas ipsas Curio mihi et alias Africa-
nas decem donavit, ne putes illum tantum praedia rustica
dare scire. tu si modo memoria ten⟨u⟩eris et Cibyratas
arcessieris itemque in Pamphyliam litteras miseris (nam
ibi pluris capi aiunt), quod voles efficies. hoc vehementius
laboro nunc quod seorsus a collega puto mihi omnia paran-
da. amabo te, impera tibi hoc. curare soles libenter, ut ego
maiorem partem nihil curare. in hoc negotio nulla tua nisi
loquendi cura est, hoc est imperandi et mandandi. nam
simul atque erunt captae, qui alant eas et deportent habes
eos quos ad Sittianam syngrapham misi. puto etiam, si ullam spem mihi litteris ostenderis, me isto missurum alios.

4   M. Feridium, equitem Romanum, amici mei filium,
bonum et strenuum adulescentem, qui ad suum negotium
istoc venit, tibi commendo et te rogo ut eum in tuorum
numero habeas. agros quos fructuarios habe⟨n⟩t civitates
vult tuo beneficio, quod tibi facile et honestum factu est,
immunis esse. gratos et bonos viros tibi obligaris.

5   Nolo te putare Favonium a columnariis praeteritum;
optimus quisque eum non fecit. Pompeius tuus aperte
Caesarem et provinciam tenere cum exercitu et consul-
⟨em fieri non vult⟩.[7] ipse tamen hanc sententiam dixit,

----

[7] *(Boot et Baiter)*

----

[4] I.e. 'for me.'   [5] Apparently with reference to some incident otherwise unrecorded. Curio's plan for a redistribution of
land in Campania (cf. Letter 87.4), even if already formed and
known to Caelius, would hardly have been known to Cicero.

[6] M. Octavius.   [7] The lands may have been owned by
Feridius senior and let to local civic corporations.

[8] This satellite of Cato had been defeated in the elections to
the Praetorship.

many times as many.[4] Curio has given me those same animals and another ten from Africa—in case you imagine that country estates[5] are the only form of present he knows! If you will but keep it in mind and send for beasts from Cibyra and write to Pamphylia likewise (they say the hunting is better there), the trick will be done. I am all the more exercised about this now because I think I shall have to make all my arrangements apart from my colleague.[6] Do be a good fellow and give yourself an order about it. You generally like to be conscientious, as I for the most part like to be careless. Conscientiousness in this business is only a matter of saying a word so far as you are concerned, that is of giving an order and commission. As soon as the creatures are caught, you have the men I sent in connection with Sittius' bond to look after their feeding and transport to Rome. Indeed, if you hold out any hope when you write, I think I shall send some more men over.

M. Feridius, a Roman Knight, is going to Cilicia on personal business. He is the son of a friend of mine, and is a worthy and energetic young man. May I recommend him to you and request you to admit him to your circle? He hopes that by a kindness which you can render with ease and propriety some lands held in tenancy by communes[7] will receive exemption from tax. You will be obliging worthy people, who do not forget a service.

I wouldn't have you think that Favonius[8] was passed over by the groundlings. All the best people didn't vote for him. Your friend Pompey is openly against Caesar being elected Consul while he retains his province and army. But speaking in the Senate he himself said that no decree

nullum hoc tempore senatus consultum faciendum, Scipio hanc, ut Kal. Mart. de provinciis Galli‹i›s neu quid coniunctim referretur. contristavit haec sententia Balbum Cornelium, et scio eum questum esse cum Scipione. Calidius in defensione sua fuit disertissimus, in accusatione satis frigidus.

83 (VIII.5)

Scr. Romae med. m. Sept. an. 51

CAELIUS CICERONI S.

1   Qua tu cura sis, quod ad pacem provinciae tuae finitimarumque regionum attinet, nescio; ego quidem vehementer animi pendeo. nam si hoc mo‹do› re‹m›[1] moderari possemus ut pro viribus copiarum tuarum belli quoque exsisteret magnitudo et quantum gloriae triumphoque opus esset adsequeremur, periculosam et gravem illam dimicationem evitaremus, nihil tam esset optandum. nunc, si Parthus movet aliquid, scio non mediocrem fore contentionem. tuus porro exercitus vix unum saltum tueri potest. hanc autem nemo ducit rationem, sed omnia desiderantur ab eo, tamquam nihil denegatum sit ei quo minus quam paratissimus esset, qui publico negotio praepositus

2   est. accedit huc quod successionem futuram propter Galliarum controversiam non video. tametsi hac de re puto te constitutum quid facturus esses habere, tamen, quo matu-

[1] *(Bengel)*

should be passed at present, while Scipio proposed that the question of the Gallic provinces should be brought before the House on the Kalends of March, with no other item attached. His speech cast a gloom over Balbus Cornelius, and I know he has remonstrated with Scipio. Calidius gave an excellent performance in his own defence; as prosecutor he was pretty unimpressive.

83 (VIII.5)
CAELIUS RUFUS TO CICERO

Rome, mid September 51

From Caelius to Cicero greetings.

How worried *you* may be about the prospects of peace in your province and the adjacent areas I don't know, but for my part I am on tenterhooks. If we could so manage that the size of the war be proportionate to the strength of your forces and we achieve as much as requisite for glory and a Triumph while avoiding the really dangerous and serious clash, it would be the most desirable thing in the world. But I know that as matters stand any move by the Parthians will mean a major conflict; and your army is hardly capable of defending a single pass. Unfortunately nobody allows for this; a man charged with public responsibility is expected to cope with any emergency, as though every item in complete preparedness had been put at his disposal. Furthermore, I do not see any prospect of your being relieved because of the controversy about the Gallic provinces. Although I expect you have settled in your own mind what you are going to do in this contingency, I thought that, since I see it coming, I ought to

rius constitueres, cum hunc eventum providebam, visum
est ut te facerem certiorem. nosti enim haec tralaticia: de
Galli‹i›s constituetur; erit qui intercedat; deinde alius
exsistet qui, nisi libere liceat de omnibus provinciis decernere senatui, reliquas impediat. sic multum ac diu ludetur,
atque ita diu ut plus biennium in his tricis moretur.

3   Si quid novi de re publica quod tibi scriberem habere‹m›, usus essem mea consuetudine, ut diligenter et
quid actum esse‹t› et quid ex eo futurum sperarem perscriberem. sane tamquam in quodam incili iam[2] omnia
adhaeserunt. Marcellus idem illud de provinciis urget [et][3]
neque adhuc frequentem senatum[4] efficere potuit. hoc
si‹c› praeterito anno Curio tribunus e‹ri›t,[5] eadem actio
de provinciis introibit;[6] quam facile tunc[7] sit omnia impedire et quam hoc Caesar i‹ique›[8] qui sua causa rem publicam non curent[9] spere‹n›t,[10] non te fallit.

84 (VIII.8)

Scr. Romae in. m. Oct. an. 51
CAELIUS CICERONI S.

1   Etsi de re publica quae tibi scribam habeo, tamen nihil

---

[2] incilicia *(Man.)*   [3] *(Vict.)*   [4] frequentiam senatus*
[5] *(Lünemann)*   [6] introi ut *(Man.)*   [7] nunc *(Rut.)*
[8] Caesari *(Kahnt)*   [9] curant *Lamb.*   [10] superet *(Or.)*

---

[1] Neither the text nor the general sense is certain. Caelius can
hardly mean that Curio in office would play Caesar's game (as in
fact he did), for at this time he expected quite otherwise. But Cu-

inform you, so that you take your decision the further ahead. You know the routine. There will be a decision about Gaul. Somebody will come along with a veto. Then somebody else will stand up and stop any move about the other provinces, unless the Senate has free licence to pass decrees on all of them. So we shall have a long, elaborate charade—so long that a couple of years or more may drag by in these maneuvres.

If I had anything fresh to tell you about the political situation, I should follow my usual practice and describe in detail both what had happened and what consequences I expected to follow. The fact is that everything has stuck in a kind of trough. Marcellus still goes on pressing his point about the provinces, but so far he has not succeeded in getting a muster of the Senate. This year thus passed, Curio will be Tribune, and the same performance about the provinces will come on the boards. You don't need me to tell you how easy it will be then to hold everything up, and how well this will suit Caesar and those who think of themselves and care nothing about the country.[1]

84 (VIII.8)
CAELIUS RUFUS TO CICERO

Rome, early October 51

From Caelius to Cicero greetings.

Although I have some matters of public import to tell

rio was unpredictable and might fish in troubled waters. Perhaps *he* might be the one to 'stand up and stop any move about the other provinces.'

quod magis gavisurum te putem habeo quam hoc: scito
C. Sempronium Rufum, mel ac delicias tuas, calumniam
maximo plausu tulisse. ⟨qua⟩ quaeris in[1] causa. M. Tuccium, accusatorem suum, post ludos Romanos reum lege
Plotia de vi fecit hoc consilio, quod videbat, si extraordi-
narius reus nemo accessisset, sibi hoc anno causam esse
dicendam; dubium porro illi non erat quid futurum esset.
nemini hoc deferre munusculum maluit quam suo accusa-
tori. itaque sine ullo subscriptore descendit et Tuccium
reum fecit. at ego, simul atque audivi, invocatus ad sub-
sellia rei occurro; surgo, neque verbum de re facio, totum
Sempronium usque eo perago ut Vestorium quoque inter-
ponam et illam fabulam narrem, quem ad modum tibi pro
beneficio dederit †si quod iniuriis suis esset ut Vestorius
teneret.†

2   Haec quoque magna nunc contentio forum tenet:
M. Servilius postquam, ut coeperat, omnibus in rebus
turbarat nec quod [non][2] venderet cuiquam reliquerat

---

1 quaeris an *(C.F.Hermann)*: quaeris qua in *(Vict.)*
2 *(Rubenius)*

---

1 This man was in Cicero's bad books; cf. *Letters to Atticus* 95
(V.2).2.   2 Why Rufus' prosecution of Tuccius should have had
priority is controversial. The Roman Games ended on 19 September.   3 On M. Tuccius Galeo see my *Onomasticon to Cicero's
Letters,* p. 99. The charge against Sempronius is unknown, but
Caelius' forecast of the outcome seems to have been correct, since
he was in exile in 44; *Letters to Atticus* 368 (XIV.14).2.

4 The nature of Cicero's involvement in this affair being
obscure (cf. *Letters to Atticus* 95 (V.2).2), the corrupt text seems
incurable.

you, I have nothing that I think you will be so pleased to read as the following. Learn that your heart's darling, C. Sempronius Rufus,[1] has been nailed for malicious prosecution to loud applause. The case? He charged his own prosecutor, M. Tuccius, with assault under the lex Plotia after the Roman Games, his idea being that, if no priority prosecution came up,[2] he himself would have to stand trial this year—and what would happen then he knew all too well.[3] He thought he might as well make this little present to his accuser as to anybody. So down he went, with no assistant prosecutor, and charged Tuccius. As soon as I hear of it, I hurry unsummoned up to the defence benches. I get on my hind legs and without a syllable on the matter in hand, I make a thorough job of Sempronius, even including Vestorius and the story of how he claimed to have done you a favour in letting Vestorius keep * * *.[4]

Now the Forum is full of another great tussle.[5] M. Servilius, having completed a career of general derangement and left nobody anything to sell, was handed over to

---

[5] The facts up to this point may be made out as follows: C. Claudius Pulcher, governor of Asia in 55–53, had been charged with extortion after his return (the case seems to have been slow in getting to court). He had paid over a sum to M. Servilius (probably a former member of his staff) to obtain an acquittal by collusion with the prosecution. He was, however, found guilty and went into exile without leaving enough assets to pay the damages assessed by the court. Pausanias, representing the provincials, then tried to prosecute Servilius on a charge of 'receiving' (i.e. receiving money extorted from the province), but the Praetor, M. Juventius Laterensis, refused leave to proceed, presumably on the ground of insufficient evidence. Caelius was acting on behalf of Pausanias, not Servilius (this corrects my Commentary).

maximaque nobis traditus erat invidia,[3] neque Laterensis praetor postulante Pausania nobis patronis 'quo ea pecunia pervenisset' recipere voluit, Q. Pilius, necessarius Attici nostri, repetundis eum postulavit. magna ilico fama surrexit et de damnatione fervente loqui est coeptum. quo vento proicitur Appius minor ut indicet [de][4] pecuniam ex bonis patris pervenisse ad Servilium praevaricationisque causa diceret depositum HS ⌐xxx⌐.[5] admiraris amentiam; immo, si actionem stultissimasque de se, nefarias de patre confessiones audisses.

3   Mittit in consilium eosdem illos qui litis aestimarant iudices. cum aequo numero sententiae fuissent, Laterensis leges ignorans pronuntiavit quid singuli ordines iudicassent et ad extremum, ut solent,[6] 'non redigam.' postquam discessit et pro absoluto Servilius haberi coeptus legisque unum et centesimum caput legit, in quo ita erat: 'quod eorum iudicum maior pars iudicarit id ius ratumque esto,' in tabulas absolutum non rettulit, ordinum iudicia perscripsit; postulante rursus Appio cum L. Lollio †transegisset†[7] relaturum dixit. sic nunc neque absolutus neque damnatus Servilius de repetundis saucius Pilio tradetur.

---

[3] maxime qu(a)e . . . invidi(a)e *(Rut.)*   [4] inpicet de *(Man.)*
[5] LXXXI *(Constans)*   [6] solet *Man.*
[7] transegisse et *C.F.Hermann*: transegit et se *Man.*

---

[6] Appius minor seems to have been allowed to revive Pausanias' charge under particular provisions of the lex Julia, with priority over Pilius' general charge under the same law, since the former stemmed from a previous trial.

[7] Appius (see my Commentary).

[8] Of acquittal. An even vote was normally considered as a ver-

me—a most unpopular defendant. Pausanias prosecuting with me as advocate on a charge of receiving, Praetor Laterensis dismissed the case *prima facie*. Then Q. Pilius, our friend Atticus' connection, charged him with extortion. It became at once a *cause célèbre* and a verdict of guilty was eagerly canvassed. Tossed up on the crest of this wave, Appius minor lays information concerning money received by Servilius out of his father's property, alleging that HS3,000,000 had been deposited to rig the prosecution.[6] The folly of it surprises you? It would surprise you more if you had heard him speak, the admissions he made about himself and his father—the former idiotic, the latter shocking.

He[7] sends the jury to consider their verdict, the same jury that had assessed the damages. The votes were equally divided. Laterensis, not knowing his law, announced the verdict of each category and, to finish up, 'I shall not call in'—the usual form.[8] He then left the courtroom, and everyone began to look on Servilius as acquitted. Laterensis, having read the hundred-and-first section of the law, which states 'the verdict of the majority of such members of the jury shall be lawful and binding,' made his entry in the record—not 'acquitted,' but the verdicts of the several categories. Appius again laid his charge; on which Laterensis said that he had arranged matters with L. Lollius and would * * *.[9] So now Servilius is neither acquitted nor

dict of acquittal, but the lex Julia, whether by accident or design, seems to have required a majority; an even vote meant that the trial was void.   [9] Laterensis' reaction to Appius' demand for a fresh trial is concealed under a corrupt text, but whatever it was it resulted in the lapse of Appius' charge.

nam de divinatione Appius, cum calumniam iurasset, contendere ausus non est Pilioque cessit et ipse de pecuniis repetundis a Serviliis est postulatus et praeterea de vi reus a quodam suo emissario, †stetio†,[8] factus. recte hoc par habet.

4   Quod ad rem publicam pertinet, omnino multis diebus exspectatione Galliarum actum nihil est; aliquando tamen, saepe re dilata et graviter acta et plane perspecta Cn. Pompei voluntate in eam partem ut eum decedere post Kal. Mart. placeret, senatus consultum quod tibi misi factum est auctoritatesque perscriptae.

5   Senatus consultum, auctorita⟨te⟩s:[9]

        'Prid. Kal. Oct. in aede Apollinis scrib. adfuerunt L. Domitius Cn. f. Fab. Ahenobarbus, Q. Cae-⟨ci⟩lius Q. f. Fab. Metellus Pius Scipio, L. Vil⟨l⟩ius L. f. Pom. Annalis, C. Septimius T. f. Qui., C. Luci-⟨li⟩us C. f. Pup. Hirrus, C. Scribonius C. f. Pom.[10] Curio, L. Ateius L. f. An⟨i⟩. Capito, M. Eppius M. f. Ter. [sal.]

        Quod M. Marcellus cos. v. f. de provinciis consularibus, d. e. r. i. c., uti L. Paullus C. Marcellus cos., cum magistratum inissent, [a. d.] ex [x][11] Kal.

---

[8] Statio *coni. SB*   [9] *(Man.)*   [10] Pop. *(Badian)*
[11] *(Gron.)*

---

[10] As a preliminary to claiming the right to prosecute the extortion case in preference to Pilius. Such contests were settled by vote of the jury.   [11] Presumably for misconduct in Asia during his father's governorship.

[12] The name, possibly Statius or Suettius, is doubtful.

[13] Meaning Caesar.

convicted, and will be handed over to Pilius the worse for wear, to be tried for extortion. Appius, having sworn good faith,[10] none the less did not have the courage to contest the right to prosecute and gave way to Pilius. He himself has been prosecuted for extortion[11] by the Servilii, and on top of this has been charged with assault by a satellite of his own, *.[12] A well-matched pair!

As regards public affairs, for a long while nothing was done pending a decision on the Gallic provinces. But eventually, after many postponements and much grave debate, during which it became quite clear that Cn. Pompeius was in favour of his[13] leaving his command after the Kalends of March, the Senate passed a decree, of which I send you a copy, and recorded resolutions.

Decree of the Senate: Resolutions

On this 29th day of September in the Temple of Apollo. Present at drafting the following: L. Domitius Ahenobarbus, son of Gnaeus, of the tribe Fabia; Q. Caecilius Metellus Pius Scipio, son of Quintus, of the tribe Fabia; L. Villius Annalis, son of Lucius, of the tribe Pomptina; C. Septimius, son of Titus, of the tribe Quirina; C. Lucilius Hirrus, son of Gaius, of the tribe Pupinia; C. Scribonius Curio, son of Gaius, of the tribe Pomptina; L. Ateius Capito, son of Lucius, of the tribe Aniensis; M. Eppius, son of Marcus, of the tribe Teretina.

Forasmuch as M. Marcellus, Consul, did address this House touching the consular provinces, it was thus resolved: that L. Paullus and C. Marcellus, Consuls, having entered upon their office, should

377

Mart. quae in suo magistratu futurae essent, de consularibus provinciis ad senatum referrent, neve quid prius ex Kal. Mart. ad senatum referrent neve quid coniunctim [de ea re referrentur a consiliis],[12] utique eius rei causa per dies comitialis senatum haberent senatusque cons. facere⟨n⟩t et, cum de ea re ad senatum referrent, ut[13] a consiliis, qui eorum in CCC iudicibus essent, s. f. s.[14] adducere[15] liceret; si quid d. e. r. ad populum pl. ve lato opus esset, uti Ser. Sulpicius M. Marcellus cos., pr., tr. q. pl., quibus eorum videretur, ad populum pl. ve ferrent; quod ⟨si⟩[16] ii non tulissent, uti quicumque deinceps essent ad populum pl. ve ferrent. u. i. ⟨c.⟩'[17]

'Prid. Kal. Oct. in aede Apollinis scrib.[18] adfuerunt L. Domitius Cn. f. Fab. Ahenobarbus, Q. ⟨Caecilius⟩ Q. f. ⟨Fab.⟩ Metellus Pius Scipio, L. Villius L. f. Pom. Annalis, C. Septimius T. f. Qui., ⟨C. Lucilius C. f. Pup. Hirrus⟩, C. Scribonius C. f. Pom. Curio, L. Ateius L. f. An⟨i⟩. Capito, M. Eppius M. f. Ter.'

'Quod M. Marcellus cos. v. f.[19] de provinciis, d. e.

---

[12] *(Hofmann)*
[13] referentur *(Hofmann)*
[14] ses. *(Hirschfeld)*
[15] abducere *Man.*
[16] *(Or.)*
[17] i.u. *(SB, auct. Constans)*
[18] scripta *(Man.)*
[19] ut *(Rut.)*

on or after the Kalends of March falling in their year
of office bring the matter of the consular provinces
before the Senate, and that from the Kalends of
March onwards they bring no other business before
the Senate either previously or in conjunction
therewith; further that for the said purpose they
may hold a meeting of the Senate upon any comitial
day and pass a Decree, and that in bringing the said
matter before the Senate they may without forfeit
incurred bring persons belonging to the panel of
300 jurors from their several juries to this House being members thereof; further, if there be need that
proposals touching this matter be brought before
People or Plebs, that Ser. Sulpicius and M. Marcellus, Consuls, the Praetors, and Tribunes of the
Plebs, whosoever of them see fit, bring such proposals before People or Plebs; and that if they do not so
do, then their successors bring such proposals before People or Plebs. Resolved unanimously.

On this 29th day of September in the Temple of
Apollo. Present at drafting the following: L. Domitius Ahenobarbus, son of Gnaeus, of the tribe Fabia;
Q. Caecilius Metellus Pius Scipio, son of Quintus, of
the tribe Fabia; L. Villius Annalis, son of Lucius, of
the tribe Pomptina; C. Septimius, son of Titus, of
the tribe Quirina; C. Lucilius Hirrus, son of Gaius,
of the tribe Pupinia; C. Scribonius Curio, son of
Gaius, of the tribe Pomptina; L. Ateius Capito, son
of Lucius, of the tribe Aniensis; M. Eppius, son of
Marcus, of the tribe Teretina.

Forasmuch as M. Marcellus, Consul, did address

r. i. c., senatum existimare neminem eorum qui potestatem habent intercedendi impediendi moram
adferre oportere quo minus de re publica p. q. ‹t.›[20]
ad senatum referri senatique c. fieri possit; qui
impedierit prohibuerit, eum senatum existimare
contra rem publicam fecisse. si quis huic s. c. inter-
cesserit, senatui placere auctoritatem perscribi et
de ea re ad senatum p. q. ‹t.›[21] referri.'

'Huic s.c. intercessit C. Coelius,[22] L. Vinicius,[23] P.
Cornelius, C. Vibius Pansa ‹tr. pl.›.'[24]

7   'Item senatui placere de militibus qui in exercitu
C. Caesaris sunt, qui eorum stipendia emerita aut
causas quibus de causis missi fieri debeant habeant,
ad hunc ordinem referri, ut eorum ratio habeatur
causaeque cognoscantur. si quis huic s. c. intercessisset, senatui placere auctoritatem perscribi et de
ea re p. ‹q. t.›[25] ad hunc ordinem referri.'

'Huic s. c. intercessit ‹C.› Coelius, C. Pansa tr.
pl.'

8   'Itemque senatui placere in Ciliciam provinciam
in VIII reliquas provincias quas praetorii pro prae-

[20] q.p. (SB)
[21] populumque (Willems)
[22] C(a)elius (Lamb.)
[23] Vicinius (Lamb.)
[24] (Or.)
[25] (Mend.)

the senate touching the provinces, it was thus resolved: that in the judgement of the Senate no person having power of veto or impediment should let or hinder that matters touching the commonwealth be brought before the Senate on the first possible occasion and that a Decree of the Senate be passed; and that whosoever offers such bar or impediment shall in the judgement of the Senate have acted against the commonwealth. If any person shall cast his veto against this Decree of the Senate, it is the Senate's pleasure that a Resolution be recorded and that the matter be brought before the Senate on the first possible occasion.

The above Decree of the Senate was vetoed by the following Tribunes of the Plebs: C. Coelius; L. Vinicius; P. Cornelius; C. Vibius Pansa.

It is likewise the Senate's pleasure as touching soldiers serving in the army of C. Caesar that the cases of any such who have completed their terms of service or who can show cause wherefore they be discharged be brought before this House to the end that their cases be taken under consideration and cognizance. If any person shall cast his veto against this Decree of the Senate, it is the Senate's pleasure that a Resolution be recorded and that the matter be brought before this House on the first possible occasion.

The above Decree of the Senate was vetoed by the following Tribunes of the Plebs: C. Coelius; C. Pansa.

It is likewise the Senate's pleasure as touching the province of Cilicia and the eight remaining prov-

tore obtinerent eos qui praetores fuerunt neque in
provincia cum imperio fuerunt, quos eorum ex s. c.
cum imperio in provincias pro praetore mitti oporteret, eos sortito in provincias mitti [placere];[26] si ex
eo numero quos ⟨ex⟩ s. c. in provincias ire oporteret
ad numerum non essent qui in eas provincias proficiscerentur, tum, uti quodque collegium primum
praetorum fuisset neque in provincias profecti
essent, ita sorte in provincias proficiscerentur; si ii
ad numerum non essent, tum deinceps proximi
cuiusque collegi qui praetores fuissent neque in
provincias profecti essent in sortem coicerentur
quoad is numerus effectus esset quem ad numerum
in provincias mitti oporteret. si quis huic s. c. intercessisset, auctoritas perscriberetur.'

'Huic s. c. intercessit C. Coelius, C. Pansa tr. pl.'

9   Illa praeterea Cn. Pompei sunt animadversa quae
maxime confidentiam attulerunt hominibus, ut diceret se
ante Kal. Mart. non posse sine iniuria de provinciis Caesaris statuere, post Kal. Mart. se non dubitaturum. cum
interrogaretur ⟨quid⟩[27] si qui tum intercederent, dixit hoc
nihil interesse utrum C. Caesar senatui dicto audiens

[26] *(Lamb.)*
[27] *(SB)*

---

[14] Voted in 53 to impose a five-year interval between the holding of a Consulship or Praetorship and the assumption of a province. The rule did not become effective until the following year
when it was enacted by law (see Letter 65, n. 1).

inces now governed by former Praetors with propraetorian rank that such persons as have held the
office of Praetor but have not previously held
command in any province, being eligible under the
Senate's Decree[14] for dispatch to provinces with
propraetorian rank, shall be dispatched to the aforesaid provinces as by lot determined. If the number
of persons qualified under the Senate's Decree for
such appointment be less than the number required
to proceed to the aforesaid provinces, then persons
having been members of the Board of Praetors
standing next in order of seniority, such persons
having previously held provincial office, shall proceed to provinces as by lot determined. If their
number be insufficient, then members of each
Board of Praetors in succession, not having previously held provincial office, shall be admitted to the
lot, until the requisite number be completed. If any
person cast his veto against this Decree of the Senate, let a Resolution be recorded.

The above Decree of the Senate was vetoed by
the following Tribunes of the Plebs: C. Coelius; C.
Pansa.

Moreover, certain remarks of Cn. Pompeius have been
noted, and have greatly raised public confidence. He said
that before the Kalends of March he could not in fairness
take a decision about Caesar's provinces, but that after this
date he would have no hesitation. Asked what would be the
position if vetoes were cast at that point, he replied that it
made no difference whether C. Caesar was going to dis-
obey the Senate or was putting up someone to prevent the

futurus non esset an pararet qui senatum decernere non
pateretur. 'quid si' inquit alius 'et consul esse et exercitum
habere volet?' at ille quam clementer: 'quid si filius meus
fustem mihi impingere volet?' his vocibus ut existimarent
homines Pompeio cum Caesare esse negotium effecit.
itaque iam, ut video, alteram utram ad condicionem
descendere vult[28] Caesar,[29] ut aut maneat neque hoc anno
10 sua ratio habeatur aut, si designari poterit, decedat. Curio
se contra eum totum parat. quid adsequi possit nescio;
illud video, bene sentientem, etsi nihil effecerit, cadere
non posse.

Me tractat liberaliter Curio et mihi suo munere negotium imposuit. nam si mihi non dedisset eas quae ad ludos
ei advectae erant Africanae, potuit supersederi; nunc, quoniam dare necesse est, velim tibi curae sit, quod a te
semper petii, ut aliquid istinc bestiarum habeamus, Sittia-
namque syngrapham tibi commendo. libertum Philonem
istoc misi et Diogenem Graecum, quibus mandata et
litteras ad te dedi. eos tibi et rem de qua misi velim curae
habeas. nam quam vehementer ad me pertineat in iis quas
tibi illi reddent litteris perscripsi.[30]

[28] volet *Teuffel*
[29] Caesarem *Weiske*
[30] descripsi *(Benedict)*

Senate from passing a decree. 'And supposing,' said another questioner, 'he chooses to be Consul[15] *and* keep his army?' To which Pompey, as gently as you please: 'And supposing my son chooses to take his stick to me?' These utterances of his have produced an impression that Pompey is having trouble with Caesar. So it looks to me as though Caesar is now ready to settle for one of two propositions—either to stay where he is and forgo his candidature this year,[16] or, if he can secure election, to retire from his command. Curio is making ready for all-out opposition to him. What he may be able to accomplish I don't know, but it is clear to me that he cannot come to grief even if he achieves nothing, his sentiments being sound.

Curio is behaving handsomely to me, and has made me a somewhat onerous present in the shape of the African panthers which were imported for his show. Had he not done that, one might have let the thing go. As it is, I have to give it. So, as I have asked you all along, please see that I have a few beasts from your part of the world. And I commend Sittius' bond to your kind attention. I have sent out my freedman Philo and a Greek, Diogenes, and given them a message and a letter for you. Please look after them and the object of their errand. How important that is to me I have explained in the letter which they will deliver to you.

[15] I.e. to get himself elected.
[16] This can only mean 'the current electoral year,' i.e. 50.

85 (II.9)

Scr., ut vid., in castris in agro Mopsuhestiae c. VIII *Id. Oct. an. 51*

M. CICERO PRO COS. S. D. M. CAELIO AEDILI CURULI DESIGNATO

1 Primum tibi, ut debeo, gratulor laetorque cum praesenti tum etiam sperata tua dignitate, serius non neglegentia mea sed ignoratione rerum omnium. in iis enim sum locis quo et propter longinquitatem et propter latrocinia tardissime omnia perferuntur. et cum gratulor tum vero quibus verbis tibi gratias agam non reperio, quod ita factus sis ut dederis nobis, quem ad modum scripseras ad me, quod semper ridere possemus. itaque, cum primum audivi, ego ille ipse factus sum (scis quem dicam)

2 egique omnis illos adulescentis quos ille [i]actitat.[1] difficile est loqui; te autem contemplans absentem et quasi tecum coram loquerer

> non edepol quantam rem egeris neque quantum
>   facinus feceris . . .

quod quia praeter opinionem mihi acciderat, referebam me ad illud:

> incredibile hoc factum obicitur.

repente vero incessi 'omnibus laetitiis ⟨laetus⟩.'[2] in quo

[1] *(Vict.)*   [2] *(Mart.)*

---

[1] After election to the Curule Aedileship Caelius could look forward to higher things in due course—the Praetorship, even the

85 (II.9)
CICERO TO CAELIUS RUFUS

Camp near Mopsuhestia (?), ca. 8 October 51

From M. Cicero, Proconsul, to M. Caelius, Curule Aedile-Elect greetings.

First my due and joyful congratulations on your present dignity and also on what may be expected to follow.[1] That they are rather late in coming is not the result of any negligence on my part but of my ignorance of all that goes on. I am in a region where news comes in very slowly, because of its remoteness and the banditry in the country. And not only do I congratulate you, I cannot find words to express my gratitude for the manner of your election, which has given us, as you wrote to me,[2] something to laugh at for the rest of our lives. When I first heard the news, I was transformed into the man himself[3] (you know whom I mean), and found myself playing all those *jeune premier* roles which he is so fond of performing.[4] It's hard to put into words, but I saw you in imagination and it was as though I was talking to you: 'Well done, egad! A famous piece of work!' The thing came to me so unexpectedly that I went on to that bit that goes 'A quite amazing thing today . . .' Then, all of a sudden, 'I walked on air. Glee! Glee!' And

Consulship. Or perhaps Cicero is simply referring to his entry into office.   [2] See Letter 79.1.   [3] Hirrus.

[4] The point of this passage is not entirely clear. It has been supposed that Hirrus was fond of quoting or reciting from Latin comedies; but why from these particular roles? Had he a propensity to pose as a dashing young gallant (he must have been in his thirties)? The authorship of the first two quotations is unknown. The third comes from Caecilius, the fourth from Trabea.

cum obiurgarer quod nimio gaudio paene desiperem, ita me defendebam:

> ego voluptatem animi[3] nimiam . . .

quid quaeris? dum illum rideo, paene sum factus ille.

3   Sed haec pluribus multaque alia et de te et ad te cum primum ero aliquid nactus oti. te vero, mi Rufe, diligo, quem mihi Fortuna dedit amplificatorem dignitatis meae, ultorem non modo inimicorum sed etiam invidorum meorum, ut eos partim scelerum suorum, partim etiam ineptiarum paeniteret.

86 (II.10)

Scr. in castris ad Pindenissum XVII *Kal. Dec. an. 51*

M. CICERO IMP. S. D. M. CAELIO AEDILI CURULI DESIG-NATO

1   Tu vide quam ad me litterae non perferantur! non enim possum adduci ut abs te, postea quam aedilis es factus, nullas putem datas, praesertim cum esset tanta res tantae gratulationis, de te quia quod sperabam, de Hillo[1] (balbus enim sum) quod[2] non putaram. atqui sic habeto, nullam me epistulam accepisse tuam post comitia ista praeclara quae me laetitia extulerunt; ex quo vereor ne idem eveniat [in] meis litteris.[3] equidem numquam domum misi unam epistulam quin esset ad te altera, nec mihi est te iucundius quicquam nec carius.

---

3 homini (*Man.*)   [1] nihilo (*Man.*)   [2] <quia> quod *Wes.*
[3] in meas litteras (*Watt:* in meis litteris *Mart.*)*

when I was taken to task for almost losing my wits with excess of jubilation, I defended myself: 'Joy overmuch, I judge . . .' In short, in laughing at him I almost came to *be* the man.

But more of this and much else, to you and concerning you, as soon as I get a minute to spare. My dear Rufus, you are Fortune's gift to me. You raise me in men's eyes, you punish not only my enemies but my enviers, making some of them sorry for their villainies and others for their ineptitudes.

86 (II.10)
CICERO TO CAELIUS RUFUS

In camp at Pindenissum, 14 November 51

From M. Cicero, Imperator, to M. Caelius, Curule Aedile-Elect greetings.

Just see how letters fail to reach me! For I cannot believe that you have sent none since you were elected Aedile, after so important and felicitous an event—expected as regards yourself, but as regards Hillus (I can't pronounce my 'r's[1]) by me quite unforeseen. And yet it is a fact that no letter of yours has come to my hand since those magnificent elections, which sent me into transports of delight. It makes me afraid that the same may be happening to *my* letters—I have never sent a letter home without another for you, than whom nothing in life is dearer to me or more agreeable.

[1] Neither, we gather, could Hirrus.

2   Sed (balbi non sumus) ad rem redeamus. ut optasti, ita
est. velles enim, ais, tantum modo ut haberem negoti quod
esset ad laureolam satis; Parthos times quia diffidis copiis
nostris. ergo ita accidit. nam Parthico bello nuntiato locorum quibusdam angustiis et na⟨tu⟩ra montium fretus ad
Amanum exercitum adduxi satis probe ornatum auxiliis et
quadam auctoritate apud eos qui me non norant nominis
nostri. multum est enim in his locis: 'hicine est ille qui
urbem . . .? quem senatus . . .?' nosti cetera. cum venissem
ad Amanum, qui mons mihi cum Bibulo communis est
divisus aquarum divortiis, Cassius noster, quod mihi magnae voluptati fuit, feliciter ab Antiochea hostem reiecerat,
Bibulus provinciam acceperat.

3   Interea cum meis copiis omnibus vexavi Amaniensis,
hostis sempiternos. multi occisi capti, reliqui dissipati.
castella munita improviso adventu capta et incensa. ita victoria iusta imperator appellatus apud Issum, quo in loco,
saepe ut ex te audivi, Clitarchus tibi narravit Dareum ab
Alexandro esse superatum, abduxi exercitum ad infestis-
simam Ciliciae partem. ibi quintum et vicesimum iam
diem aggeribus, vineis, turribus oppugnabam oppidum
munitissimum, Pindenissum, tantis opibus tantoque negotio ut mihi ad summam gloriam nihil desit nisi nomen
oppidi. quod si, ut spero, cepero, tum vero litteras publice

---

2 Literally 'there is nothing wrong with my speech'; i.e. the
topic of Hirrus dismissed *(ad rem redeamus)*, Cicero has no more
trouble with his 'r's.

3 I.e. a Triumph; cf. Letter 83.1.

But back to business (I *can* pronounce my 'b's!).[2] Your prayer is answered. You say you would have liked me to have just enough trouble to provide a sprig of laurel,[3] but you are afraid of the Parthians, because you have little confidence in the forces at my disposal. Well, so it has turned out. On the news of war with Parthia I marched to the Amanus, relying on certain narrow passes and the mountainous character of the country, at the head of an army tolerably well provided with auxiliary forces and fortified by a certain prestige attaching to my name among those who knew me not. There is a good deal of talk in this part of the world—'Is that the man to whom Rome . . . ?' 'whom the Senate . . . ?' (you can fill in the blanks). By the time I reached the Amanus, the range of mountains which Bibulus and I share between us, divided at the watershed, our friend Cassius had driven the enemy back from Antioch in a successful action (a very pleasing piece of news to me) and Bibulus had taken over the province.

Meanwhile I harried the people of the Amanus, who are perpetually at war with us, with my entire force. Many were killed or taken prisoner, the rest scattered. Their strongholds were taken by surprise assaults and burned. So in due recognition of a victorious campaign I was saluted Imperator at Issus, where, as I have often heard you say, Clitarchus told you that Darius was defeated by Alexander. I then led my army into the most hostile part of Cilicia, where I am laying siege to the town of Pindenissum, a very strong place indeed, with ramps, casemates, and towers. The siege is now in its twenty-fifth day; judged by scale and difficulty it is a major operation, one to bring me great glory in everything but the name of the town. If I take it, as I hope to do, *then* I shall send an official report. I am telling

4   mittam. haec ad te in praesenti⟨a⟩[4] scripsi ut sperares te
adsequi id quod optasses.

    Sed ut redeam ad Parthos, haec aestas habuit hunc
exitum satis felicem; ea quae sequitur magno est in timore.
qua re, mi Rufe, vigila, primum ut mihi succedatur; sin id
erit, ut scribis et ut ego arbitror, spissius, illud quod facile
est, ne quid mihi temporis prorogetur. de re publica ex tuis
litteris, ut antea tibi scripsi, cum praesentia tum etiam
futura magis exspecto. qua re ut ad me omnia quam
diligentissime perscribas te vehementer rogo.

87 (VIII.10)

Scr. Romae XIV *Kal. Dec. an.* 51

CAELIUS CICERONI S.

1   Sane quam litteris C. Cassi et Deiotari sumus commoti.
nam Cassius cis Euphraten copias Parthorum esse scripsit,
Deiotarus profectas per Commagenen in provinciam nostram. ego quidem praecipuum metum, quod ad te attine-
bat, habui, qui scirem quam paratus ab exercitu esses, ne
quod hic tumultus dignitati tuae periculum adferret. nam
de vita, si paratior ab exercitu esses, timuissem; nunc haec
exiguitas copiarum recessum, non dimicationem mihi
tuam praesagiebat. hoc quo modo acciperent homines,
quam probabilis necessitas futura esset, ⟨verebar, et⟩[1]
vereor etiam nunc neque prius desinam formidare quam
tetigisse t⟨e⟩ Italiam audiero.

    [4] *(Wes.)*
    [1] *(Wes.)*

you all this now, so that you may be hopeful that you are getting what you prayed for.

However, to return to the Parthians, we can feel tolerably pleased with the final result of this summer's operations. Next summer is an alarming prospect. So keep alert, my good Rufus. First try to get my successor appointed. But if, as you write and I suppose, that is going to be rather sticky, see that my tenure is not extended, which is easy. On politics, as I wrote to you earlier, I expect from your letters the present and still more the future. So please write everything to me in full detail.

87 (VIII.10)
CAELIUS RUFUS TO CICERO

Rome, 17 November 51

From Caelius to Cicero greetings.

We have been uncommonly alarmed by dispatches from C. Cassius and Deiotarus. Cassius has written announcing that Parthian forces are this side of the Euphrates, Deiotarus that they are advancing through Commagene into our province. For my part, the principal fear I had as regards yourself (knowing the extent of your military resources) was that this flare-up might endanger your reputation. If your military resources had been greater, I should have felt anxious about your personal safety, but, being as meagre as they are, I thought they augured retreat, not battle. I was nervous about the way such news would be received and how far the necessity would be appreciated. Nervous I still am, and I shall not stop worrying until I hear you are on Italian soil.

2   Sed de Parthorum transitu nuntii varios sermones exci-
tarunt. alius enim Pompeium mittendum, alius ab urbe
Pompeium non removendum, alius Caesarem cum suo
exercitu, alius consules, nemo tamen ex senatus consulto
privatos. consules autem, quia verentur ne illud[2] senatus
consultum ⟨non⟩ fiat[3] 'ut paludati exeant' et contumeliose
praeter eos ad alium res transferatur, omnino senatum
haberi nolunt, usque eo ut parum diligentes in re publica
videantur. sed honeste sive neglegentia sive inertia est sive
ille quem proposui metus latet sub hac temperantiae
existimatione, nolle provinciam.

A te litterae non venerunt et, nisi Deiotari subsecutae
essent, in eam opinionem Cassius veni⟨eb⟩at, quae diri-
puisset ipse ut viderentur ab hoste vastata, finxisse bellum
et Arabas in provinciam immisisse eosque Parthos esse
senatui renuntiasse. qua re tibi suadeo, quicumque est istic
status rerum, diligenter et caute perscribas, ne aut veli-
ficatus alicui dicaris aut aliquid quod referret scire reti-
cuisse.

3   Nunc exitus est anni; nam ego has litteras a.d. XIIII Kal.
Dec. scripsi. plane nihil video ante Kal. Ian. agi posse.
nosti Marcellum, quam tardus et parum efficax sit, itemque Servium,[4] quam cunctator. cuius modi putas hos esse
aut quam id quod nolint conficere posse qui quae cupiunt

[2] aliud *coni. Watt*
[3] (*SB:* fiat ⟨atque⟩ *coni. Watt*)
[4] Servius (*Man.*)

However, the news about the Parthian crossing has given rise to a variety of talk. One man is for sending Pompey out, another says Pompey ought not to be moved away from Rome. Another school of thought would like to send Caesar with his army, another the Consuls. But nobody wants to see persons not holding office appointed by senatorial decree. Moreover, the Consuls are afraid that the decree for their military appointment may not be carried, and that they will be insultingly passed over and the business handed to somebody else. For that reason they don't want the Senate to meet at all, carrying this attitude so far as to suggest a lack of conscientiousness in the public service. But whatever their motive—whether negligence or inertia or the fear I have suggested—it is respectably cloaked under the current opinion that they are uncovetous men who don't want a province.

No dispatch has come in from you, and but for the subsequent arrival of Deiotarus' letter people were beginning to believe that Cassius had invented the war so that his own plunderings would be attributed to hostile devastations—he was supposed to have let Arabs into the province and reported them to the Senate as Parthian invaders. So let me advise you to let us have a full and carefully worded account of the state of affairs out there, whatever it is, so that there is no talk of your having played into somebody's hands or kept silent about what we ought to know.

Now we are at the end of the year—I am writing this letter on 17 November. It's quite plain to me that nothing can be done before the Kalends of January. You know Marcellus, how slow and ineffective he is, and Servius too—a born procrastinator. How do you imagine they are behaving, how do you rate their capacity to put through

tamen ita frigide agunt ut nolle existimentur? novis magistratibus autem, si Parthicum bellum erit, haec causa pri-
mos mensis occupabit; sin autem aut non erit istic bellum
aut ‹t›antum[5] erit ut vos aut successores parvis additis
copiis sustinere possint, Curionem video se dupliciter
iactaturum, primum ut aliquid Caesari adimat, inde ut
aliquid Pompeio tribuat, quodvis quamlibet tenue munusculum. Paullus porro non humane de provincia loquitur.
huius cupiditati occursurus est Furnius noster. plura[6] suspicari non possum.

4   Haec novi; alia quae possunt accidere non cerno. multa
tempus adferre et praeparata mutare scio.[7] sed intra finis
hos quaecumque acciderint vertentur. illud addo ad actiones C. Curionis, de agro Campano; de quo negant
Caesarem laborare, sed Pompeium valde nolle, ne vacuus
advenienti Caesari pateat.

5   Quod ad tuum decessum attinet, illud tibi non possum
polliceri, me curaturum ut tibi succedatur; illud certe
praestabo, ne amplius[8] prorogetur. tui consili est, si tempus, si senatus coget, si honeste a nobis recusari non
poterit, velisne perseverare; mei offici est meminisse qua
obtestatione decedens[9] mihi ne paterer fieri mandaris.

---

[5] autem tum (*Rut.*)   [6] pluris (*SB*)
[7] multarescio (*Bengel*)   [8] tempus *Pluygers*
[9] decendens (ς: disced- *Or.*)

---

[1] Superseding Caesar.   [2] The eastern command.
[3] Cicero and Bibulus.   [4] He wanted a province after his
Consulship despite the law requiring a five-year interval (how he
justified this is unknown). Cicero thought he might get Cilicia;
Letters to Atticus 115 (VI.1).7.   [5] Now Tribune-Elect.

something they don't care about,[1] when they are handling what *does* interest them[2] so slackly as to give an impression of disinclination? When the new men come into office, if the Parthian war is on, that question will monopolize the first months. On the other hand, if there is no war out there, or if it is on a scale which you two[3] or your successors can handle with small reinforcements, I envisage that Curio will make his weight felt in two directions: first he'll try to take something away from Caesar, then to give something to Pompey, any little *douceur,* however trifling. Paullus, moreover, talks unconscionably about a province.[4] Our friend Furnius[5] means to oppose his appetite. More I cannot conjecture.

So much I know. Other possibilities I do not see. That time brings many novelties and changes plans I am well aware, but whatever happens, it will take place within this framework. One addition to C. Curio's programme: the Campanian land.[6] They say that Caesar is not worried, but that Pompey is strongly opposed, not wishing to have the land lying unoccupied for Caesar to play with when he gets back.

As regards your departure from Cilicia, I cannot promise to procure the appointment of a successor, but at least I will guarantee that there will be no prorogation. It will be for you to judge whether you want to maintain your attitude, if circumstances and the Senate bring pressure to bear and we cannot decently refuse. *My* obligation is to remember your parting adjuration not to let it happen.

---

[6] Curio, still at any rate ostensibly playing an optimate game, was now proposing to interfere with Caesar's agrarian legislation, as Cicero had thought to do in 56.

88 (VIII.6)

Scr. Romae m. Febr. an. 50

CAELIUS CICERONI S.

1   Non dubito quin perlatum ad te sit Appium a Dolabella
reum factum sane quam non ea qua[1] existimaveram invidia; neque enim stulte Appius, qui, simul atque Dolabella
accessit ad tribunal, introierat in urbem triumphique
postulationem abiecerat, quo facto rettudit[2] sermones
paratiorque visus est quam speraverat accusator. is nunc in
te maximam spem habet. scio tibi eum non esse odio;
quam velis eum obligare in tua manu est. cum quo <si>
simultas tibi non fuisset, liberius tibi de tota re esset; nunc,
si ad illam summam veritatem legitimum ius exegeris,
cavendum tibi erit ne parum simpliciter et candide posuisse inimicitias videaris. in hanc partem porro tutum tibi
erit si quid volueris gratificari; nemo enim necessitudine et
amicitia te deterritum ab officio dicet.

  Illud mihi occurrit, quod inter postulationem et no-
2   minis delationem uxor a Dolabella discessit. quid mihi
discedens mandaris memini; quid ego tibi scripserim te
non arbitror oblitum. non est iam tempus plura narrandi;

---

[1] quam *(Man.)*   [2] –tor ettulit *(Rut., sed* retu-*)*

---

[1] I.e., the Praetor's tribunal, for permission to proceed—the
first step in a prosecution.   [2] The second step, perhaps involving a detailed specification of the charge; but the procedure is
not exactly known.   [3] Cicero's parting commission may have
been general: to keep an eye open for an eligible match for Tullia.

88 (VIII.6)
CAELIUS RUFUS TO CICERO

Rome, February 50

From Caelius to Cicero greetings.

Doubtless the news will have reached you that Appius has been charged by Dolabella. I must say that the feeling against him is not what I anticipated. Appius has behaved rather sensibly. The moment Dolabella approached the bench,[1] he crossed the city boundary and gave up his claim to a Triumph, thereby blunting sharp tongues and looking readier for the fray than his prosecutor had expected. His hopes are now mainly pinned on you. I know you don't dislike him. How far you want to put him under obligation rests with you. If you had not had a quarrel with him in the past, you would have a freer hand altogether. As it is, if you demand the letter of the law, the standard of abstract justice without compromise, you will have to be careful not to let it look as though the reconciliation on your side was less than candid and sincere. Moreover, you can safely go the other way, if you want to do him any favours, for nobody is going to say that connection and friendship deterred you from your duty.

It comes to my mind that between the preliminary application and the laying of the charge[2] Dolabella's wife left him. I remember the commission you gave me as you were leaving,[3] and I don't suppose you have forgotten what I wrote to you.[4] Now is not the time to enter into further de-

---

[4] Caelius' letter, referred to here and in Letter 73.5, may have raised Dolabella's name for the first time.

unum illud monere te possum, si res tibi non displicebit, tamen hoc tempore nihil de tua voluntate ostendas et exspectes quem ad modum exeat ex hac causa denique.[3] invidiosum tibi sit si emanarit. porro, <si>[4] significatio ulla intercess<er>it, clarius quam deceat aut expediat fiat. neque ille tacere eam rem poterit quae suae spei tam opportuna acciderit quaeque in negotio conficiendo tanto illustrior erit, cum praesertim is sit qui, si perniciosum sciret esse loqui de hac re, vix tamen se contineret.

3   Pompeius dicitur valde pro Appio laborare, ut etiam putent alterum utrum de filiis ad te missurum. hic nos omnis absolvimus, et hercules consaepta omnia foeda et inhonesta sunt. consules autem habemus summa diligentia; adhuc senatus consultum nisi de feriis Latinis 4 nullum facere potuerunt. Curioni nostro tribunatus conglaciat. sed dici non potest quo modo hic omnia iaceant. nisi ego cum tabernariis et aquariis pugnarem, veternus civitatem occupasset. si Parthi vos nihil calfaciunt, nos [nihil][5] frigore frigescimus. tamen, quoquo modo [hic omnia iaceant][6] potuit, sine Parthis Bibulus in Amano nescio quid cohorticularum amisit. hoc si<c> nuntiatum est.

5   Quod tibi supra scripsi Curionem valde frigere, iam calet; nam ferventissime concerpitur. levissime enim, quia de intercalando non obtinuerat, transfugit ad populum et

---

[3] sane quam *Watt*   [4] *(Or.)*   [5] *(Becher)*   [6] *(Madvig)*

---

[5] As Appius' prosecutor, Dolabella would be 'in the news,' and his engagement to Tullia would attract the more attention on that account.

[6] Fixing its date, a matter of no political consequence.

[7] Cf. *Letters to Atticus* 113 (V.20).4.

tails. The only advice I can give you is this: even if you are
not against the idea in principle, don't show your hand in
any way just now. Wait and see how he comes out of this
case finally. It would not be good for your reputation if the
thing leaks out; and if any hint is forthcoming, it would get
more publicity than would be decent or expedient.[5] And
he won't be able to keep quiet about a development which
will chime so conveniently with his own hopes and will be
all the more in the public eye as he carries his business
through—particularly as he's a fellow who would hardly
hold his tongue about such a matter even if he knew that
talking would be the ruin of him.

Pompey is said to be greatly exercised on Appius' behalf. They even think he will send one of his sons over to
you. Here we are acquitting everybody. To be sure there
are screens to protect every dirty scandal. Our Consuls
are paragons of conscientiousness—to date they had not
succeeded in getting a single decree through the Senate
except about the Latin Festival![6] Our friend Curio's
Tribunate is an utter frost. But the stagnation of everything
here is indescribable. If I didn't have a battle on with the
shopkeepers and inspectors of conduits, a coma would
have seized the whole community. Unless the Parthians
liven you up a bit over there, we are as dead as dormice—
though even without the Parthians Bibulus has somehow
or other contrived to lose the odd cohort in the Amanus, so
it is here reported.[7]

A propos of what I wrote above about Curio being
frozen up, he's warm enough now—being pulled to pieces
most ardently. Quite irresponsibly, because he hadn't got
his way about intercalation, he has gone over to the demo-

pro Caesare loqui coepit legemque viariam non dissimilem agrariae Rulli et alimentariam, quae iubet aedilis metiri, iactavit. hoc nondum fecerat cum priorem partem epistulae scripsi.

Amabo te, si quid quod opus fuerit Appio facies, ponito me in gratia. de Dolabella integrum tibi reserves suadeo; et huic rei de qua loquor et dignitati tuae aequitatisque opinioni hoc ita facere expedit.

Turpe tibi erit pantheras Graecas me non habere.

89 (II.14)

Scr. Laodiceae med. m. Mart., ut vid., an. 50

‹M.› CICERO IMP. S. D. M. CAELIO AEDILI CURULI

M. Fabio, viro optimo et homine doctissimo, familiarissime utor mirificeque eum diligo cum propter summum ingenium eius summamque doctrinam tum propter singularem modestiam. eius negotium sic velim suscipias ut si esset res mea. novi ego vos magnos patronos; hominem occidat oportet qui vestra opera uti velit. sed in hoc homine nullam accipio excusationem. omnia relinques, si me amabis, cum tua opera Fabius uti volet.

Ego res Romanas vehementer exspecto et desidero, in primisque quid agas scire cupio. nam iam diu propter hiemis magnitudinem nihil ad nos novi adferebatur.

---

8 Successfully opposed by Cicero in 63. The resemblance probably lay in the wide powers proposed for the commissioners who were to execute the bill.   9 I.e. making the Aediles responsible for the regular distributions of free or subsidized grain.

10 I.e. Asiatic as opposed to African.   1 Cf. Letter 114.2.

crats and started talking in favour of Caesar. He has bran-
dished a Road Bill (not unlike Rullus' Agrarian Bill)[8] and a
Food Bill, which tells the Aediles to distribute.[9] He had
not done this when I wrote the earlier part of this letter.

If you do take any steps to help Appius, be a good fellow
and put in a word with him for me. I recommend you to
keep your hands free about Dolabella. That is the right
line both from the standpoint of the matter I am talking
about and from that of your dignity and reputation for fair
dealing.

It will be little to your credit if I don't have any Greek[10]
panthers.

89 (II.14)
CICERO TO CAELIUS RUFUS

Laodicea, mid March (?) 50

From M. Cicero, Imperator, to M. Caelius, Curule Aedile,
greetings.

M. Fabius is a man of fine character and culture, and on
very close terms with me. I have a quite exceptional regard
for him, for his brilliant intellect and scholarly attainments
go along with unusual modesty. I want you to take up his
case[1] as though it was an affair of my own. I know you great
advocates—a man must commit murder if he wants your
services. But in the present instance I take no excuse. If
you care for me, you will put everything aside when Fabius
wants your services.

I am eagerly and longingly awaiting news of Rome, and
especially want to know how you are. Because of the sever-
ity of the winter it is a long time since any news reached us.

90 (II.11)

Scr. Laodiceae prid. Non. Apr. an. 50

M. CICERO IMP. S. D. M. CAELIO AEDILI CURULI

1   Putaresne umquam accidere posse ut mihi verba deessent, neque solum ista vestra oratoria sed haec etiam levia nostratia? desunt autem propter hanc causam quod mirifice sum sollicitus quidnam de provinciis decernatur. mirum me desiderium tenet urbis, incredibile meorum atque in primis tui, satietas autem provinciae, vel quia videmur eam famam consecuti ut non tam accessio quaerenda quam Fortuna metuenda sit, vel quia totum negotium non est dignum viribus nostris, qui maiora onera in re publica sustinere et possim et soleam, vel quia belli magni timor impendet, quod videmur effugere si ad constitutam diem decedemus.

2   De pantheris per eos qui venari solent agitur mandatu meo diligenter. sed mira paucitas est, et eas quae sunt valde aiunt queri quod nihil cuiquam insidiarum in mea provincia nisi sibi fiat. itaque constituisse dicuntur in Cariam ex nostra provincia decedere. sed tamen sedulo fit et in primis a Patisco. quicquid erit, tibi erit; sed quid esset plane nesciebamus. mihi mehercule magnae curae est aedilitas tua. ipse dies me admonebat; scripsi enim haec ipsis Megalensibus. tu velim ad me de omni rei publicae

---

[1] 4 April, the first day of the festival of Cybele. Her games, as well as the Roman Games, seem to have been the responsibility of the Curule Aediles.

90 (II.11)
CICERO TO CAELIUS RUFUS

Laodicea, 4 April 50

M. Cicero, Imperator, to M. Caelius, Curule Aedile, greetings.

Would you ever have thought that I could find myself short of words—and not only the kind of words you orators use, but even this vernacular small change? The reason is that I am on tenterhooks to hear what is decreed about the provinces. I have a marvellous longing for Rome, and miss my family and friends, you especially, more than you would believe. I am sick and tired of the province. I think I have gained a reputation here such that rather than seek to add to it I should beware of Fortune's turns. Besides the whole thing is unworthy of my powers. I am able to bear, am used to bearing, greater loads in the service of the state. Then again, the threat of a great war hangs over us; this I believe I escape if I leave by the appointed day.

About the panthers, the usual hunters are doing their best on my instructions. But the creatures are in remarkably short supply, and those we have are said to be complaining bitterly because they are the only beings in my province who have to fear designs against their safety. Accordingly they are reported to have decided to leave this province and go to Caria. But the matter is receiving close attention, especially from Patiscus. Whatever comes to hand will be yours, but what that amounts to I simply do not know. I do assure you that your career as Aedile is of great concern to me. The date is itself a reminder—I am writing on Great Mother's Day.[1] On your side, please send me an account of the whole political situation as full as you

statu quam diligentissime perscribas; ea enim certissima putabo quae ex te cognoro.

91 (VIII.11)

Scr. Romae med., ut vid., m. Apr. an. 50

CAELIUS CICERONI S.

1 Non diu sed acriter nos tuae supplicationes torserunt; incideramus enim in difficilem nodum. nam Curio, tui cupidissimus, cui omnibus rationibus comitiales eripiantur, negabat se ullo modo pati posse decerni supplicationes, ne quod furore Paulli adeptus esset boni sua culpa videretur amisisse et praevaricator causae publicae existimaretur. itaque ad pactionem descendimus et confirmarunt consules se his supplicationibus in hunc annum non usuros. plane quod utrisque consulibus gratias agas est, Paullo magis certe; nam Marcellus sic respondit ei, spem in istis supplicationibus non habere, Paullus se omnino in hunc annum non edicturum.

2 Renuntiatum nobis erat Hirrum diutius dicturum. prendimus eum; non modo non fecit sed, cum de hosti⟨i⟩s ageretur et posset rem impedire si ut numeraretur postu-

---

1 Caelius, like Vatinius, prefers the plural.

2 Because the celebrating of a Supplication would take up comitial days on which he could pursue his legislative program.

3 Probably with reference to further deferment of the question of Caesar's command for which Paullus, now in Caesar's interest, had been in some degree responsible.

can make it. I shall consider what I hear from you as my most reliable information.

91 (VIII.11)
CAELIUS RUFUS TO CICERO

Rome, mid (?) April 50

From Caelius to Cicero greetings.

Your Supplications[1] have given us a nasty headache—short, but sharp. We found ourselves in a very knotty situation. Curio was most anxious to oblige you, but, finding his comitial days taken away from him on all sorts of pretexts, he said he could not possibly allow Supplications to be decreed.[2] If he did, he would appear as losing by his own fault the advantage offered him by Paullus' lunacy,[3] and would be thought to be betraying the public interest. So we got down to a compromise. The Consuls gave an assurance that they would not make use of these Supplications for the present year. You really have cause to thank both the Consuls, Paullus to be sure more than his colleague. Marcellus merely replied to Curio that he was not building any hope on these Supplications, whereas Paullus said definitely that he would not announce them for this year.

It was reported to us that Hirrus proposed to speak at some length. We got hold of him. Not only did he not do so, but when the question of sacrificial victims[4] was under discussion and he could have held up the business by

---

[4] In decreeing the Supplication the Senate would also specify the number and quality of the animals to be sacrificed as thank offerings.

laret, tacuit. tantum Catoni adsensus est, qui ⟨de⟩ te locutus honorifice non decrerat supplicationes. tertius ad hos
Favonius accessit. qua re pro cuiusque natura et instituto
gratiae sunt agendae, his quod tantum voluntatem ostenderunt, pro sententia cum impedire possent non pugna-
runt, Curioni vero quod de suarum actionum cursu tua
causa deflexit. nam Furnius et Lentulus, ut debuerunt,
quasi eorum res esset una nobiscum circumierunt et laborarunt. Balbi quoque Corneli operam et sedulitatem lau-
dare possum; nam cum Curione vehementer locutus est et
eum, si aliter fecisset, iniuriam Caesari facturum dixit, tum
eius fidem in suspicionem adduxit. decrerant[1] quidem
[qui] neque[2] transigi volebant Domitii, Scipiones. quibus
hac re ad intercessionem evocandam interpellantibus
venustissime Curio respondit se eo libentius non intercedere quod quosdam qui decernerent videret confici nolle.

3   Quod ad rem publicam attinet, in unam causam omnis
contentio coniecta est, de provinciis; in quam, ⟨ut⟩[3] adhuc
est, incubuisse cum senatu Pompeius videtur ut Caesar Id.
Nov. decedat. Curio omnia potius subire constituit quam
id pati; ceteras suas abiecit actiones. nostri porro, quos tu
bene nosti, ad extremum certamen rem deducere non
aude⟨b⟩ant.[4] scaena rei totius haec: Pompeius, tamquam
Caesarem non impugnet sed quod illi aequum putet con-

1 deserant *(Man.)*
2 quinique *(Madvig)*
3 *(SB)*
4 *(R. Klotz)*

---

5 Spinther.
6 Towards Caesar, whom Curio was now supporting.

demanding a count, he kept quiet. He merely assented to Cato, who after speaking of you in flattering terms declared himself against the Supplications. Favonius joined them to make a third. So you must thank them all according to their various characters and habits of conduct: Cato and his associates, because they merely signified their sentiments but did not put up a fight for their opinion, though it was in their power to obstruct; Curio, because he turned aside from his program for your sake. Furnius and Lentulus[5] canvassed and worked shoulder to shoulder with me as though it was their own affair, which was right and proper. I can also say a good word for Balbus Cornelius, who worked assiduously. He spoke strongly to Curio, telling him that if he acted in any other way he would be doing Caesar an ill turn; moreover, he called his good faith[6] in question. Domitius, Scipio, and company had indeed voted in favour, without wanting the business to go through. So they kept interrupting in order to provoke a veto. Curio riposted very neatly that he had all the greater pleasure in *not* casting a veto because he could see that some of the supporters of the motion did not want it to take effect.

As for the political situation, all conflict is directed to a single question, that of the provinces. As things stand so far, Pompey seems to be putting his weight along with the Senate in demanding that Caesar leave his province on the Ides of November. Curio is resolved to let that happen only over his dead body, and has given up the rest of his programme. Our friends (well you know them) do not dare to push the matter to extremities. This is the tableau, the *tout ensemble:* Pompey pretends that he is not attacking Caesar, but making a settlement which he thinks fair to

stituat, ait Curionem quaerere discordias; valde autem
non vult et plane timet Caesarem consulem designatum
prius quam exercitum et provinciam tradiderit. accipitur
satis male a Curione et totus eius tertius[5] consul⟨atus⟩
exagitatur. hoc tibi dico: si omnibus rebus prement Curionem, Caesar defendet intercessorem; si, quod videntur,
reformidarint, Caesar quoad volet manebit.

4   Quam quisque sententiam dixerit in commentario est
rerum urbanarum; ex quo tu quae digna sunt selige, multa
transi, in primis ludorum explosiones et funerum ⟨nume-
rum⟩[6] et ineptiarum ceterarum. plura habet utilia. denique malo in hanc partem errare ut quae non desideres
audias quam quicquam quod opus est praetermittatur.

Tibi curae fuisse de Sittiano negotio gaudeo. sed quoniam suspicaris minus certa fide eos ⟨esse quos⟩[7] tibi
misi,[8] tamquam procurator sic agas rogo.

92 (VIII.7)

Scr. Romae postridie quam ep. superior

CAELIUS CICERONI S.

1   Quam cito tu istinc decedere cupias nescio; ego
quidem eo magis quo adhuc felicius res gessisti. dum istic
eris, de belli Parthici periculo cruciabor, ne hunc risum
meum metus aliqui perturbet. breviores has litteras

[5] secundus (*SB, auct. Gelzer*)   [6] (*SB*)   [7] (*Wes.*)
[8] visos (*Wes.*)

---

[7] Literally 'veto-caster.'

him; he says that Curio is out to make strife. At the same time he regards the idea of Caesar being elected Consul before he hands over his province and army with strong disfavour and positive apprehension. He gets a pretty rough reception from Curio, and his whole third Consulate is being hauled over the coals. Mark my words, if they use all means to suppress Curio, Caesar will come to his Tribune's[7] rescue. If, as seems probable, they are afraid to do that, Caesar will stay as long as he pleases.

The various speeches made in the Senate are in the abstract of city news. Pick out the worthwhile items for yourself. You can pass over a lot, such as who was hissed at the games and the quantity of funerals and other nonsenses. Most things in it are of use. Anyway, I prefer to err on the generous side—better you should hear what doesn't interest you than that some matter of consequence be left out.

I am glad you are attending to the Sittius business. But since you suspect that the persons I sent are not altogether trustworthy, please act as though you were my agent.

92 (VIII.7)
CAELIUS RUFUS TO CICERO

Rome, the day after the preceding

From Caelius to Cicero greetings.

How soon you want to leave your present whereabouts I don't know, but for my part, the more successful you have been so far the more I want it. As long as you remain out there, I shall be on thorns about the risk of a Parthian war, for fear some alarm may wipe the grin off my face. This

properanti publicanorum tabellario subito dedi. tuo liberto pluribus verbis scriptas pridie dederam.

2   Res autem novae nullae sane acciderunt, nisi haec vis
tibi scribi—quae certe vis: Cornificius adulescens Orestil-
lae filiam sibi despondit; Paulla Valeria, soror Triari, divor-
tium sine causa, quo die vir e provincia venturus erat, fecit;
nuptura est D. Bruto; ⟨vir se⟩ nondum rettulerat.[1] multa
in hoc genere incredibilia te absente acciderunt. Se⟨r⟩vius
Ocella nemini persuasisset se moechum esse nisi triduo bis
deprehensus esset. quaeres ubi. ⟨ubi⟩ hercules ego minime vellem. relinquo tibi quod ab aliis quaeras; neque enim
displicet mihi imperatorem singulos percontari cum qua
sit aliqui deprehensus.

93 (II.13)

Scr. Laodiceae in. m. Mai. an. 50

M. CICERO IMP. S. D. M. CAELIO AEDILI CURULI

1   Raras tuas quidem (fortasse enim non perferuntur) sed
suavis accipio litteras; vel quas proxime acceperam, quam
prudentis, quam multi et offici et consili! etsi omnia sic
constitueram mihi agenda ut tu admonebas, tamen con-

---

[1] nondum rettuleras *(Watt)*

---

[1] Letter 88.

letter will be rather brief—I am giving it without notice to one of the tax farmers' couriers, who is in a hurry. I gave a longer one to your freedman yesterday.

Nothing new has happened really, unless you want to be told such items as the following—which, of course, you do. Young Cornificius has got himself engaged to Orestilla's daughter. Paulla Valeria, Triarius' sister, divorced her husband for no reason the day he was due to get back from his province. She is to marry D. Brutus. Her husband had not yet got back. There have been a good many extraordinary incidents of this sort during your absence. Servius Ocella would never have got anyone to believe he went in for adultery, if he had not been caught twice in three days. Where? Why, just the last place I should have wished—I leave something for you to find out from other informants! Indeed I rather fancy the idea of a Commander-in-Chief enquiring of this person and that the name of the lady with whom such-and-such a gentleman has been caught napping.

93 (II.13)
CICERO TO CAELIUS RUFUS

Laodicea, early May 50

From M. Cicero, Imperator, to M. Caelius, Curule Aedile, greetings.

Your letters, as they reach me, are few and far between—perhaps they are not getting through—but delightful. The last one[1] for instance, how wise, how full of friendship and counsel! I had in point of fact determined to act in every way on the lines you recommend, but my

firmantur nostra consilia cum sentimus prudentibus fideliterque suadentibus idem videri.

2   Ego Appium, ut saepe tecum locutus sum, valde diligo meque ab eo diligi statim coeptum esse ut simultatem deposuimus sensi. nam et honorificus in me consul fuit et suavis amicus et studiosus studiorum etiam meorum. mea vero officia ei non defuisse tu es testis, cui iam[1] κωμικὸς μάρτυς, ut opinor, accedit Phania; et mehercule etiam pluris eum feci quod te amari ab eo sensi. iam me Pompei totum esse scis, Brutum a me amari intellegis. quid est causae cur mihi non in optatis sit complecti hominem florentem aetate, opibus, honoribus, ingenio, liberis, propinquis, adfinibus, amicis, collegam meum praesertim et in ipsa collegi laude et scientia studiosum mei? haec eo pluribus scripsi quod ⟨non⟩[2] nihil significabant tuae litterae subdubitare qua essem erga illum voluntate. credo te audisse aliquid. falsum est, mihi crede, si quid audisti. genus institutorum et rationum mearum dissimilitudinem non nullam habet cum illius administratione provinciae. ex eo quidam suspicati fortasse sunt animorum contentione, non opinionum dissensione, me ab eo discrepare. nihil autem feci umquam neque dixi quod contra illius existimationem esse vellem; post hoc negotium autem et temeritatem nostri Dolabellae deprecatorem me pro illius periculo praebeo.

[1] quoniam *(Mart.)*   [2] *(Man.)*

---

[2] The Witness (e.g. to the long-lost heroine's identity) was a stock role in Attic New Comedy and Phanias a common dramatic name.   [3] One of Appius' daughters was married to Pompey's elder son, another to M. Brutus.

resolutions are strengthened when I find that wise and loyal advisers are of the same opinion.

I have a real regard for Appius, as I have often told you, and as soon as we buried our hatchet I perceived the beginning of a corresponding feeling on his side. As Consul he showed me consideration and became a pleasant friend, not without an interest in my literary pursuits. That friendliness on my side was not wanting *you* can testify. And now, I suppose, Phanias corroborates, like a witness in a comedy.[2] And I do assure you that I valued him the more because I saw he had an affection for you. Further, that I am devoted to Pompey you know, and you are aware of my affection for Brutus.[3] Why on earth should I *not* be gratified to welcome the friendship of such a man—in the prime of life, wealthy, successful, able, surrounded by children, by connections of blood and marriage, and by friends—a colleague too, who has put his learned work to the glory of our College in the form of a compliment to me? I have written at some length on this topic because your letter suggested the shadow of a doubt in your mind about my feelings towards him. I suppose you have heard some story. If so, believe me, it is untrue. There is some dissimilarity, generally speaking, between his administration of the province and my own ordinances and principles. Hence perhaps some have suspected that I differ from him out of personal animus, not from theoretical disagreement. But I have never said or done anything with a wish to injure his reputation, and after this recent trouble and our friend Dolabella's precipitate behaviour, I am ready with my intercession in his hour of danger.

3 Erat in eadem epistula 'veternus civitatis.' gaudebam sane et congelasse nostrum amicum laetabar otio. extrema pagella pupugit me tuo chirographo. quid ais? Caesarem nunc[3] defendit Curio? qui<s> hoc putaret, praeter me? nam, ita vivam, putavi. di immortales, quam ego risum nostrum desidero!

4 Mihi erat in animo, quoniam iuris dictionem confe-<ce>ram, civitates locupletaram, publicanis etiam superioris lustri reliqua sine sociorum ulla querela conservaram, privatis, summis infimis, fueram iucundus, proficisci in Ciliciam Non. Mai. et, cum primum aestiva attigissem militemque collocassem, decedere ex senatus consulto. cupio te aedilem videre miroque desiderio me urbs adficit et omnes mei tuque in primis.

94 (VIII.13)

Scr. Romae in. m. Iun. an. 50

CAELIUS CICERONI S.

1 Gratulor tibi adfinitate<m>[1] viri me dius fidius optimi; nam hoc ego de illo existimo. cetera porro, quibus adhuc ille sibi parum utilis fuit, et aetate iam sunt decussa et consuetudine atque auctoritate tua, pudore Tulliae, si qua restabunt, confido celeriter sublatum iri. non est enim

---

[3] non (*Rut.*)
[1] (*Lamb.*)

---

[1] Dolabella.

In the same letter you speak of a 'community coma.' Well, I was glad of it. It was good news that inactivity had cooled our friend to freezing point. The last little page in your own hand gave me quite a jolt. You don't say so! Curio now standing up for Caesar? Who would have thought it?—except me! For upon my soul, *I did* think it. Powers above, how I should enjoy a laugh with you!

I have completed the assizes, put money into the communal treasuries, assured the tax farmers of their arrears even for the previous quinquennium without a word of complaint from the provincials, and made myself pleasant to private individuals from the highest to the lowest. So I propose to set out for Cilicia on the Nones of May. Then, as soon as I have touched the fringe of a summer campaign and settled the troops in their stations, I intend to vacate the province in conformity with the Senate's decree. I am anxious to see you in office and feel a marvellous longing for Rome and for all my folk, you especially.

94 (VIII.13)
CAELIUS RUFUS TO CICERO

Rome, early June 50

From Caelius to Cicero greetings.

I congratulate you on the connection you are forming with a very fine fellow,[1] for that, upon my word, is what I think him. In some respects he has done himself poor service in the past, but he has already shaken off these failings with the years and, if any traces remain, I feel sure that your association and influence and Tullia's modest ways will soon remove them. He is not recalcitrant in bad

417

pugnax in vitiis neque hebes ad id quod melius sit intelle-
gendum. deinde, quod maximum est, ego illum valde amo.

2   Voles scire[2] Curionem nostrum lautum intercessionis
de provinciis exitum habuisse. nam cum ⟨de⟩ interces-
sione referretur, quae relatio fiebat ex senatus consulto,
primaque M. Marcelli sententia pronuntiata esset, qui
agendum cum tribunis pl. censebat, frequens senatus in
alia omnia iit. stomacho est [scilicet Pompeius][3] Magnus
nunc ita languenti ut vix id quod sibi placeat reperiat.
transierant illuc, rationem eius habendam qui ⟨neque⟩
exercitum neque provincias tradere⟨t⟩. quem ad modum
hoc Pompeius laturus sit, cum cognoscam. quidnam rei
publicae futurum sit, si aut non curet ⟨aut armis resistat⟩[4]
vos senes divites videritis.

Q. Hortensius, cum has litteras scripsi, animam agebat.

95 (II.12)

Scr., ut vid., in castris ad Pyramum c. v Kal. Quint. an. 50

M. CICERO IMP. S. D. M. CAELIO AEDILI CURULI

1   Sollicitus equidem eram de rebus urbanis. ita tumul-
tuosae contiones, ita molestae Quinquatrus adferebantur;
nam citeriora nondum audieramus. sed tamen nihil me

[2] cicero *(SB)*   [3] *(Man.)*   [4] *(Wes., sed post* si*)*

---

[2] The stock phrase for putting pressure upon a Tribune to
withdraw his veto, backed by the threat of suspension from office
or other coercive action by the Senate.   [3] Pompey was actually in poor health and soon afterwards fell seriously ill.

courses or lacking in the intelligence to perceive a better way. And the capital point is that I am very fond of him.

You will like to know that our friend Curio has done very nicely with his veto on the provinces. When the question about the veto was put (this was done in accordance with the Senate's decree) and M. Marcellus' proposal to the effect that representations should be made[2] to the Tribunes was the first pronounced, the House voted it down in large numbers. Pompey the Great's digestion is now in such a poor way that he has trouble finding anything to suit him![3] They have come round to accept that a person should be allowed to stand for office without handing over his army and provinces. How Pompey is going to take this I'll tell you when I know. As for what is to happen if he either resists in arms or just lets it go, you rich old gentlemen can worry!

As I write, Q. Hortensius is at death's door.

95 (II.12)
CICERO TO CAELIUS RUFUS

Camp on the River Pyramus, ca. 26 June 50

From M. Cicero, Imperator, to M. Caelius, Curule Aedile, greetings.

I am worried about affairs in Rome, with reports of rowdy meetings and a very disagreeable Feast of Minerva[1]—I have no more recent news. But the most worrying thing of all is that, whatever there may be to laugh at in

[1] 19–23 March. The disturbances were probably due to Curio's activities as Tribune.

magis sollicitabat quam in his molestiis non me, si quae
ridenda essent, ridere tecum; sunt enim multa, sed ea non
audeo scribere. illud moleste fero, nihil me adhuc his de
rebus habere tuarum litterarum. qua re, etsi, cum tu haec
leges, ego iam annuum munus confecero, tamen obviae
mihi velim sint tuae litterae quae me erudiant de omni re
publica, ne hospes plane veniam. hoc melius quam tu
facere nemo potest.

2   Diogenes tuus, homo modestus, a me cum Philone Pes-
sinunte⟨m⟩[1] discessit. iter habebant ⟨ad⟩[2] Adiatorigem,
quamquam omnia nec benigna nec copiosa cognorant.

Urbem, urbem, mi Rufe, cole et in ista luce vive! omnis
peregrinatio, quod ego ab adulescentia iudicavi, obscura
et sordida est iis quorum industria Romae potest illustris
esse. quod cum probe scirem, utinam in sententia per-
mansissem! cum una mehercule ambulatiuncula atque
uno sermone nostro omnis fructus provinciae non confero.

3 spero me integritatis laudem consecutum: non erat minor
ex contemnenda quam est ex conservata provincia. spem
triumphi inicis:[3] satis gloriose triumpharem, non essem
quidem[4] tam diu in desiderio rerum mihi carissimarum.
sed, ut spero, propediem te videbo. tu mihi obviam mitte
epistulas te dignas.

[1] pessi nun(c)te *(Baiter)*
[2] *(Taurellus)*
[3] inquis *(SB)*
[4] ⟨si⟩ (ς) non essem, ⟨et⟩ quidem *Watt*

all this unpleasantness, I cannot laugh at it with you—there is in fact a good deal, but I dare not put such things on paper. I do take it hard that I have not yet had a line from you about these matters. When you read this, I shall already have completed my year's assignment, but I hope that a letter from you will meet me on the road to tell me about the whole political situation, so that I don't come to Rome as a complete foreigner. Nobody can do this better than yourself.

Your Diogenes, whose manners I can commend, left me along with Philo for Pessinus. They were going to Adiatorix, despite reports which held out no hope of a kind or affluent reception there.

Rome! Stick to Rome, my dear fellow, and live in the limelight! Sojourn abroad of any kind, as I have thought from my youth upwards, is squalid obscurity for those whose efforts can win lustre in the capital. I knew this well enough, and I only wish I had stayed true to my conviction. I do assure you that in my eyes all I get from the province is not worth a single stroll, a single talk with you. I hope I have won some credit for integrity, but I should have gained as much of that by despising the province as I have by saving it from ruin. You suggest the hope of a Triumph. My Triumph would have been glorious enough; at any rate I should not have been so long cut off from all that is dearest to me. However, I hope to see you soon. Send me letters worthy of yourself to meet me on my way.

Scr. Sidae III aut prid. Non. Sext. an. 50

M. CICERO IMP. S. D. M. CAELIO AEDILI CURULI

1 Non potuit accuratius agi nec prudentius quam est
actum a te cum Curione de supplicatione; et hercule
confecta res ex sententia mea est cum celeritate tum quod
is qui erat iratus, competitor tuus et idem meus, adsensus
est ei qui ornavit res nostras divinis laudibus. qua re scito
me sperare ea quae sequuntur; ad quae tu te para.

2 Dolabellam a te gaudeo primum laudari, deinde etiam
amari. nam ea quae speras Tulliae meae prudentia tem-
perari posse, scio cui tuae epistulae respondeant. quid si
meam legas quam ego tum ex tuis litteris misi ad Appium?
sed quid agas? sic vivitur. quod actum est di approbent!
spero fore iucundum generum nobis, multumque in eo tua
nos humanitas adiuvabit.

3 Res publica me valde sollicitat. faveo Curioni, Caesarem honestum esse cupio, pro Pompeio emori possum,
sed tamen ipsa re publica nihil mihi est carius; in qua tu
non valde te iactas. districtus enim mihi videris esse, quod
et bonus civis et bonus amicus es.

4 Ego de provincia decedens quaestorem Coelium praeposui provinciae. 'puerum' inquis. at quaestorem, at nobilem adulescentem, at omnium fere exemplo. neque erat
superiore honore usus quem praeficerem. Pomptinus

---

¹ Hirrus.   ² Cato.

³ A Triumph, which would no doubt have been forthcoming
but for the Civil War.   ⁴ It has not survived.

⁵ In fact, Coelius must have been about thirty.

96 (II.15)
CICERO TO CAELIUS RUFUS

Side, 3 or 4 August 50

From M. Cicero, Imperator, to M. Caelius, Curule Aedile, greetings.

Your negotiation with Curio on the matter of the Supplication was a model of thoughtfulness and discretion. The result is indeed to my satisfaction. I am pleased that the thing has been settled so quickly, and also that your and my angry rival[1] gave his assent to the fervid encomiast of my official record.[2] You may take it therefore that I am hoping for the sequel.[3] Be ready to play your part.

I am glad you speak so well of Dolabella, glad too that you are fond of him. As for the features which you hope may be toned down by my dear Tullia's good sense, I know which of your letters[4] to turn up. For that matter you ought to read the letter I sent to Appius at the time on receipt of yours! But what is one to do? Such is life. The Gods bless what is done! I hope to find him an agreeable son-in-law, and there your kindly tact will help us much.

The political situation is very much on my mind. I wish Curio well, I want to see Caesar respected, I can lay down my life for Pompey; but nothing is closer to my heart than the commonwealth itself. You do not make very much of your own political role. I fancy you find yourself torn between loyalties, as a good citizen and as a good friend.

On vacating the province I left my Quaestor Coelius in charge. A boy,[5] you may say! Well, but he is Quaestor, he is a young man of noble family, and I am following an almost universal precedent. Nor had I anyone available for the appointment who had held a higher office. Pomptinus

multo ante discesserat, a Quinto fratre impe<t>rari non poterat; quem tamen si reliquissem, dicerent iniqui non me plane post annum, ut senatus voluisset, de provincia decessisse quoniam alterum me reliquissem. fortasse etiam illud adderent, senatum eos voluisse provinciis praeesse qui antea non praefuissent, fratrem meum triennium Asiae praefuisse. denique nunc sollicitus non sum; si fratrem reliquissem, omnia timerem. postremo non tam mea sponte quam potentissimorum duorum exemplo, qui omnis Cassios Antoniosque complexi sunt, hominem[1] adulescentem non tam adlicere volui quam alienare nolui. hoc tu meum consilium laudes necesse est; mutari enim non potest.

5   De Ocella parum ad me plane scripseras et in actis non erat. tuae res gestae ita notae sunt ut trans montem Taurum etiam de Matrinio sit auditum. ego, nisi quid me etesiae morabuntur, celeriter, ut spero, vos videbo.

---

[1] nobilem *Ern.*

had left long before. My brother Quintus could not be prevailed upon—but even if I *had* left him, unfriendly tongues would be saying that I had not really vacated my province after a year, as the Senate had determined, since I had left an alter ego behind me. They might perhaps have added that the Senate had designated as provincial governors persons who had not previously held such office, whereas my brother had been governor of Asia for three years. And then, as things are, I have no need to worry; if I had left my brother in charge, I should have had all manner of apprehensions.[6] Lastly, I did not so much act of my own volition as follow the example of the two most powerful men of our day, who have made friends of every Cassius and Antonius[7] who came their way. I did not so much want to attract the friendship of the young man as not to alienate him. You have no choice but to approve my decision, because it cannot be changed.

What you wrote to me about Ocella was none too clear, and there was nothing in the record![8] Your official actions are so well known that Matrinius is news even this side of the Taurus mountains.[9] As for me, unless the Etesians hold me back, I hope I shall see you all in the near future.

[6] Cf. *Letters to Atticus* 121 (VI.6).4.

[7] Q. Cassius Longinus and M. Antonius (Mark Antony) had been chosen as their Quaestors by Pompey and Caesar respectively. Normally Quaestors were assigned by lot.

[8] Cf. Letter 92.2. *Acta* in such contexts is usually referred to *acta diurna*, a sort of gazette supposedly instituted by Caesar in his Consulship; but see P. White, *Chiron* 27 (1997): 73–84.

[9] Nothing is known of this affair, apart from Letter 96.5.

97 (VIII.14)

Scr. Romae c. VI *Id. Sext. an.* 50

CAELIUS CICERONI S.

1   Tanti non fuit Arsacen capere et Seleuceam expugnare ut earum rerum quae hic gestae sunt spectaculo careres. numquam tibi oculi doluissent si in repulsa Domiti vultum vidisses. magna illa comitia fuerunt et plane studia ex partium sensu apparuerunt, perpauci necessitudinem secuti officium praestiterunt. itaque mihi est Domitius inimicissimus, ut ne familiarem quidem suum quemquam tam oderit quam me, atque eo magis quod per iniuriam sibi *[1] putat ereptum cuius ego auctor fuerim. nunc furit tam gavisos homines suum dolorem unumque m⟨e Curi⟩one⟨m⟩[2] studiosiorem Antoni. nam Cn. Saturninum adulescentem ipse Cn. Domitius reum fecit sane quam superiore a vita invidiosum; quod iudicium nunc ⟨in⟩ exspectatione est, etiam in bona spe post Sex. Peducaei absolutionem.

2   De summa re publica saepe tibi scripsi me ⟨in⟩ annum pacem non videre; et quo propius ea contentio quam fieri

---

[1] auguratum *hic suppl.* Gron. (*mallem* id *vel* hoc *post* quod): pontificatum *coni.* SB   [2] *(SB)*

---

[1] I.e. the King of Parthia. The Parthian kings bore the name of the founder of their line in addition to their individual names, like the Ptolemies of Egypt.   [2] As a candidate for the vacancy in the Augural College created by the death of Hortensius. He was beaten by Mark Antony.   [3] Cf. Letter 20.2.

[4] Translating the conjecture *pontificatum*. If right, it refers to a

97 (VIII.14)
CAELIUS RUFUS TO CICERO

Rome, ca. 8 August 50

From Caelius to Cicero greetings.

What a spectacle you have missed here! If you've made
Arsaces[1] prisoner and stormed Seleucia, it wasn't worth
the sacrifice. Your eyes would never have been sore again if
you'd seen Domitius' face when he heard of his defeat.[2]
The polling was heavy, and support for the candidates
quite on party lines. Only a tiny minority gave their backing in conformity with personal loyalties. Accordingly
Domitius is my bitter enemy. He has not a friend in the
world whom he hates more than me![3]—all the more so because he regards himself as having been robbed of the
Pontificate[4] and me as the author of the outrage. Now he is
furious at the general rejoicing over his discomfiture and at
the fact that Antony had only one more ardent supporter
(Curio) than myself. As for young Cn. Saturninus, he has
been charged by none other than Cn. Domitius.[5] To be
sure his past makes him far from popular. We are now waiting for the trial. Actually there is good hope for him after
Sex. Peducaeus'[6] acquittal.

On high politics, I have often told you that I do not see
peace lasting another year; and the nearer the inevitable

previous failure of Domitius to gain a place in the College of Pontiffs, of which he later became a member.

[5] L. Domitius' son. Cn. (Sentius) Saturninus had no doubt
supported Antony.   [6] Not Cicero's former Praetor or his son
(see Index), but perhaps a supporter of Caesar who became governor of Sardinia in 48. The circumstances of his trial are unknown.

necesse est accedit eo clarius id periculum apparet. propositum hoc est de quo qui rerum potiuntur sunt dimicaturi, quod Cn. Pompeius constituit non pati C. Caesarem consulem aliter fieri nisi exercitum et provincias tradiderit, Caesari autem persuasum est se salvum esse non posse <si> ab exercitu recesserit; fert illam tamen condicionem, ut ambo exercitus tradant. sic illi amores et <in>vidiosa coniunctio non ad occultam recidit obtrectationem sed ad bellum se eru<m>pit. neque mearum rerum quid consili capiam reperio; quod non dubito quin te quoque haec deliberatio sit pertubatur<a>. nam mihi cum hominibus his et gratia et necessitudines;[3] [cum][4] causam illam <amo>[5] unde homines odi.

3   Illud te non arbitror fugere, quin homines in dissensione domestica debeant, quam diu civiliter sine armis certetur, honestiorem sequi partem; ubi ad bellum et castra ventum sit, firmiorem, et id melius statuere quod tutius sit. in hac discordia video Cn. Pompeium senatum quique res iudicant secum habiturum, ad Caesarem omnis qui cum timore aut mala spe vivant accessuros; exercitum conferendum non esse. omnino satis <s>pati est[6] ad considerandas utri<u>sque copias et [eligendas utriusque copias et] eligendam partem.

4   Prope oblitus sum quo<d> maxime fuit scribendum. scis Appium censorem hic ostenta facere, de signis et tabulis, de agri modo, de aere alieno acerrime agere? persuasum est ei censuram lomentum aut nitrum esse. errare mihi videtur; nam sordis eluere vult, venas sibi omnis et

3 necessitudinem (*Madvig*)   4 (*Wes.*)
5 (*Madvig*)   6 pati sit (*Or.*)

struggle approaches, the plainer the danger appears. The question on which the dynasts will join issue is this: Cn. Pompeius is determined not to allow C. Caesar to be elected Consul unless he surrenders his army and provinces; whereas Caesar is persuaded that he cannot survive if he leaves his army. He makes the proposition, however, that both surrender their military forces. So this is what their love affair, their scandalous union, has come to—not covert backbiting, but outright war! As for my own position, I don't know what course to take; and I don't doubt that the same question is going to trouble you. I have ties of obligation and friendship with these people. On the other side, I love the cause but hate the men.

I don't suppose it escapes you that, when parties clash in a community, it behoves a man to take the more respectable side so long as the struggle is political and not by force of arms; but when it comes to actual fighting he should choose the stronger, and reckon the safer course the better. In the present quarrel Cn. Pompeius will evidently have with him the Senate and the people who sit on juries,[7] whereas all who live in present fear and small hope for the future will rally to Caesar. His army is incomparably superior. To be sure there is time enough to consider their respective resources and choose one's side.

I almost forgot the most interesting item of all. Did you know that Appius is performing prodigies of censorial vigour—works of art, size of estates, debt are all grist to his mill. He is convinced that the Censorship is face cream or washing soda, but I fancy he is making a mistake; in trying to scrub out the stains he is laying open all his veins and

---

[7] I.e. the rich and respectable.

viscera aperit. curre, per deos atque homines, et quam primum haec risum veni, legis Scantin⟨ia⟩e iudicium apud
Drusum fieri, Appium de tabulis et signis agere. crede
mihi, est properandum. Curio noster sapienter id quod
remisit de stipendio Pompei fecisse existimatur.

Ad summam, quaeris[7] quid putem futurum. si alter
ut⟨er⟩ eorum ad Parthicum bellum non eat, video magnas
impendere discordias, quas ferrum et vis iudicabit. uterque et animo et copiis est paratus. si sine suo periculo fieri
posset, magnum et iucundum tibi Fortuna spectaculum
parabat.

98 (VIII.12)

Scr. Romae c. XII Kal. Oct. (sed § 4 aliquanto post) an. 50
CAELIUS CICERONI S.

1   Pudet me tibi confiteri et queri de Appi, hominis ingra-
tissimi, iniuriis; qui me odisse, quia magna mihi debebat
beneficia, coepit et, cum homo avarus ut ea solveret sibi
imperare non posset, occultum bellum mihi indixit, ita
occultum tamen ut multi mihi renuntiarent et ipse facile
animadverterem male eum de me cogitare. postea quam
vero comperi eum collegam[1] temptasse, deinde aperte

---

7 ⟨si⟩ quaeris *coni. Watt*   1 collegium (*Man.*)

---

8 Or 'flesh.'

9 See Glossary. Drusus was apparently a notorious offender.

10 Appius had allegedly plundered Greece to assemble his
own art collection.

vitals.[8] Make haste in the Gods' name and man's and get here as soon as you can to laugh at our frolics—at Drusus trying offences under the lex Scantinia,[9] at Appius taking official action about works of art.[10] Believe me, you must hurry. Our friend Curio is considered to have shown good sense in not pressing his point about pay for Pompey's troops.

Well, to sum up: what do I think will happen? If neither of the two goes off to the Parthian war, I see great quarrels ahead in which strength and steel will be the arbiters. Both are well prepared, morally and materially. If it were not for the personal risk involved, Fortune is preparing a mighty and fascinating show for your benefit.

98 (VIII.12)

CAELIUS RUFUS TO CICERO

Rome, ca. 19 September (with postscript added later) 50

From Caelius to Cicero greetings.

I am mortified to have to admit and complain to you about the scurvy treatment I have received from Appius. The man is a monster of ingratitude. Just because he is indebted to me for important favours,[1] he turned against me; and being too much of a skinflint to bring himself to repay them, he declared covert war on me—not so covert though but that I heard tell of it from many quarters and saw his malevolence plainly enough for myself. But when I found

---

[1] Probably with reference to efforts on Appius' behalf when he was under prosecution; cf. Letter 88.

cum quibusdam locutum, cum L. Domitio, ut nunc est,
mihi inimicissimo homine, deliberare, velle hoc munusculum deferre Cn. Pompeio, ipsum reprehenderem et ab
eo deprecarer iniuriam quem vitam mihi debere putaram

2 impetrare a me non potui. quid ergo est? tamen, quasi[2]
* * * aliquot amicis, qui testes erant meorum in illum
meritorum, locutus sum. postea quam illum ne cui satis
facere<t> quidem me dignum habere sensi, malui collegae
eius, homini alienissimo mihi et propter amicitiam tuam
non aequissimo, me obligare quam illius simiae vultum
subire. id postquam resci<i>t, excanduit et me causa<m>
inimicitiarum quaerere clamitavit, ut, si mihi in pecunia
minus satis fecisset, per hanc speciem simultatis eum
consectarer. postea non destitit accersere Polam Servium

3 accusatorem, inire cum Domiti<o> consilia. quibus cum
parum procederet ut ulla lege mihi ponere<n>t[3] accusatorem, compellari ea lege me voluerunt †qua dicere†[4] non
poterant: insolentissimi homines summis Circensibus ludis meis postulandum me lege Scantinia curant. vix hoc
erat Pola elocutus cum ego Appium censorem eadem lege
postulavi. quod melius caderet nihil vidi. nam sic est a
populo et non infimo quoque approbatum ut maiorem
Appio dolorem fama quam postulatio attulerit. praeterea

---

[2] *lac. indicavit SB, quam ita fere supplere possis*: verum
requirerem cum Appi   [3] *(Lamb.)*   [4] qua <m digne>
dicere *tempt. SB,* qua<m sine rubore> d- *Watt*

---

[2] L. Calpurnius Piso Caesoninus, Consul in 58, elected Censor
along with Appius in 50.

[3] Text and sense doubtful.

[4] I.e. the Roman Games, which ended on 19 September.

that he had been sounding his colleague[2] and that he had talked openly to certain persons and was plotting with L. Domitius (a bitter enemy of mine these days) with the idea of presenting this little *douceur* to Cn. Pompeius— well, I could not bring myself to tax him personally and ask a man who I thought owed me his life not to do me harm. So what did I do? Notwithstanding my reluctance, I spoke to a number of Appius' friends who had personal knowledge of what I had done for him, as though enquiring as to the true facts. Finding that he did not even consider me worth the trouble of an explanation, I chose to put myself under an obligation to his colleague (an almost total stranger to me and none too well disposed, because I am a friend of yours) rather than subject myself to the sight of that supercilious monkey. When he heard of that, he flew into a rage and went on bawling that I was trying to pick a quarrel so as to use a show of enmity as a pretext for victimizing him if he failed to meet my wishes in a matter of money. Since then he has been continually sending for Pola Servius, the professional prosecutor, and talking with Domitius. They were looking for a charge on which they could put him up to prosecute me, but were puzzled to find one. So they thought they would have me put in court on a charge which they could not decently name (?).[3] They are having the effrontery to get me summoned under the lex Scantinia at the end of my Circus Games.[4] The words were hardly out of Pola's mouth when I charged Censor Appius under the same statute! It's the greatest success I ever saw. All Rome (and not just the lower orders) approves; so that Appius is more upset by the scandal than by the prosecution. Furthermore, I have instituted a claim against him for

coepi sacellum, in domo quod est, ab eo petere.

4   Conturbat me mora servi huius qui tibi litteras attulit; nam acceptis prioribus litteris amplius ⟨dies⟩[5] quadraginta mansit. quid tibi scribam nescio. scis †domitio diem†[6] tu morae es.[7] t⟨e⟩[8] exspecto valde et quam primum videre cupio. a te peto ut meas iniurias proinde doleas ut me existimas et dolere et ulcisci tuas solere.

99 (XV.7)

Scr. inter Iconium et Cybistra priore parte m. Sept. an. 51

M. CICERO PRO COS. S. D. C. MARCELLO COS. DESIG.

Maxima sum laetitia adfectus cum audivi consulem te factum esse, eumque honorem tibi deos fortunare volo atque a te pro tua parentisque tui dignitate administrari. nam cum te semper amavi dilexique, tum mei amantissimum cognovi in omni varietate rerum mearum, tum patris tui plurimis beneficiis vel defensus tristibus temporibus vel ornatus secundis et sum totus vester et esse debeo, cum praesertim matris tuae, gravissimae atque optimae feminae, maiora erga salutem dignitatemque meam studia quam erant a muliere postulanda perspexe-

---

[5] *(hic Or., alii alibi)*   [6] domi tuae teri diem *tempt. SB*
[7] est *(Festa)*   [8] te add. *Vict.*

---

[5] Claimed as public property.
[6] This postscript seems to have been added a day or two later.
[7] Letter 97.

a chapel[5] that is in his house.

I[6] am much put out by the delay of this slave who is bringing you my letter. After receiving my earlier letter,[7] he took more than forty days before setting out. I don't know what else I can write to you. You know that they are marking time at home (?). You are holding things up (?).[8] I am much looking forward to your return, and am eager to see you, as soon as possible. I ask you to take my injuries to heart, as you judge that I am in the habit of taking yours and of avenging them.

99 (XV.7)

CICERO TO C. MARCELLUS

Between Iconium and Cybistra, early or mid September 51

From M. Cicero, Proconsul, to C. Marcellus, Consul-Elect, greetings.

The news of your election as Consul gave me great happiness. I wish the Gods prosper you in that high office, and that you discharge it in a manner worthy of yourself and your father. You have always had my affection and regard, and in all the vicissitudes of my career I have had evidence of your warm affection for me. From your father also I have received a great many kindnesses—defence in bad times, furtherance in good. So I am, and ought to be, devoted to your family—the more so as that highly respected and excellent lady, your mother, has shown an active concern for my welfare and standing beyond what

---

[8] Apparently a reference to Tullia's wedding. But the text is very doubtful.

rim. quapropter a te peto in maiorem modum ut me
absentem diligas atque defendas.

100 (XV.8)

Scr. eodem loco et tempore

M. CICERO PRO. COS. S. D. C. MARCELLO COLLEGAE

Marcellum tuum consulem factum teque ea laetitia
adfectum esse quam maxime optasti mirandum in modum
gaudeo, idque cum ipsius causa tum quod te omnibus
secundissimis rebus dignissimum iudico, cuius erga me
singularem benevolentiam vel in labore meo vel in honore
perspexi, totam denique domum vestram vel salutis vel
dignitatis meae studiosissimam cupidissimamque cognovi.
qua re gratum mihi feceris si uxori tuae Iuniae, gravissimae
atque optimae feminae, meis verbis eris gratulatus. a te, id
quod consuesti, peto me absentem diligas atque defendas.

101 (XV.9)

Scr. eodem loco et tempore

M. CICERO PRO COS. S. D. M. MARCELLO COS.

1   Te et pietatis in tuos et animi in rem publicam et

could be expected from her sex. Accordingly I would earnestly solicit your regard and protection during my absence.

100 (XV.8)
CICERO TO C. MARCELLUS (SENIOR)

Same place and time as the foregoing

From M. Cicero, Proconsul, to his Colleague C. Marcellus, greetings.

I am marvellously pleased to hear that your son Marcellus has been elected Consul and that the joy you most longed for is indeed yours. My happiness is both for his own sake and because I consider you deserving of every possible good fortune. In my trials as in my successes you have always shown me conspicuous good will; indeed I have found your whole family most active and ardent for my welfare and my standing. I shall accordingly be grateful if you will convey my congratulations to that highly respected and excellent lady, your wife Junia. As for yourself, let me request you to continue to favour me in my absence with your regard and protection.

101 (XV.9)
CICERO TO M. MARCELLUS

Same place and time as the foregoing

From M. Cicero, Proconsul, to M. Marcellus, Consul, greetings.

I am thoroughly delighted that with C. Marcellus' elec-

clarissimi atque optimi consulatus C. Marcello consule facto fructum cepisse vehementer gaudeo. non dubito quid praesentes sentiant; nos quidem longinqui et a te ipso missi in ultimas gentis ad caelum mehercule tollimus verissimis ac iustissimis laudibus. nam cum te a pueritia tua unice dilexerim tuque me in omni genere semper amplissimum esse et volueris et iudicaris, tum hoc vel tuo facto vel populi Romani de te iudicio multo acrius vehementiusque diligo, maximaque laetitia adficior cum ab hominibus prudentissimis virisque optimis omnibus dictis,

2 factis, studiis, institutis vel me tui similem esse audio vel te mei. unum vero si addis ad praeclarissimas res consulatus tui, ut aut mihi succedat quam primum aliquis aut ne quid accedat temporis ad id quod tu mihi et senatus consulto et lege finisti, omnia me per te consecutum putabo.

Cura ut valeas et me absentem diligas atque defendas.

3 Quae mihi de Parthis nuntiata sunt, quia non putabam a me etiam nunc scribenda esse publice, propterea ne pro familiaritate quidem nostra volui ad te scribere, ne, cum ad consulem scripsissem, publice viderer scripsisse.

tion to the Consulship you have reaped the reward of your family affection, patriotism, and your own most distinguished and meritorious record in that office. Of sentiment in Rome I have no doubt; as for me, far away as I am, dispatched by none other than yourself to the ends of the earth, I assure you I exalt it to the skies in praises most sincere and well grounded. I have had a very particular regard for you from your childhood. On your side, you have ever desired and believed me to stand high in all respects. And what has now happened, whether we call it your achievement or an expression of the sentiments of the Roman people concerning you, very sensibly augments and enhances my affection for you, and it gives me the keenest pleasure when I hear from persons of the highest perspicacity and probity that in all our words, acts, pursuits, and habits I resemble you—or you resemble me. If only you add one more thing to the splendid achievements of your Consulship, I shall feel that you have left me nothing further to wish for—I mean the early appointment of a successor to my post, or at any rate no extension of the term which you fixed for me by decree of the Senate and by law.

Take care of your health and favour me in my absence with your regard and protection.

I still do not think I should write officially on the reports reaching me about the Parthians, and for that reason I prefer not to write to you on the subject either, even as a close personal friend, for fear that a letter to the Consul might be interpreted as an official communication.

102 (XV.12)

Scr. eodem loco et tempore quo superior

M. CICERO PRO COS.[1] S. D. L. PAULLO COS. DESIG.

1 Etsi mihi numquam fuit dubium quin te populus Romanus pro tuis summis in rem publicam meritis et pro amplissima familiae dignitate summo studio cunctis suffragiis consulem facturus esset, tamen incredibili laetitia sum adfectus cum id mihi nuntiatum est, eumque honorem tibi deos fortunare volo a teque ex tua maiorumque tuorum dignitate administrari. atque utinam praesens illum diem

2 mihi optatissimum videre potuissem proque tuis amplissimis erga me studiis atque beneficiis tibi operam meam studiumque navare! quam mihi facultatem quoniam hic necopinatus et improvisus provinciae casus eripuit, tamen, ut te consulem rem publicam pro tua dignitate gerentem videre possim, magno opere a te peto ut operam des efficiasque ne quid mihi fiat iniuriae neve quid temporis ad meum annu<u>m munus accedat. quod si feceris, magnus ad tua pristina erga me studia cumulus accedet.

---

[1] Cicero imp. (*Bengel, qui quidem* PROCOS.)

102 (XV.12)
CICERO TO L. PAULLUS

Same place and time as the foregoing

From M. Cicero, Proconsul, to L. Paullus, Consul-Elect, greetings.

I never had a doubt but that the Roman People would enthusiastically and unanimously elect you Consul in recognition of your great services to the state and the exalted position of your family. All the same, my happiness when I heard the news was more than you can well conceive. I wish the Gods prosper you in your high office and that you discharge it in a manner worthy of yourself and your forbears. I only wish I could have been on the spot to see the day for which I have always longed, and to do you yeoman service in return for your signal acts of good will and kindness towards me. That opportunity was snatched away from me by the sudden, unforeseen chance which sent me on service abroad; but I trust I may still see you as Consul administering the commonwealth in a manner worthy of your standing. To that end I earnestly beg of you to use your best efforts and prevent any unfairness to me or any extension of my year's term. If you do that, you will generously crown your past tokens of good will.

103 (XV.3)

Scr. in castris ad Iconium III Non. Sept., vel paulo post, an. 51

M. CICERO [IMP.][1] S. D. M. CATONI

1 Cum ad me legati missi ab Antiocho Commageno venissent in castra ad Iconium a. d. III. Non. Sept. iique mihi nuntiassent regis Parthorum filium, quocum esset nupta regis Armeniorum soror, ad Euphratem cum maximis Parthorum copiis multarumque praeterea gentium magna manu venisse Euphratemque iam transire coepisse dicique Armenium regem in Cappadociam impetum esse facturum, putavi pro nostra necessitudine me hoc ad te scribere oportere.

2 Publice propter duas causas nihil scripsi, quod et ipsum Commagenum legati dicebant ad senatum statim nuntios litterasque misisse et existimabam M. Bibulum pro consule, qui circiter Id. Sext. ab Epheso in Syriam navibus profectus erat, quod secundos ventos habuisset, iam in provinciam suam pervenisse; cuius litteris omnia certiora perlatum iri ad senatum putabam. mihi ut in eius modi re tantoque bello maximae curae est ut, quae copiis et opibus tenere vix possumus, ea mansuetudine et continentia nostra, sociorum fidelitate teneamus. tu velim, ut consuesti, nos absentis diligas et defendas.

[1] *(Corr.)*

103 (XV.3)
CICERO TO CATO

Camp near Iconium, 3 September (or shortly after) 51

From M. Cicero to M. Cato greetings.

In view of the close relations between us I feel I should write to inform you that a mission from Antiochus of Commagene has arrived in my camp near Iconium on 3 September with the news that the King of Parthia's son, who is married to a sister of the King of Armenia, has arrived on the banks of the Euphrates with a massive Parthian army and a large force in addition, drawn from many different nationalities; that he has already begun the passage of the river; and that there is talk of the King of Armenia invading Cappadocia.

I have not written an official dispatch for two reasons. The envoys say that the King of Commagene himself sent messengers and a letter to the Senate immediately; and I expect that Proconsul M. Bibulus, who left by sea from Ephesus for Syria about the Ides of August, has already arrived in his province, since he had favourable winds. I presume that everything will be more reliably reported to the Senate in a dispatch from him. In such a situation, with a war on so large a scale, my own principal preoccupation is to hold by my gentleness and moderation, through the loyalty of our subjects, what I can hardly hold by the troops and resources at my disposal. I hope that, as in the past, I shall have your regard and protection in my absence.

104 (XV.1)

Scr. in finibus Lycaoniae et Cappadociae XIII *Kal. Oct. an. 51*

M. TULLIUS M. F. CICERO PRO COS. S. D. COS. PR. TR. PL.
SENATUI

S. v. v. b.; e. e. q. v.

1 Etsi non dubie mihi nuntiabatur Parthos transisse Euphratem cum omnibus fere suis copiis, tamen, quod arbitrabar a M. Bibulo pro consule certiora de his rebus ad vos
scribi posse, statuebam mihi non necesse esse publice scribere ea quae de alterius provincia nuntiarentur. postea
vero quam certissimis auctoribus, legatis, nuntiis, litteris
sum certior factus, vel quod tanta res erat vel quod nondum audieramus Bibulum in Syriam venisse vel quia admi-
nistratio huius belli mihi cum Bibulo paene est communis,
quae ad me delata essent scribenda ad vos putavi.

2 Regis Antiochi Commageni legati primi mihi nuntia-
runt Parthorum magnas copias Euphratem transire coepisse. quo nuntio adlato, cum essent non nulli qui ei regi
minorem fidem habendam putarent, statui exspectandum
esse si quid certius adferretur. a. d. XIII Kal. Oct., cum
exercitum in Ciliciam ducerem, in finibus Lycaoniae et
Cappadociae mihi litterae redditae sunt a Tarcondimoto,
qui fidelissimus socius trans Taurum amicissimusque populo Romano existimatur, Pacorum, Orodi regis Partho-

104 (XV.1)

CICERO TO THE MAGISTRATES AND SENATE

Border of Lycaonia and Cappadocia, 18 September 51

From M. Tullius Cicero, son of Marcus, Proconsul, to the Consuls, Praetors, Tribunes of the Plebs, and Senate, greetings.

I trust you are well. I and the army are well.

Although receiving clear reports that the Parthians had crossed the Euphrates with virtually their entire force, I supposed that M. Bibulus, Proconsul, would be able to give you more reliable information on these matters, and therefore decided that it was unnecessary for me to send an official account of reports which concerned a province other than my own. Subsequently, however, the information reached me on unimpeachable authority, by emissaries, verbal reports, and letters. Bearing in mind the importance of the matter, as also that I have no news as yet of Bibulus' arrival in Syria and that I may almost be said to carry joint responsibility with him in the conduct of this war, I thought it my duty to write apprising you of my intelligence.

Envoys from King Antiochus of Commagene were the first to announce to me that large forces of Parthians had begun to cross the Euphrates. On receiving this report, I decided that it would be best to wait for something more reliable, since there were those who thought the king was not entirely to be trusted. On 18 September, as I was leading my army into Cilicia, I received a letter on the borders of Lycaonia and Cappadocia from Tarcondimotus, who is considered to be our most faithful ally beyond Taurus and a true friend to Rome. This told me that Pacorus, son of

rum filium, cum permagno equitatu Parthico transisse
Euphratem et castra posuisse Tybae, magnumque tumul-
tum esse in provincia Syria excitatum. eodem die ab Iam-
blicho, phylarcho Arabum, quem homines opinantur bene
sentire amicumque esse rei publicae nostrae, litterae de isdem rebus mihi redditae sunt.

3   His rebus adlatis, etsi intellegebam socios infirme ani-
matos esse et novarum rerum exspectatione suspensos,
sperabam tamen eos ad quos iam accesseram quique
nostram mansuetudinem[1] integritatemque perspexerant
amiciores populo Romano esse factos, Ciliciam autem firmiorem fore si aequitatis nostrae particeps facta esset. et
ob eam causam et ut opprimerentur ii qui ex Cilicum gente
in armis essent et ut hostis is qui esset in Syria sciret exercitum populi Romani non modo non cedere iis nuntiis
adlatis sed etiam propius accedere, exercitum ad Taurum
institui ducere.

4   Sed si quid apud vos auctoritas mea ponderis habet, in
iis praesertim rebus quas vos audistis, ego paene cerno,
magno opere vos et hortor et moneo ut his provinciis,
serius vos quidem quam decuit sed aliquando tamen,
consulatis. nos quem ad modum instructos et quibus praesidiis munitos ad tanti belli opinionem miseritis, non estis
ignari. quod ego negotium non stultitia occaecatus sed
verecundia deterritus non recusavi. neque enim umquam
ullum periculum tantum putavi quod subterfugere mallem quam vestrae auctoritati obtemperare.

5   Hoc autem tempore res sese sic habet ut, nisi exercitum
tantum quantum ad maximum bellum mittere soletis mature in has provincias miseritis, summum periculum sit ne

[1] consuetudinem (*Ferrarius*)

King Orodes of Parthia, had crossed the Euphrates with a very large force of Parthian cavalry and pitched camp at Tyba, creating great turmoil in the province of Syria. On the same day I had a letter on these same matters from Iamblichus, Phylarch of the Arabs, who is generally thought to be loyal and friendly to our country.

After receiving this intelligence, I determined to march to the Taurus, for several reasons. I realized that our subjects were in a wavering mood, poised in expectation of change; but I trusted that those with whom I had already been in contact and who had perceived the gentleness and integrity of my government had become more friendly to Rome, and that the loyalty of Cilicia would be strengthened if that area shared in the benefits of my equitable administration. I also wanted to crush the rebellious elements in the Cilician nation and to let the enemy in Syria know that on receipt of the aforesaid intelligence a Roman army was not merely not retreating but actually approaching closer.

If, however, my advice carries any weight with you, especially in circumstances which you have heard by report but which I have almost before my eyes, I would emphatically urge and warn you to take thought for these provinces even at this all too late hour. You are not ignorant of the resources and defensive forces with which you sent me out to face the prospect of a major war. It was not blind folly but a sense of shame that prevented me from declining the task; for I have never thought any danger grave enough to care to evade it by failing in obedience to your authority.

The present situation is this: Unless you send to these provinces without loss of time an army as large as you usually send to cope with war on a grand scale, there is the

amittendae sint omnes eae provinciae quibus vectigalia
populi Romani continentur. quam ob rem autem in hoc
provinciali dilectu spem habeatis aliquam causa nulla est.
neque multi sunt et diffugiunt qui sunt metu oblato; et
quod genus hoc militum sit iudicavit vir fortissimus, M. Bibulus, in Asia, qui, cum vos ei permisis<se>tis, dilectum
habere noluerit. nam sociorum auxilia propter acerbita-
tem atque iniurias imperi nostri aut ita imbecilla sunt ut
non multum nos iuvare possint aut ita alienata a nobis ut
neque exspectandum ab iis neque committendum iis quic-
6   quam esse videatur. regis Deiotari et voluntatem et copias,
quantaecumque sunt, nostras esse duco. Cappadocia est
inanis, reliqui reges tyrannique neque opibus satis firmi
nec voluntate sunt. mihi in hac paucitate militum animus
certe non deerit, spero ne consilium quidem. quid casu-
rum sit incertum est. utinam saluti nostrae consulere possimus! dignitati certe consulemus.

105 (XV.2)

Scr. in castris ad Cybistra x vel ix Kal. Oct. an. 51

M. TULLIUS M. F. CICERO PRO COS. S. D. COS. PR. TR. PL.
SENATUI

1   S. v. v. b.; e. e. q. v.

Cum prid. Kal. Sext. in provinciam venissem neque
maturius propter itinerum et navigationum difficultatem
venire potuissem, maxime convenire officio meo reique

gravest risk that all the provinces on which the revenues of
Rome depend may have to be given up. You should rest no
hopes whatever on the local levies. Their numbers are
small, and those there are scatter at sight of danger. My
gallant colleague, M. Bibulus, gave his verdict on this de-
scription of troops in Asia when he declined to hold a levy,
although you had given him permission. As for the auxiliaries supplied by our allies, the harshness and injustices of
our rule have rendered them either so weak as to be of
little use or so disaffected that it would appear imprudent
to expect anything from them or entrust anything to them.
I think we can fully depend on the loyalty of King Deiotarus and such forces as he commands. Cappadocia is a
vacuum; the remaining kings and rulers are undependable
in point both of resources and of loyalty. Few as our numbers are, I shall assuredly not be found wanting in courage,
nor yet, I trust, in judgement. What will happen no man
can tell. I pray that I may be able to provide for our safety,
as I certainly shall for our honour.

105 (XV.2)

CICERO TO THE MAGISTRATES AND SENATE

Camp near Cybistra, 21 or 22 September 51

From M. Tullius Cicero, son of Marcus; Proconsul, to the
Consuls, Praetors, Tribunes of the Plebs, and Senate,
greetings.

I trust that you are well. I and the army are well.

On arriving in my province on 31 July, no earlier date
being practicable by reason of the difficulties of travel both
by land and sea, I considered that I should best conform to

449

publicae conducere putavi parare ea quae ad exercitum quaeque ad rem militarem pertinerent. quae cum essent a me cura magis et diligentia quam facultate et copia constituta nuntiique et litterae de bello a Parthis in provinciam Syriam illato cottidie fere adferrentur, iter mihi faciendum per Lycaoniam et per Isauros et per Cappadociam arbitratus sum. erat enim magna suspicio Parthos, si ex Syria egredi atque irrumpere in meam provinciam conarentur, iter eo[s][1] per Cappadociam, quod ea maxime pateret, esse facturos.

2   Itaque cum exercitu per Cappadociae partem eam quae cum Cilicia continens est iter feci castraque ad Cybistra, quod oppidum est ad montem Taurum, locavi, ut Art<a>vasdes, rex Armenius, quocumque animo esset, sciret non procul a suis finibus exercitum populi Romani esse, et Deiotarum, fidelissimum regem atque amicissimum rei publicae nostrae, maxime coniunctum haberem, cuius et consilio et opibus adiuvari posset res publica.

3   Quo cum in loco castra haberem equitatumque in Ciliciam misissem, ut et meus adventus iis civitatibus quae in ea parte essent nuntiatus firmiores animos omnium faceret et ego mature quid ageretur in Syria scire possem, tempus eius tridui quod in iis castris morabar in magno officio et

4   necessario mihi ponendum putavi. cum enim vestra auctoritas intercessisset ut ego regem Ariobarzanem Eusebem et Philorhomaeum tuerer eiusque regis salutem et incolumitatem regnumque defenderem, regi regnoque praesidio essem, adiunxissetisque salutem eius regis populo senatuique magnae curae esse, quod nullo umquam de

[1] *(T.–P.)*

my duty and the public interest by making appropriate provisions for the army and for military security. Having made my dispositions with care and diligence rather than plenitude of means, I received reports and letters almost daily concerning a Parthian invasion of the province of Syria. I therefore thought it proper to march through Lycaonia, Isauria, and Cappadocia, since it was strongly suspected that, if the Parthians attempted to leave Syria and break into my province, they would come by way of Cappadocia, where there was least to stop them.

Accordingly I and my army marched through that part of Cappadocia which adjoins Cilicia and pitched camp near Cybistra, a town lying close to the Taurus mountains, in order that Artavasdes, King of Armenia, whatever his disposition might be, should know that a Roman army was not far from his frontiers, and that I should have King Deiotarus close at hand, a most faithful and friendly ally to our country, whose advice and material support might be of service to the commonwealth.

While stationed in that spot, having previously sent a force of cavalry on to Cilicia so that the news of my arrival might strengthen morale generally in the communes situated in that region and at the same time I might get early intelligence of events in Syria, I thought it proper to devote the three days of my halt in this camp to an important and necessary duty. I had your resolution charging me to take good care of King Ariobarzanes Eusebes and Philorhomaeus, to defend his welfare, security, and throne, and to protect king and kingdom; to which you added that the welfare of this monarch was a matter of great concern to the People and Senate—something that had never before been decreed by our House with respect to any monarch. I

rege decretum esset a nostro ordine, existimavi me iudicium vestrum ad regem deferre debere eique praesidium meum et fidem et diligentiam polliceri, ut, quoniam salus ipsius, incolumitas regni mihi commendata esset a vobis, diceret si quid vellet.

5 Quae cum essem in consilio meo cum rege locutus, initio ille orationis suae vobis maximas, ut debuit, deinde etiam mihi gratias egit, quod ei permagnum et perhonorificum videbatur senatui populoque Romano tantae curae esse salutem suam meque tantam diligentiam adhibere ut et mea fides et commendationis vestrae auctoritas perspici posset. atque ille primo, quod mihi maximae laetitiae fuit, ita mecum locutus est ut nullas insidias neque vitae suae neque regno diceret se aut intellegere fieri aut etiam suspicari. cum ego ei gratulatus essem idque me gaudere dixissem et tamen adulescentem essem cohortatus ut recordaretur casum illum interitus paterni et vigilanter se tueretur atque admonitu senatus consuleret saluti suae, tum a me discessit in oppidum Cybistra.

6 Postero autem die cum Ariarathe, fratre suo, et cum paternis amicis maioribus natu ad me in castra venit perturbatusque et flens, cum idem et frater faceret et amici, meam fidem, vestram commendationem implorare coepit. cum admirarer quid accidisset novi, dixit ad se indicia manifestarum[2] insidiarum esse delata, quae essent ante adventum meum occultata, quod ii qui ea patefacere possent propter metum reticuissent. eo autem tempore spe

---

[2] manifesta *Kleyn*

---

[1] Ariobarzanes II, murdered by conspirators.

therefore considered it incumbent upon me to convey your mandate to the king, and to promise him my faithful protection and care, adding that, since his personal welfare and the security of his realm had been commended to me by yourselves, I should be glad to learn his wishes, if any.

When I had addressed the king to this effect in the presence of my Council, he began his reply with a proper expression of profound gratitude to yourselves, and then proceeded to thank me also. He felt it as a most important favour and a very high compliment that his welfare should be of so much concern to the Senate and People of Rome, and that I should be at such pains to demonstrate my commitment and the weight attaching to your recommendation. At first he gave me to understand, to my great satisfaction, that he had no knowledge or even suspicion of any plots against his life or throne. I congratulated him and said I was delighted to hear it, at the same time urging the young man to remember the sad end that had overtaken his father;[1] he should guard himself vigilantly and take good heed for his safety, conformably to the Senate's admonition. He then took his leave, and returned to the town of Cybistra.

On the day following, however, he arrived in my camp along with his brother Ariarathes and some older persons, friends of his father's. In a state of tearful agitation, as were also his brother and their friends, he appealed to me in the name of my pledged word and your commendation. When I asked in some surprise what had happened, he said that he had received information of a manifest conspiracy, which had been kept secret prior to my arrival because those who might have revealed it were afraid to speak. But now, in the hope of my protection, a number had plucked

453

mei praesidi compluris ea quae scirent audacter ad se detulisse; in iis amantissimum sui, summa pietate praeditum
fratrem dicere (ea quae is me quoque audiente dicebat) se
sollicitatum esse ut regnare vellet; id vivo fratre suo accidere non potuisse; se tamen ante illud tempus eam rem
numquam in medium propter periculi metum protulisse.
quae cum esset locutus, monui regem ut omnem diligentiam ad se conservandum adhiberet, amicosque [in]³ patris
eius atque avi iudicio probatos hortatus sum regis sui vitam
docti casu acerbissimo patris eius omni cura custodiaque
defenderent.

7   Cum rex a me equitatum cohortisque de exercitu meo
postularet, etsi intellegebam vestro senatus consulto non
modo posse me id facere sed etiam debere, tamen, cum
res publica postularet propter cottidianos ex Syria nuntios
ut quam primum exercitum ad Ciliciae fines adducerem,
cumque mihi rex patefactis iam insidiis non egere exercitu
populi Romani sed posse <se> suis opibus defendere videretur, illum cohortatus sum ut in sua vita conservanda primum regnare disceret; a quibus perspexisset sibi insidias
paratas, in eos uteretur iure regio; poena adficeret eos
quos necesse esset, reliquos metu liberaret; praesidio
exercitus mei ad eorum qui in culpa essent timorem potius
quam ad contentionem uteretur; fore autem ut omnes,
quoniam senatus consultum nossent, intellegerent me
regi, si opus esset, ex auctoritate vestra praesidio futurum.

8   Ita confirmato illo ex eo loco castra movi. iter in Ciliciam facere institui, cum hac opinione a Cappadocia disce-

---

³ (Vict.: iam Lamb.: etiam coni. Watt)

up courage to come to him with what they knew. Among them was his brother, who loved him dearly and who had a strong sense of family loyalty. He was alleging (and Ariarathes confirmed the king's words in my presence) that he had been invited to aspire to the throne, something he could not have while his brother was alive; but until now he had been too much afraid to bring the facts into the open. Having heard this speech, I admonished the king to take every precaution for his own safety and exhorted the tried friends of his father and grandfather to take warning by the tragic fate of the former and defend the life of their sovereign with every care and safeguard.

The king then asked me for some cavalry and cohorts from my army. I was aware that under your decree I had not only a right but a duty to agree. But in view of the reports coming in daily from Syria, the public interest demanded that I should conduct the army to the borders of Cilicia as soon as possible. Moreover, now that the plot had been exposed, the king did not appear to me to need a Roman army; his own resources seemed adequate for his protection. I therefore urged him to make the preservation of his own life his first lesson in the art of ruling. He should exercise his royal prerogative against the persons whom he had found organizing the conspiracy against him, punishing where punishment was necessary and relieving the rest of apprehension. He should use the sanction of my army to intimidate the guilty rather than for actual combat. But all would understand, knowing the terms of the Senate's decree, that if need arose, I should come to the king's defence on your authority.

So I leave him in good heart. I am breaking camp and setting out on my way to Cilicia, leaving Cappadocia amid

derem ut consilio vestro, casu incredibili ac paene divino regem, quem vos honorificentissime appellassetis nullo postulante quemque meae fidei commendassetis et cuius salutem magnae vobis curae esse decressetis, meus adventus praesentibus insidiis liberarit.[4] quod ad vos a me scribi non alienum putavi, ‹ut› intellegeretis ex iis quae paene acciderunt vos multo ante ne ea acciderent providisse, eoque vos studiosius feci certiores quod in rege Ariobarzane ea mihi signa videor virtutis, ingeni, fidei benevolentiaeque erga vos perspexisse ut non sine causa tantam curam in eius vos salutem diligentiamque videamini contulisse.

106 (XV.14)

Scr. in castris post. parte m. Oct., ut vid., an. 51

M. CICERO IMP. S. D. C. CASSIO PRO Q.

1   M. Fabium quod mihi amicum tua commendatione das, nullum in eo facio quaestum. multi enim anni sunt cum ille in aere meo est et a me diligitur propter summam suam humanitatem et observantiam. sed tamen, quod ‹te›[1] ab eo egregie diligi sensi, multo amicior ei sum factus. itaque, quamquam profecerunt litterae tuae, tamen aliquanto plus commendationis apud me habuit animus

---

4 liberaret *(Ern.)*
1 *(Corr.)*

---

1 In Syria.

a general persuasion that by your policy and an amazing, if not providential, accident my advent has rescued the king from the immediate danger of a conspiracy—one upon whom unsolicited you conferred the royal title in the most honourable terms, whom you recommended to my protection, and whose welfare you decreed to be of great concern to you. I have deemed it appropriate to send you an account of the incident to enable you to appreciate from what nearly happened your own foresight in providing long in advance against that very contingency. And I have been all the more studious to inform you because I believe I have seen in King Ariabarzanes such evidences of character, intelligence, loyalty, and good will towards you as appear to justify the care and concern you have lavished upon his welfare.

106 (XV.14)
CICERO TO CASSIUS

Cilicia, latter October (?) 51

From M. Cicero, Imperator, to C. Cassius, Proquaestor,[1] greetings.

Your recommendation gives me a friend in the person of M. Fabius; but I am none the richer on his account. These many years past he has been mine absolutely, highly regarded by me for his good nature and attentive courtesy. However, I have become much the more his friend for having perceived what an exceptional regard he has for you. So his own disposition towards you, now that I am thoroughly aware of it, has been in some degree a better passport to my favour than your letter, though that too has

457

2   ipsius erga te mihi perspectus et cognitus. sed de Fabio faciemus studiose quae rogas.

Tu multis de causis vellem me convenire potuisses: primum ut te, quem iam diu plurimi facio, tanto intervallo viderem; deinde ut tibi, quod feci per litteras, possem praesens gratulari; tum ut quibus de rebus vellemus, tu tuis, ego meis, inter nos communicaremus; postremo ut amicitia nostra, quae summis officiis ab utroque culta est sed longis intervallis temporum interruptam consuetudinem habuit, confirmaretur vehementius.

3   Id quoniam non accidit, utemur bono litterarum et eadem fere absentes quae si coram essemus consequeremur.[2] unus scilicet fructus qui in te videndo est percipi litteris non potest, alter gratulationis est is quidem exilior quam si tibi te ipsum intuens gratularer, sed tamen et feci antea et facio nunc tibique cum pro rerum magnitudine quas gessisti tum pro opportunitate temporis gratulor, quod te de provincia decedentem summa laus et summa gratia provinciae prosecuta est.

4   Tertium est ut id quod de nostris rebus coram communicassemus inter nos confici⟨a⟩mus idem litteris. ego ceterarum rerum causa tibi Romam properandum magno opere censeo; nam et ea quae reliqui tranquilla de te erant et hac tua recenti victoria tanta clarum tuum adventum fore intellego. sed si quae sunt onera tuorum, si tanta sunt

---

2 consequemur ⟨

---

2 On his successful action against the Parthian invaders.

3 As often the plural refers to an individual, here Cassius' cousin Q. Cassius Longinus. He seems to have been threatened

had its effect. Anyhow, as to Fabius I shall spare no effort to comply with your request.

For many reasons I am sorry you were unable to meet me. Fond of you as I have long been, I should have liked to see you after so considerable an interval; I should have liked to congratulate[2] you in person as I did by letter; I should have liked to exchange views on such of our several concerns as either of us cared to raise; lastly, I should have liked to see a further strengthening of our friendship, which has been fostered on both sides by substantial services but interrupted, as to daily contact, by lengthy periods of separation.

Since that was not to be, we shall make the best of correspondence and get pretty well the same results apart as if we were together. Of course the satisfaction of seeing you cannot be enjoyed by letter; and the satisfaction of congratulating you would be more full-bodied if I were looking you in the eye as I did it. However, I have done so once, and I do so again. Yes, I congratulate you upon the magnitude of your success, and no less upon its timeliness, for you are leaving for Rome with the enthusiastic thanks and plaudits of your province ringing in your ears.

Then there is the third point—the exchange of views about our concerns that would have taken place had we met must be managed by correspondence. On all grounds but one I am strongly of the opinion that you should make haste back to Rome. When I left, all was quiet so far as you were concerned, and your recent brilliant victory will clearly shed lustre on your advent. But if those near to you[3]

with prosecution in respect of his ill-treatment of provincials in Spain, where he had served as Pompey's Quaestor.

ut ea sustinere possis, propera; nihil tibi erit lautius, nihil gloriosius. sin maiora, considera ne in alienissimum tempus cadat adventus tuus. huius rei totum consilium tuum est; tu enim scis quid sustinere possis. si potes, laudabile atque populare est; sin plane non potes, absens hominum sermones facilius sustinebis.

5   De me autem idem tecum his ago litteris quod superioribus egi, ut omnis tuos nervos in eo contendas ne quid mihi ad hanc provinciam, quam et senatus et populus annuam esse voluit, temporis prorogetur. hoc a te ita contendo ut in eo fortunas meas positas putem. habes Paullum nostrum nostri cupidissimum; est Curio, est Furnius. sic velim enitare quasi in eo sint mihi omnia.

6   Extremum illud est de iis quae proposueram, confirmatio nostrae amicitiae; de qua pluribus verbis nihil opus est. tu puer me appetisti, ego autem semper ornamento te mihi fore duxi; fuisti etiam praesidio tristissimis meis temporibus. accessit post tuum discessum familiaritas mihi cum Bruto tuo maxima. itaque in vestro ingenio et industria mihi plurimum et suavitatis et dignitatis constitutum puto. id tu ut tuo studio confirmes te vehementer rogo, litterasque ad me et continuo mittas et, cum Romam veneris, quam saepissime.

have loads to be carried, we must pause. Should they be such as you can cope with, then make haste—it will be the brightest feather in your cap. But if they are too heavy, you must consider. It would be a pity to arrive just at the least favourable moment. The matter is entirely for you to judge. You know your own strength. If you *can,* there is credit and popular approval to be had. But if you really cannot, you will find the talk less annoying elsewhere.

As for me, my plea in this letter is the same as in my last. Strain every nerve to prevent any prolongation of my present office, which both Senate and People fixed for one year. I press you on this point feeling that my worldly welfare depends on it. You can look to our friend Paullus, a thorough well-wisher of mine. There is Curio, there is Furnius. Do try your hardest, in the persuasion that it means everything to me.

The last of the points I mentioned was the strengthening of our friendship. On that little need be said. As a boy you drew towards me, and on my side I always believed that I should be proud of you. You also defended me in my darkest days. After you went abroad, I formed a very close friendship with your connection[4] Brutus. In your joint talents and energy I think I have a rich prospect of pleasure and prestige; and I earnestly ask you to confirm that opinion by your zeal. Send me a letter at once, and when you are back in Rome write as often as you can.

---

[4] Cassius had married Brutus' half-sister Junia, sometimes called Tertia or Tertulla.

107 (II.7)

Scr. in castris ad Pindenissum paulo post an. 51

M. CICERO IMP.[1] S. D. C. CURIONI TR. PL.

1   Sera gratulatio reprehendi non solet, praesertim si nulla neglegentia praetermissa est. longe enim absum, audio sero. sed tibi et gratulor et ut sempiternae laudi tibi sit iste tribunatus exopto, teque hortor ut omnia gubernes et moderere prudentia tua, ne te auferant aliorum consilia. nemo est qui tibi sapientius suadere possit te ipso; numquam labere si te audies. non scribo hoc temere. cui scribam video. novi animum, novi consilium tuum. non vereor ne quid timide, ne quid stulte facias, si ea defendes quae ipse recta esse senties.

2   Quod ‹in›[2] rei publicae tempus non incideris sed veneris (iudicio enim tuo, non casu, in ipsum discrimen rerum contulisti tribunatum tuum), profecto vides. quanta vis in re publica temporum sit, quanta varietas rerum, quam incerti exitus, quam flexibiles hominum voluntates, quid insidiarum, quid vanitatis in vita, non dubito quin cogites. sed amabo te, cura et cogita[tioni]—nihil novi, sed illud idem quod initio scripsi. tecum loquere, [et] te adhibe in consilium, te audi, tibi obtempera. alteri qui melius consilium dare possit quam tu non facile inveniri potest; tibi vero ipsi certe nemo melius dabit. di immortales! cur ego absum vel spectator laudum tuarum vel particeps ‹et›[3] vel

---

[1] procos. *(Wes.)*   [2] *(Wes.)*   [3] *(SB)**

---

[1] See Letter 81.2.

107 (II.7)
CICERO TO CURIO

In camp at Pindenissum, soon after 17 December 51

From M. Cicero, Imperator, to C. Curio, Tribune of the Plebs, greetings.

Belated congratulations usually pass unrebuked, especially if the omission is not due to negligence—I am far away and news reaches me late. Anyhow I do congratulate you, and pray that your Tribunate will earn you everlasting credit. And I urge you to guide and govern all your actions by your own good sense, not to be carried away by the counsels of others. No one can advise you more wisely than yourself; if you listen to yourself, you will never go wrong. I do not write this inadvisedly. I am aware whom I am addressing, I know your spirit and intelligence. I have no fear of your acting timidly or foolishly, if you defend what you yourself feel to be right.

You see, I am sure, the political situation which you have chosen (not happened) to enter—for by your own decision, not by chance, you have brought your term of office to coincide with the very crisis point.[1] I do not doubt that you are bearing in mind the power of circumstances in politics, the shifting nature of affairs, the uncertainty of events, the instability of men's sentiments, the snares and falsehoods of which life is full. But do, I beg you, give care and consideration to—nothing new, only what I wrote to start with: be your own confidant and counsellor. Listen to yourself, defer to yourself. It would not be easy to find one better able to advise others than you, and assuredly no one will better advise yourself. Ah, why am I not there as a spectator or sharer of your laurels and partner or agent in

socius vel minister consiliorum? tametsi hoc minime tibi deest; sed tamen efficeret magnitudo et vis amoris mei consilio te ut possem iuvare.

3   Scribam ad te plura alias; paucis enim diebus eram missurus domesticos tabellarios, ut, quoniam sane feliciter et ex mea sententia rem publicam gessimus, unis litteris totius aestatis res gestas ad senatum perscriberem. de sacerdotio tuo quantam curam adhibuerim quamque difficili in re atque causa cognosces ex iis litteris quas Thrasoni, liberto tuo, dedi.

4   Te, mi Curio, pro tua incredibili in me benevolentia meaque item in te singulari rogo atque oro ne patiare quicquam mihi ad hanc provincialem molestiam temporis prorogari. praesens tecum egi, cum te tribunum pl. isto anno fore non putarem, itemque petivi saepe per litteras, sed tum quasi a senatore, nobilissimo tamen adulescente et gratiosissimo, nunc a tribuno pl. et a Curione tribuno, non ut decernatur aliquid novi, quod solet esse difficilius, sed ut ne quid novi decernatur, ut et senati consultum et leges⁴ defendas, eaque mihi condicio maneat qua profectus sum. hoc te vehementer etiam atque etiam rogo.

⁴ legem *coni.* SB

464

your plans? Not that you stand in any need of such; but the measure and strength of my affection would lend me power to help you with advice.

I shall be writing more later on. In a few days' time I shall be sending couriers of my own household, since I wish to present in a single letter a full report to the Senate of the entire summer's operations, which I have conducted with considerable success and to my own satisfaction. As for your Priesthood,[2] you will learn from the letter I have given to your freedman Thraso how much attention I have devoted to this delicate and difficult matter.

My dear Curio, I have a solemn plea to make to you in the name of the unbounded kindness you bear me and I no less bear you, not to allow my tenure of this tiresome provincial post to be extended for any additional period. I took this up with you in person when I had no idea that you would be Tribune of the Plebs for the year in question, and have often mentioned it in my letters. But at that time I asked you as a member of the Senate, though to be sure a young man of the highest birth and personal influence; now I ask you as Tribune, and what is more as Tribune Curio. I do not want anything new decreed, which is apt to be difficult, but just the opposite. I want you to defend the Senate's decree and the laws of the land, and I want the terms on which I came here to stand intact. Allow me once more to make this pressing request of you.

[2] This must refer to Curio's election to the College of Pontiffs, of which his father had been a member.

Scr. Tarsi ex. an. 51

M. CICERO IMP. S. D. C. MARCELLO C.F. COS.

1   Quoniam id accidit quod mihi maxime fuit optatum, ut
omnium Marcellorum, Marcellinorum etiam (mirificus
enim generis ac nominis vestri fuit erga me semper animus)—quoniam ergo ita accidit ut omnium vestrum studio
tuus consulatus satis facere posset, in quem meae res
gestae lausque et honos earum potissimum incideret, peto
a te, id quod facillimum factu est non aspernante, ut
confido, senatu, ut quam honorificentissimum senatus
consultum litteris meis recitatis faciendum cures.

2   Si mihi tecum minus esset quam est cum tuis omnibus
adlegarem ad te illos a quibus intellegis me praecipue diligi. patris tui beneficia in me sunt amplissima; neque enim
saluti meae neque honori amicior quisquam dici potest.
frater tuus quanti me faciat semperque fecerit esse hominem qui ignoret arbitror neminem. domus tua denique
tota me semper omnibus summis officiis prosecuta est.
neque vero tu in me diligendo cuiquam concessisti tuorum. qua re a te peto in maiorem modum ut me per te
quam ornatissimum velis esse meamque et in supplica-

---

1 A branch of the Marcellus family which had passed by adoption into the Cornelii Lentuli. The best known of its members is
Cn. Cornelius Lentulus Marcellinus, Consul in 56.

2 For a Supplication.

3 M. Marcellus, Consul in 51.

108 (XV.10)
CICERO TO C. MARCELLUS

Tarsus, 51 (end)

From M. Cicero, Imperator, to C. Marcellus, son of Gaius, Consul, greetings.

Since my dearest wish has come to pass, namely that the good will of all the Marcelli, and the Marcellini[1] too—for the friendly disposition of your house and name towards me has always been extraordinary—since, I repeat, it has come to pass that the good will of your entire family can find its fulfilment through your consular office, with which my own military achievements and the credit and honour thereto appertaining have so opportunely coincided, allow me to request you to ensure that, when my dispatch has been read to the Senate, a decree[2] follows in terms as handsome as possible. That will be very easily done, for the House, as I confidently anticipate, will receive such a proposal without disfavour.

If my relations with yourself were any less close than with the rest of your family, I should make those who you know have most particular regard for me my advocates with you. From your father I have received the most signal favours; no better friend either to my survival or to my advancement can be named. As for your cousin,[3] I suppose nobody is ignorant of his attachment to me, now and always. In fact your whole family circle has always showered favours of the greatest consequence upon me. And yet you have yielded to none of your relatives in your regard for me. May I therefore specially request you to desire me to gain all possible distinction through your agency, and both in the matter of a decree of Supplication and in all others to

tione decernenda et in ceteris rebus existimationem satis tibi esse commendatam putes.

109 (XV.13)

Scr. eodem loco et tempore

M. CICERO IMP. S. D. L. PAULLO COS.

1   Maxime mihi fuit optatum Romae esse tecum multas ob causas, sed praecipue ut et in petendo et in gerendo consulatu meum tibi debitum studium perspicere posses. ac petitionis quidem tuae ratio mihi semper fuit explorata, sed tamen navare operam volebam; in consulatu vero cupio equidem te minus habere negoti, sed moleste fero me consulem tuum studium adulescentis perspexisse, te meum, cum id aetatis sim, perspicere non posse.

2   Sed ita fato nescio quo contigisse arbitror ut tibi ad me ornandum semper detur facultas, mihi ad remunerandum nihil suppetat praeter voluntatem. ornasti consulatum, ornasti reditum meum; incidit meum tempus rerum gerendarum in ipsum consulatum tuum. itaque cum et tua summa amplitudo et dignitas et meus magnus honos magnaque existimatio postulare videatur ut a te plurimis[1] verbis contendam ac petam ut quam honorificentissimum senatus consultum de meis rebus gestis faciendum cures, non audeo vehementer a te contendere, ne aut ipse tuae

1 pluribus *Man.*

consider my reputation as sufficiently commended to your care?

109 (XV.13)
CICERO TO L. PAULLUS

Same place and time as the foregoing

From M. Cicero, Imperator, to L. Paullus, Consul, greetings.

I should have wished above all things to be with you in Rome for many reasons, but especially to give you clear token of the good will I owe you both in your candidature for the Consulship and in your conduct of the office. Of your prospects of election I was always well assured, but still I wished to put my shoulder to the wheel. In office I certainly hope that you are having a comparatively easy time; but it irks me that when I was Consul and you were a young man I saw proof of your good will, while at my present time of life I am unable to show you corresponding proof of mine.

However, I think it must be fated somehow that you are always given opportunity to do me honour, whereas I find nothing but the will with which to requite you. You added lustre to my Consulship and to my return from exile; my time for military achievement has just coincided with your Consulship. So it is that, although your exalted position and dignity on the one hand and on the other the great honour I have in view, in which my public reputation is so largely involved, seem alike to require me to press a request upon you in as many words as I can muster—a request, namely, that you ensure the passage of a decree concerning my successes in the most complimentary

perpetuae consuetudinis erga me oblitus esse videar aut te
oblitum putem.

3   Qua re ut te velle arbitror ita faciam atque ab eo quem
omnes gentes sciunt de me optime meritum breviter
petam. si alii consules essent, ad te potissimum, Paulle,
mitterem ut eos mihi quam amicissimos redderes; nunc,
cum tua summa potestas summaque auctoritas notaque
omnibus nostra necessitudo sit, vehementer te rogo ut et
quam honorificentissime cures decernendum de meis
rebus gestis et quam celerrime. dignas res esse honore et
gratulatione cognosces ex iis litteris quas ad te et collegam
et senatum publice misi. omniumque mearum reliquarum
rerum maximeque existimationis meae procurationem
susceptam velim habeas, in primisque tibi curae sit, quod
abs te superioribus quoque litteris petivi, ne mihi tempus
prorogetur. cupio te consulem videre omniaque quae
spero cum absens tum etiam praesens te consule adsequi.

110 (XV.4)

Scr. Tarsi ex. an. 51 vel in. an. 50

M. CICERO IMP. S. D. M. CATONI

1   Summa tua auctoritas fecit meumque perpetuum de
tua singulari virtute iudicium ut magni mea interesse puta-

terms—yet in fact I dare not press you strongly for fear of seeming either to forget your consistent behaviour towards me through the years or to suppose that you have forgotten it.

Accordingly, I shall do as I imagine you would have me do, and be brief in addressing a request to one whose past kindnesses towards me are known to all mankind. If the Consuls in office were not who they actually are, you, my dear Paullus, would be the man to whom I should be sending to secure their most friendly dispositions towards me. As it is, the highest power and the highest influence are yours, and the relations between us are universal knowledge. Therefore I earnestly beg you to ensure that a decree in the most complimentary terms goes through concerning my successes, and as rapidly as possible. That they are worthy of recognition and congratulation you will find from the dispatch which I have addressed officially to you and your colleague and the Senate. And I hope you will regard yourself as having undertaken to look after all other concerns of mine, my reputation above all. In particular I trust you will take care that my tenure is not extended, as I requested in my previous letter. I want to see you Consul, and while you are in that capacity to attain all my hopes, not only in my absence, but also on the spot.

110 (XV.4)
CICERO TO CATO

Tarsus, end of 51 or beginning of 50

From M. Cicero, Imperator, to M. Cato, greetings.

Your exalted prestige and the respect which I have always held for your outstanding personal qualities make me

rem et res eas quas gessissem tibi notas esse et non ignorari
a te qua aequitate et continentia tuerer socios provinciamque administrarem. iis enim a te cognitis arbitrabar facilius
me tibi quae vellem probaturum.

2   Cum in provinciam prid. Kal. Sext. venissem et propter
anni tempus ad exercitum mihi confestim esse eundum
viderem, biduum Laodiceae fui, deinde Apameae quadriduum, triduum Synnadis, totidem dies Philomeli; quibus
in oppidis cum magni conventus fuissent, multas civitates
acerbissimis tributis et gravissimis usuris et falso aere alieno liberavi. cumque ante adventum meum seditione quadam exercitus esset dissipatus, quinque cohortes sine legato, sine tribuno militum, denique etiam sine centurione
ullo apud Philomelium consedissent, reliquus exercitus
esset in Lycaonia, M. Anneio legato imperavi ut eas quinque cohortis ad reliquum exercitum duceret coactoque in
unum locum exercitu castra in Lycaonia apud Iconium
faceret.

3   Quod cum ab illo diligenter esset actum, ego in castra a.
d. VII Kal. Sept. veni, cum interea superioribus diebus ex
senatus consulto et evocatorum firma⟨m⟩ manum et equitatum sane idoneum et popul⟨or⟩um liberorum regum-
que sociorum auxilia voluntaria comparavissem. interim,
cum exercitu lustrato iter in Ciliciam facere coepissem
Kal. Sept., legati a rege Commageno ad me missi pertu-
multuose neque tamen non vere Parthos in Syriam tran-

---

1 The dates ran: Laodicea 31 July–3 August; Apamea 5–9 August; Synnada 10–14 August; Philomelium 16–20 August. Cicero
seems here to give one day too many to Apamea.

feel it to be highly important to me that you should know of my achievements and not be unaware of the equity and moderation which has characterized my care for our subjects and my administration of my province. For I believe that when you are acquainted with those things I shall find it easier to win your approval for what I have at heart.

Arriving in my province on 31 July, I saw that in view of the time of year I ought to join my army with all speed. I spent two days at Laodicea, then four at Apamea, three at Synnada, and as many at Philomelium.[1] There were large gatherings in these towns, and I relieved many communes of oppressive imposts, harsh interest dues, and wrongful debt. Before my arrival the army had been scattered by a mutiny or something of the kind. Five cohorts had taken up a position near Philomelium without a Legate or Military Tribune, without even a Centurion, in command. The remainder of the army was in Lycaonia. I ordered my Legate, M. Anneius, to take these five cohorts to join the main body, and having concentrated the entire force to encamp near Iconium in Lycaonia.

Anneius faithfully carried out his orders, and on 24 August I reached the camp, having in the interval (in accordance with the Senate's decree) raised a strong force of reservists and a quite serviceable body of cavalry along with auxiliaries voluntarily supplied by free peoples and allied kings. Meanwhile, after I had reviewed the army and begun the march to Cilicia on the Kalends of September, a mission sent to me by the King of Commagene announced in a great state of excitement (but correctly enough) that the Parthians had crossed over into Syria. I was much

4 sisse nuntiaverunt. quo audito vehementer sum commotus
cum de Syria tum de mea provincia, de reliqua denique
Asia. itaque exercitum mihi ducendum per Cappadociae
regionem eam quae Ciliciam attingeret putavi. nam si me
in Ciliciam demisissem, Ciliciam quidem ipsam propter
montis Amani naturam facile tenuissem (duo sunt enim
aditus in Ciliciam ex Syria, quorum uterque parvis praesidiis propter angustias intercludi potest, nec est quicquam
Cilicia contra Syriam munitius), sed me Cappadocia move-
bat, quae patet a Syria regesque habet finitimos, qui, etiam
si sunt amici nobis, tamen aperte Parthis inimici esse non
audent. itaque in Cappadocia extrema non longe a Tauro
apud oppidum Cybistra castra feci, ut et Ciliciam tuerer et
Cappadociam tenens nova finitimorum consilia impedirem.

5   Interea in hoc tanto motu tantaque exspectatione maximi belli rex Deiotarus, cui non sine causa plurimum semper et meo et tuo et senatus iudicio tributum est, vir cum
benevolentia et fide erga populum Romanum singulari
tum praestanti[1] magnitudine et animi et consili, legatos ad
me misit se cum omnibus suis copiis in mea castra esse
venturum. cuius ego studio officioque commotus egi ei per
litteras gratias idque ut maturaret hortatus sum.

6   Cum autem ad Cybistra propter rationem belli quinque
dies essem moratus, regem Ariobarzanem, cuius salutem a
senatu te auctore commendatam habebam, praesentibus
insidiis necopinantem liberavi neque solum ei saluti fui
sed etiam curavi ut cum auctoritate regnaret. Metram et

---

[1] praesentia

alarmed by the news both for Syria and for my own province, and indeed for the rest of Asia. I therefore thought it best to take my army through that district of Cappadocia which adjoins Cilicia. Had I descended into Cilicia, I should have had no difficulty in holding Cilicia itself because of the natural features of Mt Amanus (there are two entries into Cilicia from Syria, both so narrow as to need only small forces to block them—there is no more defensible a position than Cilicia against an attack from Syria); but I was concerned about Cappadocia, which lies open from the Syrian side and is bordered by kings who, even if they are friendly to us, dare not be openly hostile to the Parthians. Accordingly I pitched camp in a corner of Cappadocia not far from the Taurus near the town of Cybistra, where I could at once protect Cilicia and hold Cappadocia, thus applying a brake to any changes of policy on the part of the neighbouring potentates.

In the midst of this agitation, with war on a grand scale in imminent prospect, King Deiotarus sent a mission to tell me that he proposed to march to my camp with his entire forces. It is not without good warrant that you and I and the Senate have always held him in the highest esteem, for he is both notably well disposed and loyal to Rome and remarkable for his lofty spirit and sound judgement. Impressed by this gesture of friendly zeal, I wrote to thank him and to urge him to make haste.

Having made a stay of five days at Cybistra for military reasons, I unexpectedly came to the rescue of King Ariobarzanes, whose welfare had been commended to me by the Senate at your instance, from the immediate threat of a conspiracy, not only saving his life, but consolidating his authority as ruler. Metras and Athenaeus (the latter the

eum quem tu mihi diligenter commendaras, Athenaeum, importunitate Athenaidis exsilio multatos ‹in›[2] maxima apud regem auctoritate gratiaque constitui, cumque magnum bellum in Cappadocia concitaretur si sacerdos armis se, quod facturus putabatur, defenderet, adulescens et equitatu et peditatu et pecunia paratus et fotus[3] iis qui novari aliquid volebant, perfeci ut a regno ille discederet rexque sine tumultu ac sine armis omni auctoritate aulae communita regnum cum dignitate obtineret.

7   Interea cognovi multorum litteris atque nuntiis magnas Parthorum copias ‹et›[4] Arabum ad oppidum Antiocheam accessisse magnumque eorum equitatum, qui in Ciliciam transisset, ab equitum meorum turmis et a cohorte praetoria, quae erat Epiphaneae praesidi causa, occidione occisum. qua re cum viderem a Cappadocia Parthorum copias aversas non longe a finibus esse Ciliciae, quam potui maximis itineribus ad Amanum exercitum duxi. quo ut veni, hostem ab Antiochea recessisse, Bibulum Antiocheae esse cognovi. Deiotarum confestim iam ad me venientem cum magno et firmo equitatu et peditatu et cum omnibus suis copiis certiorem feci non videri esse causam cur abesset a regno meque ad eum, si quid novi forte accidisset, statim litteras nuntiosque missurum esse.

---

[2] *(Hofmann, C.F.W.Mueller)*
[3] toto *(Goodyear*, alii alia)*   [4] *(Man.)*

---

[2] The Queen Mother.
[3] Of Ma-Bellona at Comana, whose power in Cappadocia was second only to the king's. We do not know his name. Archelaus, with whom he is commonly confused, was High Priest of a similar establishment at Comana in Pontus.

subject of your special recommendation to me), both sentenced to exile by the cruelty of Athenais,[2] were established by me in high favour and influence at court. There was the prospect of a major war flaring up in Cappadocia, should the High Priest[3] defend himself by force of arms, as was generally thought likely; for the young man had horse, foot, and money in readiness, and was supported by those who wanted a change of regime. I so managed that he withdrew from the kingdom. The full authority of the Palace was safeguarded without turmoil or violence, and the king settled in his royal estate and dignity.

Meanwhile, I learned from many letters and reports that a large Parthian and Arab force had approached the town of Antioch, and that a large body of their cavalry, which had penetrated Cilicia, had been cut to pieces by squadrons of my horse and the Praetorian Cohort, which had been left in garrison at Epiphanea. Seeing that the Parthians had turned away from Cappadocia and were not far from the borders of Cilicia, I led my army to the Amanus by the longest marches I could achieve. On arrival there I learned that the enemy had withdrawn from Antioch, and that Bibulus was in the town. I informed Deiotarus, who was already hastening to join me with a large and reliable body of horse and foot[4] along with his entire forces, that there appeared to be no reason for him to absent himself from his kingdom; if there was any new development I should send him a letter and messengers immediately.

[4] Armed in the Roman fashion; cf. *Letters to Atticus* 115 (VI.1).14.

8   Cumque eo animo venissem ut utrique provinciae, si
ita tempus ferret, subvenirem, tum id quod iam ante statueram vehementer interesse utriusque provinciae, pa-
care Amanum et perpetuum hostem ex eo monte tollere,
agere perrexi. cumque me discedere ab eo monte simulas-
sem et alias partis Ciliciae petere abessemque ab Amano
iter unius diei et castra apud Epiphaneam fecissem, a. d.
IIII Id. Oct., cum advesperasceret, expedito exercitu ita
noctu iter feci ut a. d. III Id. Oct., cum lucisceret, in Amanum ascenderem distributisque cohortibus et auxiliis, cum
aliis Quintus frater legatus mecum simul, aliis C. Pomptinus legatus, reliquis M. Anneius et L. Tullius legati prae-
essent, plerosque necopinantis oppressimus, qui occisi
9   captique sunt interclusi fuga. Eranam autem, quae fuit
non vici instar sed urbis, quod erat Amani caput, itemque
Sepyram et Commorim, acriter et diu repugnantibus,[5]
Pomptino illam partem Amani tenente, ex antelucano
tempore usque ad horam diei X magna multitudine hostium occisa cepimus castellaque vi[6] capta complura in-
cendimus. his rebus ita gestis castra in radicibus Amani
habuimus apud Aras Alexandri quadriduum et in reli-
qui<i>s Amani delendis agrisque vastandis, quae pars eius
montis meae provinciae est, id tempus omne consump-
simus.
10   Confectis his rebus ad oppidum Eleutherocilicum Pindenissum exercitum adduxi.[7] quod cum esset altissimo et

5 repugnantibus <hostibus> *Or.*   6 sex (*Madvig*)
7 abduxi *Wes.*

5 Set up by Alexander the Great on the bank of the river
Pyramus to commemorate his victory over the Persians at Issus.

I had come with the intention of lending aid to either province, if occasion arose. Moreover, I had already decided that the pacification of the Amanus and the removal of the traditional enemy from those mountains was of great importance to both. I therefore proceeded with this objective. Pretending to withdraw from the mountains and make for other parts of Cilicia, I pitched camp near Epiphanea, one day's march from the Amanus. On 12 October, as evening drew on, I marched the army in light equipment so rapidly during the night that by daybreak on 13 October I was moving up the mountain. The cohorts and auxiliary formations were divided into three forces, one commanded by my brother Quintus (Legate) along with myself, another by Legate C. Pomptinus, the third by Legates M. Anneius and L. Tullius. We took many of the enemy by surprise, cutting off their escape and killing or taking them prisoner. Erana, the capital of the Amanus region, which was more like a city than a village, together with Sepyra and Commoris, fell to us after a strenuous and lengthy resistance (Pomptinus was in that part of the mountains) lasting from early twilight till four in the afternoon; a large number of the enemy were slaughtered. We also took a number of strongholds by storm, and burned them. After these operations we pitched camp for four days near Alexander's Altars[5] in the foothills of the Amanus, employing the whole period in destroying whatever was left in the mountains and devastating the countryside—that part of the mountains which falls within my province.

These operations concluded, I led the army against Pindenissum, a town of the Free Cilicians. It was in a situation of great strength, perched high up, and inhabited by a

munitissimo loco ab iisque incoleretur qui ne regibus quidem umquam paruissent, cum et fugitivos reciperent et
Parthorum adventum acerrime exspectarent, ad existimationem imperi pertinere arbitratus sum comprimere eorum audaciam, quo facilius etiam ceterorum animi qui
alieni essent ab imperio nostro frangerentur. vallo et fossa
circumdedi, sex castellis castrisque maximis saepsi, ag-
gere, vineis, turribus oppugnavi ususque tormentis multis,
multis sagittariis, magno labore meo sine ulla molestia
sumptuve sociorum, septimo quinquagesimo die rem
confeci, ut omnibus partibus urbis disturbatis aut incensis
compulsi in potestatem meam pervenirent. his erant finiti-
mi pari scelere et audacia Tebarani. ab iis Pindenisso capto
obsides accepi; exercitum in hiberna dimisi; Quintum fratrem negotio praeposui ut in vicis aut captis aut male paca-
tis exercitus collocaretur.

11   Nunc velim sic tibi persuadeas, si de iis rebus ad senatum relatum sit, me existimaturum summam mihi laudem
tributam si tu honorem meum sententia tua comprobaris,
idque, etsi talibus de rebus gravissimos homines et rogare
solere et rogari scio, tamen admonendum potius te a me
quam rogandum puto. tu es enim is qui me tuis sententiis
saepissime ornasti, qui oratione, qui praedicatione, qui
summis laudibus in senatu, in contionibus ad caelum extu-
listi; cuius ego semper tanta esse verborum pondera putavi

race who have never yielded obedience even to the native kings. They were harbouring deserters and eagerly looking forward to the arrival of the Parthians, so that I considered it a matter of imperial prestige to curb their presumption, whereby others not well affected to the rule of Rome would be more easily discouraged. I surrounded the place with a rampart and moat, protecting these with six block-houses and a very large camp, then pressed the assault with an earthwork, penthouses, and towers, using artillery and archers in large numbers. By dint of much personal effort and without putting our subjects to any trouble or expense, I finished the operation in fifty-seven days. Every part of the city was demolished or burned and the population driven to surrender to me. They had neighbours no less guilty and presumptuous than themselves, the inhabitants of Tebara, from whom I received hostages after the capture of Pindenissum. I then dismissed the army to winter quarters, putting my brother Quintus in charge of stationing the troops in villages which had either been captured or were still in a state of unrest.

Now I should like you to realize that, if a motion concerning these performances is put to the Senate, I shall take it as a signal compliment if, when your turn comes, you will support the honour proposed for me. And although I am aware that personages of the highest dignity often address and receive requests in such cases, I conceive that from me to you a hint is more appropriate than a request. After all, I am writing to one whose motions in the House have again and again done me honour, and who both there and at public meetings has praised me to the skies in language of unstinted panegyric. I have always attached so much weight to your words that a single one of

ut uno verbo tuo cum mea laude coniuncto omnia adsequi
me arbitrarer. te denique memini, cum cuidam clarissimo
atque optimo viro supplicationem non decerneres, dicere
te decreturum si referretur ob eas res quas is consul in
urbe gessisset. tu idem mihi supplicationem decrevisti to-
gato, non, ut multis, re publica bene gesta sed, ut nemini,
12   re publica conservata. mitto quod invidiam, quod pericula,
quod omnis meas tempestates et subieris et multo etiam
magis, si per me licuisset, subire paratissimus fueris, quod
denique inimicum meum tuum inimicum putaris, cuius
etiam interitum, cum facile intellegerem mihi quantum
tribueres, Milonis causa in senatu defendenda approbaris.
a me autem haec sunt profecta, quae non ego in benefici
loco pono sed in veri testimoni atque iudici, ut praestan-
tissimas tuas virtutes non tacitus admirarer (quis enim id
non facit?) sed in omnibus orationibus, sententiis dicendis,
causis agendis, omnibus scriptis Graecis, Latinis, omni
denique varietate litterarum mearum te non modo iis quos
vidissemus sed etiam iis de quibus audissemus omnibus
anteferrem.

13   Quaeres fortasse quid sit quod ego hoc nescio quid
gratulationis et honoris a senatu tanti aestimem. agam iam
tecum familiariter, ut est et studiis et officiis nostris mutuis
et summa amicitia dignum et necessitudine etiam paterna.
si quisquam fuit umquam remotus et natura et magis
etiam, ut mihi quidem sentire videor, ratione atque doctri-

---

6 Probably Lentulus Spinther.

7 In 63.

8 P. Clodius.

them tinctured with eulogy of myself has represented to my mind the summit of attainment. Finally, I recall that in opposing the grant of a Supplication to a most worthy and illustrious gentleman[6] you said you would have supported it had the motion been based on his achievements as Consul in Rome; and you likewise voted a Supplication[7] to me as a civilian in unprecedented terms—not as having served the commonwealth well (that has been said of many others), but as having saved it. I pass over the fact that you took upon yourself my unpopularity and danger and all the various turns of fortune that have befallen me, and that you were very ready to go a long way further in that direction had I permitted it; that finally, you looked upon my enemy[8] as yours, and gave your approval to his destruction (yes, I fully appreciated how much you were doing for my sake), when you defended Milo's action in the Senate. On my side there has been forthcoming this much (and I do not regard it as a favour but as testimony of a sincerely held opinion), that I have not confined myself to tacit admiration of your extraordinary qualities (that, after all, is universal), but have publicly exalted you beyond any man we have seen or of whom history tells us. This I have done in all my speeches, whether addressing the Senate or pleading in court, in all my writings, Greek or Latin, in fact throughout the entire range of my literary output.

Perhaps you will wonder why it is that I should set so much store by this bauble of congratulation and honour from the Senate. I will be candid with you—our philosophical pursuits, our mutual good offices, our close friendship, the ties too between our parents, make that only fitting. If there was ever a man indifferent by nature, and still more (so at least I fancy) by understanding and instruction, to

na ab inani laude et sermonibus vulgi, ego profecto is sum. testis est consulatus meus, in quo, sicut in reliqua vita, fateor ea me studiose secutum ex quibus vera gloria nasci posset, ipsam quidem gloriam per se numquam putavi expetendam. itaque et provinciam ornatam et spem non dubiam triumphi neglexi, sacerdotium denique, cum, quem ad modum te existimare arbitror, non difficillime consequi possem, non appetivi. idem post iniuriam acceptam, quam tu rei publicae calamitatem semper appellas, meam non modo non calamitatem sed etiam gloriam, studui quam ornatissima senatus populique Romani de me iudicia intercedere. itaque et augur postea fieri volui, quod antea neglexeram, et eum honorem qui a senatu tribui rebus bellicis solet, neglectum a me olim, nunc mihi expetendum puto.

14   Huic meae voluntati, in qua inest aliqua vis desideri ad sanandum vulnus iniuriae, ut faveas adiutorque sis, quod paulo ante me negaram rogaturum, vehementer te rogo, sed ita si non ieiunum hoc nescio quid quod ego gessi et contemnendum videbitur sed tale atque tantum ut multi nequaquam paribus rebus honores summos a senatu consecuti sint. equidem etiam illud mihi animum advertisse videor (scis enim quam attente te audire soleam), te non tam res gestas quam mores ⟨et⟩[8] instituta atque vitam imperatorum spectare solere in habendis aut non habendis honoribus. quod si in mea causa considerabis, reperies me

[8] *(SB)*

---

[9] Query. Cf. *Letters to Atticus* 25 (II.5).2.

empty plaudits and the talk of the crowd, I may surely claim to be such a man. My Consulship stands witness. In that office, as in the rest of my career, I confess that I sought eagerly after the sources from which true glory might arise; but glory in and for itself never seemed to me worth the pursuing. I waived a well-appointed province and the clear prospect of a Triumph. Finally, I did not reach out my hand for a priestly dignity when in your opinion, I believe, it could have been mine without any great difficulty.[9] But after the wrong I suffered (you always call it a calamity for the state, but for myself no calamity, even an honour) it has been otherwise. I have been ambitious to receive tokens of esteem, the more flattering the better, from the Senate and People of Rome. Accordingly in this later period I was desirous of becoming Augur, something I had formerly disregarded; and I now think the honour customarily conferred by the Senate for military successes worth my seeking, although I waived it aside in days gone by.

I wrote just now that I would not make a request. For all that, I do request you earnestly for your benevolent assistance in this wish of mine, which is not without an element of an injured man's craving for balm to heal his wound. I do so, however, always supposing that you find my modest exploits not altogether paltry and contemptible—of such a kind and measure, on the contrary, that many have won the highest distinctions from the Senate for achievements by no means comparable. Furthermore, I think I have observed (you know how attentively I listen to you) that in conceding or withholding such distinctions it is your practice to pay greater regard to a commander's conduct, his principles and way of life, than to his operations in the field. If you apply such considerations in my

exercitu imbecillo contra metum maximi belli firmissi-
mum praesidium habuisse aequitatem et continentiam. his
ego subsidiis ea sum consecutus quae nullis legionibus
consequi potuissem, ut <ex> alienissimis sociis amicissimos, ex infidelissimis firmissimos redderem animosque
novarum rerum exspectatione suspensos ad veteris[9] imperi benevolentiam traducerem.

15   Sed nimis haec multa de me, praesertim ad te, a quo
uno omnium sociorum querelae audiuntur. cognosces ex
iis qui meis institutis se recreatos putant; cumque omnes
uno prope consensu de me apud te ea quae mihi optatissi-
ma sunt praedicabunt tum duae maxime clientelae tuae,
Cyprus insula et Cappadociae regnum, tecum de me lo-
quentur, puto etiam regem Deiotarum, qui uni tibi est
maxime necessarius. quae si etiam maiora sunt et in omnibus saeculis pauciores viri reperti sunt qui suas cupiditates
quam qui hostium copias vincerent, est profecto tuum,
cum ad res bellicas haec quae rariora et difficiliora sunt
genera virtutis adiunxeris, ipsas etiam illas res gestas ius-
tiores esse et maiores putare.

16   Extremum illud est, ut quasi diffidens rogationi meae
philosophiam ad te adlegem, qua nec mihi carior ulla
umquam res in vita fuit nec hominum generi maius a deis
munus ullum est datum. haec igitur, quae mihi tecum
communis est, societas studiorum atque artium nostra-
rum, quibus a pueritia dediti ac devincti soli prope modum

[9] veterem *Fuchs*

case, you will find that with a weak army I made fair and clean administration my strongest bulwark against the threat of a major war. Thus aided, I obtained results which no legions could have secured. I found our subjects thoroughly alienated and disloyal; I have made them thoroughly well affected and reliable, winning over their minds, poised as they were in expectation of change, to a sentiment of good will towards the old regime.

But I have written too much about myself, especially to you, the one man to whose ears all our subjects bring their grievances. You will learn of it all from those who feel that my system of government has brought them back to life. All, virtually with one accord, will describe my administration to you in such terms as I should most like to hear. In particular, two communities who call you their patron, the island of Cyprus and the kingdom of Cappadocia, will tell you about me. So, I believe, will King Deiotarus, with whom you have the most intimate of connections. Are not these things of greater moment? Is it not true that in all ages fewer have been found capable of conquering their own passions than of defeating hostile armies? If so, when you have added to military achievements these rarer and more difficult kinds of merit, it will surely be in your character to rate those very achievements of higher account and desert than they would otherwise have appeared.

In conclusion, as though lacking confidence in the efficacy of my plea, let me make Philosophy my advocate with you—than which nothing in my life has been more precious to me, nor have the Gods bestowed any greater gift upon mankind. Think then of the pursuits and acquirements we have in common and to which we have been devoted heart and soul since we were boys. We two almost

nos philosophiam veram illam et antiquam, quae quibusdam oti esse ac desidiae videtur, in forum atque in rem
publicam atque in ipsam aciem paene deduximus, tecum
agit de mea laude; cui negari a Catone fas esse non puto.

Quam ob rem tibi sic persuadeas velim, si mihi tua sententia tributus honos ex meis litteris fuerit, me sic existimaturum, cum auctoritate tua tum benevolentia erga me
mihi quod maxime cupierim contigisse.

111 (XV.5)

Scr. Romae post. parte m. Apr. an. 50

M. CATO S. D. M. CICERONI IMP.

1   Quod et res publica me et nostra amicitia hortatur
libenter facio, ut tuam virtutem, innocentiam, diligentiam,
cognitam in maximis rebus domi togati, armati foris pari
industria administrare gaudeam. itaque, quod pro meo iudicio facere potui, ut innocentia consilioque tuo defensam
provinciam, servatum Ariobarzanis cum ipso rege regnum,
sociorum revocatam ad studium imperi nostri voluntatem
sententia mea et decreto laudarem, feci.

2   Supplicationem decretam, si tu, qua in re nihil fortuito
sed summa tua ratione et continentia rei publicae provisum est, dis immortalibus gratulari nos quam tibi referre

alone have brought the old authentic philosophy, which some regard as an amusement of leisure and idleness, down into the marketplace, into public life, one might almost say into the battlefield. This companionship of ours pleads with you on behalf of my renown. I do not think Cato can in conscience say no.

Take it then, if you please, that, should the honour for which I ask in my dispatch be accorded to me by your voice in the House, I shall regard myself as having attained my dearest wish through the weight of your prestige and through your good will towards me.

111 (XV.5)
CATO TO CICERO

Rome, latter April 50

From M. Cato to M. Cicero, Imperator, greetings.

Patriotism and friendship alike urge me to rejoice, as I heartily do, that your ability, integrity, and conscientiousness, already proved in great events at home when you wore the gown of peace, are no less actively at work in arms abroad. Accordingly, I did what my judgement allowed me to do: that is to say, I paid you tribute with my voice and vote for defending your province by your integrity and wisdom, for saving Ariobarzanes' throne and person, and for winning back the hearts of our subjects to a loyal support of Roman rule.

As for the decree of a Supplication, if you prefer us to render thanks to the Immortal Gods in respect of provision taken for the public good by your own admirable policy and administrative rectitude, not at all the result of chance,

acceptum mavis, gaudeo. quod si triumphi praerogativam
putas supplicationem et idcirco casu⟨m⟩ potius quam te
laudari mavis, neque supplicationem sequitur semper
triumphus et triumpho multo clarius est senatum iudicare
potius mansuetudine et innocentia imperatoris provinciam quam vi militum aut benignitate deorum retentam
atque conservatam esse; quod ego mea sententia cense-
bam.

3 Atque haec ego idcirco ad te contra consuetudinem
meam pluribus scripsi ut, quod maxime volo, existimes me
laborare ut tibi persuadeam me et voluisse de tua maiestate quod amplissimum sim arbitratus et quod tu maluisti
factum esse gaudere.

  Vale et nos dilige et instituto itinere severitatem diligentiamque sociis et rei publicae praesta.

112 (XV.6)

Scr. Tarsi post. parte m. Quint. an. 50

M. CICERO S. D. M. CATONI

1 'Laetus sum laudari me' inquit Hector, opinor, apud
Naevium 'abs te, pater, a laudato viro.' ea est enim profecto
iucunda laus quae ab iis proficiscitur qui ipsi in laude vixe-
runt. ego vero vel gratulatione litterarum tuarum vel testi-

---

[1] Cato as a Stoic believed in a Providence, but in ordinary language and thought the ideas of fate, providence, gods, fortune
(more or less personified), and chance were much confused at this
period.

[1] See Letter 22.7.

rather than to put it down to your own credit—why, I am very glad of it. If, however, you regard a Supplication as an earnest of a Triumph, and on that account prefer the praise to go to accident[1] rather than to yourself, the fact is that a Triumph does not always follow a Supplication. On the other hand, the Senate's judgement that a province has been held and preserved by its governor's mild and upright administration rather than by the swords of an army or the favour of the Gods is a far greater distinction than a Triumph; and that is what I proposed in the House.

I have written to you at some length on this subject (contrary to my normal habit) so that you may realize, as I most earnestly hope you will, my anxiety to convince you of two things: firstly, as touching your prestige, I desired what I conceived to be most complimentary to yourself; secondly, I am very glad that what you preferred has come to pass.

Good-bye, remember me kindly, and follow your chosen course, rendering to our subjects and to the state their due of a strict and conscientious administration.

112 (XV.6)
CICERO TO CATO

Tarsus, late July 50

From M. Cicero to M. Cato greetings.

I think it is Hector in Naevius who says 'Glad thy praise doth make me, father, praise from one that praisèd is.'[1] Praise is pleasant, you will agree, when it comes from those who have themselves led honoured lives. Yes, I assure you that the congratulatory terms of your letter and the testi-

moniis sententiae dictae nihil est quod me non adsecutum
putem, idque mihi cum amplissimum tum gratissimum
est, te libenter amicitiae dedisse quod liquido veritati da-
res. et si non modo omnes verum etiam multi Catones essent in civitate nostra, in qua unum exstitisse mirabile est,
quem ego currum aut quam lauream cum tua laudatione
conferrem? nam ad meum sensum et ad illud sincerum ac
subtile iudicium nihil potest esse laudabilius quam ea tua
oratio quae est ad me perscripta a meis necessariis.

2   Sed causam meae voluntatis (non enim dicam cupiditatis) exposui tibi superioribus litteris. quae etiam si parum
iusta tibi visa est, hanc tamen habet rationem, non ut nimis
concupiscendus honos sed tamen, si deferatur a senatu,
minime aspernandus esse videatur. spero autem illum ordinem pro meis ob rem publicam susceptis laboribus me
non indignum honore, usitato praesertim, existimaturum.
quod si ita erit, tantum ex te peto, quod amicissime scribis,
ut, cum tuo iudicio quod amplissimum esse arbitraris mihi
tribueris, si id quod maluero acciderit, gaudeas. sic enim
fecisse te et sensisse et scripsisse video, resque ipsa decla-
rat tibi illum honorem nostrum supplicationis iucundum
fuisse, quod scribendo adfuisti. haec enim senatus consulta non ignoro ab amicissimis eius cuius ⟨de⟩ honore agitur
scribi solere.

Ego, ut spero, te propediem videbo, atque utinam re
publica meliore quam timeo!

_____

² A Triumph.

monial you gave me in the House represent to my mind the sum of attainment. I am particularly flattered and gratified to feel that you were glad to accord to friendship what you would have had no hesitation in according to truth. And if many (not to say all) members of our society were Catos (the marvel being that it has produced *one*), how could I think of comparing the triumphal car and crown with an encomium from you? To my way of thinking, and by the unbiased and delicate standards of a philosopher, nothing can be more complimentary than that speech of yours of which my friends have sent me a copy.

But I have explained the reason for my inclination (I will not say 'desire') in my previous letter. Perhaps you did not find it altogether convincing; at any rate it means that I do not regard the honour[2] as something to be unduly coveted, but at the same time that, if proffered by the Senate, I feel I ought by no means to spurn it. I trust, furthermore, that in view of the labours I have undertaken for the public good the House will deem me not unworthy of an honour, especially one so commonly bestowed. If it so turns out, all I ask of you is that (to use your own very kind expressions), having accorded to me what in your judgement is most complimentary to myself, you should be glad if what I prefer comes about. Your actions, your views as expressed in the Senate, your letter, and the very fact that you were present at the drafting of the decree are clear evidence to me that the grant of the Supplication in my honour was agreeable to you. For I am well aware that such decrees are usually drafted by the closest friends of the persons honoured.

I shall see you soon, as I hope, and only pray we meet in a better political atmosphere than I fear we shall.

113 (VII.32)

Scr. fort. Laodiceae m. Febr. vel Mart. an. 50

M. CICERO S. D. VOLUMNIO

1   Quod sine praenomine familiariter, ut debebas, ad me epistulam misisti, primum addubitavi num a Volumnio senatore esset, quocum mihi est magnus usus; deinde εὐτραπελία litterarum fecit ut intellegerem tuas esse. quibus in litteris omnia mihi periucunda fuerunt praeter illud, quod parum diligenter possessio salinarum mearum a te procuratore defenditur. ais enim, ut ego discesserim, omnia omnium dicta, in his etiam Sestiana, in me conferri. quid? tu id pateris? nonne defendis, non resistis?

2   Equidem sperabam ita notata me reliquisse genera dictorum meorum ut cognosci sua sponte possent. sed quoniam tanta faex est in urbe ut nihil tam sit ἀκύθηρον quod non alicui venustum esse videatur, pugna, si me amas, nisi acuta ἀμφιβολία, nisi elegans ὑπερβολή, nisi παράγραμμα¹ bellum, nisi ridiculum παρὰ προσδοκίαν, nisi cetera quae sunt a me in secundo libro de oratore per Antoni personam disputata de ridiculis ἔντεχνα et arguta apparebunt, ut sacramento contendas mea non esse.

---

¹ παρὰ γράμμα *Whibly*

---

1 'Eutrapelia,' defined by Aristotle as 'cultured insolence.' The *cognomen* Eutrapelus was personal and descriptive, Volumnius being a well-known wit.   2 'Salt' *(sal)* = 'wit.'

3 P. Sestius notoriously lacked *sal*; cf. *Letters to Atticus* 141 (VII.17).2.

4 The Greek word used means 'charmless.'

113 (VII.32)
CICERO TO VOLUMNIUS EUTRAPELUS

Laodicea (?), February or March 50 (?)

M. Cicero to Volumnius greetings.

As you headed your letter in familiar style (and quite right) without first name, I was at first inclined to wonder whether it might not be from Senator Volumnius, with whom I have much acquaintance. But its *eutrapelous* quality[1] gave me to understand that it was yours. The contents all made most agreeable reading, with one exception: as my agent-in-charge you are not careful enough in protecting my property—my *salt mines!*[2] You say that since my departure every witticism, whosoever it be, not excluding even Sestius' efforts,[3] is fathered upon me. Well, do you allow this? No opposition, no resistance?

I had hoped to have left my various categories of *bons mots* so clearly branded as to be recognizable at sight. But since Rome is so full of scum that the most banausic[4] of jests will find someone to relish its elegance, in friendship's name bestir yourself! If there be no pungent *double entendre,* no tasteful hyperbole, no pretty pun,[5] no comical surprise; if the other varieties which I discussed through Antonius'[6] mouth in the second volume of my treatise *On the Orator* shall not appear neatly pointed and *secundum artem:* why you may go bail that the thing is not mine.

---

[5] Strictly, a joke depending on letter substitution, as in Manutius' example from Terence *inceptio eat amentium, haud amantium.*

[6] Apparently a slip on Cicero's part. The section on jokes in the *De Oratore* is in fact given to C. Julius Caesar Strabo.

Nam de iudiciis quod quereris, multo laboro minus. trahantur per me pedibus omnes rei; sit vel Selius tam eloquens ut possit probare se liberum, non laboro. urbanitatis possessionem, amabo, quibusvis interdictis defendamus; in qua te unum metuo, contemno ceteros. derideri te putas? nunc demum intellego te sapere.

3   Sed mehercules extra iocum valde mihi tuae litterae facetae elegantesque visae sunt. illa, quamvis ridicula essent, sicut erant, mihi tamen risum non moverunt. cupio enim nostrum illum amicum in tribunatu quam plurimum habere gravitatis; id cum ipsius causa (est mihi, ut scis, in amoribus) tum mehercule etiam rei publicae, quam quidem, quamvis in me ingrata sit, amare non desinam.

Tu, mi Volumni, quoniam et instituisti et mihi vides esse gratum, scribe ad me quam saepissime de rebus urbanis, de re publica. iucundus est mihi sermo litterarum tuarum. praeterea Dolabellam, quem ego perspicio et iudico cupidissimum esse atque amantissimum mei, cohortare et confirma et redde plane meum; non mehercule quo quicquam desit, sed, quia valde cupio, non videor nimium laborare.

As to your grumbles about the trials, I am much less concerned. Every defendant may go to the devil for aught I care. Selius[7] may wax eloquent enough to prove himself freeborn—it doesn't worry me. But my property in wit is another matter. Let us protect that for pity's sake! Get any court order you like. The only rival I fear in this field is yourself, the rest I despise. You think I'm poking fun at you? Very good, I perceive *now* that you are a man of sense.

But really, joking apart, your letter struck me as most entertaining and elegant reading. One part though, however amusing (and it was certainly that), did not make me smile. I am anxious for that friend of ours[8] to carry all possible weight in his career as Tribune, both for his own sake (as you know, I am very fond of him) and also, I may add, for the sake of the commonwealth, which, however poor my return, I shall never cease to love.

Well, my dear Volumnius, now that you have made a start and see that I appreciate it, write to me as often as you can about affairs in Rome and the political situation. I enjoy the way your letters talk. Furthermore, do encourage and confirm Dolabella in his sentiments towards me, which I perceive and judge to be those of sincerely affectionate good will. Make him mine entirely—not, to be sure, that anything is lacking. But keenly desirous as I am, I don't think I am labouring the point unduly.

7 Unknown.
8 Curio.

Composed in ZephGreek and ZephText by
Technologies 'N Typography, Merrimac, Massachusetts.
Printed in Great Britain by St Edmundsbury Press Ltd,
Bury St Edmunds, Suffolk, on acid-free paper.
Bound by Hunter & Foulis Ltd, Edinburgh, Scotland.